POSTNATIONAL MEM
AND WAR

This book examines the phenomenon of modern memory as a reaction to total war, an aspiration to truth-seeking provoked by the independent forces of modern war and collective violence which is transnational, or postnational, in character. Using examples from prose and poetry, film and theatre, painting and photography, and music and the popular arts, the author traces a narrative path through the events of the twentieth century, defining the tradition of modern memory in terms of its essentially anti-militaristic, anti-war character, as expressed in the manner in which it represents recalled violence and atrocity. Through a series of thematic discussions of two world wars, the Shoah, urbicide and nuclear weapons, *Postnational Memory* explores the formation of transnational memory, drawing on examples from industrialized societies, with a focus on memory of real events and their reproduction in literature and the arts, often including personal recollections that link the self to the represented past. As such, by asking how the concept of modern memory is constructed through the victims of war and genocide, the book constitutes an alternative to national memories and hegemonic, militarist or ethnocentric histories. Surveying the emergence of new, transnational forms of remembering the past, it will appeal to students and scholars of sociology, memory studies and peace studies, as well as those working in disciplines such as modern and international history, cultural studies and military studies.

Nigel Young is Professor Emeritus of Sociology and Research Professor in Peace Studies at Colgate University, USA. He is the editor in chief of the *Oxford International Encyclopedia of Peace* and co-editor of *Campaigns for Peace: The British Peace Movement in the 20th Century*. He is the author of *Nation State and War Resistance*, *On War, National Liberation and The State*, and *An Infantile Disorder? The Crisis and Decline of the New Left*, and the co-author of *Pacifism in the 20th Century*.

Memory Studies: Global Constellations

Series editor:
Henri Lustiger-Thaler, Ramapo College of New Jersey, USA and Ecole des Hautes Etudes en Sciences Sociales, France

The 'past in the present' has returned in the early twenty-first century with a vengeance, and with it the expansion of categories of experience. These experiences have largely been lost in the advance of rationalist and constructivist understandings of subjectivity and their collective representations. The cultural stakes around forgetting, 'useful forgetting' and remembering, locally, regionally, nationally and globally have risen exponentially. It is therefore not unusual that 'migrant memories'; micro-histories; personal and individual memories in their interwoven relation to cultural, political and social narratives; the mnemonic past and present of emotions, embodiment and ritual; and finally, the mnemonic spatiality of geography and territories are receiving more pronounced hearings.

This transpires as the social sciences themselves are consciously globalizing their knowledge bases. In addition to the above, the reconstructive logic of memory in the juggernaut of galloping informationalization is rendering it more and more publicly accessible, and therefore part of a new global public constellation around the coding of meaning and experience. Memory studies as an academic field of social and cultural inquiry emerges at a time when global public debate - buttressed by the fragmentation of national narratives - has accelerated. Societies today, in late globalized conditions, are pregnant with newly unmediated and unfrozen memories once sequestered in wide collective representations. We welcome manuscripts that examine and analyze these profound cultural traces.

Titles in this series

13. London and the Politics of Memory
In the Shadow of Big Ben
Stuart Burch

14. Heritage, Memory, and Punishment
Remembering Colonial Prisons in East Asia
Shu-Mei Huang and Hyun Kyung Lee

15. Postnational Memory, Peace and War
Making Pasts Beyond Borders
Nigel Young

https://www.routledge.com/sociology/series/ASHSER1411

POSTNATIONAL MEMORY, PEACE AND WAR

Making Pasts Beyond Borders

Nigel Young

For Peter.
December 2019.
in peace –
Nigel ...

Routledge
Taylor & Francis Group
LONDON AND NEW YORK

First published 2020
by Routledge
2 Park Square, Milton Park, Abingdon, Oxon OX14 4RN

and by Routledge
52 Vanderbilt Avenue, New York, NY 10017

Routledge is an imprint of the Taylor & Francis Group, an informa business

British Library Cataloguing-in-Publication Data
A catalogue record for this book is available from the British Library

Library of Congress Cataloging-in-Publication Data
Names: Young, Nigel, 1938- author.
Title: Postnational memory : peace, war; making pasts beyond borders / Nigel Young.
Description: 1 Edition. | New York : Routledge, 2019. | Series: Memory studies: global constellations | Includes bibliographical references and index.
Identifiers: LCCN 2019026241 (print) | LCCN 2019026242 (ebook) | ISBN 9780367110963 (hardback) | ISBN 9780367110970 (paperback) | ISBN 9780429024801 (ebook)
Subjects: LCSH: Memory–Social aspects. | War and society–History. | War in art. | War in literature. | Transnationalism.
Classification: LCC HM1033 .Y68 2019 (print) | LCC HM1033 (ebook) | DDC 303.6/6–dc23
LC record available at https://lccn.loc.gov/2019026241
LC ebook record available at https://lccn.loc.gov/2019026242

ISBN: 978-0-367-11096-3 (hbk)
ISBN: 978-0-367-11097-0 (pbk)
ISBN: 978-0-429-02480-1 (ebk)

Typeset in Bembo
by Integra Software Services Pvt. Ltd.

MIX
Paper from responsible sources
FSC® C013056

Printed and bound in Great Britain by
TJ International Ltd, Padstow, Cornwall

This book is dedicated to Antonia Young, and the rest of my family, especially my cousin Wendy Price. But also it is for all those of you, both named and unnamed in what follows, who (and will know who you are) supported, participated, advised and helped in this collective project and *Memory Journey*: long may it continue from here.

FIGURE 0.0 Cover art by Iri and Toshi Maruki, *The Hiroshima Panels: XII Floating Lanterns*, 1969. Maruki Gallery for the Hiroshima Panels, Saitama.

The ceremony depicted in the panel in memory of the souls of about 200,000 atomic bomb victims takes place every 6 August on the anniversary of the bombing. Thousands of paper lanterns inscribed with personal peace messages are set afloat down Hiroshima's Motoyasu river, passing directly in front of the Atomic Bomb Dome.

CONTENTS

IMAGES

PREFACE

Ways of remembering and the role of text

This is an exploration of a particular tendency in contemporary memory that I believe has not, and cannot be, understood fully by traditional sources, and I have used the following three alternative approaches.

The first, presented in personal vignettes and stories, is based on direct experience of sites, visits, places, memories of war, conversations about and relationships beyond, nationality.

The second, more familiar path is to interrogate key transnational texts – many lesser known, such as in film, Peter Watkins' *The Journey*; in art, *The Hiroshima Panels* painted in Japan by the Marukis; and also the photography of Del Tredici and Khaldei. Other postnational representations are better recognized, including the films of Resnais and Lanzmann's *Shoah*; also expressionist art from Munch to Kiefer, most especially Kollwitz and Otto Dix; the theatre of Joan Littlewood; and the writing of those who fought, such as Sassoon and much poetry of war, and in prose from Orwell and Hemingway, and post-war from W. G. Sebald.

My third source are the truth-telling, often anonymous or unknown, voices of victims, witnesses, survivors. The civilian memories of nurses, such as Vera Brittain, stretcher bearers, prisoners of war, refugees, who testify to both atrocity and barbarism, as well as acts of compassion that cross borders. I have learnt much from scholars, theorists and historians of memory; but for the most part, this book is not a conversation with them.

I was particularly touched by the personal permissions granted to me in messages from or by relatives of many writers and artists, including the late Gavin Ewart, Terrence Des Pres, Gerard Rondeau and H. S. Williamson, and support from Peter Watkins, Piet Chielens, Peter Dale Scott and Peter Balakian, who has fought against forgetting of the Armenian catastrophe and others.

It is said that our collective memory has been both democratized and civilianized – but if so there is still a long way to go – and this book represents a contribution to that journey. Echoing Peter Dale Scott, who urged us to rescue the reality of the Indonesian genocide, as part of our path towards sanity; living honestly requires memory work (see epigraph page 179).

PART 1

Memory and counter-memory

PROLOGUE

A modern memory?

The form memory takes, and what we forget, influences our intentions and actions for the future. A fiercely truth-telling voice and graphic images emerged to respond to the atrocities that overshadowed twentieth-century history. It is clear that over time memory has come to play a more important part in our lives both public and private. Less prevalent is the idea that the way we remember differs from the past. This book describes the modern postnational form of such remembering that emerged with total war after 1914.

Another dimension of this process is that it represents an intentional use of interpretations of the past. Modern memory finds no apology acceptable for genocide and military excess. Such construction of alternative memory, at times perhaps even a counter-memory, has an alternative social possibility in mind, quite unlike most history. The contention of this book is that key elements of such memory work play a transformatory and cathartic role. This is expressed through the intermediary voice of literature and art.

As this voice and these imageries increasingly find receptive constituencies, recalling the past becomes both an agency of changing our cultural consciousness and an ingredient in that restructured feeling. In touching potential transgenerational audiences to further the spread of such constructed memories, it is representations – our pictures of the past – that changes the way we feel about the present.

Vignette:
Being there – a Cotswold Vignette 'Adlestrop'

IMAGE 0.1 Adlestrop former train station sign, Gloucestershire, England. The old sign has been placed here at the village bus stop almost a mile from the railway line. A plaque with Edward Thomas's poem of that name and a memorial is placed in the shelter. (see *Poems of Edward Thomas* (Oxford, 1978)).

Yes. I remember Adlestrop—
The name, because one afternoon
Of heat the express-train drew up there
Unwontedly. It was late June.

'Adlestrop' the poem was published after the poet's death in 1917, in *Poems*. Three years earlier the poet, Edward Thomas, had passed through the station on a hot day in June, two months before war began. He wrote the poem the following January.

My grandfather, early in his career, was a travelling dentist in the Cotswolds – he travelled in a pony and trap – once he was stuck all night in a snow drift in a hamlet above Andoversford until he, and his transportation, were dug out. Before 1914 he certainly visited his surgery in Moreton-in-Marsh and went on to Stow, a mile from Adlestrop. But whether he ventured as far as there, I'm not sure. At least we know there was already a railway station. But, his proximity, like Thomas, extended further: he fought in France, being wounded and gassed several times, once near the Somme – a service experience in the Great War that he had in common with Edward Thomas. But he survived, with much German lead shrapnel in his limbs.

Until first I read the poem the name of this village didn't mean much to me, although I had spent late summer holiday weeks nearby in Rissington as a child. And then we went through the village on a school history trip I recall (I organized it). We were there to see the 'Rollright stones', Chastleton House, Compton Wynyates and then onto Edgehill but, only, via Adlestrop; indeed, that's the point of 'Adlestrop', it's the later remembering – the moment – as much as the place, and all the unanswered questions and faded images of a station – between Oxford and Worcester – memorized in time, in June 1914.

And willows, willow-herb, and grass,
And meadowsweet, and haycocks dry,
No whit less still and lonely fair
Than the high cloudlets in the sky.

It is an unlikely shrine and I wonder what the locals make of the increasing numbers who visit it. We also struggle to rediscover it physically. Lost in the brambles there is no longer a station at Adlestrop and the site was, when last I visited, largely overgrown. It may have been a collateral victim of Dr Beechings 1960s railway cuts; though it is not on a branch line. Quite away from the village itself it is difficult for people to find the place now. But the name plate for the station platform was saved. It sits at the back of the village bus shelter, with a plaque for Thomas, and the words of the poem – strangely incongruous.

Thomas remembered much more than the name of course; that is the point of the poem and its symbolism. And then all that is not named, or said, or spoken about: the subsequent horrors of Flanders or the Somme – the huge machinery of unfolding events around which birds still sang; and this unspoken reference back to 'pre-war', to the last summer. It is a key aspect of a memory that we can now call 'modern' because it sat at the cusp of a new sensibility; a new way of thinking about a present passing, as it becomes memory. The moment is recollected not as a dream but as an image: one that impels us to think about the imperative to recall, perhaps framed as pastoral, but essentially as transition.

> And for that minute a blackbird sang
> Close by, and round him, mistier,
> Farther and farther, all the birds
> Of Oxfordshire and Gloucestershire.

And not far away from Adlestrop, in the glorious summer of 1944, a six-year-old boy stood and watched the endless lines of trucks and jeeps and tanks trundling in convoy down the country road towards Cirencester and the Southern coast. My father just said 'Something big is going to happen'. It did; in Normandy.

And so pastoral Adlestrop is one trigger for what I mean by modern memory and subsequent reconstructions of it. And for what reason? That moment? A change in consciousness? The poem? Or the 'great' events in which they were set? A metaphor for unexplained disruptions? And why does a chance halt in a named – but unexperienced – and now lost, Gloucestershire village station, become a notable cultural marker in modern collective experience?

> The steam hissed. Someone cleared his throat.
> No one left and no one came
> On the bare platform. What I saw
> Was Adlestrop—only the name

INTRODUCTION

Defining 'modern memory'

In order to separate this evolving form of collective memory from other shared memories, the term 'modern' helps distinguish it from 'traditional', folk or communal memory, and also from 'state' memory, when that was typically formed as a national historical memory. As new nationalisms arise, the new, alternate postnational remembering co-exists, uncomfortably even, in tension, with them.

Four prime traits help define modern memory. First is its 'truth-telling' and truth-seeking character especially in the way it represents an unheroic, unromanticized view of the past; specifically in expressing the reality, in words and images, of modern war and state violence. That quest for a voice, a language, was led by victims and witnesses, those who 'were there'.

Second, I stress the uniquely postnational and critical character of this memory work. It has arisen as an alternative to the national and state-ordered memories that predominated for over a century. Essentially that aspect of this memory is anti-militarist, even anti-war. It increasingly represents a constructed civilian alternative to military and violent nationalist narratives.

Third, this creative form of remembering is marked by its typically non-violent, universalist and empathetic character. This trait is especially evoked by what I describe as both real and represented 'recognition scenes'. These are moments of identification or empathy with the humanity of 'the other'. Engaging another 'self' - with a human 'enemy', as person, especially when such acknowledgements occur in a conflict situations - constitutes the epitome of the *recognition-memory*, postnationalism implies.

Finally, although I do not link this alternative memory-making to specific *individual* identities, or a 'collective identity', or even to a particular social group's or generation's shared memory, the use of memory as a search for authentic representation of past events undoubtedly involves *personal* autobiography, and self-reflection. It equally reflects the experiences of a succession of political generations, both shared and contested.

Each of these four characteristics – the truth-telling voice; the cosmopolitan framing of past events; the images of empathetic interaction; and, not least, the personal responsibility for memory construction - can be related to one ideal. That is a transgenerational cultural vision of peace: a democratizing, political aspiration to transcend war and militarism that has matured over a century.

This book avoids the usual foci of modern academic work in memory studies – for example, work on trauma and post-trauma. But inevitably such paths of memory represent in part a response to the mass suffering associated with the violence of modernity, and the scars of atrocity and modern genocide in particular

Iconic visual representation of such violence – what one might describe as the 'Guernica' syndrome (which I discuss in Chapter 10, see endnote 5) – has been potentially and actually crucial to the growth of such new form of collective memory. As a result, the images of war, holocaust and peace are central to the argument of this book. In this, the arts and literature of modernism play a key role; however, memory is expressed in many styles and forms, not least in the popular arts. Those who created them were often directly touched by these traumas, events and personal experiences.

From among these memory-workers I have chosen to focus on victims, witnesses and survivors. I use such sources to build a picture of the past, rather than the representation of the victors, the military 'brass' or political decision-makers – or even professional historians. This allows a greater possibility of de-territorializing memory – of moving to a past beyond borders.

1

A MEMORABLE ENGAGEMENT

Vignette:
Kennington at Laventie

There is a marvellously contradictory but striking painting in the Imperial War Museum in London, it represents a group of crestfallen British soldiers in a ruined French village in the snow in 1915. For me it sums up perfectly that puzzling moment, especially in this case for Britain, when the link between past, present and future has been ruptured. It was becoming clear to millions in Europe by 1915 that a great divide had been crossed and an era ended. The changes had been accelerating for decades especially in Austria, France and Germany. Yet there is still a sense of loss, bewilderment and dislocation from the past. This painting is no modernist statement. Eric Kennington had been there in January 1915 as a soldier. *The Kensingtons at Laventie* was painted in traditional ways, employing oil on glass, giving the brilliance of some of the Renaissance artworks. There are even echoes of a fashionable salon painting (after all Kennington was a Royal Academician). But it represents a stark truth: of exhausted, dejected British 'officers' and 'men', defeated as much by cold as by German guns. This is no 'Bank Holiday lark'. The awkward pose of the white-faced figure, bandaged, lying on the snow, is the nearest artistic image to a modernist element in the picture.[1] Yet neither the subject nor the moment is 'traditional'. It is not glorious, chivalrous or patriotic. The image speaks the language of the popular soldier's song – "We're here because we're here, because we're here because we're here (ad infinitum)." No illusions, no reason, no logic, just bafflement. One soldier carries what at this point might be seen as his iconic, if somewhat pointless, war trophy: it is a handsome, and now dysfunctional German helmet of the kind worn early in the war. But it is at best a consolation prize. There's no sense of triumph amongst the group of soldiers.

IMAGE 1.1 Eric Kennington, *The Kensingtons at Laventie*, 1915. The sense of disillusionment in the picture can be compared with the equally sombre images by Nevinson and Williamson. © Imperial War Museums (Art IWM ART 15661).

The painting seems memorable, not least because it depicts a specific moment less than six months into the 'Great' War. Pondering over catastrophes, the pressing need for a new way of remembering such moments like these has become obvious to those directly involved in such debacles, and also to onlookers. The moment of puzzlement symbolizes the familiar search for a fixed point in a continuous conjunction of past and future: the use of recollection in order to decipher who we are and where we are in that flux of time and experience. It is such a moment revisited. And there is irony in that Laventie is geographically close to one of the sectors of the continuous battlefield where the spontaneous and remembered Christmas truce or winter ceasefire of a few weeks earlier is best documented. By January reality returned; the war was not over by 25 December as had been widely predicted. The slaughter gradually resumed, and accelerated not only in Laventie, but also in hundreds of villages like it.

Never included in anthologies of World War One poetry, because it has no specific reference to the conflict, is the poem 'Adlestrop'. The title of Edward Thomas's well-known memory piece is symptomatic of that new sensibility. It refers to a chance moment on a hot summer's day at a Cotswold railway station in June 1914. Written about eight months later, it famously came to symbolise the same disjuncture between the worlds of 1914 and 1915.

> No one left and no one came
> What I saw was Adlestrop – only the name[2]

Written before going to the front, the image of the country station at Adlestrop seems to capture retrospectively that sense of transition: from a pastoral – though not sentimental – remembrance moment, to its likely eventual recollection on the battlefields in France. A remembered England as it was, compared with a dawning awareness of the reality of the Western Front in 1915. Not perhaps entirely coincidentally, the poem was written in the same month that Kennington was in Laventie.[3]

The war to end war – and its legacy

Like the poppies populating the summer mud of the battlefields, modern memory generates shoots everywhere from the remains of the 1914–18 European civil conflict. The unanticipated scale of loss is captured in two lines from *The Waste Land*:

> A crowd flowed over London Bridge, so many,
> I had not thought death had undone so many.[4]

Historically, no other war, perhaps no other such event, has had such a profound and widespread cultural effect. This was *especially* true in northern and western Europe, where it intensified an existing crisis of social memory. Any attempt at understanding the emergence of new forms of remembering in the modern era inevitably first centres on this, the so-called 'Great' War. The war is significant for its symbolic character and its relation to modernity. But it is its structural implications and their long-term global impact that have become ever clearer over time.

Infused with a sense of loss of a traditional past, a new remembering was a reactive, but not in the main reactionary, response. It reacted to both military and civilian worlds, and not least to the impersonality of modern, mass mechanized war-making. Because of the nineteenth-century revolutions in transport and communications it was the first worldwide war, and its sociological effects were inevitably more universal in scale and resonance, as was the more universalist memorialising and representing of it.

The decades 1776 to 1815 saw the first great rupture of early modernity; and its effects were widespread, but the first decades of the twentieth century saw a social revolution on a quite overwhelming scale. Militarism and modern organization, through the 'national' mobilizations for the Great War, created the structures and technological preparedness for totalism, for a second world war, and for the eventual mass civilian destruction of the 1940s culminating in nuclear weapons. It prefigured such killing both in cities and in death camps or forced labour – in factories, or as draftees in combat; it marked the subsequent civil wars in Russia, in Spain, and across Asia and the Pacific– even before the bombing of 1940. It was a war waged beyond November 1918, more or less continuously – often as civil wars for another thirty-one years, and it marks the essential backdrop for any analysis of how modern memory evolved.

Not only was the Great War as transformational as 1789 to 1815 was for Europe, it was indeed a world event: a war of six old empires – French, British, German, Russian, Austro-Hungarian and Ottoman. With conflicts spanning the globe and mass armies fighting globally, it drew participants from five continents. For example, largely unnoticed, hundreds of thousands of labourers from China were brought by ship and helped construct the trenches of the Western Front. The war involved large numbers of combat troops from Africa, India, Australasia and the Americas.

But in another sense it was also a war of the nation states: older ones such as Britain and France, newer ones such as Germany and Italy – and the USA. For the emergent nations in the old Empires such as Turkey, Canada, Australia, New Zealand and South Africa, the war was equally about new 'national' identity. The sites of memorials at Anzac Cove and elsewhere on the Gallipoli peninsula for Australia and New Zealand (and Turkey), those in France at Vimy Ridge, Beaumont Hamel and Newfoundland Park for Canada and Delville Wood for South Africa are sites of national loss and tragedy. A Turkish national identity and memory also arguably began with Kemal Ataturk, fighting the allies, in the Dardanelles. Annually and increasingly marked by, sometimes ambivalent, even controversial ceremonies of remembrance, these are the first and in many ways key 'national' sites of memory for these states. For others this identity formation and symbolism is more ambiguously remembered and these new memories are commemorated on or about such European battlefields. For Ireland, and Ulster, in particular, the new memories are of division and conflicted allegiances after the 1916 rising, and the mixed loyalties of Catholics and Protestants, Republicans and Unionists, north and south.

State driven as it was, there was a cultural logic to the war and its context which pushed the world beyond both empires and new nations in the direction of more global identification, and as well as towards a gradual renaissance of transnational European identity. Such contrasting tendencies confront both war and many aspects of modernity. Whilst new empires emerged from the war as several old empires, Ottoman, Russian and Austro-Hungarian, collapsed, it is pressure for post-colonial statehood that accelerates; and also the hegemonic rise of two great powers – one capitalist and one state collectivist. These follow different trajectories, with their own 'public histories', which are confirmed in the cultural stand-off of the nuclear Cold War. In contrast, the more short-lived fascist imperial aspirations and projects (Italy, Spain, Japan and Germany) lead directly to confrontation with both of them: the USA and USSR, in the wars of 1936–45. In different ways through these procedures each were shaped by the 1914–18 conflict, they are marked by divergent and contested public memories.

An archetypal war

This was the first fully photographed war, as well as the first literate one.[5] Many critics and commentators have stressed how the archetypical quality of 1914–18, that imprinted in itself the memory, derived from the mass distribution of photographic images of the war, especially on the Western Front. In Vernon Scannell's words:

> Wherever war is spoken of
> I find
> The war that was called 'Great' invades the mind

The 'theatre of war' was enacted in hundreds of miles of lines of parallel trenches, across France and Belgium, often only yards apart. We engage with scenes of the unprotected soldiers living in them facing often continuous artillery and machine gun fire; the catastrophic casualties suffered, the often appalling daily conditions of life, as well as the terrible and ironic proximity both to 'home' (normality) and to 'the enemy', made this quite unlike any other violent conflict in human history. But was this a model of mutual, assured destruction sufficient in itself to stamp a mark on a public memory so widely and deeply? Was the impact of these horrors on social consciousness in several continents (almost all of the countries of Europe, and of the British Commonwealth) sufficient to transform collective remembering?

Beyond its physical reality, the iconic character of the war was created, represented and transmitted culturally by the genius of memory-makers; building on their new insights from the battlefield, this memory came to constitute an alternative narrative or 'myth' of war. It was sustained by an extraordinary creative responsiveness not only in the arts, as well as the letters and images from the Front, but also by popular songs and humour. The starkly dramatic battlefield photographs paralleled the terse truthfulness of much war writing. So too did the revelatory painting of the war artists at the Front (many of them 'official'), but especially the expressionist drawings by two German soldiers. Together they created a shared, imagined 'memory': a representation of war. It was one that came to transcend borders.[6]

Poetry was an especially important part of this in Britain and the English-speaking world. School students first encountered the Great War not so much from reading history, as through a poem (probably Sassoon, Owen, Macrae or Brooke), or prose (again Sassoon's trilogy of 'memoirs', or Robert Graves's retrospective *Goodbye to all That* (1929)[7]). At home, family photographs include pictures, not of the trenches but of a son, a father or grandfather or a nurse in uniform, or a memento of the war, such as shell cases on the mantelpiece. By the second half of the twentieth century, paintings such as Paul Nash's *We Are Making a New World* or prints and sculptures by Käthe Kollwitz began to acquire similar public status as familiar and symbolic representations not only of a hopelessly tragic, wasteful war, but also its disastrous results.

Vignette:

'The Bradford Pals' – a community of loss

Even before 1918, memory 'communities' in Britain and on the continent were forming, focused on bereavement. Eventually, this bonding was symbolized by the names of dead on local war memorials; a plaque; a list of the 'fallen' which also appeared in places of work as well as schools, hospitals, churches and stations. My college has one, so does Charing Cross Station in London for its staff casualties – a departure point for troops. Even the smallest villages marked their losses. Similar elective affinity groups formed around such collective mourning projects occurring across Europe, in different forms, groups and pilgrimages. In a dislocated society, it was a memorable bonding, defying the processes of change across continental Europe. Iconic communities of mourning defy national frontiers: the memories they carry are not those specified by race, religion or state identification.

In modern memory formation such communalism is symbolized even by single streets in one city – Bradford, Yorkshire in northern England is such an example. Here memories were associated with the veterans, the dead and the survivors of 'Old Pals' associations. They were part of Kitchener's Army, the recruited 'Pals' battalions. These existed in many cities in England after 1914, not least to recruit from amongst the many hundreds of volunteers. From cities such as Bradford, thousands of these 'pals' died, often together, especially in July 1916. The 'Bradford Pals' lost over a thousand dead during the Somme fighting, most on the first day of 1 July. In 2016 a centennial memorial was erected for them in Artois near the main battlefield. These were brothers, neighbours and friends; dozens from a single street of terraced houses, such as Arncliffe Terrace. That loss included several sons from the same family – many killed in the initial hours of the attack. Many hundreds more were badly wounded, some missing and never found. They had 'joined up' together, and to the same regiment, in this case mainly the sixteenth and eighteenth battalions of the West Yorkshires and there was a vivid sense of communal loss both in these battalions at the front and at home. The following months saw thousands more casualties, and hundreds more deaths. Until the 1980s the Bradford Pals had their own section in Bradford's local museum, and there is still a headstone in the city square, as well as the memorial in France; in 2014, there was an exhibit in the cathedral.

But even in the detailed accounts of two local military historians, neither of them mainly focusing on losses, the story of the Pals is a dismal and appalling story.[8] There is nothing uplifting about the disillusion and suffering of thousands of ordinary men, caught up in a process far larger than their experience or their local community. The image is not of heroism but stoicism. The palpable disenchantment started soon after 1914, long before leading to the Bradford Pals disasters at Serre and Gommencourt on the Somme. These dispiriting experiences are portrayed in the grim-faced photographs and the understated witness stories. These were 'pals' surviving in comradeship but *in extremis*, as the survey of the remembered dead revealed. Amongst the losses, some were shot (even if drunk) for 'desertion', leaving the trench and not finding their way back.

But the dead were replaced by new cogs for the machine. Of the 35,000 Bradford war dead, thousands were from these same volunteers. In soccer, Bradford City's 1914 team was top of the football league in England and cup winners. Announcements and declarations by players at football games turned matches into recruiting rallies and as a result thousands volunteered. Sixteen 'City' players joined up, nine of them 'Pals', and six died.

There is another irony in the disasters of the Pals because it coincided with the beginning of Bradford's decline as a successful textile city. For a century, like many industrial areas, Bradford had grown from a chain of villages into a city. The handcraft workers became mechanized and the villages industrialized. Around the factories, these communities grew together. The villages became parts of a city, but over decades new communities, 'urban villages', evolved with soccer teams, later a rugby and cricket team, and multiple clubs and chapels, and from these the 'Pals' battalions were recruited. This chapter in military history ended in the 1960s (before 1914, the professional army had developed from enlistment).

Perhaps as the recent memorial on the Somme suggests, this represents part of the ongoing work of memory that links a changing city to these iconic communities of mourning and a danger of forgetting in an ongoing journey of understanding.[9]

Such a story also represented a new era in British war experience – and a democratization of memory. Before 1914, the army had an understandably bad profile of low life, drunkenness, brutality and criminality. The professional army had only developed from enforced enlistment, including convicts, mercenaries and soldiers subject to impressment, giving the army its previously evil reputation. But with Kitchener's civilian army, the national volunteerism of 1914 represented a radical departure. Such a choice was based on patriotic appeals, which represents a break with the past. These civilian recruits replaced centuries of a brutal and often semi-criminal and coerced military. Symbolic communities of civilian loss, like Bradford's, were part of a more widespread popularization in remembering: the shared loss of a citizen army whose experience, which nevertheless raised more questions than gave answers, changed public memory forever.

The roll calls of place: memory sites

Amongst the most important mnemonics, the role of place looms large. The names of places emerge from the Great War with special resonance – partly because of the war's often static quality, and the memorials and cemeteries that mark the sites. These are not so much 'battles' as 'sites of experience' – memories of 'being there': not famous for a victory or defeat as much as representing a passage in an imponderable event. Like the roll calls of atrocious 'battles', these sites of memory, of mass trauma, are rehearsed in film, poetry and political theatre. It is hard to accept, constructed as it was, that this was, as some assert, a 'romanticized' view of war.[10] Many writers begin to capture this sense of the special meaning war gave to a hamlet named on a trench map: Mametz, St Eloi, Zonnebeke, Vlamertinghe, Warnencourt, Serre, Laventie, Gericourt, Craonne. Each name recalls an image, a moment; each is engraved as part of a memory of war.

It was over two years before the pacifist writer Vera Brittain and her friend Winifred Holtby could visit her fiancé Roland's grave at Louvencourt. This was in 1921 before fully organized battlefield tours to France and Belgium were developed (Image 1.2). Brittain describes how as they drove from Amiens, where she had nursed in the war, they read makeshift village signs "incredulously" and with "chill excitement" as they drove from Albert to Bapaume: 'Cléry, Villers-Brétonneux, Péronne, Grivesnes, Hédauville'. Places either known by her now-dead men, her friends, her brother and her fiancé, or places where those men whom she had nursed[11] were wounded when she worked in Etaples and elsewhere.

Such haunting lists appear in many guises. In literature they are the key memory locators of 1914–18. In Scannell's evocative poem 'The Great War' (1962), the "Fateful commentary of Distant Guns" is recorded by names –

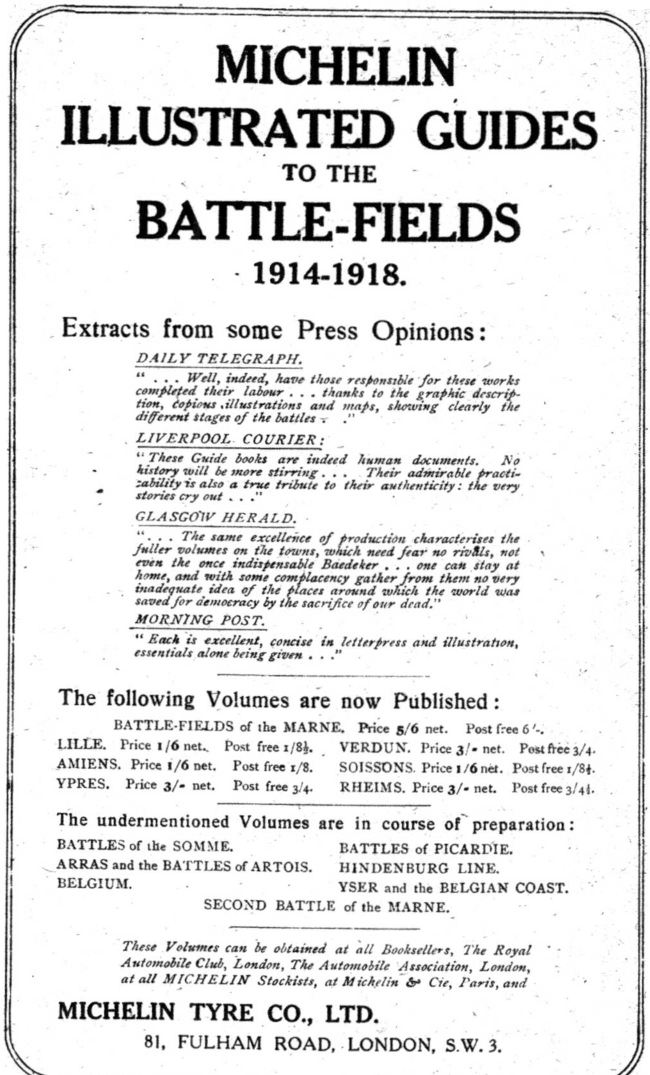

IMAGE 1.2 *Michelin Illustrated Guides to the Battlefields 1914–1918* 'Ypres', published in 1919. At first they were not commercially successful, and not until the mid-1920s did such tourism become popular.

Passchendaele, Bapaume, Loos and Mons, the place names of conflict.[12] Much later in Pat Barker's novel, *Regeneration* (1991), there is a scene before the silent soldier, Callan, is administered electric current treatment to deal with 'mutism' caused by his shell shock. Dr Yealland cites more specifically (to show Callan's capacity for endurance), the battles he fought in: "Mons, the Marne, Aisne, First and Second Ypres, Hill 60, Neuve-Chapelle, Loos, Armentieres, the Somme and Arras" (a daunting, fictional record that few would have survived!).[13] In Sandburg's (1918) poem, 'Grass',[14] it grows both over "Ypres and Verdun". Later Paul Fussell acutely remarks on the onomatopoeic sounds of such names as Passchendaele (the 1917 battle in a Flanders swamp) evoking the 'splash', and 'passion' of that 'slaughter in the mud'.

Such a sombre catalogue of battles was also intoned by the Nazis at the Nuremburg Nazi Party rally of 1934. As the drums roll, each battle name is read out: the tone is of loss, solemnity, veneration, memory, by and for a new generation of fighters. As the battle standard is slowly lowered, one of the 'future soldiers' (still in the labour battalion) intones the list of places: *Wie eins vor Lutticht* (Liege), *Bei Langemarck, Bei Tannenberg, Vor Verdun, An der Somme, An der Una* (Aisne), *In Vlandern.* The village name Langemarck carried special meaning because of the death of thousands of young volunteers near there, early in the war, including the artist Kollwitz's son Peter and some of the fictional characters in Remarque's novel *All Quiet on the Western Front.*[15]

Nothing so new about all this perhaps; the roll call lists of battles on regimental standards or at veterans rallies have long been a familiar part of military ritual. Except that in most cases these new place names are not battles as such, but associated with conflicts and experiences of many kinds – temporal and spatial signposts in a general region. Some such as 'the Somme', which covered over fifty miles and several years (not just 1916), resonated in a particularly unmilitary way. Many of the lithographs in Otto Dix's notable *Der Krieg* (War) series (a set is in the British Library) are identified with specific places such as Mericourt or Cléry-sur-Somme where he fought as a machine gunner (Image 1.3).[16]

There is no triumphalist version of the Somme – for any army, any state – and not only the Somme, but also Flanders, Artois or Verdun, or the often appalling, half-forgotten Chemin des Dames and the attrition of spring 1917. Siegfried Sassoon's writing often fixes on such places: men "slogged up to Arras"; or constructed parapets at Mametz; or meditated near Albert about the Battle of Somme.[17] In *Aftermath* he insists that we remember these moments. He notes that the physicality of the war is located in names of sites rather than people. The names of places become lastingly significant regardless of what happened there – whether a mundane day at the front, another poet Edmund Blunden passing the Chateau at Vlamertinghe, or a sudden July killing, or a mindless protracted slaughter. For Hemingway it was Fosalta: his often-quoted remarks from *A Farewell to Arms* ring especially true of these remembered sites:

> Abstract words such as glory, honour, courage or hallow were obscene beside the concrete names of villages, the numbers of roads, the names of rivers, the numbers of regiments and the dates.[18]

IMAGE 1.3 Otto Dix, *Seen at the Steep Slopes of Cléry-sur-Somme*, 1924. Der Krieg series. Dix served as a machine gunner at Cléry. The complete series 'Der Krieg' is on view at Historial de la Grande Guerre, Péronne, France, near the Somme. Sprengel Museum Hannover. © bpk/DACS. Photo: Stefan Behrens.

There was another hidden reality beneath these ruined cities towns and villages, even as the sites were fought over. It was to occur again on a vastly larger scale after 1940. Cowering in a troglodyte world, of cellars and sewers, basement city vaults and other hiding places were refugees – and the infirm, injured and incapacitated, the elderly and the insane, who could not, or would not, leave. Geoffrey Winthrop Young who worked with the Quaker ambulance team in France and Belgium describes in his memoir, *The Grace of Forgetting*, a bizarre reality discovered under the ruins of Ieper (Ypres). It was not publicized at the time, and was not well known afterwards, nor were the fates of the elderly, women, children and the demented – many refugees from the battlefield who the medics found there, and of whom many died.[19] Otto Dix met the insane in such ruined desolation and subsequently drew them. Decades later De Broca's 1960s film *King of Hearts* (1966) created a satire around such abandoned lunatics in a small French town, implying that the real lunacy was war itself.

Modernity and modern war

'Modernist' orientations in painting and music that hinted at war had preceded the outbreak of the fighting. Some premonitions had indeed been foreshadowed in artistic expressionism after the 1880s. Dominated by portrayals of impending apocalypse, this art is ambiguously related to the emergence of a modern memory and its precursors. The art is not only darkly prophetic, but also nihilistic and violent, and some of it expresses a worship of 'force', an idea representing a symbiosis of war, conflict and the art of revolt.[20] A debate persists on whether the Great War was the main source of the idea of the 'modern', or was predicated on the pre-emergence of modernity. It has been proposed that the images of cultural 'modernism' *emerging before 1914* played a part in shaping the war ideologically.

Ironically, some avant-garde art did become a component, a modernist dimension, of war itself. Indeed, Modris Eksteins (1989) argues that the war of 1914 in itself is pre-figured in aspects of early modernism – even in the new Russian ballet and Igor Stravinsky's musical forms in *The Rites of Spring*; it reflected the new technologies and used new techniques; in its threatening rhythms and drumbeats, a revolutionary music is accompanied by 'war' imagery. In the decade before the war, this imagery marked the new styles of *futurism* vorticism and cubism in particular, but more generally marks some popular art and music in the same years.[21]

'Pre-figured' in this evolution, these semi-abstract styles entered the war in forms such as the dazzle strip camouflage on ships,[22] representing the technological narrative. The 'modern' was a dimension of 'war culture' in the disassembled shapes of Wyndham Lewis's vorticist paintings, or C. W. Nevinson's 1914–18 futurist angularity (see his image of French troops, *Returning to the Trenches*, Chapter 9, Image 9.1). This became part of the memorable imagery of the war, just as much as its spaces and absences.[23]

The pre-1914 cataclysmic premonitions of modernist art are a key part of the new consciousness. Post-war, it is reflected in Eliot's poem *The Waste Land*, and is paralleled by a transatlantic modernism. Alyson Booth argues, "We read modernism without fully realizing the extent to which it handles the bones of the war 'dead'."[24] In her *Postcards from the Trenches*, she traces the idioms of modernism as a having important origins in the trenches: "What soldiers said of the Great War has become part of what modernism is." It is also clear that war provided a setting for the further growth of style. As in *The Waste Land*, or in vorticism, a 'modern memory' of the war was a conflict experienced often in starkly modernist terms. At the same time modernism itself was or became profoundly haunted by the war, not least in Woolf's novels.

After 1918, a 'modernist' version of memory of the conflict became a key cultural and political presence across the social spectrum. This becomes clear in the contrasting usages of World War One memory in the USA. After the American entry into the war, both war poets and writers epitomize this mood:

Hemingway and Sandburg, but also Randolph Bourne and then John Dos Passos in his *1919* (1932).[25]

Modern memory work continues to evolve in such transatlantic interactions, but often in a contentious, conflicted and critical context. In Italy, fascism inherited parts of modernist imagery, even whilst the war was fought. Such images represented aspects of early modernism, especially in Marinetti's 'futurist' work, which continued under Mussolini's hegemony.[26] Later the German veteran, Ernst Junger's fictionalized memoir, a paean to violence (*Storm of Steel*, 1929) embodies similarly brutalist recollections of fighting at the front.[27] His first person account is undeniably modern: its deeply militarist voice, echoes the Nazi worship of force, celebration of armed conflict, and the thrill of combat.

Even in Eliot's *The Waste Land* itself, the war imagery *is* inescapable. Like many other modernist texts, Eliot's is a poem about the ruptures of modernity: metaphors for the void, the loss, the fear of the future predominate. The acute spaces of this lifeless landscape, the detritus and the physical spaces imaged in the poem, are indubitably the killing fields of the Great War – and prophetically, those still lying ahead. As an Anglo-American conservative, Eliot's stark modernist account reflects a more general transatlantic watershed in sensibility. It was part of a mood of reflectiveness, and was also articulated in the stylistically innovative prose of both Ernest Hemingway and Virginia Woolf. As in expressionist art, the fragmentation and emptiness of modernity was represented, and even mocked, by Eliot's poetry, just as it was mirrored in Woolf's novels. By the time they wrote, 'memory' (and forgetting) had become associated with the painful issues plaguing the modern 'self', and the loss of purpose that accompanied these. These represented in fiction and in social criticism, are often influenced by Freudian analysis: dreams and nightmares, repression and revelation are never far away, and with these, representations of pasts and pasts lingering in the present.

In this interpretation, the 'modern self' is depicted as an alienated one, stranded in a disconnected present. It represents an identity in a new space, no longer anchored in a familiar time-continuum. These changes of modernity sever even the temporary communities formed by war; they reflect a desperate search for belonging and attempts to re-position the individual self in the setting of a modern and an impersonal mass society. It is a separation even seeking community in conflict, such as briefly found in the transitory world of trench war. Reinventions of identity also involve the rise of populist movements with their own manipulations of memory and repackaging of the self. Some are clearly marked by generational experience as was the post-war generation in Germany. The sense of isolation of the modern stimulates the rise of such movements, many of them succeeding in creating the sense of ersatz community that is another part of modernity. Others sought collective closure and consolation through memorializing the victims of the war. For a generation that survived the war, this mayhem of scattered memories from the 1920s to the 1930s illustrate both kinds of constructed community; but they also show

how a generation's war memory could be politically turned to serve, on the one hand, the pacifist and anti-militarist causes, and, on the other, the nationalist and militarist traditions.[28] They co-existed and clashed with momentous consequences.

The problem of the war memorial

The war memorial movement, especially in Britain, had a strong local and non-official dimension. In almost every community after 1918 a grassroots and spontaneous response to the losses of the war were focused on creating memorials and other 'foci' for mourning and collective events of remembrance.[29] These were group memorials, but they were rarely 'nationalist' memorials or patriotic plaques even though a tricolour or a reference to the fatherland or *la patrie* might be involved. There were also individual memorials such as Käthe Kollwitz's unique contributions to modern memory to which I will return again in this book. Most remembrance of the war is in fact sedate, dignified and linked to the past, largely by employing conventional, classic or religious language and inherited symbols not modernist forms. Such new 'remembering' rarely abandons all traditional forms or images in the interwar years. For example, war memorials often included representational sculptures. These dominated tens of thousands of towns and villages, not only in Britain and France, but also across Europe.

In the case of Kollwitz, she incorporates various inherited images – for example the classical *Pieta* – and some reference late medieval religious art. But her usage is boldly expressionist and secular, not sacred, especially in Flanders: when she could finally deal with her personal grief, the anti-militarist, internationalist artist chose to express this in a more sombre imagery. To mourn loss of her son, Peter, who had died at Roggevelde in the first months of the war, a few miles north of Langemarck, the notable *Grieving Parents* memorial comprised self-portrait figures of herself and husband. Peter's grave was later relocated, eventually sited in Vladslo (1932); it is in an almost exclusively German war cemetery, and like other symbols of mourning, the sculpture is still a mixture of modern and traditional elements.[30] But it articulates a new form of postnational memorializing:[31] both private and yet transcending the specific loss (Image 1.4).

The images are profoundly and painfully universalist, yet not otherworldly. These images like most of her art clearly merge her humanism and her life experience of grief, war and poverty with artistic formalism. It is this that secures her work from the sentimentality of which it has been sometimes accused The memorials from the 1918 to 1940 period challenge a simplistic dichotomy of 'modernity' and 'tradition', in remembering twentieth-century wars and atrocity, and show the survival of traditional forms after 1918, despite co-existing with modernism.[32]

Yet Fussell and Winter are right to see this modern memory as a critical memory. World War One was less a catalyst for heroic memories than an occasion for bitter and revisionist ones; in the words of the poet "never such

IMAGE 1.4 Käthe Kollwitz and her husband, Karl, by the kneeling statue of the grieving parents in 1932 in Flanders. The statue of herself (the other parent) has not yet been erected. The grave of the Kollwitz's son, Peter, lies in front of them. Both statues were later relocated to the larger military cemetery at Vladslo. By permission of IFF.

innocence again". Many post-war monuments were not celebratory, neither are they explicitly critical. For example, there was no expressionist or other sculptured depictions of the *gueules cassées* (the people with broken faces) or other markers of the brutal wounds of war; the human figures may be solemn, but they are, with few exceptions, whole.

The state or Nationalist groups continue to put up statues to commemorate or celebrate 'victory'; but this movement of more democratized memory, after 1918, creates memorials for a community to mourn, to remind a new generation to show or express the civic solidarity of a locality. It reveals at times a more sceptical public memory after 1918, and this was even more true after 1946 and the Holocaust. The post-modern critique of Walter Benjamin was opposed to concealing or replacing the devastating trauma of war. It must not be diverted or screened by monuments or commemorative ritual.

In the next chapter, I discuss loss, disappearance and absences, sixty years after the Great War: in the context of late modernism, and with controversies about memorialization of atrocities especially the Shoah, the concept of an alternative, a counter-monument, or even anti-memorial arose. As James Young in his work on holocaust memorials remarks, the problem was how to depict vast absence and loss.[33] Sometimes sites for memorials are no longer even 'places' but voids; for example, Birkenau is largely space, and it is Auschwitz that is a 'place' four miles away. Lists of names denote absences, but monuments draw attention to their own presence. It was rare for a 1914–18 war memorial to depict absence, though Edwin Lutyens's attempted to do that in several famous examples.

Memorializing can be honest, but it cannot comfort the bereaved. This is illustrated by the ambiguous styles of two of Lutyens's monuments to the missing and the dead in London and at Thiepval on the Somme, which I discuss again later in this book. Lutyens's cenotaph in London (1920) appears as a fusion of classical and modernist elements:[34] mixed genres from memorial sculpture to architecture, their forms at first only marginally influenced by modernism. Expressionism is also truthful, but it remembers rather than heals; in Käthe Kollwitz's 'parents', it both mourns and reminds.

Perhaps the clear link of memorial art to modernism comes to fruition finally in the 1930s. This is represented in Constantin Brancusi's ultra-modern, abstract stone and wood 'Monuments to the fallen, 14–18' (1937–38) exemplifying an absolutely 'new' memorial form. Constructed in Tirgu-Giu, Roumania,[35] and completed only just before the next war began in 1939, it memorialized an almost forgotten disaster ready for the next catastrophe.[36]

A modern war and the social critics: Paul Fussell to Jay Winter

Until the 1970s, the connections made in this interpretation of memory of 1914–1918 went unrecognized, or at least unacknowledged, by most cultural and literary critics. One can exaggerate his role, but Paul Fussell's book *Great War and Modern Memory* in 1975 helped change attitudes by putting a notion of 'modern memory' on the critic's conceptual agenda. Whether intended or not (and Fussell subsequently made clear he was quite the American warrior-patriot), this book provided a profound source for disentangling the war-ism of modern culture by focusing on the new language of memory, and the role of irony in creating mnemonics about war in general. Other critics, like him, see the Great War as the source of 'the modern'.[37]

Fussell's critical use of the term 'modern memory' placed it firmly in the public sphere. But he did not attempt to define it except by implication.[38] In his conclusion, his reference to one literary critic, Northrop Frye is, however, suggestive. It confirms that this approach is all about changed social consciousness – a new more holistic way of presenting and dealing with the past with perhaps an echo of Proust's big picture.[39] Fussell presents this corpus of literature as deeply critical of militarization in general, but he does not explicitly associate modern memory with 'anti-war', but mainly with scepticism and a new demythologizing of war, and a new 'truth-telling' voice about it.

In North America major writers on this period after Fussell, such as Eksteins and Winter, have dealt with the evolution of memory in its relation not just to this war but also to modernity itself. The momentous quality of the changes in human lives surrounding the 1914–18 conflict, the cultural watershed it represented, means that 'remembrance' of the war, after 1918, becomes a mass social phenomenon across Europe and beyond. A growing corpus of critical work such as Fussell's landmark volume, as well as the emergence of a creative 'genre' in literature, re-addressed the cultural centrality of the entire war. It was seen not merely as a geo-political event, but also as a moral and cultural moment. It attempts to answer the obvious question of any war 'called great', how it became and remains for many societies the memorable conflict: the 'mnemonic war', even an archetype, in a wholly changed environment.

Central to popular life, this remembering was expressed in new, often eclectic forms. For example, the war comprehended a transition in social class structure and this is illustrated in powerful metaphors by Jean Renoir's film *La Grande Illusion* (1937). The film depicts two characters, a French and a German aristocrat, as the 'heroes', but they represent the old, dying orders of chivalry and honour in Europe; it is other characters – the nouveau riche, the Jew, and the proletarian – who survive.[40] In an era which provided a setting for the growth of modern attitudes, Renoir depicts the war as representing the end of an old order of aristocratic privilege, and even the last epoch with a notion of the 'heroic'.

This change is echoed in the work of major memory-makers referenced in this book, such as Dix, Hemingway, Sassoon and Kollwitz: even if the poets and artists are indeed saying new things – telling 'bitter truths' – they are less often using the frameworks, symbols and references from the past to do so. In Chapter 3, I discuss this new voice of memory that avoids the use of classical literature or romantic pastoral images. Other than in memorials, a religious or sacred imagery is far more rarely used to tell this 'truth'. Poets such as Sassoon described chivalry's "nose being ground deeper in the mud".[41] In numerous war memoirs the 'heroic' is demolished – notions of an honourable sacrifice are demystified. The victims are demeaned or lost in mangled wastes of flesh. Individual acts of bravery are made meaningless in an anonymous, technologized slaughter. There is an enduring tension; if the language of honour and heroism, even 'chivalry', is retained, even for the anti-hero it is at the same time subverted by truth-telling with a new vocabulary.[42] Perhaps this contradiction is resolved to some degree after 1945, but a tension endures: Yossarian, in the post-1945 novel *Catch 22*, or the semi-auto biographical Billy Pilgrim in *Slaughterhouse 5* become the fictional embodiment of those anti-heroes. Notions of the heroic become ironic in their characterization as in the surrealism of the context, the madness of the trenches.[43]

The precedent for targeting a whole society and its civilians, as nuclear weapons do, was foreshadowed both in the starvation of Germany (1916–19) by blockade, and Trenchard's 'terror bombing' raids in Africa and the Middle East.[44] These raised issues for the limits of 'just war' theory in light of modern state technology aimed at non-combatant populations. On the German side, both the Zeppelin raids and the sinking of the *Lusitania* provided occasions for asking further ethical questions about war, 'modernity' and progress. The 'home front' began to be a potential target; the implications of this unravelled further with techniques of aerial terror bombing after 1918. Of course, changing norms of cultural life and war continued to be debated long after 1918 and a result, from the 1920s moral and legal issues of 'national' and international security, was challenged by new internationalist perspectives, including the move to abolish war (Kellog) and the League of Nations – and, after 1945, the UN. World War One provided the first modern archetype of mutual assured destruction: images, such as the *underground* shelters of 1940 or 1944–45, prophetically depicted in Henry Moore's Blitz sketches and prints point both forward to potential failure of nuclear deterrence, and back to the experience of the trenches.

For the re-dedication of the bombed Coventry Cathedral (twinned with Dresden's bombed Frauenkirche in 1962), Benjamin Britten's *War Requiem* was performed. It combined the Latin mass with Wilfred Owens's 1914–18 poetry – including parts of a key poem 'Strange Meeting'. This, an engagement with the dead, was depicted in Derek Jarman's later 'silent' film of the requiem. Each conveys the same deep involvement with the earlier war; the sense of universal loss it invoked, as well as the aspiration towards acknowledgement, reconciliation, even redemption after conflict.[45]

The emergence of a variety of new forms of public memorializing from that subsequent conflict coincided, despite the Cold War, with the pan-European project. As this emerged, it was strongly influenced by memories of war. Its evolutionary course continued despite threats and setbacks, and its existence was particularly linked to public memory, and memorizing. Even an emergent 'European memory' was postulated.

Memorial sites of the Great War were chosen as key places of symbolic political encounter across Europe. The names of the dead were intoned within poetry, prose and at public events. Garton Ash observed that Europe was still remarkably close in the 1990s to the context of 1914, the tensions of nationalism and the ethical issues of the catastrophes of 1914 and 1940 still challenged the relevance of much contemporary scholarship.[46] For Russia (for a variety of reasons) as well as Poland, Yugoslavia, Ukraine, and even Germany, as well as the other central, South East European countries, the appalling scale of deaths in 1940–45 to a degree overshadowed memories of the traumas of 1914–18. So did representations of the war in the Pacific for the United States in the 1940s; yet it was North American historians who played a key role in refocusing attention on the events of 1914–18.

War as mythology

The war of 1914–18 was called 'great' because more than any event it was this that colonized imaginations in its aftermath. This archetype even endured after 1945, since these collective, transgeneration memories in Britain, France and the

Commonwealth often encapsulated both wars, as do the memorials themselves. As a World War Two soldier Scannell's poem, 'The Great War', suggests,[47] memory looks back to the earlier catastrophe as the 'marker': the ground from which such special remembering sprang. Like Scannell, Paul Fussell was also a World War Two veteran.

A renewed sensed necessity for rediscovering memory, which emerged in the mid-1950s, owed much to the threat of the atom bomb. Paradoxically, the shadow of nuclear weapons created a context for a revival of interest in the Great War. Renewed focus on texts, art and images from the 1914 cataclysm had already begun, again across Europe. A key context was the Western nuclear disarmament campaigns (of 1957 onwards). By the 1960s there were a number of widely circulated collections of the poetry of, and books about, the conflict. One of the most important critical narrators, 'myth' makers and analysts of the European conflicts was A. J. P Taylor.

A classic Whig sceptic and an early opponent of British nuclear weapons in the 1950s, Taylor particularly popularized the still dominant 'Lions led by Donkeys' image (or 'myth') of the Great War so disliked by more conservative and establishment historians such as Samuel Hynes.[48] It was especially promulgated in Taylor's popular *The First World War: An Illustrated History* (the captions were humorous, sardonic and almost brutally cynical).[49] It was one of the key revisionist texts about the war, widely read, with multiple editions. Taylor was not of course the only source of this archetype, whose origin dates back to the war itself; it has been continued by others. The concept of a socially rooted memory-construction of these wars and its influence was in part drawn from the methodology of such radical, revisionist historians, and the emergence of cultural studies.

Simultaneously, in critical cinema, by directors including Joseph Losey and Stanley Kubrick in particular, but also in iconoclastic theatre, popular songs and folk ballads, the memory was infused with new and radical vitality.[50] The popular songs of 1914–18 often contained an anti-war and sarcastic component: they had not entirely been forgotten. These enjoyed a public revival. The songs had been especially sustained in Britain as long as 'music hall' singers remained alive to perform them, often with audience participation. After an emotional evening at the Albert Hall in 1927, the writer H. V. Morton remarked, "We did not realize until last night that the songs we sang in the army were bits of history".[51] This interest in such popular elements in counter-normative culture continued, and not only amongst liberal elites. Even though attention shifted somewhat in the context of the Vietnam War, Jon Silkin's *Out of Battle* (1972)[52] on World War One poetry and then Fussell's *Great War and Modern Memory* (1975) followed later by Modris Ekstein's *The Rites of Spring: The Great War and the Birth of Modern Age* (1989)[53] were just some of the numerous published works that helped reinforce this framing of 'modern memory' in the social imagination amongst a literate public.

Continuing ever since, the Great War was part of museumization: in London, in the 1980s and 1990s, World War One exhibits and displays at the Imperial War Museum (IWM) were enhanced (including a 'Trench experience' exhibitionary *mis en scene*[54]). The IWM's display of, mainly British, Great War art of the period was acknowledged as the jewel of the whole collection.[55] A decade later an international art exhibition at the Barbican, London (1991)[56] was a another marker which included some of the IWM paintings, but focused its concerns more on the avant-garde aspects and international scope of the art of World War One. This was a major and remarkable pan-European display, and included rare Russian contributions.

All this exemplified what was seen by some as constructing a continuing 'cult' of World War One and led to substantial controversy. As a traditional historian, Samuel Hyne's *The Great War Imagined* was a serious critique of this.[57] He viewed it as 'a war in the imagination': one that had been concocted and accepted, at least unconsciously, as an anti-war representation. This was perhaps made intentionally, as an enduring template: it constituted a 'myth' of remembering; a memory 'that never dies'. Hynes further described how it was determinedly imaged, sustained and elaborated by revisionist history. But beyond Hynes's thesis, an artificial, even invented, 'memory' was cultivated to be remembered afresh in each new generation. Even during and after the subsequent episodes in the continuous war of 1914 to 1945 in Europe, especially the civil war in Spain, it seems that such a counter-memory expanded to mythologize or romanticize other conflicts. Such transgenerational threads of memory were then supposedly woven into a chain of memory work.

In so far as this was constructed intentionally, it can be fairly described as myth, and has been criticized by radicals and conservatives alike. Nevertheless Hynes does acknowledge that such an alternative 'myth' of the Great War was not entirely artificial, but it grew from the genuine experience from the war itself, and in opposition to an inherited and more traditional 'framing' of the war as 'noble', 'heroic' and 'just'. This is true of much of modern memory, not only in the case of the memory of the Great War; it is in a sense part of ongoing 'myth' making. That is to say that construction of memory in this way represented an alternative method of assembling facts and experiences to *history*. It is not any less 'true' than the conventional (e.g. 'public') myths of military or national history. Sociologically, if it is seen to be 'true' – or seeking transformative truth – then it will have, despite its constituted character, social and cultural consequences. Following the idea of 'social myth' derived from George Sorels' classic pre-1914 social theory, such 'imagined' alternatives are powerful as both motivators and inhibitors of collective action.[58]

This idea is very obviously close to describing an overall constructionist approach to much of modern or postnational memory itself. Even if its roots lie before the Great War, and however inchoate its post-war evolution, the emergence of an alternative remembering is at first selectively linked to a 'war memory'. Either it points to a society's own potential collective repression of memory, or to the uncomfortable presence of forgotten or silenced trauma. Notably, in sociological analysis, the very idea of 'collective memory' reflected actual 'war-remembering' of the years after 1914. It was perhaps a personal reconstruction that the sociologist Maurice Halbwachs did not acknowledge as an individual one; but his theorizing about collective remembering was a direct product of that experience, one which he had endured together with a million others.

The new memory work after 1970 produced particularly trenchant interpretations, and these reminded the literary world in particular just how culturally 'memorable' the war had in fact been. It was remembered because it was absurd, 'ridiculous' and its moments and situations were 'ironic'.[59] The significance of the sarcastic or sardonic way in which it was recalled by many of its ordinary participants reflected a growing public undermining of the 'expected' image of military conflict. For so many ordinary soldiers the traditional language and imagery of honour, patriotism and military virtues were subverted. Despite the need to forget, the war poets, the artists and the memoirists, by expressing that human anguish and shared pain and loss, continuously located it in the war experience; they even transcended it in their celebration of compassion and humane recognition. In the next chapter I discuss silencing, denial and the repression of war experience that was paralleled with the 1940s. But modern mass war was so surreal, so world shattering, that it could not easily be forgotten. For a minority the war constituted a (potential) epitaph to 'war' as a human invention, at least in the field of culture. The irony of the phrase a "war that will end war" was not lost on those who survived.[60] One, admittedly utopian, response was mass pacifism, to which I turn in Chapter 4.

Beyond irony or a *Satire of Circumstances*, the Great War is remembered because it was a truly tragic world event. In the full classical sense of tragedy: it represented a fall from grace, grounded in human flaws and folly, or hubris. There are parallels with the European Holocaust, but rather than a tragedy of individuals the drama presented itself as a collective social tragedy – an unanticipated event or series of events of unknown proportions – which was met with the ignorance, incomprehension and arrogance of entrenched power. This enactment and its transparent stupidity was far more than a merely satirical or ironic engagement. In that the 1914–18 war has its universal, mnemonic quality and its archetypical significance, more than a century later this explains the war's lasting effects on our social memories.

Notes

1 See image caption and in Richard Cork, *A Bitter Truth: Avant Garde Art and the Great War* (New Haven, 1994).
2 Edward Thomas in *Poems of Edward Thomas* (Oxford, 1978).
3 Thomas died at Arras in 1917.
4 T. S. Eliot, *The Waste Land* (1922).
5 The 'literate' war is stressed by Paul Fussell in *The Great War and Modern Memory* (Oxford, 1975), especially ch. 5. The photographs of war gave veracity to remarkable events such as the Christmas truce of 1914. Modris Eksteins, *The Rites of Spring: The*

Great War and the Birth of the Modern Age (Boston, 1989); Malcolm Brown and Shirley Seaton, *The Christmas Truce* (London, 1984).

6 The two German soldiers and artists, Otto Dix, a machine gunner, and also Georg Grosz, are memory-makers I return to several times in this book.

7 The autobiographical Robert Graves, *Goodbye to All That* (London, 1929) had been preceded by Edmund Blunden's *Undertones of War* (London, 1928).

8 R. N. Hudson, *The Bradford Pals* (Bradford Libraries, 2000); David Raw, *Bradford Pals: A Comprehensive History of the 16th, 18th and 20th (Service) Battalions of the Prince of Wales' Own West Yorkshire Regiment 1914–1918* (Barnsley, 2005), an exhaustive and at times critical survey based on numerous sources, interviews, witness statement, regimental histories and by experts on the War.

9 Worthy of research is, except for the 2000 publication by Bradford Library, the apparent caesura in memorializing of the Pals between the mid-1980s and the 2014 anniversaries (and a small exhibit in 2016 in Bradford Cathedral).

10 Raphael Samuel is right to stress the ambivalence – noble, tragic, futile, heroic – but 'romantic'? Raphael Samuel, *Theatres of Memory* (New York, 1994).

11 Vera Brittain, *Testament of Youth* (London, 1933), pp. 488–89.

12 Scannell (1984), in Stallworthy (1987).

13 Pat Barker, *Regeneration* (New York, 1991).

14 See J. Stallworthy, *Oxford Book of War Poetry* (Oxford, 1987).

15 Eric. M. Remarque, *All Quiet on the Western Front* (New York, 1958).

16 Richard Cork, *A Bitter Truth: Avant Garde Art and the Great War* (New Haven, 1994) contains multiple references on Dix, see especially *Der Krieg (Nocturnal Encounter with a Lunatic)*. See Image 1.3.

17 Siegried Sassoon, *Memoirs of an Infantry Officer* (New York, 1930).

18 Ernest Hemingway, *A Farewell to Arms* (New York, 1957).

19 Geoffrey Winthrop Young, *The Grace of Forgetting* (London, 1953).

20 Cork (1994); Jay Winter and Blaine Baggett, *The Great War and the Shaping of the 20th Century* (New York, 1996); Jay Winter, *Sites of Memory, Sites of Mourning* (Cambridge, 1995).

21 British war paintings are symptomatic of that same dimension in art. Cork (1994), especially pp. 132–39, 208–10, Gertler W. Nevinson, p. 137, Wyndham Lewis, pp. 225–27.

22 Cork (1994). Yet Spencer's memorial work was far from a worship of war: his paintings indeed express an almost surreal pathos in describing war and post-war, not least the resurrection of the dead. See the Burghclere Sandham memorial chapel wall paintings.

23 Alyson Booth, *Postcards from the* Trenches (Oxford 1996), Introduction, pp. 4–11.

24 Ibid., on corpselessness, and pp. 10–11.

25 Dos Passos's stream of consciousness prose-poem refers to pre-1914 and pre-1917 re-imagining years of transition.

26 George Mosse, *Fallen Soldiers: Reshaping the Memory of the Great War* (Oxford, 1990) stresses this aspect. Adrian Gregory attempts to create a taxonomy from these tendencies, including Fussell and Eksteins (but not Winter's work). See A. Gregory, *The Silence of Memory: Armistice Day, 1919–1946* (1994).

27 Ernst Junger, *The Storm of Steel* (London, 1929). Junger's work was bitterly attacked by Walter Benjamin.

28 See image of the British Legion Veterans' Parade, Ypres (p. 73) On pacifism in the 1920s and 1930s, see Peter Brock and Nigel Young, *Pacifism in the Twentieth Century* (Syracuse, 1999), also in Martin Caedel, *Pacifism in Britain, 1914–45: The Defining of Faith* (Oxford, 1980).

29 Like Jay Winter (1995); Annette Becker, *Maurice Halbwachs: Un Intellectuel en Guerres Mondiales 1914–15* (Noesis, 1994), Preface by Pierre Nora, and Mosse (1990). In chapter 8, I also show experience of this search for consolation and closure.

30 See Winter (1996), Becker (1994) and Mosse (1990).
31 Cork (1994), Epilogue.
32 A key point made by Jay Winter (1995). There is in Winter's case sometimes contradictory or critical ambivalence in relation to the modernity of remembrance of the war, not only in relation to Lutyens's monuments, but also to Sassoon's poems or expressionist art. Key examples, in Dix, especially and in Kollwitz's output can be deployed in the debate about modernity and memorializing of the Great War to underline the ambivalence of expressionism.
33 See James Young, *Texture of Memory* (New Haven, 1994).
34 Thiepval is a more radical response by Lutyens.
35 Brancusi, see Cork (1994), Epilogue, pp. 310–13. Roumania (pre-1975); Romania (post-1975).
36 The London Cenotaph retained a public classical Roman referent (a 'catafalque') but is so highly original and innovative that few would recognize it as a Roman form.
37 But Fussell, despite his stress on the anti-militarist nature of Great War literature, like many veterans, in 1945, welcomed the use of the atomic bomb on Japanese cities.
38 Others, in particular Jay Winter in his cultural history of the war, made more effort to elaborate the concept of modern memory. See also Northrop Frye, *Anatomy of Criticism* (Princeton, 1957).
39 One might say 'The world in a tea cup': the smallest momentary mnemonic can highlight a social milieu, the spirit of an epoch time past, time future – in Proust's case, the hierarchy of manners and its class base.
40 Jean Renoir's film *La Grande* Illusion (1937). The title was derived from Norman Angell's book *The Great Illusion* (1909).
41 Sassoon (1930).
42 Paul Fussell, *Wartime: Understanding and Behaviour in the Second World War* (New York, 1989). See also Chris Hedges, *War Is a Force That Gives Us Meaning* (New York, 2002).
43 Kurt Vonnegut, *Slaughterhouse Five* (London, 1970); Joseph Heller, *Catch 22* (London, 1962).
44 See Sven Linquist for references to origins of strategic bombing in 'Colonial' experiments by the RAF, and in the first use of bombs on cities and afterwards in colonial wars: Sven Lindquist, *A History of Bombing* (London, 2002).
45 *War Requiem* (1989), dir. Derek Jarman (film), Benjamin Britten (composer).
46 See Winter and Baggett (1996), T. Garton-Ash, *A History of the Present* (London, 2000), and Keith Lowe, *The Fear and the Freedom: How the Second World War Changed Us* (London, 2017).
47 Scannel (1984) in Stallworthy (1987) and in Winter (1995).
48 A. J. P. Taylor's 'First World War Myth' is countered by Samuel Hynes in *A War Imagined* (London, 1990).
49 A. J. P. Taylor, *The First World War: An Illustrated History*, 1st edition (London, 1963). As Winter remarks, in North American PBS series (and a subsequent and much edited British version) he brought the Great War to a mass audience in a way that, if consciously or not, was a sceptical construction. In promoting further analysis of these memories, Winter has been particularly influential in several books (and a television series). In remembering the war, Sites of Memory, challenged a simplistic dichotomy of 'modernity' and 'tradition'.
50 Joseph Losey's *King and Country* (1964) and Stanley Kubrick's *Paths of Glory* (1957) were part of an active regeneration and revision of Great War memory in cinema, much of it involving an anti-war critique and eventually involving revived interest into the cinema of war post-1918 (Gance, Milestone, Pabst and Renoir).
51 Adrian Gregory, *The Silence of Memory* (1994), p. 82, quotes H. V. Morton, *In Search of England* (London, 1927). See also Winter (1995).
52 John Silkin, *Out of Battle: The Poetry of the Great War* (London, 1972).

53 See Eksteins (1989); who questions the demise of 'honour' until later in the war. See also Winter (1995) who continues these debates.
54 To be paralled by the 'Blitz experience' about the 1940s life of civilians.
55 Envied by Art Galleries worldwide as were its World War One poster archives.
56 Cork (1994).
57 Hynes (1990).
58 Georges Sorel, *Reflections on Violence* (1908; Glencoe, 1950).
59 See Fussell (1975).
60 H. G. Wells, *The War that Will End War* (New York, 1914).

2

'THE GREAT SUNK SILENCES'

The nature of forgetting and the unbearable pain of recall

Forgetting

> *And when they ask us … and they're certainly going to ask us*
> *And when they ask us, how dangerous it was,*
> *Oh, we'll never tell them, no, we'll never tell them.*
> (Sung to the popular tune *'They Wouldn't Believe Me, They Wouldn't Believe Me'*)[1]

The mass trauma of 1914–18 created a need to forget, and a silencing amongst those returning from war. A much bemedalled member of the Bradford Pals, Harry Roberts refused to talk about his experience afterwards.[2] Walter Benjamin remarked that men returned from the battlefield at the end of the war were grown silent – poorer in communicable experience.[3] E. M. Remarque talks of a generation of men destroyed by the war. A sense of hopelessness accompanies a numbing of memory.[4] I have suggested the impact on a British city, Bradford. In writing more recently about the lost generation, Jay Winter illustrates in countless cities and towns how, after 1918, whole communities were often silenced by grief.[5] But however painful and delayed, an imperative of communal reconstruction of memories confronted all individual survivors. In a way that is often imperceptible, individual stories are simply woven into a collective narrative, one I will attempt to summarize. The recall is much more difficult in communities when faced by dispersal, denial and cultural amnesia. Amongst Armenians after 1915, or subsequently among survivors of the European Shoah, numbing and repression became the norm; forgetting is the default response to such pain, especially as for exile communities this can take several generations to overcome.

IMAGE 2.1 Richard Attenborough, *Oh! What a Lovely War!*, 1969. The child asks, "Granny, what did Daddy do in the war?" The women, the survivors, picnic among poppies and crosses as the reincarnated male members of the 'Smith family' reassemble on the day of the Armistice.

The result of exposure to trauma and atrocity is often numbing. As the daughter of a holocaust survivor responds to Claude Lanzmann's question:

> 'What died in him in Chelmno?'
>
> 'Everything died. But he's only human, and he wants to live. So he must forget. He thanks God ... That he can forget. And let's not talk about that.'[6]

It is ironic that Halbwachs, the major twentieth-century sociologist of collective memory, appears to have repressed his own shocked reactions to his experience. He witnessed and shared the traumas of battle in 1914–18 and as Annette Becker suggests, his failure to include collective memory of the war in his post-war writing published on the subject may reflect a personal guilt and denial. As he implied, simply he could not "speak the unspeakable."[7]

Forgetting is a key aspect in the sometimes delayed and agonized construction of modern memories, in whatever form, whether after 1918, 1945, or of later disasters. It is a crucial theme in the writing of some of those who fought: amongst them Owen, Rosenberg and Thomas died. Perhaps even more tragically, Ivor Gurney survived, but in his post-war poems he delusionally continued to fight the terrifying war in his imagination. Eventually placed in a psychiatric hospital, Gurney still could not find closure; such symbolic illusions were symptoms of a withdrawal from the world. But for some major memoirists, such as Sassoon who survived, forgetting was impossible. As has been observed, the language of modern memory does not easily heal trauma, but it may transcend it. Even *in extremis*, some art points to therapeutic, even redemptive, paths from conflict. Such ways may also provide a vocabulary of and motivation for resistance.[8] For the generation of 1918, a personalized, but not always inward-looking grief could present itself as a form of opposition to state-ordered atrocity; and even, if only implicitly, to the institution of war itself.

For the last twenty-six years of his life, Walter Benjamin was haunted by a spectre of an anti-war protest: the suicide by gassing of his two closest friends in the student movement, Fritz Heile and Rika Seligson. They killed themselves on 8 August 1914 upon the announcement of mobilization for a war they opposed. Mythologizing these traumatic losses, both personally and in his writing, Benjamin used these civilian deaths to resist both the screen provided by commemoration of the war dead and later the cult of the fellowship of battle-front life (*Fronterlebnis*). Both paths denied in his view the horrific nature of actual combat. In fact Benjamin did not refuse military service in 1914, though later he avoided and evaded it. But a sense of actual guilt seems to have pursued him after the war, centred on the sacrificial but ultimately impotent gestures of his friends. He had survived to give public witness, but others had not – the private trauma obsessed him as an encapsulation of the overall public horror of 1914–18.[9] For some returnees, a voluntary silencing of memory represented a stubborn acceptance of the incommunicability of the traumas experienced; for others, such as Benjamin and Sassoon, some form of public witness was required. Sassoon demanded that those searing experiences be acknowledged, specified and remembered. His bitter 1919 poem *Aftermath* represents his heart-felt manifesto against forgetting. It ends with the lines:

> "Have you forgotten yet?
> Look up, and swear by the green of the spring that you'll never forget."[10]

Acknowledged in the ironic British song *Oh We'll Never Tell Them!* is the impossibility of relaying the reality of fighting to civilians, and even to close relatives, either at the time or after return. It expressed and popularized what a whole generation began to recognize, just how terrible the experience had been, a trauma too shocking for everyday recall or description. Though life had to go on, it left, in Sassoon's phrase, a 'haunted gap in your mind'. Such words also articulated the fact that soldiers felt unable to speak of their experiences of war, even to those closest. My grandfather never spoke of the war to my grandmother, and to me only in his final years. The song was a poignant reminder of such silenced memories.[11] Many thought it unseemly for those who did not experience the Great War, or as David Jones puts it, were not 'there', to even talk about it.[12]

Many returning veterans, scarred by a burned-in-disbelief, can only communicate by silence, a 'refusal to tell lies about the war'. Hemingway's Harold Krebs in the story *Soldiers Home* finds that his exaggerated tales of his war experience turned to denial and disillusion with the civilian's at home, uninterested in the realities: "A distaste for everything that had happened to him in the war set in because of all the lies he had told". He is unable to cope with family and friends.[13]

The pain of recall

For Sassoon, Remarque and Hemingway denial is part of the subject matter of post-war. Only the condition of 'wordlessness' can be itself written about. Literature is an occasion for depicting the incapacity of language to communicate. For the soldier back home from the war, modern mass killing and genocide have become in that sense indescribable. Silence, for example at remembrance parades, such as that observed at the Cenotaph on 11 November 1919 and at subsequent Armistice Day ceremonies and rituals worldwide, seemed perhaps the only appropriate response.[14]

But silence did not always denote forgetting. In generating memories, Vera Brittain talks of "drowning in a black wave of memory" and of "a war that obstinately refuses to be forgotten". The silence of the November remembrance rituals partly acknowledges a silencing of memory. But more generally the suppression of images of past conflict because the general need to forget was widespread in the decade after 1918.[15] Involuntary mutism, epitomized in symptoms of shell shock subsequently becomes a literary metaphor for collective, largely consensual forgetting.[16] Even the field services postcard with its 'tick the boxes' approach to war experience had represented a systematic form of silencing at the Front. It censored all but the most banal facts of survival, such as 'I am being sent down to the base', and a warning ('if anything else is added, the postcard will be destroyed').

In such ways war and genocide restructured not only remembering, but also modes of forgetting; and not only for the veterans and victims, but also the secondary observers and witnesses – wives, descendants (grandchildren), relatives and lovers. Kollwitz's decade of struggle to complete her universalist epitaph to her son Peter is emblematic of that challenge of filling the void.

Ghosts returned

Both at home and at the sites of death, preserving the memory of loved ones killed took many forms: memorials, visits to cemeteries once these were created, pilgrimages to battlefields or to the monuments there. But the absences were too hard for some and conventional mourning insufficient. Whilst the dead left records, photographs and diaries, there was also another kind of 'not letting go', and of maintaining that past as it was: in the many attempts to keep the dead victims of the war alive, not in memorials, and in cemetery visits, but by invoking a physical presence through Spiritualism and conversations with the dead. It constituted a widespread cultural mood and movement during and after the war.[17] Summoning up the ghosts or spirits of those departed sustained a significant cultural movement (spiritualism) and an imagery that haunted much art, post-war cinema and prose.[18] Film director Abel Gance in *J'Accuse* (1919) invoked the dead, returned.[19] To be shadowed by loss, by intimations of the past, was not new in 1918, and culturally such memories had often been represented in the nineteenth century as illusions, fantasies and nightmares. Even before any widespread knowledge of the discovery of the unconscious, and before the search for the lost generation after 1918, there was a felt sense of a need to raise the dead, to reawaken the ghosts of a forgotten, repressed or distorted past. The contradictory need to forget the horrors of the war existed in tension with a refusal to accept that loss of those one knew: close family members, sons, brothers, close friends – it was an impossible and unresolvable paradox.

These haunting spirits are evoked throughout the arts: in poetry, painting and other media, such as in cinema. Gance's two versions of the film *J'Accuse* (remade in the 1930s) were calculated to condemn the attitudes of the home front. The symbolic rise of the dead confronts civilians and relatives: they demand a proper memorial to their suffering. By using serving soldiers, Gance chose to give a sombre reality to the construction of an apparition – members of a 'dead army'. This battalion of cinematic ghosts, like the 'spooks' in Charles Sorley's poem, arise to confront us.[20] In the 1936 version, the ghosts return to specifically accuse and haunt us, the living, rather than to comfort the bereaved. They are superimposed against the backdrop of the Douaumont Ossuary ('the boneyard' memorial) on the Verdun Battlefields. Some scenes were shot with the realities of the slaughter, still close at hand in 1918 and with military cooperation. Gance borrowed combat troops on Furlough or on leave from the French Army as 'extras', even though his film warned against war. Beyond the pathos of the poets, some of these part-time actors returned to the Front after filming (Image 2.2, on p.38).[21]

Spirits are depicted at such war monuments to the dead as at Douaumont, and in rituals for the bereaved like those at Ypres (Ieper). At the nightly Menin Gate memorial ceremony to the missing, which started in the 1920s (and, except for 1940–44, has been continuous ever since), thousands of relatives and communities come to mourn. Some of the sites are represented as peopled by ghosts of the lost by the Australian popular artist Longstaff. His haunted paintings are at the Australian war memorial in Canberra: one depicts the spectres of troops returning to the Menin Gate at Ypres at night (Image 2.3), and another, skeletal figures on Vimy Ridge at Arras.

Such ghosts shadowed not only those involved in spiritualism as a movement, but also writers such as Virginia Woolf in her life and novels, such as *Mrs Dalloway*. Attempts to communicate with the souls of the dead were widespread: neither Conan Doyle nor Rudyard Kipling and other figures could come to terms with such loss, of sons, loved ones. In November 1918, Harold Owen had such an 'other-worldly' experience at the moment his brother Wilfred was killed. Vera Brittain talks of being haunted by those she lost. They needed to forget, but could not.[22]

In a more covert way, these spirits occupied the minds of those who, like Sassoon, wrote memoirs and autobiographies. Sassoon derives from what he calls his "dreams from the pit" some of his finest verse about the war. The bereaved

IMAGE 2.2 Abel Gance, *J'Accuse*, 1919. The ghosts of the war dead are summoned from their graves and battlefields to give silent accusation.

IMAGE 2.3 Will Longstaff, *Menin Gate at Midnight*, 1927. Australian War Memorial. Typical of the ghost pictures and spirit images of the time, Longstaff painted similar scenes of Vimy and the Somme, and many more sites of memory.

too became secondary witnesses. Generational memories of veterans and victims – and mourners too – were relived in visits and pilgrimages. The nightmares and delusions of returned veterans were the same dreams that psychiatrists treating neurasthenia had explored during the war in several countries. Many of these like W. H. Rivers started deploying Freud's analysis to probe them. In Otto Dix's lithographs, the nightmare dead of all sides come back to haunt the artist himself, and the survivors.[23] Like Edvard Munch, these echo an expressionist obsession with death and dying. Like Munch before, the veteran Dix drew both what he saw in the recent past or what he had sketched at the time – not just what he sees in the present. Together with fellow artist Georg Grosz, who had also fought, he depicted the physically maimed, the crippled, and disfigured veterans and the criminality of the aftermath. After 1918, many images show begging on German or Czech streets, and some depict sadistic murder, as did Max Beckman. These brutal spectres were a living memorial to the physical and mental scars of the fighting.

Such appalling images in the photographs collected by Ernst Friedrich, and are also recorded by the artists, included grotesques – the '*gueules cassées*'. Those

IMAGE 2.4 Otto Dix, *Die Skatspieler* (Skat Players). Such destroyed faces (*gueules cassées*) were also depicted by Henry Tonks and the photographs published in Ernst Friedrich's notorious book on war. Nationalgalerie, SMB, Verein der Freunde der Nationalgalerie. ©bpk/DACS. Photo: Jörg P. Anders.

men with broken faces haunted almost every town and city in Europe. They were a constant ugly reminder of the costs of war. It is a portraiture which, with few exceptions, is never depicted on war memorials. In Germany, Georg Grosz, Dix (who used the photogaphs), Max Beckman and many more portray them as gargoyles and the savage images are used to shock. In Dix's painting of *The Skat Players*,[24] four grossly 'repaired' officers play cards together (Image 2.4).[25] In these scenes, people are juxtaposed with the maimed and disfigured. These pictures condemn not just the horrors of the conflict, but also those held responsible: the war profiteers and bureaucrats, the generals and politicians. Prostitutes too trade on these unlovely castaways of war. In Berlin, a legless man approaches a painted whore. In London however, Henry Tonks, of the Slade School, created drawings which were meticulous academic medical portraits of them.

Spaces of loss

Ways of forgetting such horror are also linked to the modernist imagery of spaces – a void left by traumatic loss. Allyson Booth explores such absences[26] and links both to memorial architecture – and the literary 'spaces' in such post-war writing as Virginia Woolf's *Mrs Dalloway*, or *To the Lighthouse*.[27] On an empty battlefield, Gance's cinematic battalion of ghosts, or later Longstaff's spectral painted army, are awakened to condemn the complacency at home. But few war monuments attempt to deal with that space. As noted, a memorial's aim in James Young's view is not to call attention to its own presence, but rather to 'past events' – since those are no longer present. In other words, its role is to direct imagination to a 'remembered' absent historical past, or at least a re-imagined one, but not to an edifice.[28] It is hard not to see Lutyens's Thiepval memorial and its huge, hopeless spaces as constituting as much an intrusive, condemnatory statement as a monument to the missing of the Somme (Image 2.5). Facing mourners and local residents alike, it draws attention to the infamously problematic losses of the battlefield of 1916. That is perhaps why local people feel unduly burdened by this almost monstrous reminder of the lost. It is neither comforting nor comfortable.[29] It is certainly 'unavoidable'.

For Booth, loss is most tellingly represented by such constructed spaces – Thiepval is a shrine to loss and it is not in any sense healing. Perhaps a presence of that emptiness can give some closure: as Lutyens's cenotaph in London, or as the absences in Virginia Woolf novels. But at Thiepval there is no reassurance. It is just a mnemonic arch amongst smaller arches – a framed view of an endless vacant lot, and beyond an ordered no-man's land. Lutyens's vistas provide a desolate site for contemplating one of the most problematic collective absences of a problematic war.[30] The poet, Carl Sandburg's metaphorically uses grass to represent covering such buried memories of loss (see poem *Grass*). In re-foresting, the gradual covering up and grassing over of memorable sites at the Somme, Ypres, Verdun or the Chemins des

IMAGE 2.5 Thiepval Memorial to the Missing of the Somme Battlefields, Somme, France. The memorial was designed by Sir Edwin Lutyens, built starting in 1928, and unveiled on 1 August 1932. It commemorates the 72,000 men of the UK and South African forces with no known graves, who died in this Somme sector before 20 March 1918, the vast majority between July and November 1916. Note the 'spaces' in the arches. Photo: Andrew Matthews/PA Archive/PA Images.

Dames make the physical reminders disappear: some do so under junk yards, shopping malls, car parks or even the plough; Thiepval buries it under its own pile of bricks, and a semblance of order.

> Two years, ten years, and passengers ask the conductor
> 'What place is this?'
> 'Where are we now?'[31]

Many of these spaces of loss, like the remains of death camps, crumble and are half-hidden by grass or trees; nature reclaims even some of the most toxic landscapes. After a century, the poisonous hills around Verdun have begun to recover. Deer leap the fences of Birkenau, rabbits scuttle past the ruins of the crematoria, the birch trees survive. Later in this book, I will discuss the indomitable Yves Gibeau, who scoured the ridge west of Reims, collecting objects as a way of memorizing the slaughter. The detritus is stacked along the sides of country roads; each year farmers still churn up shells, bones and skulls, and occasionally they find or set off an unexploded shell, mine or bomb; sometimes there are still casualties. This has continued for a century. Such an event is depicted in Bertrand Tavernier's film *La Vie et Rien d'Autre* during a search for the missing after 1918.

Nowadays the excavated ordnance is left on the side of roads to be collected, but there are still dangerous areas left, especially in woodlands, caves or tunnels. A hundred years after the battles, sixty tons of metal debris from 1914–18 is still dug up annually around the Somme; Gibeau filled his priest's house with such remnants, reminders of the troglodyte world. Even now at Verdun, remains still surface, or are found in projects on the archaeology of the recent past which continue as the soil slowly recovers and is worked again by farmers.

Missing in action

Almost a century after their burial a whole platoon of British skeletons from the same regiment, laid out side by side, was uncovered in northern France. Despite modern methods, not all have yet been identified. By 1918, literally millions of names of the missing or body parts without identification were listed. Millions died without trace, without witness even. Before modern DNA tests, it was rarely possible to match these remnants or identify more than a tiny minority of them. If there was a body, it was buried anonymously, often in a mass plot: '*unbekannte deutsche Soldaten*', or unknown British soldier. In Commonwealth countries, the epitaph if not 'No known grave' was 'Known only to God'. Later with such corpselessness came the reinvention of the concept of 'Missing in Action'. For many in the USA at the end of the Vietnam War, MIA was a new concept and indicated an American exceptionalism, since in Europe missing in action had become the norm in the mechanization of mass war after 1914. Tens of thousands of horses and men disappeared on the muddy battlefields of Ypres alone by autumn 1917. But the use of DNA since the 1980s has made the identification of discovered remains, whilst still incomplete, a very different and more precise process in the twenty-first century.

This was a process, part of a democratization of memory: the spaces occupied by missing in action, for example. Unidentified remains created a presence constituted by nameless bodies, or body parts, or skeletons. But without bodies, faces or identity, they at least now had their own individual lists of names as memorials.[32] In Tavernier's story, the issues that arise involve funding memorials for these remnants of the loved, lost ones. It is set as a drama in northern France after 1918. It reflects the real political story of impassioned debates at the time about where the dead should be taken and how they should be memorialized, and by whom. In France this was usually in the hometown or village: a community of loss would claim its own. But between 1918 and 1923, what to do with the rest of the unfunded dead still remained controversial and a diverse issue. Many were buried on site, like the vast majority of British and Commonwealth dead. To leave them or dig them up and rebury them elsewhere was a difficult choice. Even in France, many poorer families and widows could not afford the cost of any removal in any case. But bodies continued to be exhumed, and many moved, for at least twenty years or more, on all sides. But some, certainly by then, had no families to own them, and it was not just a case of burying:, but which was the right body? And which one was to be the impeccable 'Unknown Soldier'? Even a corpse or body part had to be the right one: often a ghoulish exercise. Tavernier's film reflects those tensions but celebrates the will of the survivors.

Such searches for lost relatives and lovers had started well before the Great War ended, and it continued long after 1923 – an official completion date. Relatives, including grandchildren and great-grandchildren, have returned ever since, though in many places such visits were interrupted between 1940 and 1945. The German occupation of Belgium and France, where mass graves of unknown German soldiers also existed in collective graveyards such as Langemarck, prevented other visitation. The vast British and Commonwealth cemeteries, included both the unknown soldiers and the missing of the wars and the latter were usually in individual plots, not mass graves (Image 2.6).

As reminders of the scale of the slaughter, one of the largest fields of the unknown is Tyne Cot, at Passchendaele ridge near Ypres. Since the British decided to bury almost all on the battlefield, the inscription 'A Soldier of the

IMAGE 2.6 Members of the Women's Auxiliary Army Corps carrying wreaths to place on the graves of British soldiers buried at Abbeville, 9 February 1918. This was the site of a large hospital. The local people, French and Belgian, also placed wreaths in the years during and after the war. © Imperial War Museums (Q 8471).

Great War: known only to God' appears commonly not only on these graves, but also in large and small cemeteries for tens of miles in each direction.

Many of the initial graveyards were 'consolidated' into much larger ones.[33] A few states, including the USA, returned most of their dead to the home country, but in Britain there was consensus to keep most in war cemeteries near where they were killed, mostly with no funeral in the home country (Image 2.7). Whilst the Germans too buried many on the spot, others were taken home.

As I have indicated, each belligerent nation had to decide both what to do with the 'unknown soldiers' unidentified bodies and how to memorialize those missing with 'no known grave'. The missing in action were given various national memorials and monuments, as at Verdun (Douaumont, and its Ossuary), or the Commonwealth War Graves Commission at the Menin Gate at Ypres, Delville Wood, Thiepval on the Somme or at the Cenotaph.[34] But recently, near Arras, at Notre Dame de Lorette, an alternative transnational, if not postnational memorial has been created for those from all sides killed in the region. A huge symbolic steel memorial ring was erected in 2011, remembering over 600,000 victims.

The sociologist Paul Connerton has focused on the historical importance of such bodily rituals as these in the ceremonies that are crucial to collective

IMAGE 2.7 Maurice Langaskens, Funeral Cortege. On view at the Cloth Hall, In Flanders Fields, Ypres. Several such pictures were painted in prisoner of war camps in Germany. By permission of IFF.

memory, though he concentrates on elites and symbolic individuals, not ordinary soldiers. This process has become more dramatic because of the spaces created by the facts of corpselessness. Re-enactment ceremonies, pilgrimages to special sites and anniversary events and commemorations, not least burials and re-interments, have been the norm. The Great War rituals relate to acknowledging these absences, and voids. The faceless battle landscapes of Nash, Nevinson, William Orpen, and in France, Felix Vailloton and others are prophetic: they prefigure the photographs of the wastelands of Treblinka, Dresden, Stalingrad and Nagasaki. No longer 'battlescapes' in a traditional sense, only forms of abstraction, such as Kiefer's painted collages, will be appropriate – more metaphor than depiction. Given the lack of bodies, the empty landscapes of modernism are also inevitably occupied by more elusive images: ghosts, symbolic empty tombs or catafalques. They are therefore 'vulnerable', to reinterpretation, to counter-memories and to counter-monuments – even to co-optation in populist moments. In the tradition of critics such as Benjamin, they screen, potentially denying the validity of traditional memorializing for such atrocity.

A more precise location for this pain is in the domestic voids of loss: the empty room of the departed soldier, for example a son, remaining as it was the day they left, back to the Front. When news came of Peter's death in 1914, the Kollwitz family left his bedroom as it was, intact, and they then held annual rituals on his birthdays and at Christmas with a candle for each year, added after his death.[35] Such a room is similarly preserved in the French village of Belabre. In an old house, a bricked up room was rediscovered and opened up in the 1950s. It contained the room of Hubert Rochereau, an officer killed in Flanders in April 1918, almost exactly as he had left it when he returned to the war. In addition his uniform, his personal possessions and his *Croix de Guerre* were added – his devastated family turned these into a permanent memorial and sealed the room. They left the property in 1975 and it was only discovered twenty years later by new owners who broke open the walled-up entrance.[36]

Securing such preservation of memorizing spaces and moments of loss is always a risky process – as witness the heroic attempts to preserve Yves Gibeau's house and collection in Craonne after his death. It was rescued, and preserved for twenty years, by the photographer and filmmaker Gerard Rondeau. But now it is lost. An even more sobering example is the more recent story of Ferdane Qukezi's creation of a memorial near Gjakova in Kosovo. During the Kosovo conflict, in 1999, Serb paramilitaries seized and 'disappeared' six members of her family: her husband, four sons and a nephew. She froze the pain at the moment of their departure by sealing the house. She moved nothing in the house, preserving it just as it was when they all left. But later her husband's relatives tried to repossess her home (and 'museum') and to destroy her act of 'memory work'.[37]

Memorials in many countries also use forms such as empty tombs to symbolize the unknown and unidentified. In central London, such a space, the 'catafalque', was created at a more public site. The Cenotaph in Whitehall was at first temporary, representing all those with 'no known grave' (Image 2.8).

IMAGE 2.8 The Cenotaph at Whitehall, 1920. The arrival of the gun carriage bearing the Unknown Warrior at the Cenotaph, Whitehall, for the unveiling ceremony by King George V, 11 November 1920. It was the first major Remembrance Day silence. Under the memorial designed by Edwin Lutyens lies an empty tomb. The "unknown warrior" is buried in Westminster Abbey nearby. © Imperial War Museums (Q 31513).

Lutyens's structure was built to encase it in stone. Yet in addition to this 'tomb', nearby the body of an actual 'unknown soldier' was still placed in a Westminster Abbey tomb.

Though based on the model of a classical monument, in Lutyens's minimalist design the overall image appears modern. Held there from 1920, a minute's silence at 11 am on 11 November, the mnemonic time when the Great War ended, marked the annual Cenotaph ritual in Britain. With it, a public movement of support, the memorial event became, like the monument itself, permanent. Later the main traditional event, in London was moved from the eleventh of the eleventh itself, to "Remembrance Sunday" (the nearest Sunday to the 11th). Similar events have been held in dozens of other countries, not least in France and Canada.

On the Champs-Élysées in Paris, as at Westminster, an unidentified corpse had been chosen from a number,[38] to symbolize all those lost. The body of this unknown was placed under the Arc de Triomphe, having been selected after nine coffins arrived at a ceremony in the citadel at Verdun (see Image 2.9). However, there was always a risk of it being the wrong body: the unknown soldier, after all, might have been a deserter. As a result the final choice was made from eight - or possibly only six - caskets at Douaumount in 1920.[39]

IMAGE 2.9 Bertrand Tavernier, *Life and Nothing But* (*La vie et rien d'autre*), 1989. In 1919 the unknown soldier has been chosen from six coffins at the Citadel in Verdun to be taken to Paris. Similar events took place in other countries, the most recent in Australia (1992).

Trauma and loss

It is hardly surprising, following Freud, that the story of modern memory should often be told in terms of post-trauma – both individual and collective: decades after the Shoah the overlapping fields of both the Holocaust and Trauma Studies increasingly dominated memory work, and to some extent they still do. But these various responses to the collective loss of 1914–18 do not easily fit these frames of trauma theory: conversations with the dead, spiritualism, self-repression, the obsession with corpses (present or absent), the preserved space (rooms of loved ones left empty), the repetitive pilgrimages and searches – the focus on spaces and absences (so well observed by Allyson Booth) are only a few of the multiple forms of response of both the survivors and the bereaved.

In the 1920s and 1930s the escapist mood of spiritualism and communicating with the dead was widespread and even accompanied the visitations to sites, which continued unabated into a third or fourth generation. In some places the memorial events have grown larger over the years, and acquire a charismatic quality. One could see this ritualistic mood as threatening to undermine or replace the very project: an alternative demythologizing tradition of modern memory would be vitiated by such routinization of grief. However it was saved by the way memory work interpreted, inverted and even transcended those responses in anti-militarist projects and cultural creativity that countered conventional modes of remembrance.

Numbing, the denial of loss and the repression of war experience, represents a familiar response to trauma. The widespread phenomenon of suppressed memory that also followed the Shoah for victims (survivors), bystanders and perpetrators alike, seems to be both cause and effect of a new kind of longer-term self-consciousness about the relationship between trauma, shock and remembrance. After 1945, repressing the recent atomic past in cinema can be paralleled, with holocaust amnesia: both are explored in Alain Resnais's films *Night and Fog* and *Hiroshima mon Amour* (see Chapter 9).[40] In the latter, the protagonists are two lovers – one a Japanese architect from a survivor family from Hiroshima, the other a woman, a French peace journalist scarred by war memories in occupied France. They recognize in each other's very different experiences of trauma they are both marked by those memories. In Chapter 9, I will discuss how this recall is painful and repressed; but for both of them it is linked to place: to the scenes and sites of suffering. The need to forget is balanced by an urge to remember, to represent, to acknowledge a reality, but to recall experience beyond representations alone.

Mute resistance: trauma and rebellion

In her *Regeneration* trilogy – through real and fictional figures Rivers, Prior, Owen, Sassoon, Yealland, Callan, Burns, Anderson and others – the British novelist Pat Barker offers us a series of questions about war, science and progress – and memory. She links these to the repression and recovery of remembering – and of war traumas. Psychotherapy globalizes the study of traumatic recall and it involves interface with alternatives. The ethical paradoxes presented in these three novels are also able to provide us with admirable metaphors of war and memory loss. By counterposing problems of medical science (i.e. shock treatments–electrodes) as opposed to the more humane Freudian 'talking cure' (psychotherapy), she explores tensions symptomatic of a cultural, and implicitly political, crisis. In both cases methods are used to mend the victims of technological trauma (shell shock) but present an ethical dilemma: in returning them to their memory of events. It may also then return them as 'cured' of symptoms of trauma, and as fit to face again its cause, the hell of modern technologized war. Barker's use of non-Western, anthropological sequences suggest this is a particularly Western civilizational value crisis (1914–18).[41]

Loss of memory caused by shocking experienced events – for example, by Barkers main fictional, character Billy Prior – represents a principal theme of the novels. Developed from the specifically documented story of the treatment and rehabilitation of shell shock by Dr William Rivers, it details 'talking the cure' therapies at the Craiglockhart Hospital near Edinburgh.[42] Rivers specifically addressed the spiritual ghosts that haunted his patients.[43] Insofar as the development of mutism in soldiers can be interpreted as a form of, albeit unconscious, rebellion against the experience of war, it is as a 'mutiny of silence'. As the state takes away the mutism, it simultaneously crushes the resistance to continuing combat. In *Regeneration*, one such process is illustrated by Barker's description of the mute Callan, undergoing electric-shock therapy (Image 2.10). Rivers describes his experiences of watching Yealland's treatment to cure him; in Barkers words, "He [Rivers] was witnessing the silencing of a human being". In the

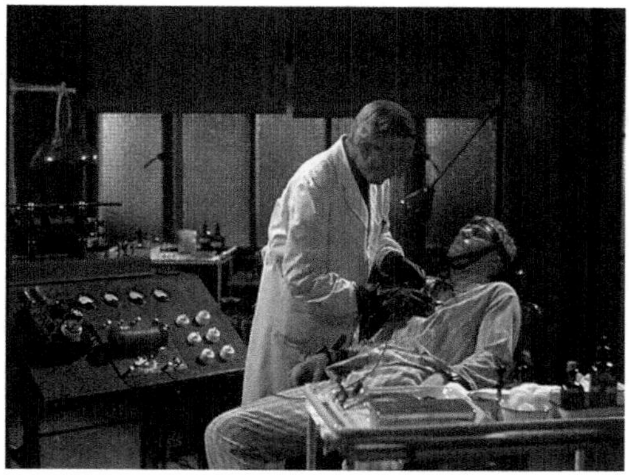

IMAGE 2.10 Gillies MacKinnon, *Regeneration*, 1997. An Electric current treatment used to deal with the neurasthenia of 'shell shock' is illustrated, as Dr W. H. Rivers (Jonathan Pryce) watches Yealland 'cure' Callan of mutism. The film is based on Pat Barker's novel with same title, first published in 1991.

film, which draws from two novels, these words, "taking away his silence", are spoken to Sassoon by Rivers (who is acted by Jonathan Pryce in the film representation, *Regeneration*[44]) when the therapist returns from London to Craiglockhart.[45]

At different times, wide varieties of treatment were used from psychotherapy to electro-static shock. But there was another solution to shell shock: execution for cowardice or desertion.[46] How to diagnose and treat the symptoms of memory loss as a medical/psycho-social condition, its recognition and definition (often described as hysteria) differed in each country. Freud commented on similar treatments in Germany, saying that the process misunderstood the condition. Loss of memory, which also sprang directly out of such shell shock, led to research on the condition and its differing effects and symptoms. It proved a complex syndrome: indications varied even by rank, or social background. Michel Foucault's later work on discipline is highly relevant to analysing the medical scientific–techno-military complex as it has developed since the nineteenth century.[47] It can be related to modern work ethics, bureaucracy and the 'total' institutional approaches, which are used by states to deal with war-induced trauma and subsequent neurasthenia, or indeed political dissent when treated as a psychiatric disorder, as by several states including the Soviet Union.

Treatment (cure) led to some military recognition of an inconvenient syndrome (neurasthenia), but generally there was an impatience with it for creating extra problems when a 'just war' was to be won. The military-mind set and technology that produced some techniques,[48] was essentially that of repairing cogs in a machine; hardly what Freud had in mind, though he was reluctant to criticize such work by medical colleagues.

The continued recurrent nightmares of such veterans and their traumatic stories meant that such moral and political issues and debates were carried forward to debates in later wars. Controversies continued; for example, over French use of torture in Algeria, and later post-traumatic stress disorders, Abu Ghraib, and the 'Gulf War syndrome'.[49]

Re-constructions of such generational experiences, which reawaken forgotten pasts, represent, in part, a de-construction of a patently unsatisfactory 'history' of atrocity. The project of alternative remembering encapsulated by Barker's novels replenishes – perhaps even partly replaces – the public archive in such cases. Her work bridges several mnemonic genres and is perhaps an effective prosthetic.

Subterranean narratives

In part this same project could be attempted in a search for oral testimony, diaries and stories, providing sites of resistance to the dominance of other hegemonic narratives. Below the surfaces, physical and mental unknown, or unspoken accounts exist of the hidden aspects of war.[50] I have referred to the founder of the Quaker Ambulance volunteers in World War One, Winthrop Young. He described rescuing wounded, sick and dying civilians in Ypres 1914, including children, 'from dark, noisome, airless, cellars'. As in so many cities in modern war, there was no provision for them:

> The Civil population of the war zone – ought in every military preconception simply not to be there.
>
> In that seeming emptiness of desolate grey and shell blistered streets – to discover all going on around and under us, unseen and unheeded: a subterranean population, hopeless, often lightless living on what they might and breeding disease, they were being killed and wounded 'when a direct hit smashed down.'[51]

Foreshadowing cities in World War Two and more recently in Syria, Young's memoir remarks on the silencing of these people; it is a metaphor for the suppression of experience. Such testaments as these, written from 'the wasteland', emerge at the very time when our awareness of memory began to grow more sensitive:

> Even speech or any power to express emotion seemed to have been lost by many of them. Many were refugees from the surrounding country villages, they could not survive the uprooting from their homes: they died later in our wards like plants – torn from the soil – others clung to the cellars and were killed there, daily by the bombardment.[52]

Modernist attempts to confront such 'bitter truths' wrestled with multiple post-war pasts narrated in autobiographies. They illustrate the self-reflexive dilemmas of modern memory-making – which ask why do we 'stir the roots of pain'? [53]

The difficulty and problem of such recall, whether in a psychiatric interview or in this corpus of autobiography, such as those of Graves or Blunden, becomes clear. Otto Dix said that he revisited his shocking (autobiographical) experience in his prints and paintings *Der Krieg* 'to exorcise the ghosts'. Often the only inhabitants found near the battlefield were indeed the insane: Dix depicts the deranged *Mad Woman of Sainte – Marie-a-Py* with her dead child. Another of his lithographs depicts *A Nocturnal Meeting with a Lunatic* (Image 2.11).[54]

These were some of the 'ghosts' of war incapable of following orders to evacuate. In some of Dix's 'war' scenes, trapped in small dugouts under constant bombardment, many of the combatants too appear to have lost their wits. Suicide was not uncommon in the trenches.[55]

Georg Grosz used the weapons of the post-war irony in his cartoons to probe that memory suppression – and to express his anger at what he remembered.[56] When others chose to forget for some, such as Grosz – as in his prints *Eccoe Homo* – it was essential to recall; it stirs an unconscious and involuntary

IMAGE 2.11 Otto Dix, *Nocturnal Meeting with a Lunatic* (Nächtliche Begegung mit einem Irrsinnigen), Part 22 of the series *Der Krieg*. The themes of madness, ghost-like creatures – often civilians – appear in a number of images in not only Dix's, but also his contemporaries' work. Kupferstichkabinett, SMB. ©bpk/DACS. Photo: Volker-H. Schneider.

remembering because memory can become shrouded in mental illness or dulled by alcoholism, or both. As the post-war music hall song put it, "Just another little drink, another little drink won't hurt at all", that was another path to forgetfulness, and Hemingway was not the only memory worker to follow it.

Sassoon, after 1918, had dedicated himself to oppose forgetting:

> But the past is just the same – and War's a bloody game.....
> Have you forgotten yet? ....
> Look down, and swear by the slain of the War that you'll never forget.[57]

Sassoon's work reveals layers of memory, some numbed by drink or morphine, but his continuing bitterness about the War proved to be the spur to most of his further writing. Such obsession, even 'madness' was a spur to a creative response to the trauma; the surreal images of Stanley Spencer's paintings, and David Jones's drawings, poems and prose, seem to invoke an insanity. In Gurney, the war continued as delusion, as if it had never ended; it was the form which his madness took, and Brittain talks of her breakdown after the war as crossing the thin line between normality and insanity.[58]

Silence, denial, and the thirty-one year war

As critics suggest, whilst such modern re-orientations of memory, in the years 1915–25, is in part 'modernist' in form, in part it also represents a reaction to modernity's excesses and the sheer brutalism of it. The agents and carriers of new memory traditions represent a range of social groups in various layers of civil society; they employ everyday clichéd and often sacred forms to express their anguish, but theirs is a more self-conscious unease. Their mode of construction largely depends on the summoning up of an individual experience as loss. The new remembrance work in this context is typically defined in terms of sudden recall of a moment, of bearing witness or giving testimony, but it is a truth-seeking exercise that may also be prophetic – a warning of recurrence. Accompanying the phenomenon of mass public rituals of remembrance, such alternative 'truth-centred' memory work emerges as a counter-cultural response to any patriotic celebration of 'victory'. It suggests writers and artists do as much as the psycho-analytic tradition to restructure our feelings about past events.

In the short run, and for personal loss, the acerbic, ironic angry harshness of much of this modernist creativity may be 'truthful', but as Winter rightly argues it is not therapeutic.[59] This is a dilemma: more traditional salves help the wounds, but at the expense of a long-term transcendence. But insofar as a postnational even post-militarist recognition of trauma and its causes constitutes a key component of modern memory, it offers only limited hope of redemption. But does it also hint at a transnational strategy of political change, making internationalism both more democratic and more concrete? This includes a collective response beyond individual loss, or communal bereavement and shock. For example, after 1945, such memory was an integral component in the process of cross-border reconciliation in Europe. A strong memorizing component marked the twinning of bombed cities: Coventry and Dresden for example. The wars come to be seen increasingly as European: as one overall shared trauma, not a purely national one. It is also transgenerational: neither silencing and denial, nor the exorcism of ghosts ends with war or memory booms in the late 1920s and early 1930s. It returns in the later 1950s, which I discuss in Chapter 4: Modern memory, once stimulated, continued to develop alternative forms of representation to confront new traumas.

At times, it seems as if the insights and revelations of psycho-analysis were following the cultural shift, not leading a new quest for understanding memory and forgetting. The dialectic between recovery and recognition of a silenced past and acknowledgement of a troubled present – as well as consideration of a more honestly envisaged and critical future – can be seen emerging in these four decades of trauma and repression: they mirror the complexities of private and public forgetting. The new generational traumas of the 1940s appear to create a *caesura* in memory in the evolution between the late 1930s to the early 1950s; but it now seems the tradition had continued in its own subterranean existence only to re-surface more than a decade later. Despite the numbing and repression that accompanied war and atrocity in the 1940s (explored in Chapters 6 and 7), responses to World War Two were deeply influenced by the memory culture of the 1920s and 1930s.

Denial, as well as comprehensive silencing, returned in 1945 not only across Europe, but also across Asia, especially in Japan, China and Korea. Similarly traumatic repression was the norm across Stalin's Soviet Union in the 1940s and 1950s, thus repeating patterns of the 1920s, with renewed terror. Meanwhile the subsequent lack of debate about nuclear weapons globally after 1945 parallels previous censored experience. Repressed memories of war and the gulags as well as holocaust denial in Central and Eastern Europe; the continuing amnesia in Turkey about both world wars, the Armenian genocide; and in much of the West, silence about the European Shoah prevailed. Such repression did not end easily. In Germany, France, Russia, Japan and also in Spain during and after the Spanish Civil War, collective and private silencing affected whole societies. Recurring public and private denials of Stalin's appalling record up until 1953 and even beyond; denial of mass crimes and atrocities in colonial Africa, India and South East Asia, and then silence over such massacres as those in 1965 in Indonesia,[60] or disappearances in Argentina, remained commonplace.

As will be discussed in more detail in Chapter 8, like Spain, post-war Austria, in particular, remained haunted by an unacknowledged, or rarely acknowledged past. Indeed in much of eastern and Central Europe since the fall of the Soviet Union, the process of recovery of memory has proved a long, incomplete and complex process; for example, there was less continuity after 1989 from the dissident movements than anticipated, and new dialectics came into play. But the mass silencing of memory first appeared in the aftermath of the Great War.

Notes

1 A popular song; it was later used by Richard Attenborough at the end of his film *Oh! What a Lovely War!* (1969), sung amongst a sea of poppies and white crosses.
2 Documentation from Harry Roberts Papers, Bradford Peace Museum, Archive.
3 Walter Benjamin, *Illuminations*, Introduction by Hannah Arendt (New York, 1968), p. 84.
4 E. Remarque, 'Preface', *All Quiet on the Western Front* (New York, 1958).
5 Jay Winter, *Sites of Memory, Sites of Mourning* (Cambridge, 1995), ch. 2; and Jay Winter, 'Kinship and Remembrance in the Aftermath of the Great War' in Jay Winter and Emmanuel Sivan, *War and Remembrance in the Twentieth Century* (Cambridge and New York, 2000), ch. 2.
6 Lanzmann interviews Mordechai Podchlebnik, the only survivor of Chelmno, from the first phase. Claude Lanzmann, *Shoah* (New York, 1985), English edition, p. 4.
7 Annette Becker, *Maurice Halbwachs: Un Intellectuel en Guerres Mondiales 1914–15*, Preface by Pierre Nora (Noesis, 2003). Halbwach's lack of acknowledgement of how the relationship between his own work on collective memory and his obviously shattering experiences of the events he witnessed in 1914–18 is an example of such repression.
8 Winter (1995), Introduction p. 5 and pp. 26–27.
9 Martin Jay, 'Against Consolation: Walter Benjamin and the Refusal to Mourn', in Winter and Sivan (2000).
10 Siegfried Sassoon, *Memoirs of an Infantry Officer* (New York, 1930).
11 The symbol of the opiate poppy, which offered sleep to forget the horror. Paul Fussell, *The Great War and Modern Memory* (Oxford, 1975), discussion of poppies, pp. 246–54.
12 Fussell (1975), quoting David Jones.
13 Ernest Hemingway, 'Soldiers' Home', in *In our Time* (New York, 1925), pp. 66–67.
14 Adrian Gregory, *The Silence of Memory* (Oxford, 1994). This contrasts with the noisy scenes of 11 and 12 November 1918, commented on by Virginia Woolf; Vera Brittain *Testament of Youth* (London, 1933).
15 Brittain (1933).
16 Pat Barker, *Regeneration* (New York, 1991). The metaphor is more explicit in her *The Ghost Road* (New York, 1995).
17 Winter (1995).
18 Winter (1995); on Abel Gance's film *J'Accuse*, see pp. 15–24.
19 For several references to these films, see Eksteins's essay 'Memory and the Great War', in Huw Strachan, ed., *World War I: A History* (Oxford and New York, 1998).
20 The film was remade with sound in the 1930s.
21 Winter (1995), pp. 15–24, 55–57; also in Jay Winter and Blaine Baggett, *The Great War and the Shaping of the 20th Century* (New York, 1996), pp. 384–87.
22 Brittain (1933), 'Survivors not Wanted'. Similarly Woolf was deeply affected by the death of Julian Bell in the Spanish Civil War.
23 See examples of such phantom figures in Otto Dix's *Der Krieg* series in Richard Cork, *A Bitter Truth: Avant Garde Art and the Great War* (New Haven, 1994), pp. 272–80.
24 Dix's *Skat Players* is discussed in Cork (1994), pp. 254–55. See illustration.
25 Cork (1994), see images on p. 286 (plate 383).
26 Allyson Booth, *Postcards from the Trenches* (Oxford and New York, 1996).
27 Allyson Booth, (1996), Virginia Woolf, *Mrs Dalloway* (London, 1925) written after the war. 'Jacob's room' becomes such an empty space, when the war kills him at the end of the book. The closure is ambiguous, not reassuring.
28 Young James, *Texture of Memory* (New Haven, 1994), see Introduction.
29 On the Images of Thiepval monument, see discussion in Booth (1996), pp. 36–37 and Winter (1994), pp. 105–08, and in Chapter 9 of this book.

30 In an imaginary flight the Angel of history (*the Angelus Novus*) of Klee and Benjamin might appropriately have been driven past Thiepval, even hovered there. But the Angel would have viewed, not so much the valley of the Somme, as beyond it, the emptiness. See Chapter 14.
31 Carl Sandburg in Jon Stallworthy, ed., *Oxford Book of War Poetry* (Oxford, 1987), p. 168.
32 Whilst DNA still matches a few, most remain lost, forever unidentified.
33 As the Germans did at Vladslo, where Peter Kollwitz was buried.
34 See 2013 Year Book of the 'In Flanders Fields' Museum, Ypres (IFF, Ieper) in Dutch and English.
35 See Winter and Sivan (2000), ch. 2.
36 On Belabre/Rochereau, see Kim Willsher, 'French Town Tries to Save First World War Soldier's Room', *The Guardian*, December 2014; also Winter and Baggett (1996); on Peter Kollwitz's room, see Winter and Sivan (2000) p. 57.
37 Nita Luci and Linda Gusla, 'Our Men Will Not Have Amnesia', in S. Ramet, ed., *Civic and Uncivic Values in Kosovo* (Budapest and New York, 2015), p. 214.
38 Gregory (1994); Winter and Baggett (1996) shows nine soldiers' coffins at Verdun, pp. 380–89. But some of the exhumed bodies were not included in the selection. From these, one was chosen as the Unknown Soldier.
39 The political controversies over the 'unknown soldier' is depicted in the end of Tavernier's film with the choice of one of the coffins at a ceremony at Verdun to give symbolic closure. But the use of DNA has made the discovery of such remains a very different process at the end of the twentieth century.
40 Resnais/Duras script of *Hiroshima mon Amour*. See Chapter 9 (Places past remembered: Nevers And Hiroshima) and further reference in Chapter 7.
41 Examples worldwide since from Algeria, Rwanda, the West Bank, East Timor, all present continuing studies of trauma and silencing.
42 Pat Barker describes the work of Dr W. H. Rivers using Rivers'a own work and notebooks as background.
43 Craiglockhart, as described in Winter and Baggett (1996). 'Anthem for Doomed Youth', one of Wilfred Owen's best-known poems, was drafted while he was a patient at Craiglockhart, where he was being treated for shell shock. Sassoon who, as another patient treated by Rivers, commented on and helped revise the poem which mourns the young men yet to die in the war. Owen himself was killed in November 1918, shortly before the Armistice. See Barker (1991).
44 Also titled *Behind the Lines* (in some versions).
45 Note image from director Gilles McKinnon's film *Regeneration* (1997) (based on Barker's Trilogy).
46 Statistics on executions in *Shot at Dawn* (exhibition), In Flanders Fields Museum IFF. A special display was sponsored on these in Ieper and in the IFF yearbook. One such occurrence is portrayed in Joseph Losey's 1964 film *King and Country*, which narrates a story similar those of one of Bradford's executed 'Pals'. On all sides the contradictions of 'humane cures' and cruel punishments deepened debates about conscientious objection.
47 Michel Foucault, *Discipline and Punish: The Birth of the Prison* (London, 1977), English version.
48 Using some scientific data and statistics at the time.
49 Henri Alleg, *La Question* (London, 1958). Similar debates about trauma were linked also to the Aids epidemic, euthanasia or the effects of testing new weapons, or using them. Franz Fanon's discussion of torture in Algeria, following Henri Alleg's books, was also linked to case studies of silencing and trauma of both torturers and victims, as well as those treating them.
50 Such as those mentioned in chapter 1 from Geoffrey Winthrop Young's *The Grace of Forgetting* (London, 1953).

51 G. W. Young (1953).
52 Ibid.
53 Brittain, Sassoon, Graves – later, Orwell; and in fiction (Hemingway, Remarque), by journalists (Gellhorn), in poetry (Sassoon), and filmmakers (Gance, Tavernier, Resnais, Ophuls, Franju, Lanzmann).
54 For *Nocturnal Meeting with a Lunatic*, see Cork (1994).
55 Dix explicitly describes his engagement with such scenes in his art as *memories*. Much German expressionism was similarly cathartic. On Dix, see Cork (1994).
56 And in his series *Ecce Homo*, intended to provoke others to action.
57 Siegfried Sassoon, 'Aftermath', in *Collected Poems* (New York, 1949).
58 Brittain (1933).
59 Winter (1995), Introduction.
60 Deplored by Peter Dale Scott for example in his *Poetry and Terror: Politics and Poetics in Coming to Jakarta* (Lanham, MD, 2018).

3

MEMORY'S NEW VOICE

'The truth untold'

> "A man's brains splattered on
> A stretcher bearer's face;
> His shook shoulders slipped their load"
>
> (Isaac Rosenberg, 'Dead Man's Dump')[1]

Almost from the beginning, an imagery and language was required that was appropriate for relaying a new experience of war in the autumn of 1914:

> The rats; and the stench of corpses rotting in front of the front-line trench.[2]

News of the war was often censored, whether by official censors of letters and photographs from the Front, or self-censorship. The messages home did not reveal the physical and mental scars even when those who returned spoke. The new voice had to break silences: when truth-telling voices emerged, they did not always find receptive audiences. This confronted the rebellious representations of Siegfried Sassoon, who was one of the major architects of the new memory. But he insisted that all confront the new truths about war.

This reality was best revealed in the Great War by those who fought in it, and described it as experience as did Sassoon and Dix. Only such a terse, sparse vocabulary and imagery as theirs could meet the need for a fresh, unromantic voice – one that, by freeing itself from classical reference, could speak honestly about trauma and atrocity. In the same way Dix did so using visual representation. For any poet in a belligerent country, such articulation could be scandalous: for a decorated serving officer such as Sassoon to use it, was even more unbelievable in the midst of a 'patriotic' war. In most belligerent states, both his deeds and his words would be treasonable, as some thought they were in Britain.

Here we confront the search for truth as a defining characteristic of modern memory. It is a 'way of truth-telling about war' that provides a base for an alternative narrative of 1914–18: to shock and reveal:

> The place was rotten with dead; green clumsy legs
> High-booted, sprawled and grovelled along the saps
> And trunks, face downward, in the sucking mud
> Wallowed like trodden sand-bags loosely filled;
> And naked sodden buttocks, mats of hair
> Bulged, clotted heads slept in the plastering slime,
> And the rain began – the jolly old rain![3]

This was a tradition of veracity, building on the nineteenth-century precedents of Walt Whitman, Thomas Hardy or Rudyard Kipling. Such an honesty began to replace much military and nationalist patriotic rhetoric, or the classic euphemisms of *dulce et decorum est (pro patria mori)*. It was finally formed in the battles of 1914, and such is the literary language in which the war has been best remembered. Descriptions of the shaping experiences of the bloodletting were sustained by a matter-of-factness: they parodied the bureaucratic reports of war ministries, or pronouncements by the general staff, such as Douglas Haig's assertion about 'walking through the enemy lines' at the Somme.

At Arras, Sassoon's dialogue between 'General' and squaddies is entirely unpretentious:

> The General
> 'Good-morning, good-morning!' the General said
> When we met him last week on our way to the line.
> Now the soldiers he smiled at are most of 'em dead,
> And we're cursing his staff for incompetent swine.
> 'He's a cheery old card,' grunted Harry to Jack
> As they slogged up to Arras with rifle and pack.
> But he did for them both by his plan of attack.[4]

Blunt speech is, for writers and poets, part of *the* new vocabulary: plain diction typically stripped of religious and pastoral reference, potentially giving a more universal appeal, as Sassoon's verse illustrates; and it was also often deeply ironic in its inversions of the sentiments and images of honour and heroism. In one instance, he develops a sardonic response and chorus in 'They'. It is one of several bitter conversations, exposing the complacent ignorance of civilian England. The Bishop tells the 'congregation' that the returning soldiers will have 'changed', having fought in a just cause - and a chorus of troops responds:

'We're none of us the same!' the boys reply.
'For George lost both his legs; and Bill's stone blind;
Poor Jim's shot through the lungs and like to die;
And Bert's gone syphilitic.'[5]

Here again, Sassoon is mocking the smug hypocrisy, the denial – the double standard – it is a dialogue with those not listening. The reason for deafness is not the lack of an adequate or appropriate language, but that no one wants to listen to the truth of war – it is all too unpleasant. In Sassoon's 'Glory of Women' this indifference is also located in different gender roles, as an invocation of the chasm between the war and the euphemisms of the home front:

You love us when we're heroes, home on leave,
Or wounded in a mentionable place.[6]

As Paul Fussell's ensuing analysis of this genre shows, much is built around binary structures: 'home' (front) and the battle 'front'; civilians and soldiers; officers and men; men and women; the enemy and 'us'. These serve to demonstrate multiple – and not necessarily synchronized – memory narratives. They enable a more radical, revelatory form of 'true representation'.[7] Sassoon's transparency succeeds not just because of its direct, plain speech and irony, but also because of this construction. Using the binary device of the conversation ('us and them'), these dialogue relationships (sometimes tertiary) set alive the social oppositions of 'General' and 'men' (ordinary soldiers); male soldiers and female civilians; a Bishop and a congregation of soldiers. Similarly in Hemingway's short story *Soldiers Home*, a disenchanted and probably agnostic returned soldier Harold Krebs converses with his devoutly religious mother.[8] This method – a dialogue of oppositions – appears subsequently in much war fiction and war poetry, and such oppositions provide remarkable templates for demythologizing conflict.

In his 1975 survey, Fussell saw the war itself as so ironic as to mock the inherited language of classical verse. It made the chivalric or heroic appear absurd and irrelevant, as linked to a militarized memory, which revels in hyperbole and high diction. In his poem 'Dead Man's Dump', Isaac Rosenberg recalls 'A man's brains splattered on a stretcher-bearers face'.[9] Romance dwells with personalized chivalry not with such graphic language and imagery of victimhood: it is profoundly challenged by this new pared down voice – both soldierly and civilian. Honest description, mixed with savage pity, it is an expression of the plight of the common soldier on all sides: the universal victim. This victimhood is articulated in Reinhard Koselleck's later work.[10]

In the previous chapter, I argued that to describe the 'myth of the memorable war' as romantic is mistaken.[11] Accounts of it may indeed be nostalgic, mythical, remorseful and often marked by a naïve pathos, but any romance left in the war died in the early experiences: of Mons, at Laventie, or on the Marne. The loss of romance and Edwardian idealism is symbolized by Rupert Brooke's death, felled not by bullets but by disease. Far from creating a sentimental, cliché-ridden version of the Great War, the economy of language in new prose (Hemingway) and in poetry (Sassoon, Sorley, Rosenberg, Gurney) captured stark, immediate and often shocking images of war experiences. For example, in graphic and original voices in modern prose, poetic recall for Ivor Gurney's 'dear friend' summons his blooded fatal wound: it is "that red wet thing I must forget".[12] Elsewhere in the images of such wounds, natures blood red poppy is juxtaposed with flesh.[13]

The use of civilian language and imagery, sometimes vernacular, is foreshadowed pre-war in Kipling's *Barrack Room Ballads* and his Tommy Atkins or in Hardy's *Drummer Hodge*; or even earlier, in Whitman's compassionate poems of the 1860s US Civil War.[14] It is continued by Sassoon's honesty about serving soldiers.[15] The language of the Tommy is at first about the enduring ambiguity of a 'mercenary army' – the hypocrisy towards the old 'contemptibles' which endures into a conscript era,[16] or an era of voluntary enlistment.

By mid-1916 in Britain, and in late 1917 in America, when conscription started, the new armies did not match the stereotypes of either the professionals or mercenaries any longer. Across Europe, from 1914, they were ordinary, often simple, and mostly conscripted men as well as the civilian volunteers (such as the *Pals*); and, after them, the enlisted troops and conscripts whom they later fought beside. From cities and villages in France and Germany, and in Italy, and a dozen more countries, these were men drafted into war – as they had been for very much longer almost everywhere else in Europe except Britain. Then, the USA: they did not choose a war some regarded as wrong, but most accepted it.

'The pity war distils'

Whitman's work had already described the pathos of a mass civilian-involved war of the 1860s: the voices of draftees in an internecine conflict, in a contrast to the patriotic doggerel of the broadsheets.[17] Amongst most *litterati*, however, this was not a topic for poetics; for example, Pound and Yeats unlike, later, Eliot had no great interest in war as a subject. Despite their originality, they failed to effectively distance themselves from the patronizing pretentions that marked much of the inherited tradition of high literature, the so-called 'literary canon'. At a time of immense change and genocidal disasters, in a European catastrophe for which others sought the right words, critics have argued that Pound and Yeats remained ambivalent, aloof and self-absorbed, if not cynical, in a poetry dismissive both of 'pity' and memories of war.[18] This is perhaps aesthetically understandable given that there are immense difficulties in any use of language to describe modern war. Terse phrases such as 'blown to pieces' best describe the sheer physicality and bodily disappearances. The mechanization of killing makes most verbal descriptions inappropriate for those who 'fight', or had 'fought'.

In the 1970s, Jon Silkin, in particular, articulated the salience of the new language and its sparse immediacy in Sassoon, Owen, Rosenberg and Gurney – and David Jones's wonderfully apt term 'thisness' is used by Silkin to describe this aspect of voice. 'Thisness' is not merely the use of English vernacular, but is also the actual use of plain words – not in a sense of literary construction or allusion, but in relation to everyday usage and our communication about events to authenticate feelings and thus memories. It is an idiom of veracity uncontaminated by literary reference, media cliché, or received or borrowed phrases. An example of such honest communication is an illiterate soldier who is thought to give the best descriptions of the horrors of the Great War because he has not read anything – only heard and used the spoken word detached from words borrowed or read, unless encountered in conversation. It suggests that, despite the story of Sassoon's amendment of Owen's draft of *Anthem for Doomed Youth*, conversations with peers may be a poet's and writer's problem too in their search for truth-telling.[19] Evading high diction, the working-class poet Rosenberg has a 'conversation' with a 'droll' and 'cosmopolitan' trench rat. No lies there!

Sassoon himself argued that as a result Rosenberg modelled his words with a "fierce energy"[20] – the very 'thisness' – the 'lived-in' words that were the only language possible to 'reshape' a culture. Similarly, Ernest Hemingway reproduces this personal, immediate speech in several of his memorable post-war vignettes of such conflict (in *Our Home*), the following one being of a trench experience:

> While the bombardment was knocking the trench to pieces at Fossalta, he lay very flat and sweated and prayed oh Jesus Christ get me out of here. Dear Jesus please get me out. Christ please please please Christ. If you'll only keep me from getting killed I'll do anything you say. I believe in you and I'll tell everyone in the world that you are the only thing that matters. Please please dear Jesus. The shelling moved further up the line. We went to work on the trench and in the morning the sun came up and the day was hot and muggy and cheerful and quiet. The next night back at Mestre he did not tell the girl he went upstairs with at the Villa Rossa about Jesus. And he never told anybody.[21]

Aspirations to a truth-telling in relation to a memory of personal horror had been represented by Edvard Munch's painting of death simply because it was 'what he saw': a depiction of trauma, just like Dix's. In contrast Eric Kennington's painting of his fellow soldiers at Laventie is more sombre but detached. But, Williamson's stark simple painting of a *A German Attack on a Wet Morning, April 1918* (see Chapter 10, Image 10.5) graphically depicts, as described to me by his son, the specific moment when he was wounded (for the second time in the war). The artist as witness is still alive to remember, and paint that recall of memory: the retreating figure holding his left arm is in fact the artist.

These contrasts pose the question of whether in such a painting or in writing using the language of 'thisness' can also aspire to challenge the bifurcation of different kinds of culture: high and low, elite and mass, or 'popular'; or private and public creativity. The dissolution of such divisions is one aspect of modernism and accelerated with the rupture with the past symbolized by the Great War. However, the emergence of the 'modern' and finding this new, more honest, voice clashed paradoxically with the initial dominance of a cultural modernism that was in the main as elitist as the canon.

Imaging war

A mark of a truth-telling voice is the understatement - simply made – and, as in Hemingway's bleak and stark stories - of 'thisness'; it is most suited to narrate a clearly sceptical view of war. In some the mood sometimes suffuses a whole work – such as in Hemingway's *In Our Own Time*,[22] or *Farewell to Arms*. Yet Hemingway's journey to understanding war, and truth-telling, was also an erratic autobiographical quest. To some extent, Hemingway is his Krebs character, and other of his anti-heroic persona. Seven years after witnessing the disaster at the battle of Caporetto (1917) on the Isonzo Front, Hemingway's prose seeks to explore and narrate his own exaggeration and deception.[23] In uncovering his own, in some cases faked, war experiences, he also finds truth about war itself, and how and why we construct our myths about it.

In most of Sassoon's wartime poems, especially the collection, *Counter-Attack*, this voice blends with stark scepticism, but a more traditional language is fused with less accessible passages, just as in Eliot or Jones.[24] The classical and the ordinary, the sacred and profane are combined. In context, *The Waste Land*'s recall of war imagery is inescapable and obviously about a stirred memory. Eliot's 'Boneyard', with 'the rattle' of the dead men's lost bones, is such a mixture of popular and esoteric reference:

> White bodies naked on the low damp ground
> And bones cast in a little low dry garrett
> Rattled by the rat's foot only...[25]

As in Gurney or Sorley, the 'new' voice appears suddenly – a word or image to shock, to stress a moment, an event 'burned-in', or a surprise encounter – a face recognized amongst those killed, Wilfred Owen invokes the image of a tunnel to hell where he recognizes a 'strange friend', a dead 'enemy' who speaks (the conscript he killed). It says, "I am the enemy you killed, my friend".[26] In Charles Sorley's poem *Millions of the Mouthless Dead* a 'spook' appears.[27] It is a phrase or an image, or a this single word, that leaps out of context to jar the reader into a consideration of the words we use to relay memorable experiences, both banal and indescribable. There are events so awesome and terrible that to silence us may be the purpose of writing. In the search for the lost victim amongst the piles of corpses, the subject encounters a moment of shock – the vision of a ghost that cannot be forgotten: "Should you perceive one face that you loved heretofore. It is a spook. None wears the face you knew". In Chapter 5, I refer at length to Owens's 'German Conscript' who appears almost as an apparition in *Strange Meeting*, yet it is a scene of recognition:

> Then, as I probed them, one sprang up, and stared
> With piteous recognition in fixed eyes,
> Lifting distressful hands as if to bless
> And by his smile, I knew that sullen hall
> By his dead smile I knew we stood in Hell.[28]

Soldiers home

It is the spare understatement of this new tone that paradoxically moves us. In the iconic scene depicting Harold Krebs sitting at breakfast, Hemingway's enlisted returnee has missed his heroes' welcome as he returned late from the war. The anti-climax is palpable, his war photos are pitiably unmemorable, his stories are of no interest to those back home, or those who remained behind. They even seem ridiculous. For Krebs and generations of returnees, the mood becomes sullen, resentful and silent, as their experience is not validated:

> He enlisted in the Marines in 1917 and did not return to the USA until the second division returned from the Rhine in the summer of 1919. There is a picture which shows him on the Rhine with two German girls and another corporal. Krebs and the corporal look too big for their uniforms. The German girls are not beautiful. The Rhine does not show in the picture.[29]

Nursing her emotional scars and memories in 1918, Vera Brittain returned from war service to student life. She found a similar disinterest in the enormity of what she had seen, amongst her younger contemporaries at Oxford – Brittain was deeply depressed by civilian attitudes and was stimulated to write about them.[30]

In his Krebs vignette, Hemingway, like Sassoon's *The Glory of Women*, mocks the denial, stupidity and duplicity in civilian life, not least at home and including parental or spousal attitudes to the war. Harold's mother is only concerned with his 'moral' state after Europe and his failure to look for a job. Her interest in the war is totally absent:

> 'I have prayed for you. I pray for you all day long, Harold'... Krebs looked at the bacon fat hardening on his plate.

Hemingway's laconic description is one of the most memorable yet banal images of 'post-war',[31] a classic repression of war experience. In the breakfast scene, Krebs can only stare at the food, as his mother lectures him on God, and the moral pitfalls associated with military service. The imagery, like the irony of the German expressionists' cartoons, demythologize the heroic picture of war, and its aftermath. This iconoclastic vocabulary of war writers is paralleled in the shockingly brutal imagery of much war art. Subsequently Dix and Grosz depicted this in urban or civilian settings. In one famous drawing, "*I Serve (Evening Off)*", Grosz's uniformed veteran leans against a tree smoking a cheroot as he gazes, blankly, at a bloated corpse half-submerged in an industrial river (Image 3.1).

In his diary, one 'official' war-artist, Paul Nash, wrote about painting as a 'bitter truth' after experiencing the Passchendaele battlefields (1917). He felt the need to communicate this memory in poetic yet authoritative depictions of

IMAGE 3.1 Georg Grosz, *I Serve (Evening Off)* (*Ich Dien* [*Feierabend*]), from the portfolio *God with Us* (*Gott mit uns*), 1919, published 1920. Grosz shared Dix's scepticism of the war and public attitudes to it. © Estate of Georg Grosz, Princeton, N.J./DACS.

empty, faceless landscapes, shattering any heroic imagery of the battle.[32] So too, much later, does Dix's major work *Flanders 1917* (after *Le Feu*) (1934), and the savage trench images recalled by Dix and Grosz. Both the sullen despair of the *Flanders* painting (Image 3.2), and especially the Dix's print series, *Der Krieg*, are drawn from recollections of these immersions in the war; Dix's fellow soldiers huddle in a mud-filled shell crater; it is an image reminiscent of Owen's verbal representation of soldiers, "bent double, like old beggars under sacks", in his poem *Dulce et Decorum Est*[33]: not chivalric splendour, but barbaric debasement.

Even 'Flanders' mimics, ironically, a Renaissance battle painting and, as has been emphasized, not all the new 'remembering' abandoned traditional forms or images. Even if as pastiche, the new survives with the old, but the traditional order is nevertheless challenged by those depictions. The realities of the modern technology of destruction in the first years of fighting presages a dramatic break not only with inherited codes of honour but also inherited imagery of triumph.

IMAGE 3.2 Otto Dix, *Flanders 1917* (*Flandern 1917*), after Henri Barbusse. 1934–36. Based on Barbusse's book *Le Feu*, the scene is of the Ypres salient 1917. It remarkably survived both the Nazis and allied bombing. It is reminiscent of Altdorfer's battle scene from the sixteenth century. Nationalgalerie, SMB. ©bpk/© DACS. Photo: Jörg P. Anders.

Transitions and truth-telling

Jay Winter has similarly documented how the survival of sacred, religious codes and language in the inter-war years still enveloped acts of mourning and remembrance, both public and private, in Britain and the rest of Europe after 1918. In memorials and rituals the new and the inherited were often mingled. This is how, at least in the language of mourning and memorial architecture and ceremonies of remembrance, a traditional, and in many cases a spiritual voice, often remained the obvious choice. But this had become far more muted by the spring of 1945.

In the decades after 1918, the transitions in 'truth-telling' I have described take on new forms and functions in the construction of memory – beyond the new literary voice of 'thisness'. This expression was still often mixed with military symbols and traditionalism. But their survival disguises the fact that in general these practices were in rapid decline, not least because the power of tradition in general was waning. In an era of totalism and massification, of techno–bureaucratic 'newspeak', and of the distanced language of 'Final Solutions', the depersonalized jargon of a new mechanized militarism prevailed. The task of a new language was not so much to debunk hyperbole and rhetoric, as to re-humanize a language drained of true reference.

During the exterminations of the 1940s, a letter from an SS officer documented in the film *Shoah* is an example. It describes a group of Polish Jews being gassed in a van as 'the load'.[34] Truth-telling's role was now not only to challenge euphemisms of this new kind, but also to reinsert humanity where it has been lost. The European Holocaust has multiple examples of bureaucratic language, where the only truth is what is accidently uncensored. An SS letter gives a chilling lesson in the obscuring of genocide in technicism: but there is one mistake – 'the load' 'screams'![35]

Orwell's anti-ideological plea in *Politics and the English Language* was also a call for a 'truth-telling' as a response to specific examples of the uses of Stalinist 'newspeak' and 'double speak' that he encountered, especially as a volunteer in Spain. But he later saw it replicated in and after the war of 1939 in media language, and this was deployed in his critique of the total state in *1984*.[36]

The RAF allied strategic bombing vocabulary in the 1940s was equally impersonal: the phrases 'Administering the dose' in order to 'Blot out Bremen' were part of the terrorist language of urbicide used by Bomber Command in a typical British briefing session, before 'one "1,000 plan" [i.e. bomber] operation' on Germany. 'The dose' was in fact burning ordinary people alive, in their tens of thousands, sometimes the 'medicines' administered were chemicals such as phosphorus, as at Pforzheim.[37] The American 'Strategic Air Command' inherited such a technical newspeak from these World War Two killing machines. In the 1960s, the drained language of long-distance killing in Vietnam spoke of the 'delivery of ordnance to co-ordinates', destroying unseen (often civilian) targets and depersonalizing the potential victims, just as nuclear missiles were expected to do.[38]

Truth-seeking and memory work re-born

It is notable that, in the wake of World War Two, Germans (Austrians to a much lesser extent) developed existing terms as a rich and sensitive vocabulary around the issues of memory and mourning, acknowledgement and denial: '*Mahnmal*', '*Denkmal*' and '*Gedenkstätte*'. This response to historical experience all marked the problems of writing 'true memory': '*Trümmerliteratur*' (writing from the ruins) was a work of '*Trauerarbeit*' (mourning work). And in a society that was traumatized, shocked – *betroffen* – this too was a conscious search for a truth-telling voice. It was a process that would take over half a century to evolve, as native German speakers refined and developed an inherited language for it.[39]

In light of this, modern memory aspires to answer Adorno's question about an appropriate language to speak about modern genocide, one that equally applies to total war and urbicide, especially as transferred into a nuclear age and, potentially, omnicide: instead of the monument, the counter-monument; instead of the canon, 'thisness'.

The free and colloquial verse of Allen Ginsberg's poem *Howl* (1955) was one attempt to break the silence about nuclear weapons of the 1950s ("America go fuck yourself with your atom bomb").[40] For hipster poetry and prose, the received canon of English literature now seemed largely irrelevant to dealing not only with mass bombing of civilian targets, but also with the possibility by the 1950s of a thermonuclear wipe-out. Perhaps the canon was being displaced by a multi-genred one that enabled a more appropriate recall of the recent past to imagine a holocaust that had not yet happened: a thermonuclear holocaust.

Amongst the novels that best spoke of aerial war and of the 'fury of aerial bombardment' of cities, were two American books: Joseph Heller's *Catch 22* and Kurt Vonnegut's *Slaughterhouse Five*, both continued the sardonic and vernacular traditions of Sassoon and Hemingway.[41] A memorable scene in *Catch 22* is at the rear of a bomber: it is remembered for an iconic conversation between the anti-hero, Yossarian, and the unknown gunner, Snowden, after he is hit. A dialogue proceeds both before and after the crew's realization of the fatal wound, and continues even to the moment of death. This sequence's terseness and stark immediacy needs a language as staccato as the firing of the machine gun that the anonymous gunner, Snowden, was supposed to use. Wordiness will not do – and this passage of almost monosyllabic communication is the closest words can do to replicate shock and terror amid the noise of battle: "Help him Help him; – Help who?" – "Help the bombardier" – "I am the bombardier, I'm alright" – "Help him. Help him" etc.[42] (The pilot is ordering Yossarian, the bombardier, to save the nameless Snowden in the rear of the plane). And then comes the dying Snowden's repetitions of "I'm cold, I'm cold", and Yossarian's repeated, almost tender, repeated response "There, there, there, there", and his "You'll be alright kid".[43]

Such a voice is notable not only for the inclusion of such *staccato* vocabulary, but also, as I have exemplified in Sassoon and in relation to Hemingway, its essential humanity and its construction of multiple conversations. In other binary or tertiary dialogues, such as Henry Reed's World War Two cameos *Naming of Parts* and *Judging Distances*, memory is evoked to illustrate the renewed tension between this 'mechanized' war and a civilian vignette of 'pastoral' peace. Between the private self (the human) and the soldier self (the *warrior*), Reeds's contrast involves a gruff 'conversation' occurring in 'basic training': the soldier-poet is "easing the spring of his rifle and the sergeant is telling him, 'you can do it quite easy'" (with his thumb).

Another imagined dialogue with a real, but distanced 'other' occurs in Virginia Woolf's 1940 blitz essay, *Thoughts on Peace in an Air-Raid*. She invokes the thoughts of the young German bomber pilot "trapped in his machine" flying over her. Trapped in her London flat, she invents a dialogue as she hears the planes with their 'hornets drone' about to deliver their potentially "fatal sting".[44] Later Des Pres would imagine the 'bored' H-bomber crews flying over New York.

A memento, written in Gothic script but in colloquial German, from a sweetheart ('Steffi'), is found on a soldier's body in a World War Two poem *Vergissmeinnicht*: it is a trope of recognition. The South African poet Keith Douglas addresses the corpse in the Western desert: a 'lover', singled for death.[45] I shall return to such dialogues, and other conversations, since they represent a significant device in modern memory writing. As I try to show in Chapter 5, they demonstrate 'recognition scenes' beyond boundaries – an empathy for 'the other', the 'enemy, living, dying or dead': for example, when in Douglas's piece, a letter from home (Steffi's) is found on the German, or when a captured German bomber pilot (as in Wolfe's essay) is downed, but not lynched – and instead is "given a cup of tea". The artist aspires to converse with the enemy; the bond of humanness is re-joined even in extremity.

Pat Barker returned to the Great War as a theme again after her 1990s widely read *Regeneration* trilogy. She describes it as 'telling truth' and as her most important aim; in her three linked World War One novels, some of her language is reminiscent of Hemingway's vignettes, or Sassoon's short poems; she continues that tradition at the end of *Ghost Road* in describing the infamous clash on the Sambre Canal late in 1918, an action in which the poet Owen was killed. Her fictional narrative describes how Billy Prior, her unheroic central character, reacts as the attack fails: "banal, simple, repetitive thoughts ran round his mind. 'Balls up, Bloody mad, Oh Christ'."[46] And the familiar wartime reaction, a resort to the divine in crisis, is a common one: "Jesus make it stop" (that was the title of another 1914–18 poem), and like the words spoken by Hemingway's alter-ego in the Italian trench at Fossalta.[47]

The memorably climactic scene in Barker's novel *Ghost Road* epitomizes this diction *in extremis*: a hospital-ward confrontation is recorded between a patriotic father and a dying, brain-damaged soldier-son, Hallett.[48] Not only is speech virtually impossible, but the victim's sentiment is at first denied. Barker fictionally introduces W. H Rivers, the psychotherapist, who painfully witnesses this further silencing. Barker describes other "damaged brains and drooping mouths" which "jargoned and gobbled" out the 'chorus' started by Hallet; these were the words *Shot Varfet* ('It's not worth it'); and these were the "mangled words" that 'faded' as he died. 'Oh but it is!' responded the father.[49]

I have reviewed how the increasing cultural disillusion after 1915 saw the spread of this kind of 'truth-telling', its de-bunking idiom and imagery. This memory genre first arose during the early twentieth century in a world that was changing. As war became more common by its later decades, a wider public accepted an increasingly 'modern voice' in remembering it – in novels, poetry and film. Over the four decades from 1918, an anti-war mood slowly, if episodically, undermines – or infects – the untested language of the *Oxford Book of English Verse*. In a later epilogue to his 1975 book, Fussell commented that 'English literary traditions' seemed less central by the 1980s. But this was only because, by the 1970s and 1980s, this other, authentic and more postnational voice was more broadly acknowledged as quite independent, both of English literature and of British national experience, indeed of 'English' as *language*. Thus a new voice was clearly recognized, by critics, analysts and audiences alike, as a currency of representation not only as important as 'the canon', but also more crucially as a significant and more universal genre in its own right.[50]

Notes

1 Isaac Rosenberg, 'Dead Man's Dump', in Jon Silkin, ed., *Book of First World War Poetry* (London, 1979), p. 211.
2 Siegfried Sassoon, 'Aftermath', in *Collected Poems* (New York, 1949). It is hardly an exaggeration to describe Sassoon's output after 1918 as an extended project in memory work, which explains the central role he occupies in my analysis.
3 Siegfried Sassoon, 'Counter Attack', in Jon Silkin, ed., *Book of First World War Poetry* (London, 1979).
4 Siegfried Sassoon, 'The General', in Jon Stallworthy, ed., *Oxford Book of War Poetry* (Oxford, 1987), poem 124, pp. 177–78.
5 Sassoon, 'They', in Stallworthy (1987), poem 121, p. 176.
6 Sassoon, 'Glory of Women', in Silkin (1979), p. 132.
7 But in his section on problems of factual representation and testimony, he cautions against the suspension of critical judgement. Paul Fussell, *The Great War and Modern Memory* (Oxford, 1975).
8 Ernest Hemingway, 'Soldier's Home', in *In Our Time* (New York, 1970), p. 69.
9 Rosenberg, 'Dead Man's Dump', in Silkin (1979), p. 211.
10 R. Koselleck, *Sediments of Time: On Possible Histories* (Stanford, 2018).
11 As Raphael Samuel did in *Theatres of Memory* (New York, 1994).
12 Ivor Gurney, 'To his Love', in Silkin (1979), p. 115.
13 In death, as in art and literature.
14 Even Longfellow and Mark Twain who contributed to this change.
15 The voices of Sassoon's soldiers make them heirs of Kipling's character, 'Tommy' from *Barrack Room Ballads and Other Verses* (London, 1892). This forerunner literature is discussed in Silkin *Out of Battle* (London, 1972) and in Fussell (1975).

16 Even though uttered with an upper-class officer's background, Sassoon's voices are universally accessible. Kipling's vernacular had been used to point up the demeaning of the tough professional soldiers in Victorian England, and the hypocrisy of the marginalization of 'redcoats', who did the work of the regular army. And it is a theme that long predates Kipling's Imperial redcoats, and accompanied their dubious reputation.
17 Vaughan Williams in his 1921 Pastoral Symphony uses 'the last post' ('taps') as a war referent. Even before 1914, he had set Whitman's poem about Veterans to music, and his service in the war resonated in his post-war music, though he did not talk about it.
18 Yeats's vision of death for an Irish airman is not really about war, or its recall, it is an image abstracted from war.
19 Fussell (1975).
20 Quoted by Silkin (1979), who who sees a search for the authentic as the purpose of Rosenberg's exploratory language.
21 Hemingway (1970), ch. vii, 'Vignette', p. 67.
22 Hemingway, *Farewell to Arms* (New York, 1957), *In Our Time* (1970).
23 Sassoon's poems ('The General', 'Them' and much of the poem 'Counter-Attack').
24 T. S. Eliot, *The Waste Land and Other Poems* (London, 1922).
25 Fussell notes that there were parallel issues of exaggeration in Robert Graves' *"Good-bye to all that"*.
26 The encounter is in Owen's poem 'Strange Meeting'.
27 Charles Sorley, 'Millions of the Mouthless Dead', in Silkin (1979), p. 89.
28 Owen, 'Strange Meeting', in Silkin (1979), p. 196 (see Silkin's commentary).
29 Hemingway (1970), p. 69.
30 Vera Brittain, *Testament of Youth* (London, 1978), ch. X, 'Survivors not Wanted'. This chapter describes her return to Oxford and her depression; it reflects the difficulties of communicating war experiences of nurses as well as soldiers to a new generation which had no understanding of it.
31 Ibid.
32 Richard Cork quotes Paul Nash in 'Introduction', *A Bitter Truth: Avant Garde Art and the Great War* (New Haven, 1994), p. 8.
33 Wilfred Owen, 'Dulce et Decorum Est'. See in Stallworthy (1987). See discussion of Dix in Cork (1994). The image in Otto Dix's 1917 painting *Flanders* (see Image 3.2 and caption) is based on Henri Barbusse's graphic memoir of the war '*Le Feu*'.
34 Claude Lanzmann, *Shoah* (film script – English edition) (New York, 1985), '*The Saurer*' gas vans need alterations, and the SS are requesting changes to the vehicles, pp. 92–94.
35 Ibid. 'The Load' describes the human 'cargo' during the gassings, pp. 92–94; the error is to describe 'screams' (cries). I return to this in Chapter 6.
36 George Orwell's 1946 essay, *Politics of English Language* 1984 is included in *Collected Essays* (New York, 1968).
37 Gwynne Dyer in *PBS War Series* (London, 1985), part 1 'The Road to Total War'; and see also in W. G. Sebald, *On the Natural History of Destruction* (German edn 1999; New York, 2003).
38 The phrase is Tom Stoniers from his writing about the Vietnam War.
39 For an incisive analysis of these diverse terminologies, see Andreas Huyssen, *Twilight Memories in an Era of Amnesia* (New York and London, 1995) and *Present Pasts: Urban Palimpsests and the Future of Memory* (Stanford, 2003). Ian Buruma also has multiple references to this variegated vocabulary in his *Wages of Guilt* (New York, 1994).
40 Alan Ginsburg, *Howl and Other Poems* (San Francisco, 1956) – still a prophetic voice.
41 Kurt Vonnegut, *Slaughterhouse Five* (London, 1970); Joseph Heller, *Catch 22* (London, 1962).

42 Heller (1962).
43 Ibid., pp. 428–29.
44 Virginia Woolf, 'Thoughts on Peace in an Air Raid' (1942), in *Death of a Moth and Other Essays* (San Diego, New York, London, 1970), p. 243.
45 Keith Douglas, 'Vergissmeinnicht', in Stallworthy (1987), pp. 202 and 207.
46 Pat Barker, *Ghost Road* (New York, 1995), pp. 272–73.
47 The remark 'Jesus Make it Stop' is in the partly auto-biographical *vignette* in 'Fossalta', in *The Short Stories of Ernest Hemingway*, 2nd edition (New York, 1953).
48 As a more recent exercise in this genre, Vonnegut had used a similar device in *Slaughterhouse Five*.
49 Barker, at the end of *Ghost Road*, pp. 273–75.
50 Fussell, *Great War and Modern Memory* (postscript to later editions).

4

GENERATIONS OF MEMORY

War Booms and Memory Booms

Memory booms

Modern memory does not emerge as the representations of a single 'group', or of a single generation, nor can it be summarized as solely the composite memory cultivated by unique, creative individuals. Whilst it can be interpreted as including expressions of a series of generational and transgenerational memories, each generation carries divided and competing memories of trauma and atrocity: for example there is *no* single generational identity, or memory linked to World War One. But there is nonetheless a thread that binds one kind of generational memory of, for example, a shared war, to others.

Ambiguous remembering of the war lived on long after the battlefields had grassed over: not only in the war memorials and rituals, but also in uniformed movements, especially the fascist *Squadristi* in Italy, and the German *Freikorps* and their successors and through the veterans associations and 'legions' in many countries (Image 4.1).

Such associations led to the birth of the Nazi movement and party, both in Germany and in Austria, and to fascism in Italy. These were, as were the anti-war, pacifist groups, more specifically generational movements, invoking and mythologizing both negative and affirmative memories of the battlefront.[1] This analysis confirms the recurrent and cyclical nature of memorizing: even if contested, new memory movements still re-emerged, up to twenty years after events. These processes in turn chime with the revival of past templates and cultural memories and its literature becomes popular again even decades later. For one key memory-maker, Eric M. Remarque, the task was to demythologize a generational experience.

IMAGE 4.1 Antony d'Ypres, Pilgrimage, 1928. The British Legion in the main square in Ieper (Ypres). These visits to the Menin Gate multiplied in the 1920s, including veterans and relatives. The ruined Cloth Hall is in the background. By permission of IFF.

In his novel *All Quiet on the Western Front*, Remarque wrote of a destroyed generation:

> This book is to be neither an accusation nor a confession, and least of all an adventure, for death is not an adventure to those who stand face to face with it. It will try simply to tell of a generation of men who, even though they may have escaped shells, were destroyed by the war.[2]

Each generation of memory tends to refer back to earlier phases of memory-building. My point here is to attempt to name those generations and their stories. This may give some temporal framework to these cycles, both of 'boom' and of latency in the growth of new sensibilities of the past. Easily explained by intervening traumas, lapses between memory booms, periods of denial, silencing and forgetting are part of the narrative. However spasmodic and disconnected, these non-contemporaneous memories are in fact linked, as I hope to show. More complex is to interpret the cycles of remembering and what inspires them. Repression and revelation are never far away, and with these, representations of pasts, and pasts lingering in the present.

Karl Mannheim's famous essay on political generations of 1928 gave a theoretical basis for this: he shows how a body of ideas, interpretations or representations of society can develop as and from a generational experience.[3] Usually these influences occur in later teenage years and early twenties – unlike theories of childhood experience they shape political viewpoints and attitudes. Between life within the parent family and the experience of parenting there is typically a hiatus, a freed space, even irresponsibility for intellectual evolution and innovation. For example, those born between the early 1930s and early 1940s would have had a childhood memory of WW2 but a political baptism as teenagers in the post-war era, the 1950s, and early 1960s.

But Mannheim's analysis is partially flawed: like Halbwachs's sociology of collective memory, Mannheim homogenizes a cohort as a 'group'; in this case it is a 'generation-unit' and its memory. But this is misleading: the event or experience may be shared – as was Remarque's or Halbwachs's or Junger's – but the way memory is interpreted and used by people differs: their 'affinity' is in fact heterogeneous, so there is no unified 'identity of responses' to a memory of such common experiences as Mannheim states. For example, it may be transgenerational. In most ways Käthe Kollwitz was not of the 'post-WW1 generation'. Her work spanned the industrial struggles of the late nineteenth century and was influenced by a Christian social ethic. But her personal loss in war placed her expressionist art, and her politics, in the post-1918 evolution of memory and in a central place in creative modern memory work.

I have detected three identifiable generational memory cycles described in this book – each follows and filters major collective traumas. The first major example treated here is the contentious war-memory boom of 1928–36. In each case after 1918, 1945 and 1972–75, these booms follow a delayed response to traumatic events. About a decade elapses: ten years after each war ended in Europe. For example, a decade after 1945: the opening of the camps, the war in the Pacific, and the Hiroshima–Nagasaki bombs, the second wave emerged. The third reaction is more complex, but surfaced ten years after the end of the US ground war in Indochina in 1972 (or the fall of Saigon in 1975). This watershed had also coincided with the decline of the era of new radical movements of the 1960s, themselves both cultural links to the previous generation of modern memory, and progenitors of the third wave.

War and political memory 1920–1940

Though still inchoate, two specific, dramatically opposed, paradigms for collective memory of war had evolved by November 1918. The first is the militarism of remembering typifying the fascist movements in Europe, and the precursors of the Nazi Party in Germany, such as the *Freikorps* and the Stahlhelm. Their memory of the war is rooted in the militarized comradeship of the battlefront.

Some interpretations of the 'modern self' depict it as an alienated one, stranded in a disconnected present. It represents an identity in a new space, no longer anchored in a familiar time-continuum. These changes of modernity sever even the temporary relationships formed by war: they are reflected in a desperate search for belonging and attempts to re-position the individual self in the setting of a modern and an impersonal 'mass society'. It is a separation even seeking community in conflict, such as briefly found in the transitory world of trench war. Reinventions of this mythical identity also involves a sense of solidarity; in the rise of populist movements with their own manipulations of memory and repackaging of the self, some are clearly marked by their generational experience. The sense of isolation of the modern stimulates the rise of such movements; many of them succeed in creating the sense of *Ersatz-community* that is another part of modernity. The post-war generation was one. Others sought collective closure and consolidation in mourning, or through memorializing the victims of the war. For the generation that survived the war, this mayhem of scattered constructed memories in the 1920s and 1930s illustrate both. But they also show how a generation's war memory could be turned to serve both the pacifist and anti-militarist causes, and the nationalist and militarist traditions.[4] They co-existed and clashed.

Rather than being contradictions or incompatible, both major historical interpretations of the impact of war memory are in fact correct. The small pacifist, or socialist internationalist movements that survived the Great War, or regrouped after it, confronted large fascist chauvinistic movements (and also left-wing militaristic groups) wedded to violence. Yet, each movement used War memory and imagery in their propaganda. Another incipient and starkly alternative anti-war memory, growing much slower in the 1920s, was rooted in painfully emerging often traumatized memories. Though not synchronic, these memorializing generational movements were strangely parallel, if not overlapping, phenomena, often locally based and merging in some occasionally ambiguous remembrance events. Where the participants agreed was on the profound significance of what had occurred. Portrayals of past conflict surface with increasing vigour and mass appeal in the late 1920s and early 1930s. The two polar types co-existed; representations with many variants in the spectrum, and other forms of war memory. There was, as well, a continuing mass silence. But both versions reach their peak at about the same time (1928–34), confirming both the cyclical and the complex character of memory movements.

On the far right, fascism had, from the start, glorified nationalism, violence and militarism. In its political beginnings after the war, it exploited combat memories of the returned veterans who, across Europe, formed revolutionary groups: political, veteran, and military organizations – notably the German *Freikorps* in 1918, and in Italy the *Squadristi*, which formed the base of Mussolini's march to power. Symbolic of their glorification of the war, Italian memorials erected after 1919 reflect their nationalist triumphalism and its imperial nostalgia.

As this illustrates, generational memories of traumatic experience are rarely unitary. Bifurcation of a generation's memory of war, as well as of contrasting combat soldiers' and civilian experience, is perfectly exemplified in Germany in the 1920s and 1930s. Patriotic militarism is counterposed to the bitter anti-war work of veterans such as Otto Dix, Georg Grosz and E. M. Remarque – or civilians such as Kollwitz, who challenged the 'Front Kampfers' celebrations of military comradeship, past, present and future. These were symbolically re-enacted by the parades of veterans, such as the Stahlhelm and uniformed new recruits, portrayed in *Triumph of the Will*, Riefenstahl's (1935) film of the 1934 Nuremburg Rally.

In Germany, Hitler and the early Nazis had successfully exploited the mythology of heroic fellow soldiers as 'stabbed in the back': 'betrayed' in 1918, by the Jews, Communists and Socialist Internationalists, led by the so-called 'October' or 'November criminals'. Whilst those returning, or returned, troops, who joined paramilitary groups, provided the prime recruiting ground for the founders of the fascist movements in Germany, Italy and elsewhere, equally, many millions of returning soldiers initially joined the ranks of the international leftist opposition across Europe. These included the revolutionary Spartacists who supported the anti-war internationalists, Liebknecht, and ultimately Rosa Luxemburg.[5] Indeed, much besides human lives were destroyed by the polarization and continuing political violence of 1918–36. A holder of an Iron Cross, Hitler's own 'biography', *Mein Kampf* (1926), epitomizes the bitter response of many such German veterans to their thwarted aspirations. They were unified in an unacknowledged defeat, but after the extremes of four years of dangerous combat which they had survived, their yearning for renewed comradeship, even conflict, was a spur to a new nationalist militarism.

Like millions of veterans, Adolf Hitler could not let go of the experience of the war. As he recounts in his *Mein Kampf*, on hearing the bitter news of defeat in hospital, his reaction to the Armistice was to pledge to start his political career.[6] Twenty-two years later, at the fall of France, his gleeful grin appears in the iconic photograph of him in occupied Paris near the Eiffel Tower. To stress the point that a memory of a victory once lost was now apparently regained, the Third Reich chose a mnemonic site, richly symbolic, for the formal surrender of France in 1940. It was the same memorable space – the railway carriage at Compiegne – where the 'October' criminals had agreed to sign the Armistice of November 1918.

Culture wars

In stark contrast to the Nazi cult of the past, in such rituals as annual rallies celebrating the combat experience, others used other more sober military rituals to honour the fallen. Rejecting triumphalist nationalism, an increasingly mass-based pacifism also emerged that called for a total abolition of war in the 1930s. Internationally such visions were institutionalized in the Kellogg–Briand pact, outlawing war. Illustrating the tensions between benign and pathological responses to the past, this contest is symbolized by the political controversy over Remarque's novel, *All Quiet on the Western Front* (1929). Though the author claimed he did not "accuse the war",[7] it was nevertheless a banned and even burnt book, several years before Hitler became chancellor. Physical clashes occurred after 1932, even in cinemas, when the film was shown. Remarque's semi-autobiographical book made a global impact and sold millions, but like the novel, Lewis Milestones' (1930) Hollywood film of it, was attacked and censored in Germany before 1933, despite winning an Oscar in the USA. This was symptomatic, showing of how contestation over war memories were profoundly and actively controversial ones. In 1931, the film was first blocked by German conservative authorities, including Konrad Adenauer as pre-Nazi mayor in Cologne (and later, post-war, chancellor).[8] When the books were burnt by the Nazis in Berlin, Remarque's was included.[9] When the book was filmed in the USA, with Lew Ayres as the protagonist Paul Baumer, its narrative was unequivocally 'liberal',[10] demythologizing combat memory – and with sympathy for the 'enemy'. It was a counter-perspective that deeply affronted the Nazis. Ayres himself became a Pacifist and later an American conscientious objector in World War Two.

The manufactured cult of the 'slaughter of the innocents' – as the thousands of young student volunteers killed at Langemarck in Flanders were represented – was widespread and typical of the shared mythology. Early in the war and faced by veteran British machine gunners (October 1914), the story of killing was sustained, in part, as a legendary martyrdom of youth for the fatherland. These are the same victims, including some thousands of students, who are depicted in Remarque's novel yet from another anti-militarist perspective. The ages on the gravestones in the area – seventeen, eighteen, nineteen, twenty – do still attest to the youth of many of those buried in Flemish cemeteries. But, contrary to the myth, the majority of the victims around Langemarck were not particularly young, nor lacking experience or training, as was Peter Kollwitz. Large numbers were ordinary soldiers, just as were those (many professionals) killing them.[11]

Together with such myths, Hitler's *Mein Kampf* and the rhetoric of National Socialism present a starkly anti-pacifist, ultra-nationalist alternative memory of war. This mode of remembering is articulated in one 1914–18 veteran's account: Junger's book *Storm of Steel* – on his brutal war experience – represents a modernist, but quasi-fascist account of the violence.[12] Equally, Leni Riefenstahl's film of Nuremberg 1936 perfectly captures the use of this combat re-enactment at the Nazi rallies; in some still shocking scenes in *Triumph of the Will*, these acts of collective memorializing were in part rituals of remembrance. In these propaganda events Goebbels emphasized this celebratory comradeship –for purposes of both re-dedication and revenge. The dedication to the 'fallen comrades' of the Great War is depicted not in shrill, but in remarkably sober tones – it is the 'militarization of memory'.[13]

These Nuremberg party spectacles, the key representational moment of Nazi manipulated remembering, were enabled by, and enhanced, the use of absolutely new media. Riefenstahl's cameras capture extreme moments with technical perfection. How conflict remembered is exploited by such imagery, and the way it can be enhanced by film is captured incisively in her record of the party rallies. It was a lesson in Goebbels's propaganda not lost on the allies, especially in the USA, who used it in their war documentaries. The film lends charisma to the event, and 'the heroes', but not least to Hitler. Staged by the architect Albert Speer, in a powerful media event and a ritualized 'theatre of lights', the generations of veterans stand together with the uniformed front-fighters of the future. The new battalions listen as the names of the World War One sites are remembered. At each new standard

IMAGE 4.2 Leni Riefenstahl, *Triumph of the Will* (*Triumph des Willens*), 1935. Hitler (top left) touching the standards and recalling the battles of 1914–18 in the notorious Nazi propaganda film depicting the party rally in Nuremberg in 1934, including both veterans and new recruits.

symbolizing 1914–18, Hitler touches the flags, then salutes, signifying a rededication of a comradeship formed on the battlefront (Image 4.2); they are ready for a new combat – this was the *Frontkämpfer* (combat soldiers) version of memory mobilized.

War and anti-war

It was clear by 1929, that, despite the spate of anti-war novels, plays and films, and with *All Quiet on the Western Front*, as the best-known example, whilst 'the war boom' was by no means entirely patriotic, it did not represent the predominance of a benign or anti-militarist mood. Nevertheless in Germany, as in other countries, there were strong counter-memories: with pacifist, anti-militarist and anti-nationalist variants. Even before 1918, the voices against war such as Rosa Luxembourg, even in her prison writings, had expressed this opposition. Following the war, on the Left the forceful anti-fascist cartoonist, collage-maker and Dadaist John Heartfield parodied Hitler, and provided a critical, socialist rejoinder to Nazism, ridiculing them in brutal posters and savage illustrations for newspapers, he deplored the collapse of the supposed peace arrangements post-1918.

After publishing his graphic pictorial collection of images of mutilated and dead, *War against War* (1924),[14] the virulently anti-militarist and anarcho-pacifist Ernst Friedrich worked to create an 'Anti-Kriegs Museum' in Berlin. In 1933 on the night of the Reichstag fire, Nazi storm troopers broke into the museum and smashed and looted the anti-war exhibition and photographs. Soon after Friedrich was imprisoned, and the anti-war museum was destroyed, but he was permitted to go into exile, where he continued his agitation. But with true Nazi irony, the museum of 'war horrors' was subsequently used as a Gestapo interrogation and torture centre. Friedrich's son continued his work after the war, and the museum was re-established on the same site in Berlin.

The war boom generation

Despite their fragmentation, these representations need to be seen as inter-generational memories. They represent an important basis not only of 'modern memories' in general, but also of a new tradition of remembering war that first emanated from those who survived the Armistice of 1918. As a generational memory, the Great War is sustained in real or fictional biography and autobiography and by relatives and civilian participants. Many, such as Remarque and Hemingway, I have cited earlier. In England, Vera Brittain, Robert Graves, Edmund Blunden and Siegfried Sassoon epitomized that generational narrative. Brittain's personal story, *Testament of Youth*, an account of nursing the victims from both sides of the conflict and of her own personal bereavements, was read aloud at meetings in towns all over Britain from the 1920s onwards as a witness to the suffering on all sides and to solidarity with the wounded.[15] Also in England, plays typified by Sherriff's *Journey's End* (1929) represented a similarly regretful anti-war memorizing, and shared the mood not only of Brittain's autobiography but of many lesser-known war memoires by survivors.[16]

Perhaps because of the prevalence of silencing and numbing, in this generation the influence of this cohort of anti-militarist veterans even on the peace and pacifist movements seems to have been limited, or at least largely indirect. There were reciprocal effects: Remarque, as an ex-soldier for whom, like Sassoon, it was important never to forget the horrors, wished to tell of 'a generation of men' who even though they may have escaped shells were 'destroyed by the war', but he was never politically engaged. Nor was Walter Benjamin, who had volunteered in 1914 alongside his generation to be with friends, but later avoided and evaded service. Nevertheless he felt a sense of solidarity with those opposed to the war, and whilst never an explicit pacifist, was traumatized by both the death of friends and the war itself.

In Germany, the expressionist work produced during the 1920s and up to 1936, and then detested and stopped by the Nazis, followed the same trend, including work such as Max Beckman's *Going Home (from Hell)* and Otto Dix's *Prague Street* (1920) and *Der Krieg* (1924) and, most importantly, his *Flanders 1917* (1934–36). From 1934, much of this anti-war art was attacked, branded degenerate and in a number of cases masterpieces, including major works by Dix and Barlach, disappeared, were destroyed or were burnt.[17]

Some of these miraculously survived both war and the Nazis, as did Georg Grosz's *Pillars of Society* (1932) and Dix's *Flanders* (now in Berlin). Some of Kollwitz's later work also survived from this post-1933 period. But tragically some of the greatest anti-militarist works in Germany were destroyed first by the Nazis, after 1934, then by the 1939–45 war and the aerial bombardments. Allied bombing destroyed much of the greatest anti-war art, including major work by Kollwitz, Dix, Barlach and Grosz.[18] Nevertheless, whether it survived or not, such imagery old and new was crucial to spreading an alternative representation of war memory of a critical kind, at least amongst liberal and educated elites in Europe, both before and after 1945.[19]

There is essentially the same memorial contestation in England and Germany. In Britain, it is exemplified in theatre in the 1920s. A number of plays between 1920–36, not only *Journeys End*, had a strong pacifist orientation. At the same time the art of Otto Dix, Georg Grosz, Käthe Kollwitz, and Ernst Barlach in Germany, – and C. W. Nevinson, Paul Nash, William Orpen and many more in Britain were all implicitly anti-militarist. Some of the best known of these visual images, such as Kollwitz's Grieving Parents (1932), John Sargent's Gassed (1918–19), Nash's The Menin Road (1919) and Wyndham Lewis's A Battery Shelled (1919), were all created after the war. Important British art that reflected the war continued to appear between 1918 and 1938. In 1919 Stanley Spencer painted Travoys, and later his remarkable set of paintings covering the walls of the Sandham memorial chapel, Burghclere as murals, work increasingly acknowledged after World War Two. An anti-fascist memory, in an existential clash with the militarization of the recent past by the veterans, the British Legion, and then by Mosley's black shirt fascists, finds common imagery across borders. I have shown how the movements of the internationalist Left (until 1937) and the proto-fascist nationalist right across Europe had both effectively used 'the War' experience as a justification for their politics and actions. In the 1920s the result was that social consciousness and memory was fractured Left, Centre and Right.

Memory divided

Further fragmented with the crisis of 1936 in Spain, many internationalist, non-Stalinist, non-pacifist groups, like the majority of the British Independent Labour Party on the Left, supported the Republicans. In a rehearsal for the clash between the Axis and Russia, in what was seen to be legitimate armed resistance to Franco's nationalists coup, led by part of the army; political dualism was replaced by a continuum, a range of anti-fascist civil actions. With the rise of Stalinism across the Left in Europe, especially with regard to the war in Spain, these proved to be no longer the same political formations by the mid-1930s. Opposition to German militarism after 1934 was replaced by a span of methods, evolving from non-violence to eventually, armed resistance. But from 1933 to 1936, with the polarization in Germany, Spain and Italy, the movements fissured yet again, and this time between pro-, and anti-war positions on the Left, which split the peace movements. In several countries the political centre collapsed as a direct result. It was a disaster for pacifism, not only in Europe: but it also had implications for the coalition supporting the Republic and the 'popular front'.[20]

Forms of mass popular pacifism still survived in France, and to a significant but lesser extent in the USA, Britain, and several other countries in Europe. Debates about the wisdom of anti-fascist violence and of re-armament sharpened the splits in all the Left movements, which had already divided after the revolutions of 1917/18. However, the cause of Republican Spain helped initiate the construction of another radical tradition of 'internationalist' memory of war and with it the often confusing myths of 'the Spanish struggle'. These ambivalences evolved, – embodied in the writing, not only of Orwell and Hemingway, but also of Gellhorn, Borkenau, Brenan, Malraux, and in Auden's poetry.

The evolution of ways of remembering was interrupted in 1936–37, both by opposition to war and by a struggle against fascism that had separated from it, and, by 1940 formed adversarial divisions in radicalism. These were symbolized by the Nazi/Soviet pact and the tragedy of Poland. Peace positions now inhabited different trajectories, histories, symbols and interpretations of the past. As in 1914, the large pre-1940 Peace Movements, both pacifist and non-pacifist, had split, and then, even in democratic polities, began to collapse. Given widespread authoritarian advances, that process was even more decisive and complete in 1940 than it had been in 1914.

Powerful memories of the Great War, however, did not entirely die: remnants of anti-militarist organizations of the inter-war years continued to carry these reminders even underground into the full-scale war of 1940. The pacifist wing of the peace movement, in France until 1940 and in Britain even after, was still sizeable, but now even more divided. It lost ground to Left internationalists – for example, Trotskyist and other anti-fascist resistance groups – and then to support for the war. Moreover, unlike 1915, there was no significant re-emergence of wartime pacifism in 1940, though there were in Britain alone 60,000 conscientious objectors to military service of whom 7,000 were imprisoned (and similar numbers in the USA).[21] These enjoyed a significant infrastructure from religious and secular groups in support and some leading public figures also supported them – notably a few particularly opposed the strategic bombing of cities. This aspect of peace culture is relatively unknown, and does not fit dominant narratives. It generates a retreat into communitarianism, emigration, or both. Elsewhere it supports resistance to occupation.

Indeed, given the context of 1918–39, there was never likely to be an effective anti-militarist action after the 1920s, given the legacies of Versailles, the breaking of pre-1914 internationalism at the outset of war, the consequences of the post-war settlements, and the rapid spread of fascism in the 1920s. So by the mid-1930s, the failure of the pacifist stance appeared inevitable, given the militarist (and ultimately armed) alternatives to it, and the physical confrontations that ensued. What is less acknowledged is that the anti-pacifist left in the democracies failed equally miserably, unless one includes those battalions supporting Stalin and the Soviet Union. Yet even these Communist parties were deeply divided by the Hitler–Stalin pact, the purges, and much else in the decades after Spain, and up until the post-war crises, after 1953, 1956 and the events in Hungary.

It will be clear from this, and my previous discussion of the 1920s and 1930s that it is misleading to use binary, let alone unitary, frameworks for studying generational memory. Divisions in memory culture vary over time, from the universal versus particularistic mode of remembering to the cosmopolitan versus national/ethnic perspective on war; or from a militarist perspective contrasted with 'pacific' or non-violent methodology of action. However ineffective the broad peace movement was before 1918 and to the mid-1930s, it did represent a transnational peace dimension in public opinion; the traditions of war resistance transcended many national allegiances in Europe, North America and wider. For example, Gandhi's non-violent movement gained widespread support. Adhering to both liberal and socialist internationalist principles of universalism, such perspectives stressed attempts at reconciliation, and co-operation – or at least conflict transformation.

Yet even using these more refined categories of political culture, we risk oversimplifying. As critics, such as Adrian Gregory in his *Silence of Memory* and others observe, in discussing remembrance [in Britain], war could be remembered not just in two or three, but also in a multitude of ways.[22] In other words, it is how that memory was used politically, and methodologically, that is the most useful basis for viewing the plural culture of remembering, and it is a deeply contested phenomenon. Many theories of war memories lack such sociological insight even of already bifurcated societies. By this I mean that contradictory forms of social and cultural change may occur and co-exist simultaneously. These are signified by mixed icons juxtaposed, such as white and scarlet poppies, red flags and swastikas. Even on the Left, Picasso's *Dove of Peace*, co-existing with the hammer and sickle – or more radically with broken rifles, suggest how ambiguous symbols can be memorably deployed in political conflict, often alongside **national** flags. They are signs, not only of political discord, but also of divided, fragmented perceptions of their meanings as mnemonic devices for reading the past and present politically, and of envisioning future change.

What was hard to ignore by more detached observers was the structural continuity of twentieth-century war, genocides and holocaust, noted after 1945 by authors such as Hannah Arendt. This context, and these linkages, have a central bearing upon the modernity of memory. Even before 1940, mobilizations for the two world wars were clearly related to each other, not only politically and in military technology (tank warfare, aerial bombing and submarine war), but also culturally. The thirty-one-year war from 1914 to 1945 saw continuing conflicts across the globe, from Spain and North Africa, the Mid and Far East, and the Pacific. Arendt's prescient polemic hints at the broader implications of the structure of totalitarianism through this era. But after her, such analysis needed further exposition structurally and sociologically to specify those linkages.[23] As I have stated (Chapter 1), militarism and modern state organization was vastly enhanced in the mobilization for the Great War and created the structures and the technological (and social) preparedness for the mass civilian destruction to come after 1940. It was foreshadowed in (aerial bombing) cities, in death camps (Armenia) and in forced labour (conscription) for mandatory work in factories, or slave labour and as draftees in combat.

At the heart of this process was the destruction of the inherited distinction implied by international law, between civilians and combatants. This emergent process, characteristic of total mobilization, entailed loss of civil liberty and the physical merging of the 'front' and the 'home front' in war. It presages urbicide, the incineration of cities, the Shoah and later 'low-intensity' warfare. As a key factor, both in the rise of our new forms of memory of collective trauma and in attempts to represent them and heal their consequences, these emergent continuities are too often left implicit and unacknowledged in social and cultural theory.[24]

A second 'post-war' generation: the memory boom of the 1950s

Despite widespread political repression of such memory before and after 1945, cultural spaces survived and signs of memory construction reawakened. After the initial numbing and emotional paralysis engendered especially in the years from 1943 to 1945, a basis for remembrance was gradually re-established by the early revelations of the camps (such as film of the liberation of Belsen) and the awareness of the increasingly indiscriminate mass bombings of civilian targets (1944–45), including Hiroshima and Nagasaki. But it took many decades to find some appropriate balance between what was acknowledged, what was memorialized and what was quietly left to rest or pass away with the witnesses and silent survivors.

The generation of those born before World War Two, and who grew up in the 1940s, were as much puzzled as radicalized by these experiences. Once again reactions differed widely; trying to make sense of a decade historically and existentially was not easy since it was novel: as others have observed, "the most terrible decade in a most terrible century".[25] Those who lived through World War Two in belligerent countries, especially in cities, were inevitably marked in some way by it. For those survivors who were bombed, tortured, raped, mutilated or imprisoned, it was a burnt-in experience. The gut response of mild to acute panic at the sound of air-raid sirens is a familiar one, a common reaction, but one learned amongst those who experienced aerial war. It is one that is shared by contemporaries across many borders. In the 1950s and 1960s, the new alternative voice of memory was particularly rooted first in the experience of people who had been directly or indirectly involved, both as civilians and as 'civilians in uniform' (conscripts and draftees). Long after 1945, these witnesses included millions of refugees and ex-prisoners of war and those who had been conscripted for war or imprisoned for avoiding service. By the 1950s, with the Algerian and Indo-Chinese War in France, or those performing national service in Britain, in Egypt (1956), Cyprus, Aden or Kenya, or serving in UN armies in Korea, a re-awakened generation was formed that represented a new cohort of reactive memory, and a new generation of not uncritical veterans.

Intergenerational transmission of memories from these decades becomes a significant factor in shaping the generational politics of memory that emerged in the mid-1950s and continued for over a decade. This not as easily tied to a single war experience as the boom of the late 1920s, but to a series of contests and traumas. It included memory-makers who had been old enough to have fought in Spain or to be World War Two combatants (such as Paul Fussell, Kurt Vonnegut, Henry Reed, Vernon Scannell, Edward Thompson, or those killed such as Keith Douglas). Even non-combatants had been adult witnesses such as Iri and Toshi Maruki. It also especially involved those who had early memories of urban bombing: 'children of the blitz'. Mostly born in the 1930s, they had lived enough to be aware of World War Two traumas of war, refugees, genocide or personal exodus. There were also those memory-creators, such as W. G. Sebald and Anselm Kiefer, who were born at the end of the war but not yet of the baby-boom generation. They were nevertheless teenagers in the 1960s. Even without any direct personal memory of the war, fully aware of the extent of the destruction, such events profoundly affected the revival of memory work.

This generational memory comprised both the atomic bomb and the imagery of death camps. A decade later, growing up during the post-colonial wars in Indo-China, Palestine, Korea and Algeria; the early crises of the Cold War, Berlin 1953, Budapest 1956 and the Berlin 1960–62 culminated in the Cuban Missile crisis: 'a smell of burning in the air'. The Egypt/Israel Six-Day War in 1967 added to an accumulating sense of tension and threat.

In the UK, France and Germany, the early New Left was shaped by a decade of such events: these experiences helped re-structure consciousness. A new wave of popular memory work evolved. This was never a studied, opinionated or even analytical production, such as that of late modernism (or post-modernism in the 1980s to 1990s). Moreover the response of the 1950s and 1960s lacked any unifying agenda or any collective self-consciousness. Given reference to still recent trauma, some had predicted there would be 'no poetry after Auschwitz' (Adorno). Initially the social mood, with some exceptions (Britain's welfare state of 1945–50), was even less optimistic than after 1918. But however pessimistic in terms of social progress, it was marked by a changing cultural life that, as in the 1950s in the West and Japan, cannot be easily summarized. Beyond the terminology of modernity, 'modernism' or *modernist*, the artistic output of this post-1945 generation was marked by pathos, rage, sometimes despair: often resentment, even bitterness. In Stalin's Soviet Union and other total states, it also comprised the courage of humour, irony, satire and prophesy. The literature of 'engagement' encompassed acts of resistance, of testimony and of bearing witness, or at least heeding the warnings of the survivors.

As in the 1930s, memories became increasingly *'committed'* politically: a main impulse was ultimately both oppositional and future-oriented, the purpose was to 'prevent forgetting'. By the 1960s, this was not carried by the veterans' generation alone. It was more an expressive, existential reaction to events. Whilst not programmatic, a politicized memory was inevitably selective. As a voice of civil society, it sustained structures of feeling beyond the state. This was contested, especially by repressive regimes such as those dominated by the Soviet Union under Stalin and in its satellites.

The new engaged memory, at first inevitably politically radical, was also contested by key actors. In the West, for example in the USA, and Israel after 1948, memory focused on the European/Jewish Holocaust, and the Nazi past; there was less concern with witnesses of conventional, or atomic, bombing. Following the somewhat constructed discovery of the partial, but remarkable and moving Anne Frank diaries, the Shoah narratives gradually touched the public mood[26] (I return to deal with this later in Chapter 6). Other witnessed traumas, not least the previously suppressed experiential art and testimony and literature of Japan's atomic survivors after 1953, also became available and more influential. The story of Sadako, the girl stricken by leukaemia, and the paper cranes she made and her death (Image 4.3) was a typical parallel to the Anne Frank story.[27]

The stories of both the Hibakusha (atomic bombing survivors) and the concentration camp victims and witnesses were linked to a growing concern with – and belated preservation of, their sites of suffering. This new cohort of remembrance, and the private and public mourning that followed, were especially focused on Auschwitz-Birkenau in Poland, as well as at Hiroshima and Nagasaki. These memorials represented a dominant cultural construct for both popular and elite audiences. Memory sites gradually became places of secular pilgrimage in the 1950s,

IMAGE 4.3 Robert Del Tredici, Sadako's paper cranes, 1984. These are the handiwork of Sadako Sasaki. When she was twelve years old, Sadako contracted leukemia from earlier exposure to the atomic bomb. She did not wish to die. She refused all painkilling medication and took literally a Japanese proverb that says: 'If you fold 1,000 paper cranes, you will get whatever you wish'. She folded 645 of the tiny birds before she died. In *At Work in the Fields of the Bomb*, image 42. © Robert Del Tredici.

though some were from the outset 'political sites' of memory, they also became 'sacralized' over time.[28]

A major memorializing source of this second generational boom in the 1950s was a project born out of French 'engagement'. It was, contradictorily, both more consciously political – influenced by the Marxist Left, yet less extreme in its forms than the cultural contests of the 1930s. Unlike the utopianism of the pacifist peace movement of the 1930s, it was replaced by a more pragmatic approach using 'counter-memory' as a tool in building cooperation and linkages at the grassroots. The same impulse supported transnational institutions both in Europe and beyond. It was not so much counter-hegemonic as an alternative; it was made from a coalition of popular community groups and avant-garde generational milieux. Living in turbulent times, politics became part of their biographies and memory-making process. But its roots in pre-war experience was not necessarily apparent to that student generation of the 1950s, still grappling with the *grand narratives* of World War Two, the Shoah and the Cold War. In the context of 1956, even during the Suez and Hungarian crises, denial and silence continued about the growing global nuclear threat, as well as of the ravages of colonialism on three continents.

After 1953, with attempts at change in east and central Europe, largely non-violent street protests erupted; through these, and other acts of witness, such as Jan Palach's suicide by self-immolation, new markers of dissent were established. But as in the West, if it existed, 'memory work' was an underground project which lacked self-consciousness until eventually articulated by Kundera, Wolf, Sakharov and others. But like memory resurgence in the West, it was uncritical, arbitrary and often spontaneously 'situationist'; it accumulated materials and critically appreciated a collage of texts or *samizdat* and Polish film, especially Wajda. But in France, Alain Resnais's films (1956–59) on Hiroshima and the camps amplified both Duras's scripts and Franju's *Hôtel des Invalides* (1953) (discussed later) as key moments in a repertoire which saw a cross-border transmission of memory – images of cities (especially in photography), Berlin, Warsaw and Budapest, and other sites, associated in an apparently random way. Accompanied by new reportage in film, theatre and poetry especially, such images of memory became cultural fashionable. To accompany *'new wave'* cinema, there was a philosophy (existentialism), as well as a fledgling 'angry theatre' and poetry in Britain. New poetry, both there and in 'hipster' America, and as well as a 'free cinema' movement, all became associated with generational identities, and in it a celebration of popular images of working-class 'kitchen sink' culture and life. Retrospectively it is easy to over-interpret the transnationalism of such shared cultural experience. This inter-generational project represented a unique cultural fusion of post-World War Two responses, and was shared not only by an educated white minority emerging in the West.[29] But to conflate the experiences of these two decades into widespread restructuring of consciousness about renewing the past can appear a contrived and value-laden exercise.

However, one clear example of authentic identification with the past is the widespread 1950s revival in appreciation of the soldier poets of both wars.

This was not just British 'Trench poetry', but a rediscovery of war in the poets, of the 1930s and 1940s such as Keith Douglas, Henry Reed and W. H. Auden. It accompanied a more systematic search for oral witnesses. The quest for testimony began: linked to a new popular and oral history. The 1960s interest in the Great War and popular culture was a memory revival that spread to countries where that war had not previously been memorialized on a significant scale. For a generation that had encountered both wars, and war in general, through literature rather than history, it was culturally transformative.

Such was the context; the paradox of two separated generations living for the present – a mood prevalent in the 1920s, and then repeated in the more politically aware forms – or the hipster ethos, of the 1950s and 1960s. This cultural renewal coexisted with a fascination with the past. The result was a dramatization of time remembered as in Phillip Larkins's 'MCMXIV' and by the construction of multiple new memory pieces. The best-known theatrical example in Britain was perhaps Joan Littlewood's memory metaphor *Oh! What a Lovely War!*, to which I will return in some detail in Chapter 10. It was in part a trope linking nuclear weapons to the memory of mutual military attrition. Such productions, also in cinema, marked a widespread resurgence of anti-militarist sentiment (1956–65) accompanying opposition to rearmament, nuclear escalation, and imperial ventures from Algeria, and Suez to the two Indo-China wars.[30]

Whilst such memories of the Great War remain recurrently 'generational', even in the 1930s, 1940s, 1950s and 1960s, they then continued transgenerationally long after the death of the last veterans. The testimony of survivors or witnesses of events also became culturally enlisted as 'the past in the present'; as the last of these from 1918 died and those of 1945 grew fewer, the continuation of contemporary memory work owed much to individual and collective longevity, reinforcing the third generation effect. Especially in the Western world, and in Japan, Russia and even China, veterans and survivors lived longer to testify: the memorials became better presented and preserved (though no less controversial), and new ones were constantly created.

An intentional and oppositional memory-making that had timidly emerged in the late 1940s was transformed by this series of visionary image-makers and popular historians. It signified that an alternative postnational memory generation was emerging. The documentary impact on a generation unaware of the Holocaust, e.g. of Resnais's *Night and Fog* (1955),[31] and other works were key ingredients in cultural re-framing. Similarly, first film footage of Hiroshima, which coincided with the first visits (1950s) of *Hibakusha* (Japanese atomic bomb survivors) to the West, encouraged the flourishing of new or recycled mnemonics of war, and icons of peace, as well as the invention of new ones. These became spurs to an evanescent anti-atom bomb movement, and are at first part of a predominantly non-violent counter-culture. Moreover, as global decolonization spread, a more transnational and multi-cultural memory became a possibility. Whilst modern memory remained largely a project of Western industrial societies and reflected European, and especially English-speaking, experience and activism, there were major exceptions. The modernizing industrial society in Japan slowly evolved its own memorial culture after 1945. Constructed mainly in response to the Hiroshima and Nagasaki bombings, it began an interchange with Western peace movements in the late 1950s which became highly politicized. These sustained a global cross-fertilization that helped transnationalize the framing of an alternative modern memory as a more universal project: but it remained a compromised and ambiguous one, ethnically and ideologically, in the Cold War context.

Repression of information about atomic weapons, East and West, was perceived by many radicals as an official 'conspiracy of silence'. It was partially broken on the stage, in art and in literature, as well as in 'free cinema' and in new-wave film. The revision, reinvention or re-interpretations of inherited images – included in the language and symbols of war and peace. There is a growing intentionality in this; the creation of a sceptical, more cosmopolitan and non-aligned alternative to a dominant corpus of militarized memories. In the 1950s and 1960s the German new Left self-consciously embodied it; and in France, for whom the bitter continuities of 1914, 1918 as well as 1940 were hard to ignore, such memory work helped pave the way for the eventual generational outburst of 1968, and the overthrow of De Gaulle.[32]

'Counter memories' and populism

In the wake of the 1960s movements and decades of protracted wars in Indo-China and Middle East, a third stage, the most recent memory surge occurred. It was one that could be clearly seen as an heir to the 1960s generation – yet was discontinuous with it. It arose with the second Cold War (1979–90), and I will return to it in Chapter 10 and 11. But, as in the 1930s, and in contrast to the second boom, a 'reactive memory', which returned to the politically tribal past of nationalism, also re-appeared after 1989. Especially in eastern and Central Europe, the role of 'memory' as part of reactive identification politics played a key role in the resurgence of chauvinistic nationalist movements in the former Yugoslavia, especially Croatia, Serbia, and then later Kosovo (Kosova) and also in the republics of the former Soviet Union and its satellites and allies, such as Hungary. This raises questions about postnational trends and the continuing contested nature of modern memory in subsequent generational experiences – from the second Cold War (1979–85) and after the end of it (1989–2000).[33]

For any generational analysis the story is perhaps too recent to assess; the contours less clear – and the innovations vast. Various memory booms seem now to continue in successive overlapping waves and in various forms at the millennium. Individual memory was enhanced by tapping into global archives online; the process was both increasingly global and confused. In researching the evolution of social change movements, my analysis, which has focused on cycles of social protest, generational politics and episodic shifts, shows that cultural and social movements have their own life spans. But after decline they may be reborn, years later, in new forms; the same is true of the representations of the past (memories) that accompany them. But to analyse contemporary generations of memory in a detached and comparative way, and which takes into account the gendering of memory cultures since the 1970s, this detachment is problematic. So, at this point, my discussion of memory is confined to the three cycles, the 1920s/30s, 1950s/60s, and then later, to a lesser degree by the 1980s, when a global archive of material became accessible electronically to millions worldwide.

The main cultural movements of memory-making discussed in this book were cyclical: each lasted about a decade, some more between 1928 and 1934, 1952 and 1964, and 1975 and 1985. The latest memory boom from the late 1980s, whose demise was frequently predicted, seems to have lasted somewhat longer and perhaps represents a more enduring part of modern culture and global communication. It now comprises overlapping but different movements – especially the women's movement, but including other cultural and academic ones. The reasons for these booms probably still have more to do with individual life cycles and the key experiences of generations than further changes in collective memory per se, though the boom in social media has had effects not yet fully understood.[34] For all its theoretical problems, Mannheim's work on generations poses key questions of exactly how, when and where we 'make memory', based on key individual experiences, forged in our teens and twenties. It is also arguable that given different generational trauma (of childhood) these can be formed from much younger memories, and still be equally salient to the reconstruction of collective memory later.

Caveats about the varieties of memory surge, emerging in popular communication and social media are needed. After the third boom the *cult of memory* may have become a victim of its own success, evolving in the 1990s into heritage and other saleable commodities, even kitsch. This can be illustrated by the Great War commemoration of 1914–18 in Britain, where it almost appeared that the surfeit of memory was serving to vitiate the whole project.

As a symptom of this overload, the English 'poppy' obsession appeared in the form of a mass pottery centenary sculpture, displayed at the Tower of London in August 2014. It provided what was perhaps fitting for some, and moving, or for others, a depressingly populist, epitaph to the memory work of previous generations. A notable public memory piece, marking a centenary at a military site – an early medieval castle – it was largely detached from any history of memory or of war. Equally distant were the prevalent scholarly debates of the 1980s and 1990s on memory. This event at the Tower was simultaneously a part of a burgeoning popular memory interest, exploiting social media and part of the war heritage business; it was a populist, conservative project and promoted by a patriotic media, and I will return to it in Chapter 11.

Like the boom in memory tourism however, a more serious shift in educational priorities, uses of technology and also grassroots approaches to modern history accompanies the 'war heritage' business, and with it a revival of local and family history, constructed often by using the internet. Like the grass on the battlefields, such virtual installations, rebuilt structures and monuments, can screen the past from view. Detached from the authentic memory of trauma, the hundreds of thousands of ceramic poppies might be judged as constituting a similar denial of the scale of the real events: the kind of wrapping up of the past that Benjamin had feared in the 1920s.

Similarly, the constantly repeated filmed image of the Twin Towers destroyed in New York City, subsumed the masonry and girders in the instant, organic present of 9/11. Like the mushroom cloud, it entered the pantheon of iconic and evanescent remembrance, even as it was erased – a trauma blitzed from memory in a symbolic war on terror. Each cycle of remembrance may develop its own cultural response and specific generational connectedness with possible futures. But as stated at the outset, a generation is not in itself a unified mnemonic community: it is the movements and communities who respond to the past, within that generation, that can act to restructure sensibilities about an experience. Cultural and social movements are subject to periodic transformation and change, even in their construction and self-reflection on events – these all are variables. 'Modern memory' as an act of post-national intentionality remains like the rebel dream: half fulfilled, half fading. It faces its monsters, past, present and future, and those monsters are to some degree the rebels' own creations.

Notes

1 George Mosse, *Fallen Soldiers: Reshaping the Memory of the Great War* (Oxford, 1990).
2 Eric. M. Remarque, 'Preface', *All Quiet on the Western Front* (New York, 1958).
3 Karl Mannheim, 'The Sociological Problem of Generations' (1928), partially excerpted in Olick et al., eds, *Collective Memory Reader* (Oxford, 2011).
4 See image of the British Legion's Veterans' Parade, Ypres. On pacifism in the 1920s and 1930s, see Peter Brock and Nigel Young, *Pacifism in the Twentieth Century* (Syracuse, 1999). Also in Martin Ceadel, *Pacifism in Britain, 1914–45: The Defining of Faith* (Oxford, 1980).
5 These splits deepened the polarization of the new Weimar republic, with the Spartacist uprisings starting in 1918. Karl Liebknecht and Rosa Luxemburg were assassinated during the failed German revolutions. Both had opposed Germany's entry into the war, and were imprisoned for their anti-militarist agitation and killed by the right-wing *Freikorps* (1919). Some of Luxemburg's collected letters are excerpted in Jon Silkin, ed., *Book of First World War Prose* (London, 1979). These are an important memory document of the war. After Liebknecht's death (1919), Kollwitz produced a memorial piece, 'Gedenkblatt'. Ursula von Trotta's film *Rosa Luxemburg* (1986) evokes the prison memories especially graphically. On the *Freikorps*, see Mosse (1990); and J. P. Nettl's biography of Luxemburg, *Rosa Luxemburg* (Oxford, 1966) remains the definitive account.

6 Hitler's account is summarized in Adolf Hitler, *Mein Kampf* (Berlin, 1925) and discussed in chapter IX in Modris Eksteins, *Rites of Spring: The Great War and the Birth of the Modern Age* (Boston, 1989), and in Jay Winter and Blaine Baggett, *The Great War and the Shaping of the 20th Century* (New York, 1996).
7 Modris Eksteins, 'Memory and the Great War', in H. Strachan, ed.,*Oxford History of the Great War* (Oxford and New York, 1998), and Eksteins (1989).
8 Remarque (1958) and Eksteins (1998). As a collector and cinema buff, Goebbels probably kept secret copies of both book and film. These culture contests are well analysed in Eksteins (1989), on the work of the 1920–30s (chapters IX and X).
9 Eksteins (1998) and Eksteins (1989), especially chapter IX.
10 Remarque (1958).
11 See Mosse (1990), pp.71–76
12 Remarque (1958), and see Eksteins (1998), ch. IX 'Memory' (on Remarque); Hitler (1925); Ernst Junger, *Storm of Steel* (London, 1929), and see commentary in Mosse (1990) on this version of the war.
13 The image of Hitler is reproduced in Eksteins (1989). See also film *Triumph of the Will* (Riefenstahl, 1936).
14 Ernst Friedrich, *War Against War* (Seattle, 1987).
15 Vera Brittain, *Testament of Youth* (London, 1933), and see Adrian Gregory, *The Silence of Memory: Armistice Day, 1919–1946* (Oxford, 1994).
16 R. C. Sheriff, *Journeys End* (London, 1929).
17 A number of these destroyed works are discussed in Richard Cork, *A Bitter Truth: Avant Garde Art and the Great War* (New Haven, 1994).
18 One destroyed masterpiece Ernst Barlach's 'Hovering Angel' now restored to Güstrow cathedral had a remarkable renaissance (see Chapter 14).
19 Subsequently, Anselm Kiefer re-assumed the weight of responsibility of this extraordinary expressionist *oeuvre* in his work after 1970, also dominated by war memory. On Kiefer's art as a contemporary reflection of this tradition, see Andreas Huyssen, *Twilight Memories in an Era of Amnesia* (New York and London, 1995), ch. 11, especially pp. 210–15 and pp. 224–27.
20 At the same time, Pacifism was crushed in Japan with the expansion of war in the 1930s.
21 Peter Brock and Nigel Young, *Pacifism in the Twentieth Century* (Syracuse, 1999), esp. pp.156–57 and pp. 171–78. See also Rachel Barker, *Conscience, Government and War: Conscientious Objection in Great Britain, 1939–45* (Abingdon, 1982).
22 Gregory (1994), see 'Introduction'.
23 The innovative work of Arendt contributes to an important structural framework for any overall analysis. An émigré from Germany to France, then to the USA, she was influenced by the Frankfurt school. A philosopher, political theorist and sociologist and comparative historian, she described the evolution and continuities in the structures of modern violence, total war and the modern nation state and their authoritarian character. Whilst she did not write about either memory or modernism directly her analyses are a key context for understanding modern memory. In her major work, *The Origins of Totalitarianism* (New York, 1951), she implicitly connected war and genocide. On memories of the Shoah, see her *Eichmann in Jerusalem: A Report on the Banality of Evil* (London, 1963, see 2006 edition). Amplifying Arendt's work on modern state power, the American political sociologist C. Wright Mills's analyses of the social, military political 'power' elites and interplay with corporate ones complements other overall empirical macro-analysis of modern state power. I return to these issues in Chapter 6. Other participants in these debates have included Zygmunt Bauman and Jurgen Habermas.
24 It was accessibly articulated and popularized in Winter and Blagget's extensive work on the Great War and the PBS (and also BBC) TV documentary series on the Great War, both of which implicitly reflect the macro-analysis of Hannah Arendt's *Origins*

of Totalitarianism. See Winter and Baggett (1996); and then PBS series *The Great War* (edited version by the BBC).

25 Eric Hobsbawm, *Age of Extremes* (New York, 1998) begins with a series of epitaphs on the dark experiences of the century, which are almost universally pessimistic. I return to this in the final chapter.

26 Anne Frank, *Diary* (New York, 1952). Many powerful documentary interviews followed.

27 Robert Lifton, *Death in Life: Survivors of Hiroshima* (New York, 1968); see his account of Sadako's illness, and death – a story relayed to Western readers in the late 1950s.

28 Quite unlike the 'battlefield tourism after 1918, which at first, like the Michelin guide to them, was a business failure (though this would later change); this was genuine memory tourism. On battlefield tourism, see Winter and Baggett (1996), especially the image of tourists on the battlefield, and see the cover of the Michelin Guides to the battlefields (Image 1.1).

29 Counter-memory is implied in T.W. Adorno, *Prisms* (Cambridge, MA, 1981), which also refers to Auschwitz. The idea is taken up by twenty-first century critics.

30 With sceptical incisiveness A. J. P. Taylor played a key role as a populist historian, entrepreneur and TV lecturer. Taylor was also as interested in culture as history in educating public memory on such topics as nuclear war. A sardonic iconoclast, he admired, *Oh! What a Lovely War!*, and subsequently dedicated his 1963 Penguin History of the 1914–18 War to Littlewood, its producer on stage in London in the East End. On both Taylor and Littlewood, see later discussions in Chapter 10.

31 Resnais's title *Nuit et Brouillard* (*Nacht und Nebel*) is derived from the chilling phrase written on the transportation wagons used for deporting Jews to the camps to which they were assigned- under cover of night, and fog.

32 In the same period, the American New Left developed its own narratives.

33 The Iraq or Gulf Wars; the USA after the 2001 Twin Towers attack.

34 Mannheim's early experience in the Weimar Republic was clearly a model for his analysis, and perhaps should be included along with the precursors discussed later.

5

STRANGE MEETINGS AND COSMOPOLITAN SYMPATHIES

Recognition scenes as epitome of postnational memory

> I am the enemy you killed, my friend.
> I knew you in the dark: for so you frowned.
> Yesterday through me as you jabbed and killed.
> I parried; but my hands were loath and cold.
>
> Let us sleep now...
>
> (Wilfred Owen, *Strange Meeting*)[1]

The rise of modern nationalism shattered European society into state-ordered shards. As A. J. P. Taylor observed, by 1910 passports and hard borders were symbols of this closing. Even more than the problem of physical frontiers, the linkage of universalism to the idea that the world was somehow progressing had already fragmented amongst elites by the late nineteenth century. The horrors of industrialism and urban squalor that had also accompanied the rehearsals for mass industrial warfare in the USA in the 1860s and the genocidal nature of imperial expansions both there and across Africa and Asia had become apparent. But the widespread dreams of liberal internationalists, and the attempts to implement socialist transnational organization (e.g. of the Second International) which confronted the new nationalism, could not in the event transcend the growing patriotic allegiances revealed when the moment of mobilization occurred. The image of mass enthusiasm for war is part of the accepted mythology of 1914, it is greatly exaggerated, and the mood faded quickly, but the cultural identification with each country was real.

Nevertheless whilst a trans-European culture had survived into a new century, it was tempered by a realization of impending crisis and thus provided a background for the melancholy and pessimism of *fin de siècle* Europe. Out of this emerged Viennese psychology, as well as early expressionism and symbolism in art. In the last decades of five old empires, Hannah Arendt describes how the emboldened nation-state broke the last vestiges of post-enlightenment cosmopolitanism. It was a factor that sealed the future fate of millions of Jews.

In the longer term, after the cataclysm of 1914–45, subsequent tentative rediscoveries of a redemptive if more cautious empathy invoked a universalism of common loss, if not a renewed idea of 'progress'. This was to be the immanent appeal of a project implicitly creating an alternative – a 'modern memory'. The mood of this creative process was not hopeful but resistant, not sentimental but compassionate. In the tradition of Camus, by the 1950s such a project eventually represented in part the celebration of defeat, of heroic loss, of 'flowers for the rebels failed'. The concept of empathetic recognition represents the, at least momentary, acknowledgement of a common humanity, often *in extremis*, that keeps hope alive and lasts long after all else about the situation is forgotten. In the way this process is represented as a symbolic past. Such emblematic encounters are remembered and these remain far beyond the 'real' event itself to become iconographic 'tropes'. They are the devices by which real, or fictionalized, encounters are forged into enduring images of compassion and solidarity that have a resonance beyond patriotic appeals and myths.

Antony Jay appropriately terms such collective memory a mystery.[2] The often unknowable motives and methods of collective memory construction, which become so central to later memory analysis, remain largely imponderable. What is clear is that in relation to a dominant group memory, the creative process has a capacity to transcend national or other 'belonging identities'. In an extreme form, such enclosed identities, with their layers of protectiveness, constitute a dimension of Adorno's paranoid 'authoritarian personality' theory in which collective submersion of the 'self' defends it against an 'other', or others, which compensates for a weak or absent core identity.[3] In this analysis, an alternative memory tries to confront both collective victimhood and vengeful patriotism, with a global and potentially redemptive identification steering war memories towards more benign purposes, and by presenting a model of human recognition and bonding, rather than revenge, it makes possible a shared acknowledgement of loss and trauma and of reconciliation.

Each such *recognition scene* portrays a particular mode by which a more universalistic image of a relationship, occurring amidst or following trauma, is imprinted on a mnemonic past. Through the arts and literature, it is then encapsulated in the representation of the cathartic moment. It is when enemies become human again – at least temporarily. As in the *Iliad*, the concept of mutual recognition in war developed as early as the concept of the warrior itself. But this is often not a chivalric recognition of an 'honourable' enemy, but the acknowledging of a common fate, a shared a history of victimhood. Such an empathetic framing is used, though ambiguously, at the close of Stanley Kubrick's important early film, *Paths of Glory*, dealing with French soldiers in World War One and based on the real events on the Chemins des Dames.[4]

This is a scene which seems at first to offer a recognition of common humanity, but we doubt, lest Kubrick, ever the sceptic if not cynic, has created ambiguity. French troops are about to go back to the trenches, after the execution of scapegoats; like 'lambs to the slaughter', they are reminiscent of the glum images of French soldiers in Nevinson's paintings, trudging back to the Front. But the *poilus* in a café are permitted first to listen to a beautiful young German woman (Christiane Harlan), who sings (in German) 'The Faithful Hussar' ('*Der treue Husari*'), a sardonic song about doom and love (Image 5.1). Apparently the tearful girl has been captured, or 'conscripted', and is now forced to sing. At first men jeer her, but as her emotion, and the music, draw slowly their attention and *their* tears, Kubrick shows the scene of empathy, across nationality: they are, as we are, moved, yet they probably do not understand the words. As the film finishes the men return to the butchery, and the same song is repeated, played by a military band. The moment is exceptional, but the war goes on regardless. Is this a fake recognition scene? Or is Kubrick the realist reminding us not to succumb to sentimentality about the context of a passing acknowledgement of our shared humanity? Like the Christmas truce it is a moment of exception, a dawning empathy in a context of ruthless, impersonal and nationalist bloodletting. Like all such events, there are many narratives, many scenarios and many possible interpretations.

Another less ambivalent and more authentic case of recognizing common humanity across tribal division occurs in Vera Brittain's auto-biographical *Testament of Youth* (1933). In 1917 Brittain was unexpectedly moved into a ward nursing the German wounded, many dying. Her account of a period when she was nursing these prisoners provides one especially moving cameo. She had

IMAGE 5.1 Stanley Kubrick, *Paths of Glory*, 1958. Tears follow jeers: a captured German girl singing in German a soldier's song 'The Faithful Hussar' to French troops in an *estaminet*, about to be called to return to the battlefield in a bittersweet moment of borrowed time.

enough German to converse with them, and she had nicknames for them: 'Fish', and 'Hyacinth'. She writes with compassion, detail and concern about their agonies and deaths. But it is a passing episode and she was transferred again, involuntarily from that ward, without explanation, but without ever forgetting the experience;[5] and she spoke of it publicly after the war, with often mixed responses, since anti-German feeling had not entirely dissipated.

From literature, cinema, film and the representation of such actual events, the work of modern memory illustrates the varied nature of specific recognition scenes but suggests a more universal canvas. The perceptive work of Northrop Frye, *Anatomy of Criticism*, is one key to the concept of 'recognition scenes': he is a literary critic, but in an almost Bergsonian (or Proustian) voice he invokes timeless moments out of time: "The contrast between the course of a whole civilization and the tiny flashes of a significant moment."[6]

He notes these moments not only in Proust, but also in Eliot's *The Waste Land*, and the last works of Virginia Woolf. A similarly striking recognition occurs in her *Death of a Moth* (*Thoughts on Peace*), when Woolf identifies, during the Blitz, with the young pilot trapped in his machine circling above her and London, trying to kill her. She appeals to the mental fight, and if shot down, she would be glad if he was given a cup of tea.[7] In fact one was, and so were others. But elsewhere he would have been lynched, and many were.[8]

The other

Vignette:
Eugen Gehweiler

He arrived on a Sunday afternoon early in 1946 with two others in their drab POW uniforms. He, a bespectacled artist from the Neckar valley, north of Heilbronn with Gustl Walter, a hairdresser from Schwäbisch Hall. And Herr Kemp, who had been a judge in the Third Reich, and was their minder (he returned to the East when they were repatriated in 1948 and we never heard of him again). Their prisoners of war camp was outside town. They did agricultural work. Eugen was, in civilian life, a graphic designer and it shows in the inscription in the atlas that they gave me as a Christmas gift in the wintry Christmas of 1947 (Image 5.2). We invited them to spend Christmas Day with us as a family. They arrived, for us unexpectedly, on the 24th (their Christmas) whilst family preparations were beginning for the celebration on the 25th. This cultural difference – celebrating Christmas on the 24th, Christmas Eve, reminds us that it was German celebrations on 24 December 1914 that led on to the Christmas Truce on the 25th. So we had two 'Christmas' celebrations; they returned the next day for a memorable dinner.

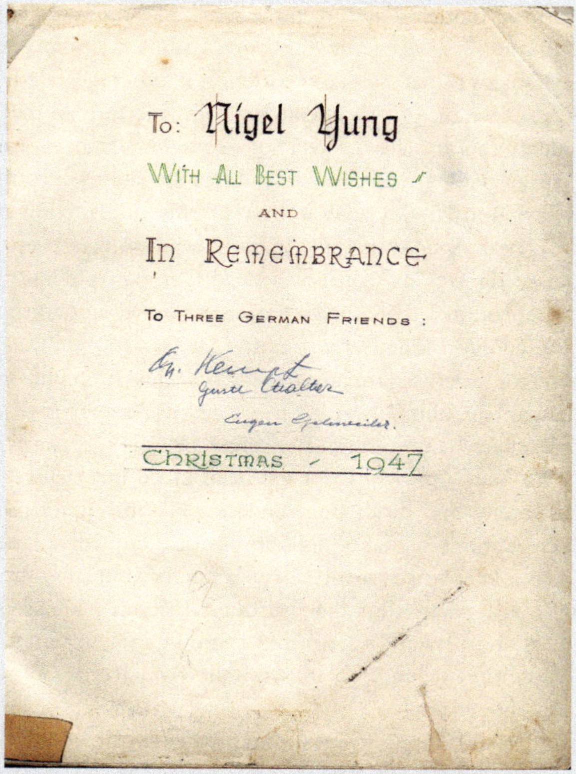

IMAGE 5.2 A gift to the author, an atlas signed by three German prisoners of war, 1947. One of the signatures belongs to Eugen Gehweiler. Photo: Nigel Young.

Eugen was the sociable articulate member of the group. He had been stationed in the Lofotens, took hundreds of photographs (sadly lost), but spoke little of the war; he had been captured in Holland in 1945. I still have photos of him and his family from Heilbronn, where I spent a long summer in 1952, and Gustl cut my hair. The scars of war in Heilbronn, Stuttgart, Pforzheim and Frankfurt were plainly visible. Remaining in contact with him and the Gehweiler family ever since, his daughter, Ursl, survived in a retirement home near Lake Constance with pictures of her proud father in his Wehrmacht uniform. But for the family after 1944, life was hungry and hard. My last meeting with him in the 1980s before he died was over some glasses of Warsteiner in Ingolstadt, in the bar at the railway station. He never wanted to see England again, but we were friends for over three decades.

The phrase 'recognition scenes' was Frye's, but Paul Fussell employs it in a broader way: these empathetic moments are not mere recall, like those triggered by Proust's *Petite Madeleine*, nor do they necessarily reproduce a moment of retrospective remembering, such as Thomas's halt at Adlestrop station. It is rather as a real-life, or fictional, or even contrived experience of an encounter with 'the other': 'the enemy'. Such engaged, lived identification is characteristic of a counter-memory, or many counter-narratives, that challenge the negative myths and representations of conflict.

One of the best-known Great War uses of this humanizing device was in Wilfred Owen's poem *Strange Meeting*; it invokes a conversation with a soldier killed. The poet recognizes the spirit as a dead German (a conscript in the first version) who is encountered in 'hell', a trench tunnel underground, and tells him "you are the enemy I killed, my friend".[9]

The film director, Derek Jarman, transcribed this moment in a fusion of poetry, music and silent film. Owen's *Strange Friend* ('enemy as friend') appears, accompanied by poetry and music (Benjamin Brittain's *Requiem*). But in the third medium – cinema – the conscript has been killed but is alive. The recognition scene is of enmity and death transcended; and the reunion is depicted, not implausibly given Owen's sexuality, as homo-erotic empathy. Jarman opens his meditation with spoken words from Owen's poetry, but after that only music and sung text. It is a silent film that, through Brittain's music, sets the Latin words of the mass and Owen's poetry, but without spoken narrative.[10] Cinema presents this recognition scene with its symbolic embrace, which becomes both universal and acutely personal.

Robert Jay Lifton interprets these moments as revelatory encounters which acknowledge a shared fate, a common humanity.[11] It is perhaps the role for a modern memory beyond borders to help, by the representation of recognition of this fate, to construct a more general culture of solidarity. Such recalled images, alternative myths of conflict, have, thanks to such work, become central to an alternative cultural remembering. In that way our enemy stereotypes start to be replaced by a transnational/universal acknowledgement of the other. Such themes recur in poems, paintings, plays and photographs; the recognition scene is a device that operates especially effectively in prose narratives or biography. For example, auto-biographical moments become iconic encounters, occurring in Orwell, Hemingway, Graves and Keith Douglas. An empathy with the adversary in combat is revealed: the enemy image is deconstructed both mythologically, and experientially. But the task of transcending otherness facing postnational memory is immense, and it is the visual representation that is often the most successful, since it, like music, does not 'territorialize'.

We select consciously beyond difference in memory-making; a shared individual, or sometimes group, experience of suffering and trauma has to be epitomized. Such constructs can rarely directly reproduce a mutually testified personal memory of each individual shared experience – though this is, in theory, possible. But they create an archetype, one that aspires to reproduce these in opposition to powerful chauvinist and antagonistic collective memories. The process itself has a symbolic capacity: that potential – to transcend national belonging identities – can remind us of past collective human relationships and counter-narratives – *a peace history*: memories that are otherwise lost.

December, 1914: throwback to the past or revelation?

During the twentieth century, at certain, perhaps fortuitous, moments such myths become, almost unbelievably, historically concrete. Some are well, and mutually, documented in now deservedly famous historical events. Such scenes present us with surprising, peaceful and memorable recognitions of 'the other, the enemy'. Because of letters and photographs, and popular film and popular music, one of the most celebrated and timeless moments we know of began on 24 December 1914; it was in France and Belgium on the Western Front. There had been calls for an armistice, as many had expected the war to be 'over by Christmas'. There was an urgent need to bury the dead, with many bodies still lying in no-man's land. The process of ceasing fire had started in any case several days before the 24th. The Pope and many other religious leaders had been calling for a ceasefire, or even an official truce for the December festivals.

Despite these appeals, this so-called 'Christmas', unofficial, truce or 'spontaneous armistice' was remarkable and unexpected. Given the alignment and proximity of the combatants, it was, and will probably remain, one of the largest such simultaneous fraternizations in the history of warfare. It occurred between several vast armies stretching, though discontinuously, along large sections (possibly up to two-thirds) of the Western Front – troops highly armed with deadly mechanical weapons. In fact these encounters lasted from just a few hours to one or two days (25th to 27th), and in a few places, even up to a week. In some sectors, they continued even longer, in the form of local 'live and let live' arrangements. Though never on the same scale, these arrangements continued or were repeated in various places throughout the war.[12]

These various collaborative events and relationships are clearly documented, even in British Regimental histories. However, there are major factors explaining these 'recognition events' that have often been neglected. It can be forgotten how widespread was the internationalism and anti-militarism that existed in European societies before August 1914. This attitude had accompanied the spread of radical socialist ideas in the 1880s and the growth of the Leftist labour unions. The long-term unpopularity of military conscription, in most European states, which had mostly imposed compulsory service, was combined with mass opposition to growing nationalist, jingoist and pro-military sentiments.

Because of the myths of August 1914, the evidence is ignored that such movements still involved tens of millions of people in the first decade of the twentieth century. These were not pacifists in any strict sense: the socialist movement and parties, and radical unions had mobilized millions of supporters and members and most were not opposed to violent resistance. Their leaders passed

IMAGE 5.3 Christmas truce in no-man's land on the Western Front in December 1914. "A friendly chat with the enemy" British and German soldiers photographed together between the trenches during the spontaneous armistice, which was foreshadowed in informal truces after 19 December that arranged to bury the dead. National Army Museum, London.

an ambitious and radical anti-militarist resolution at the Second International's Conference, in Stuttgart. It, somewhat ambiguously, proposed a strategy, including general strikes and non-cooperation, to prevent war. Mass peace movements of a more pacific, liberal kind overlapped with social democracy, and also existed in most belligerent countries. In France, the socialist orator Jean Jaures was a dominant figure in the internationalist peace movement across Europe. There was outrage and widespread despair when he was murdered shortly before the war began. Of the German socialists, by August 1914 only Liebknecht and Luxemburg and a few other Left leaders publicly opposed the war declaration, though hundreds more supported them. In Britain, Keir Hardie and Philip Snowden did the same, and the Independent Labour Party and some key labour and liberal leaders opposed war, and indeed British involvement was not a foregone conclusion.

Many authors who have written about the following December events ignore this pre-mobilization dimension of Europe at war. As a result some critics have interpreted this 'Truce' as merely an anachronistic throwback to nineteenth-century attitudes, an adherence to codes of honour towards opponents, and chivalry in war: this is Modris Eksteins' view. But except perhaps for some officers, the solidarity of the fraternization had little, if anything, to do with any sudden gentlemanly outpouring of chivalry. Whilst it revealed genuine and understood respect for fellow soldiers, the victims of war, the wounded – and the unburied dead of both sides – it was also as much an expression of the survival of cross-national solidarity, and an early sign of disillusion with the war and its protagonists, especially by erstwhile members of the mass Labour unions and parties. These 'Socialists with no fatherland' found themselves forced into a war, and faced with the fellow working people they were being ordered to kill. As Dolleans, the French syndicalist, wrote from a trench in 1914, about his conscription: "I did not have the strength of character not to go, although I did not recognize frontiers or fatherland. I was afraid, it's true, of the gallows. I was afraid."[13] Many of those with the machine guns were neither volunteers nor professional soldiers, but forced to fight, and they were horrified by what they encountered.

It is a huge irony that the only place where these links, human and political, could be, and eventually were, forged in actions was in the incredibly unlikely arena of the battlefield itself. Volunteerism had quickly decreased in belligerent countries in 1914, as casualties accelerated, and with it came the rapidly declining legitimacy of the war itself, in both its aims and its strategies. Voluntary enlistment was replaced by the draft. In the four years, conscription became an increasingly unwilling process, not least in Britain, and enlistment was a poor alternative. As evasion of service and strikes rose, so did the first outbreaks of mutiny, desertion and widespread self-harm. In Europe, as Joll observes, the anti-militarist internationalists, their spirits and hopes broken in 1914, soon began to re-group – even during the war, some organized in exile in Sweden, Holland, Switzerland, even London. Those emigres included French syndicalists, German intellectuals, Russian anarchists and revolutionary Marxist exiles, such as Lenin. These gradually recovered a voice and began to preach 'war against war',[14] or indeed at the Zimmerwald conference a revolution to stop war. Such a situation hastened the eventual breakup of armies in mutiny and desertion: in 1917 this spread first to the French armies, to the Russians, to Italy and then to other countries: in September, 1918, it reached the German navy, then the army; and finally at the end even the British. There were no armies left in Europe by November 1918 that were free of such dissent. As in Russia, millions simply voted with their feet and walked home from the war, even before the Armistice.

But iconic as the scenes in Flanders and France in 1914 and 1915 were, such memories of fraternization are not peculiar to the Western Front. Similar events have been documented not only in 1915 and later in the war on many fronts, but of course they also occurred in scores of later wars, including in Indo-China and Serbia/Croatia. Each example is different, it is often triggered by a chance event, or a recognition of common interest beyond nation or *ethnie*. This existed especially against bad conditions, over-eager officers, or the need to share resources. On the *Chemins des Dames*, German and French soldiers extraordinarily shared the same water supply underground in the Caverne du Dragon, (1915–17) despite being in daily combat of a ferocious kind; co-operation was negotiated by the soldiers themselves fighting in caves.

In a discussion at the innovative and anti-militarist Historial de la Grande Guerre Museum in Peronne (on the Somme), I commented that excellent as its first three exhibition rooms were, there was not a single mention of the Christmas truce of 1914–15. A curator commented that it was just a few days in a war that lasted over four years and killed ten million and that such truces were not typical of the war.[15] However, Frye might have agreed with my response on hearing this, which I later wrote as a letter to the director:

> But that is the whole point, the exceptional event poses memory as a moment of departure from 'history'; from 'believed narrative' it sustains the possibility of an alternative, in the most unlikely circumstances; it is a revelatory moment of the possible and perhaps the desirable.

Each such revelatory scene – real, historical, semi-autobiographical or imagined – portrays a particular way in which a modern universalistic memory of relationship in trauma is imprinted through the past, and encapsulated in a redemptive flash, a moment, when enemies become human again (Images 5.4 and 5.5).

IMAGE 5.4 Canadian soldier sharing a cigarette with a German prisoner. Likely to have been near Passchendaele in Belgium in 1917. Georg Metcalf Archival Collection, Canadian War Museum (CWM 19930065-531).

IMAGE 5.5 A wounded soldier from the Durham Light Infantry shares a cigarette with a wounded German prisoner during the Mareth line battle, 22–24 March 1943. © Imperial War Museums (NA 1344).

Throughout this book, I suggest how real-life stories of these abound.

It is a theme systematically explored by social psychologists; for example, Sam Keen and Robert Jay Lifton both deploy demythologizing narratives from life in trying to demolish 'Enemy Images' – hostile stereotypes of 'the other'.[16] Evidence from child education suggests that some such hostile images can be subverted at an early age: as is revealed in biography and autobiography.

Vignette:

An espresso memory – a coffee moment recalled

An unlikely place to evacuate a small boy from the Blitz, the back garden abutted on a large railway marshalling yard – twenty-four hours of the endless din of shunted wagons, track to track, coupling to coupling. The childhood dream was to become 'a shunter'. Although a hundred miles from London, bombers flew overhead many nights, on missions to Birmingham and Bristol, Cardiff and Coventry. The air-raid warning sirens sending a lifelong shudders of terror that long survived the war. A major aircraft factory lay eight miles away and was hit (my father and aunt had a near miss). On their way back home the bomb aimers would drop any unspent load around us. One night a whole street on the opposite side of the tracks was hit (Image 5.6). I watched it burn from an upstairs window in my grandparent's house. My Uncle Cyril flew similar raids for Bomber Command on their cities.

IMAGE 5.6 John Boorman, *Hope and Glory*, 1987. The London Blitz. Two wars are linked by mimicking images from a similar 1917 photograph. By recycling the Great War images for World War Two, the director stresses the visual continuity of the wars; the home front is now the battlefield.

My grandparents' battered back garden wall was built of red brick; it had a ladder of notches in it, up which several generations of kids climbed, to get the view of the trains, and the hills beyond. The men who worked the yards there when I was a child were Italians; bronzed prisoners of war, their garb imprecisely remembered now. But they were brown-faced men, dark curly haired, captured after the fall of North Africa and they were brought to England in 1943. They chatted to me, made me pipes to play from reed. Missing their kids, we made friends, and they helped, lifting me from the wall and down the steep grass embankment beside the railway. And then the smell: that aroma – in their steamy hut – What was it? – Strong, dark, pungent and unforgettable. Mugs of it, large white enamel mugs.

Years later, a version of espresso arrived in England: frothy coffee in ugly plastic glass cups. It tasted bad and that smell did not register then either. My real 'coffee moment' came many years later, when coffee really made it from the Mediterranean via Seattle, and package holidays, and cheap flights. Then that sense brought back to me a memory and it transported me to that hut on a railway yard in 1944: those friends, ex-soldiers, and those times. I suppose the coffee must have come to them from families, sent in Red Cross parcels? After all what could be a more precious gift, to remind one of home, than real, black espresso!

Other wars, and other fellow victims, recognized are a common theme. A Vietnam war veteran and officer William Broyles, the author of *Brothers in Arms*, recounts encountering a possible Vietnamese enemy in a military tunnel. It was his duty as an officer to blow it up. His sensed contact with the supposed other was so strong that he urged the 'soldier' to leave (in Vietnamese), rather than be killed. He warns him, or her, again and again to 'get out' before exploding a grenade. It may have been imagined, but the urge not to destroy the human enemy is authentic.[17] Virginia Woolf's 'enemy' in the London Blitz was imagined thousands of feet above. We non-combatants shared our space with the German bombers overhead, as Germans did in German cities.

But for a combatant, when 'the enemy' is thousands of feet or more below, or miles in the far distance, not only is personal physical engagement with 'the other' impossible, but also even in imagination it is stretched or screened. It can only occur later – for example, post-war in arranged meetings of ex-combatants – or solely in correspondence, or as fantasy or fiction as vaguely remembered pasts. But even in modern war, collective recognition, as in 1914–18, can still occur in close proximity. For example, in low-intensity conflict it did to some degree in Algeria, in Vietnam and in Croatia/Serbia (Yugoslavia) in the 1990s, and since then, even Afghanistan. So called 'unconventional' war still allows for occasional unconventional contacts, but communication is totally excluded by the missile technology of nuclear deterrence, or long distance, high altitude air-strikes: it is left to the 'mental fight'.

In contexts of technological barbarism, any concept of 'positive peace' which involves such active and particularly redemptive communication, may require or at least involve such reconciliation stories. These need to represent moments in conflict, illustrate an identification with the 'other'. In this way, in a film, or poem, the enemy image is replaced by alternative transformatory, empathetic memory images. In these scenes of 'the enemy', as a trope of postnationalist representation, it is central to remembering. These 'others', when promoted in cultural forms, often include an engagement drawn from an individual's own past, including, like mine, some childhood experience held in common. But whether remembered and reconstructed, individual moments of both real and fictional recognition, can, through these means create a sharing process. This becomes a part of a collective memory that inevitably reconstructs our views of the past. These contribute in turn to the highly political divisions and contests over history.

When recalled, 'recognition scenes' represent images central to our cultural remembering, such iconic experiences of war are likely to be transnational and universalistic ones. The process of postnationalizing memory deploys these tropes of remembrance to illustrate empathetic identification. The 'enemy image' is deconstructed mythologically. Joseph Campbell has suggested we demythologize 'the other' by using this method, and in this we also reveal ourselves. Campbell gives as an example a scene from popular culture, and from an often quite violent cinema: Luke Skywalker kills Darth Vader (the monster image) in the film *The Empire Strikes Back*, but the face he sees is not Vader's face, but his own, a mirror image of 'the killer in the killed'.[18] Something of Skywalker's own humanity is destroyed in causing the death. Robert Jay Lifton suggests that similar identifications are crucial in real life.

Recognition often occurs in chance meetings. Orwell's encounter with the (real) Italian soldier in Catalonia, Hemingway's meeting with the real-life Old Man (at the Bridge on the Ebro). Both meetings are in the context of the close contact experience of the Civil War in Spain.[19] Individual veteran's stories and journalists' accounts of conflict personalize and universalize these actual moments with an individual 'other'. Such recall is often a telling comment on the unwilling role of civilians, conscripts, or volunteers at war. Humanized by a recognition of other uniformed civilians of a similar age, conscripted into a common destiny, part of that fate may be to meet in future political recognition scenes. In Owen, Remarque, Pabst or Douglas there is a shared victimhood even in death, that points to reconciliation.

By using cinematic flashback, G. W. Pabst brilliantly deploys the device in his film of contradictory solidarity. *Kameradschaft* (1931) is a film of a mine disaster: a French miner sees his German rescuer as a German attacker. Based on a real event, during an underground fire and explosion along the border in the Saar/Lorraine region of France, it constructs a trans-European memory. Metaphoric scenes can become a collective, symbolic rehearsal – gestures towards a more postnational recognition of a shared fate. The climactic scene is used to illustrate both the solidarity and the residual fear of French and Germans, engaging metaphorically, under the national frontiers, during the emergency.[20] The coalmine stretches underground across the frontiers, mimicking the Troglodyte world of the 1914–18 trenches and dugouts. Yet the moment of encounter is inverted, or reversed. The German rescue team, in the endangered mine, breaks through the 1914 frontier wall, bricked up at the start of the war – and still bricked up years after the wars end. It represents the boundary beneath: a psychological frontier being crossed to help groups of French miners trapped in the burning mine. Pabst uses a sudden flashback to the horror and fear of combat of the Great War, of 1914–18: it provokes the terrified French miner to grapple with his surprised German rescuer (Image 5.7). As he breaks through, the French miner sees the rescuer's respirator as reminiscent of the gasmask of an attacking German enemy in the trenches. It is 'the other'. In his frenzy, he images that memory and he has – once again – to try instinctively to kill his saviour.[21]

One of the most effective memory devices or creative tropes of personal interaction is one that illustrates an interactional empathy. A clear example is when, in a revelatory moment, a letter and a photograph bring a reminder of the past of the other, which brings a sense of identification and shared humanity. These reflect similar discoveries made in reality. My grandfather found them in 1917, on Turkish corpses. Drawn from Henri Barbusse's own experiences are several such recognition examples. These stories, reproduced in his literary work *Le Feu*, reflect his traumatic memories from the battle of the Marne, where he found moving family letters on German corpses.[22]

IMAGE 5.7 G. W. Pabst, *Comradeship* (*Kameradschaft*), 1931. A trapped French miner grapples with his German rescuer during mine disaster. The flashback takes him to the conflict of 1914–18, and the enemy wearing a gasmask; the metaphor is drawn from a real event.

This same device often appears in art: a discovered message or love note, a family photograph, or a memento on a body. Paul Baumer discovers photos, an ID card and letter on Gerard Duval's body. The climax of the shell hole encounter in Remarque's novel is Paul's dialogue with the French corpse (Image 5.8). As the central scene in the film version, it is one of recognition: and it involves personal biography, which then reinforces the sense of identification. Using the victim's pencil, Baumer writes down Duval's address and pledges to write to his family:

> I have killed the printer Gerard Duval. I must be a printer. I think confusedly, be a printer, printer.

IMAGE 5.8 Lewis Milestone, *All Quiet on the Western Front*, 1930. Paul Baumer and Gerard Duval in a shell crater. The young German asks the dying Frenchman to forgive him.

Representations of universalist experiences of war – when encountering the dying 'enemy' – aspire to dissolve national distinctions. Striking narratives in war literature involve such mnemonic conversations: the living and the dead, a conversation with a corpse, or a phantom.

A similarly iconic experience, involving an anonymous, real but dead German was recalled in a Keith Douglas's 1940s desert poem, *Vergissmeinnicht*.[23] It describes his physical encounter in the North African desert with a young soldier. The poet finds, on the body, a love message – a note from 'Steffi' – and a photograph with two words on it:

> Look. Here in the gun pit spoil
> the dishonored picture of his girl
> who has put: Steffi. Vergissmeinnicht,
> in a copy book gothic script.

Lines in each of these recalled moments remind us of Owens's 'you are the enemy, I killed, my friend'. These poet-combatants, as in multiple real-life examples, recognized 'the other', either as a friend or a fellow victim of war. In these ways, scenes of recognition entail the antagonist acknowledged as an individual: human; a person.

In 1976 the folk singer, songwriter Eric Bogle, after visiting the cemeteries in northern France and Flanders, wrote a popular anti-war requiem, *No-Man's Land*. Like Owens's poem, Bogle's lyric was a conversation with the dead. It involved a series of questions addressed to one victim – in this case an unknown nineteen-year-old Willy MacBride, who died in 1916. The imagined dialogue with the dead soldier takes place beside his gravestone. The song about him, later renamed *The Green Fields of France*, became one of the most powerful anti-war songs in English, and became immensely popular, especially widely performed in Ireland (though Bogle was in fact Scottish). It was re-constituted and reworded as a salute to the tragedies of all the hundreds of thousands of Irish troops from north and south, before and after 1916, who fought and died in the war. These memories, not least of the Somme, are portrayed in the murals of Belfast. But the song could provide similar identification elsewhere, not only in Scotland, but also responded to universally. The director of the Flanders Fields museum in Ypres has so far identified the graves of at least eighteen Willie MacBrides from the belligerent countries – and others claim there are many more. If he is not quite the universal soldier of another song, the very name MacBride transcends the boundaries of Ireland, Scotland, England and most of the former Commonwealth countries, such as Canada, as well as the USA.

This example reminds us that memories of peace movements, and of non-violent actions, and resistance to war constitute something of an anti-militarist tradition of memory. Effective peace memorials are few; whilst there are war memories, we cannot speak of a 'peace memory' as such. But there are memorials to conscientious objectors, there is one in Richmond Castle, Yorkshire.

Some non-violent activists are commemorated, from civil rights movements such as Medgar Evers, murdered in Jackson, Mississippi. We should talk of peace traditions, of these empathic moments of acknowledgement and of a humanity across division that transcends the traumatic events of collective violence.

Recognition scenes, real and constructed, are a key source for modern memory. They are also at the core of any attempt to construct a *culture of peace* and to de-militarize post-industrial consciousness, an issue returned to in Chapter 11. In India this has started to be museumalized with M. K. Gandhi's emphasis on non-violence whose aim was not least to keep open the possibility of communication with the other, the opponent (not enemy) during conflict. As Hannah Arendt similarly observes when violence begins, human dialogue, language and therefore the discourse of politics ends. A truth-telling memory recalls that sustaining of conversation in conflict, even in the extremity of violence; it represents an aspiration towards reconciliation.

Instances of common humanity in war relates also to a larger search for identity beyond chaos, a constant theme of drama since Classical Greece. In his *Genealogy of Morals*, Schopenhauer argued that the recognition of the self emerges in our opposition to the other. As in a mirror, the way in which our past is represented is made specific by the reflection on individual biography prompted by encounters with other 'forked creatures'. As in Shakespeare's major tragedies, they occur even in the most acute situations. Such encounters especially during war and disaster are recognizable historically far beyond any event itself. These 'strange meetings' can, and have, become universalized: as iconographic tropes. They are the most effective devices, real or fictionalized, which can be turned into archetypes, models of possible, not necessary behaviour. In this a postnational memory can attempt the civilizing task of constructing a positive myth of human recognition beyond divisions. We are fortunate that it is a historically evidenced myth, and in Kenneth Boulding's words, 'what exists is possible'. There are many actions that have existed that may still be possible, once we can represent and re-enact them. That is a task for modern remembering.

Notes

1 Wilfred Owen, *Strange Meeting*, in C. Day Lewis, ed., *The Collected Poems of Wilfred Owen* (London, 1963), and see Paul Fussell, *The Great War and Modern Memory* (Oxford, 1975).
2 Antony Jay, 'Against Consolation: Walter Benjamin and the Refusal to Mourn', in Jay Winter and Emmanuel Sivan, *War and Remembrance in the Twentieth Century* (Cambridge and New York, 2000), p. 221.
3 T. W. Adorno, E. Frankel-Brunswick, David Levinson and R. Sanford, eds, *The Authoritarian Personality* (New York, 1950).
4 The film was based on the novel by Humphrey Cobb, *Paths of Glory* (London, 1935).
5 Vera Brittain, *Testament of Youth* (London, 1933), pp. 339–46.
6 Northrop Frye, *Anatomy of Criticism* (Princeton, 1957), p. 61.

7 Virginia Woolf, 'Thoughts on Peace in an Air Raid', in *Death of a Moth and Other Essays* (London, 1970). Witnesses have articulated a sense of reciprocal relationship with bomber pilots, especially those shot down. And, yes, as in Virginia Woolf's example, treated humanely.

8 I remember describing this type of conciliatory event to a survivor of the air raids on Tokyo, and my own experiences of socializing with the enemy at about the same time. He was shocked at such a neutral attitude: "We would have lynched them!" And indeed, one of the *Hiroshima panels*, painted by the Japanese artists Iri and Toshi Maruki, depicted a similar scene: *The Lynching of the American Prisoners of War*, in the *Hiroshima Panels* (panel xiii). See I. and T. Maruki, *Hiroshima Panels: The Joint Works of Iri Maruki and Toshi Maruki*, 2nd edition (Saitama, Japan, 1991).

9 Jon Silkin, ed., *Book of First World War Poetry* (London, 1979), pp. 196–98 on Owen, and pp. 65–66. Jon Silkin discusses the possibility that the more specific (and political) 'German Conscript and my friend' rather than the more universal 'the enemy I killed, my friend', which was the final version. But more salient is the encounter itself, and the empathy for injured males – bodies in pain; on this aspect of the war and poetry see Fussell (1975), chapter 'Soldier Boys', and Elaine Scarry, The *Body in Pain* (New York, 1985).

10 Benjamin Britten, *War Requiem* (1962).

11 Robert Lifton, quoted in Sam Keen, *Faces of the Enemy* (New York, 1988).

12 There are now available multiple accounts of the Christmas Truce; the fullest in a single volume is still Malcolm Brown and Shirley Seaton, *Christmas Truce: The Western Front December 1914* (London, 2010). See also T. Ashworth, *Trench Warfare 1914–18: The Live and Let Live System* (New York, 1980).

13 James Joll, *The Second International, 1889–1914* (London, 1974), p. 178.

14 Joll (1974), see text of *Stuttgart Resolution*, printed as an appendix.

15 A view endorsed by the distinguished French historian of the period Annette Becker.

16 See Keen (1988) for a discussion of enemy images.

17 William Broyles, *Brothers in Arms: A Journey from War into Peace* (New York, 1986).

18 Joseph Campbell, *The Power of Myth* (New York, 1988).

19 Opening of George Orwell, *Homage to Catalonia* (London, 1962); Ernest Hemingway, 'Old Man at the Bridge', *The Short Stories of Ernest Hemingway*, 2nd edition (New York, 1953), p. 78.

20 The studio reconstructed scenes of a French coalmine; the German rescue event is set in the 1920s, shortly after the war.

21 Pabst's film *Kameradschaft* was based on an actual historical event, one of the worst industrial accidents in mining history, the Courrières mine disaster in 1906 in France, where rescue efforts after a coal dust explosion were hampered by the lack of trained mine rescuers. Expert teams from Paris and Germany – miners from the Westphalia region – came to the assistance of the French, but still 1,099 died, including children.

22 Henri Barbusse, *Le Feu* (*Under Fire*) (London, 1988); and E. M. Remarque, *All Quiet on the Western Front* (New York, 1958).

23 Keith Douglas, '*Vergissmmmeinicht*', in Jon Stallworthy, ed., *Oxford Book of War Poetry* (Oxford, 1987), no. 203, p. 268.

PART 2

Against forgetting – retrieving a borderless past

6

MEMORY AFTER THE 'SHOAH'

Holocaust and total war

Total war, mass bombing of civilians and genocide left numbing aftermaths. But a refusal to allow the European Holocaust to go unnoticed, or denied after 1945, was a key moment of renewed truth-telling and indeed in the reconstruction of modern memory. The revelations of the camps, especially in Poland, and the aerial destruction of cities, dominated memory production after 1945. Recent critics have argued over whether merging the analysis of memories of the war and of the Shoah are justified. Analysing Holocaust memory in the context of total war is related to a concept of 'totalism' and the analyses of Hannah Arendt and her political sociology of 'totalitarian' regimes. Overcoming denial about a novel, monstrous European but largely Jewish atrocity, the Shoah involved reviving memory work in a context of further reappraisal of the nature of modern wars. But this placement alongside, or as part of, memories of war and military occupation often proved to be controversial. My approach accepts the view that the European Holocaust should be seen as a template for a global concept of modern genocide, which has become a postnational cipher of particularist barbarism. But historical remembrance sustains an over simple representation of the genocidal process. A significant proportion of the slaughter did not occur in the six death factories (extermination camps) but was scattered eastwards in rural sites, face-to-face killings or smaller massacres in local ghettoes. The Einzatsgruppe killing squads operated across the villages of Eastern Europe, beyond Poland, where the similarities with urbicide disappear.[1] This genocide can be compared more with Armenia or, subsequently, Rwanda and Cambodia.

How we frame such iconic events is a central issue. One of the most difficult tasks facing anyone writing about modern memory is to assess the role and contribution of these Holocaust memories overall, but eventually also their changing relationship with the new state of Israel and the Jewish diaspora. Given the specific focus of this book, my approach emphasizes one side of the issue, an analysis of the universal or cosmopolitan as against the particularistic framing of the Shoah/or Holocaust, and whether in national or postnational, or secular or religious terms.

As this suggests, an attendant problem given the vast scale of holocaust literature is that of selectivity: how can one do justice in one chapter, to memory of atrocity on such a scale? Remembering the Holocaust has become central to modern memory not least because it acts as a template of collective trauma worldwide. As against the particularization or nationalization of it, recognizing the Shoah or Holocaust as a universal *lieu de memoire* invokes a framework for understanding of genocide *globally*.[2] This archetype, whilst it acknowledges the unique quality of both the specific Jewish Shoah and the larger Central European Holocaust as a whole, structural analysis also universalizes and deterritorializes it. As a historical paradigm, Levy and Sznaider have argued, the Holocaust becomes a global trope.[3]

Developments such as 'Holocaust Studies' or 'Trauma Studies' tend to compartmentalize such collective killing of civilians into different categories or events, giving them particularity, but distinct from a history of cultural remembrance as a whole. In an odd way, both the Nazis and the Western allies both collaborated in this fragmentation of memory. The latter almost conniving in a silence about the genocide: partly because it was being judged in the context of the larger 'Holocaust' of World War Two and total war, and partly because it was politically inconvenient in a context of reconstruction in Europe. For example, in 1948, the French/Jewish journalist and filmmaker Lanzmann was prevented by authorities in Berlin from giving a seminar on anti-Semitism, requested by students. The silences of both totalitarian and 'open' societies were similar in that regard.

In another case, the 1943–44 allied aerial photographs of Auschwitz/Birkenau and other camps were kept secret and did not become well publicized until the 1980s; for example, at the US Holocaust Museum. As in Japan, allied occupation in Germany (and Austria) meant censorship, and despite trials, included repression of the representation of both war memories and acknowledgement of atrocity. At the time, the use of depersonalizing techno-military language to describe the events was common on all sides. It was not just Nazi silencing that ghettoized the exterminations – it was, in the Polish diplomat Jan Karski's words, 'another world' and an unreported, silent universe separated by far more than electric fences, Ghetto walls, or selection ramps.

By far the largest proportion of those dying in camps were Jewish citizens of occupied European states. But those arguing the uniqueness of the Jewish Holocaust have been accused of privileging that memory over millions of other victims. It should not have been necessary for critics to re-emphasize in writing on memory, now or then, that the Shoah (a biblical term) was not solely a Jewish event, nor was it merely a continuation of traditional anti-Semitism. In that sense, the process was indeed unique but as Arendt indicates, symptomatic of larger social-structural forces.[4]

Problematic also is the universal figure of 'the victim' – the Jews as stateless, 'the exile', alienated, scapegoated and sacrificial. It is one that rises above national narratives. This archetype is central to Sartre's *Reflection on the Jewish Question* (1946).[5] Yet he does not refer to the Holocaust directly. Attempts to control and frame the Holocaust were pursued not by one state, but several states, and at least two religious traditions for the rest of the century.

This controversy was first to be exacerbated by the 1961 Eichmann trial, which publicized Nazi crimes and Jewish victimhood. The victim's genuinely iconic transnational 'universalism' as a culture or religion was, in this way, partly vitiated by the needs of narrower nationalist chauvinist claims.[6] This was less true of the transnational cultures of Roma and Sinti.

In the longer term, Israel, and Zionism in particular, sought to possess this memory as a more ethnically specific and politically legitimating narrative. This revision partially undermined the profile of Jews as non-state victims of a specific and totalitarian state. In later decades, increasingly by the 1980s, Israel aspired to the role of protectors of the Holy Grail of Holocaust memory.

Totalism as paradigm

In confronting memories and denial of the traumas of the 1940s, a brief conceptual detour at this point in the book is necessary. The political sociology of twentieth-century violence provides an essential context for understanding cultural process and how it frames the past. It raises the issue of whether the narrative of 'modern memory' can comprehend remembering worldwide, structures of collective violence and modern genocide – together with a potential of global nuclear war. This needs to be acknowledged as a sensitive issue; in other words, can we compare atrocities, such as modes of genocide, without privileging one in terms of a measurement of excess – as if statistics of trauma and suffering were either possible or acceptable criteria? Can we juxtapose actual events (embedded in memory) with potential ones; in other words, imaginatively extrapolating prophecy from memory, as warning or prediction?

The whole of World War Two was a global civilian holocaust, and the military losses in war were catastrophic, not least in Russia and China. Yet the urbicidal worldwide destruction of cities was on an entirely new scale; much of it from the air, such as Coventry, Rotterdam and Tokyo, and finally Hiroshima and Nagasaki, but it was duplicated or extended by land war, as in the ultimate destruction of Warsaw and Berlin.

In this context, imbricating the memories of the 1940s European/Jewish Holocaust in a 'world war' imagery represents to many a problematic approach. Yet subsequent critics, directors, writers and artists from R. J. Lifton, Alain Resnais and subsequently Jürgen Habermas, Terrence des Pres, and more recently W. G. Sebald, Anselm Kiefer, J. Winter or Andreas Huyssen, this seems only natural. No disconnect is seen in framing war memory, to include death camps, targeting civilians in cities and villages, on land, from the air, selectively and randomly. The mass bombing of the largely civilian urban targets of Hiroshima and Nagasaki was only unique technologically: as part of a totalizing process. The universalism of this is implied in the threat of future wars – potentially fought with genocidal weapons.

Given my brief of considering postnational memory, my concern here is both to analyse and globalize our understanding of collective memory. Here I have consciously chosen to juxtapose the recollections of both modern war and genocide: to view their total violence as related historical processes. This has been judged inappropriate by some critics; the analysis is a controversial one because it might imply an equivalence ethically, structurally or culturally. It is true that urban and aerial blitzkrieg, and implementing final solutions to a 'Jewish problem' are distinct modes of atrocity. As at Hamburg and Nagasaki, urbicide is random, individually if not 'nationally'. In this way it does not discriminate between victims, as opposed to the selective *'Shoah'* which is relatively targeted. Supposedly this distinguishes the phenomenon of modern *genocide* from modern *war*, including the use of atomic weapons, which are ultimately indiscriminate, even if territorially 'selective'. For example, a potential nuclear war could even be accidental or unintended: the victims may be random, 'collateral' in an unanticipated catastrophe.

Yet all illustrate such 'totalism'; their historic roots are clearly shared, and their structural affinities are sociologically real; their cultural context is also the same; which shapes common memory. Their victims, bystanders and perpetrators share this milieu of mutual witnessing, or denying, modern mass killing; and typically, whatever their specific experience, overall they name that time as 'the war'. It is true that the Holocaust was never just about death in a totalistic death factory, but also in the vast but scattered local annihilations of the Eastern Front. Yet those were only a step beyond the comparable depredations of Armenian genocide, spread across and beyond Turkey, Anatolia and the Syrian Desert, as Balakian reminds us.

Political sociologists since the 1950s have repeatedly depicted modern total war and modern genocide as the 'Siamese twins' of modernity, and the degree to which they stressed this overlap is contestable; but it is consistent with Hannah Arendt's historical work on the total state. Latterly usages by such as Zigmunt Baumann and Jay Winter support this interpretation.[7] Yet the same dilemma exists amongst other memory scholars. Can one discuss the comparison, even fusion, of remembering such atrocity beyond these structural similarities? These are unimaginables, and so far, few amongst academic critics venture to compare them, or discuss the implications for shared memory.

A postnational memory, truth-telling or truth-seeking, that deals with 'modern' forms of mass killing and totalism is, inevitably, dominated by such controversies and political agendas – particularly ethnic and nationalist ones (see discussion in Chapter 9). But in totalitarianism, the state narrative becomes the master narrative; it becomes independent of history – as the past, as counter-memory, is obliterated. The logic of totalism has no 'memory agenda', but its techno-bureaucratic dynamic eliminates authentic memory and private witness, or marginalizes it as irrational or utopian. It censors inconvenient public testimony as obstructive, even treasonable – as counter-propaganda. Central to the task of Holocaust memory is the revelatory project defying erasure.

In totalizing or totalitarian regimes, official images and statements, or silences, compete with unofficial stories or whispered rumours of atrocity. In the initial acknowledgement of crimes and victimhood, in such survivors' testimony, or posthumous accounts written by victims, it is witness that becomes central. But this is never unproblematic.[8] The literary genre of victims and survivors analysed by Des Pres, especially the memories of Primo Levi and Eli Wiesel, writing in terms of both personal witness and victim testimony, was an uncomfortable exercise in linking a represented past to a present.[9]

I have acknowledged that at their extremes, modern genocide and modern war, including the use of atomic weapons are different phenomena. Yet to reiterate my point from Chapter 1, structurally and culturally, total war and the total state have grown together, as modern war is turned against civilians, not least 'the enemies within' (Jews, or communists, and gays, Roma, or other minorities). Those selected for elimination by the state, such as Armenians in 1915, did not 'fit in'. Most groups 'selected' are typically chosen because they are portrayed or perceived as not accepting a national or ideological frame. In Stalinism, it was Kulaks, 'Trotskyists' – even Jews. Elsewhere stateless groups, such as Kurds, Armenians, Roma, and now Palestinians, exemplify affronts to myths of unity. This is a topic I return to in Chapter 11.

Hannah Arendt discusses the mass killings and Stalinist excesses in the Soviet Union and Eastern Europe alongside Nazi crimes, and implicitly acknowledges the totalism of each. It is true that totalitarian states such as Stalin's Russia and Nazi Germany turned militarized violence inwards, even before external war began. Yet almost all of these excesses of modern genocide, Armenia, the final solution after 1942, and later the Khmer Rouge's Indo-China war genocide in Cambodia, all occurred in a context of other wider wars – or of civil wars, as in Rwanda.

Part of the arsenal of state terror is uncertainty; the essential element of unpredictability exists within it. There was already a view in Poland from 1940 that 'Poles were next', and that they were the real and ultimate target of the Reich in seeking 'living space' in the East. But by 1942, it was the Jews, who like Roma, were vulnerable, easily identifiable and would not seriously resist removal. Moreover, whilst they were many millions of Jews, they were not tens of millions; it was agreed the 'solution' could be achieved alongside the war effort. Yet as Martin Gilbert notably points out, it is easily forgotten how the worst cruelties were being meted out not to Jews, other Slavs, or Roma/Sinti, but to Soviet prisoners of war, whose intentionally prolonged and agonizing deaths at sites from Austria to Russia, betray a selective sadism whose 'logic' remains known only to the perpetrators, but to apply logic to banal extermination and racial hierarchy is misplaced.

At times, collective memory of these processes become intermeshed as both fact and myths. However repressed the recall becomes, the plight of a Nanjing or a Srebrenica was as much determined by the fact that they were strategic targets of modern war as that the atrocity there was genocidal in character. In each case, as in the 1940s, armies or other military groups are principle perpetrators, even if only particular parts of an army, or special units (like the *Einzatzgruppe*), were mainly responsible. For example we now acknowledge that, once again, as in the historic past, systematic rape became another essential instrument, even a weapon, of modern war, not just a peripheral, incidental and regrettable accompaniment.

Whilst obviously such brutality takes a variety of forms, the images of total war and totalistic killing often share a bizarre commonality – for example, material similarities that inform a shared and overlapping memory of trauma. One major example of this was the use of gas or other chemicals. Whilst urbicide and genocide are different 'final solutions', with arguably distinct agendas, they are hard to separate in the collective imagination. Holocaust occurs within a military frame of two total wars, and other civil violence, war and conflicts. There is clearly a continuity of representations in remembering the process globally, not just its structural linkages.

In this analysis, I prefer to use the general term 'totalism' to embrace both 'total' war and other processes that inform 'totalitarianism' but are independent of it. In this way, I stress the contributions of 1914–45 and beyond, structurally – not only in the totalitarian violence of Stalinism, Nazism and eventually in some other fascist states, but also in the mass destruction of civilian life by other means than death camps and mass executions. Collective memories of these processes differ, but the structural affinity is essential to my argument – about a common 'modern' civilian memory of collective violence: that it is of a totalism that 'universalizes victimhood', whilst the perpetrators remain tied to a particular, specific social base, usually a nation state.

Hannah Arendt: war and genocide

Arendt is a key figure for anyone analysing such modern memory work, though her work has proved controversial.[10] For example, her report on the Eichmann trial was a key part of the publicizing of the Holocaust itself, but also in stimulating the heated debates about the implications of the trial. Contested concepts developed, such as 'the banality of evil', and it also highlighted the role of the Israeli state itself as the judge and jury.

But her work on the events in Jerusalem needs to be placed in the context of her major historical work, the *Origins of Totalitarianism*, which has a special focus on the cultural role of anti-Semitism. Whilst the book does not address either memory, or war, directly, Arendt's main survey covers several other major factors conjoined in the violent exercise of power in the first half of the twentieth century: imperialism, nationalism and the modern state – all impacted by racist ideology. In particular she sees anti-Semitism as an underlining historical force. But whilst continuities from 1914–18 are hinted at, war as an autonomous and dynamic structural factor is notably missing. Why?

The links between the 'explosion' of 1914 and the 'total' structure inhabited by totalitarian regimes and movement ideologies are certainly clear. But it serves Arendt's thesis better to see World War One as the destructive force creating the classless caesura. The alternative suggested here is to include war as being an ongoing and critical part of the structural narrative of 'totalism' that marks both regimes and cultural organization.[11] Whilst most of these belligerent states are not 'totalitarian' in the form of Arendt's ideal–typical construct, nevertheless both institutionally and technologically they presage the 'factories' of killing of the 1940s. Arendt's thesis sees totalitarian regimes and ideologies as arising in a *vacuum*, in the atomized *space* left by a destruction of class society – caused not least by war. This post-war lacuna becomes in effect a 'mass' society of isolated individuals.[12] This view of war as an institution rightly stresses its destructive, negative characteristics. But it omits its innovative, *'constructive'* and dynamic aspect: the mobilization of masses for industrial war, and obedience, to new forms of bureaucratic state power. The connection with totalitarian violence is clear, but in Arendt's thesis it remains at most implicit, something beyond the ideologies and specific regimes that fit her archetype of 'totalitarian'.[13]

The Holocaust as memory and myth: constructing the 'Shoah'

Collective remembering has often been ambiguously constructed around sites, and individuals, as well as key events (such as the post-war trials): remembering people – Anne Frank, Adolf Eichmann, Oscar Schindler – or the places they related to – the camps at Belsen and Auschwitz, but also Buchenwald, Dachau, and holocaust memorials such as Yad Vashem.[14] Whilst the last, in Israel, is not a site of atrocity any more than the hidden annex on the Prinsengracht, it has become, since the 1940s, a symbol of the complexities of Israeli-Jewish memory of the Shoah. Both secular and religious, official and informal, universal and particular, it stands in contrast to the evolution of the sites at Auschwitz, as places of global memory.[15]

After 1945 this memory evolved from the first publication of parts of Anne Frank's diary in 1947, through Resnais's breakthrough Holocaust film, *Nuit et Brouillard* (*Night and Fog*, 1955), to the publicity surrounding Adolf Eichmann's trial in 1961, and Arendt's report on it. But the acknowledgement of the Holocaust was notable also for both its slow pace and a widespread complicity in suppressing of evidence. Despite the initial Nuremberg trials, for over a decade the predominant response was silence. The first major scholarly account, in 1961,

Raul Hilberg's, *Destruction of the European Jews*, attracted far less attention at the time than the work deserved.[16]

Remarkably it was not the Holocaust or its perpetrators that were on trial at Nuremberg – or even the Nazi state – it was war and war crimes. Even here, Ben Ferencz, the young trial lawyer, and subsequent campaigner for world peace through world law and international justice, had to take up the newly discovered crimes of the *Einzatzgruppe* almost single-handed, as a personal responsibility for fear they would be forgotten.[17]

Much of my stress is on holocaust memory images – and I have particularly focused here on film, rather than literature: Bernstein, Resnais, but especially Lanzmann, are my key texts, which may be idiosyncratic. Yet the new voice of modern memory is represented here too in resolving these tensions over repression: the testimonies of witnesses to Holocaust, forced between memory and amnesia, are central to this rediscovery. In the *Survivor*, Terrence Des Pres invokes Eli Wiesel, Primo Levy and the poet and survivor Paul Celan and individual witness literature. Together with Robert Lifton and Bruno Bettelheim, others focus on the psychology of camp inmates.[18] By adding the nuances of survivor witness in Europe, Israel, and the USA, they help confront an ongoing silence about a denial of events of the Shoah, often based on guilt, trauma, or political advantage.

In Wiesel's words, the genocidal expunging of cultural moments, the physical attempt to revise, or eliminate history, is an attack on memory which only the witness, the survivor, can perhaps resist through oral or written testimony. A typical lack of response in the 1950s to such attempts to combat denial was not confined to the perpetrators or the guilty.

The Anne Frank diaries and similar accounts were, in part, a conscious, continuing attempt, with support of some in the Jewish diaspora, to revisit the witnesses and survivors – or at least surviving texts and artefacts. Small groups worked to develop them: often with publications, visits to sites, sacred spaces and evolving museums, such as Yad Vashem (1953). Multiple visits to the many sites of genocide make the role of *place*, not only in the six Polish death sites a key factor to overcoming forgetting and the reconstruction of trauma.

The link of Holocaust in cinema to totalism was best first illustrated in France by Resnais's documentary. It created an archetype of mass murder and the banality of the process. Like Resnais, other new wave directors and writers expressed their concern about such unfinished business in Germany: the failure of de-Nazification, and the rush to let bygones be bygones. (Alfred Hitchcock had been involved in the first 1945 film of Belsen.) The cyclical character of memory and denial is an often marginalized aspect of social and cultural process and the danger seen was a new cycle of memory, once again repressed or denied, as with the 'forgetting' of the Armenians in the 1920s, since continued by the Turkish state.

It is not easy to describe how or explain why this process occurs: at the time retrospective remembrance of devastating events are first reconstructed, or re-discovered; then distorted, forgotten or denied, and re-discovered again a decade, or many decades later. The annihilation of Armenians had been the most widely publicized ethnic crime of the period of World War One, yet this was a memory that in 1915 had not, perhaps could not, be then maintained, as Hitler allegedly boasted in 1939 (referring to Poles).[19] The need for modern commemoration, 'to bury the dead', is for an acknowledgement – by a wider world – that they died.

By 1955 there was certainly no doubt of the identification of the Holocaust as a largely Jewish event. But as a frame of visual interpretation, Resnais's highly original feature, *Nuit et Brouillard* (*Night and Fog*) integrated other aspects of modern organization and society into an abstract cinematic essay imagining atrocity.[20] At times, with its innovative use of minimalist music and polemical commentary, it bordered on sensationalism. But it was highly influential and engaged, rather than propagandistic. It was initially banned in France for visually indicating French official collaboration. It was provocative in several other ways. Whilst the Star of David is visible and the imagery of Jews as victims *was* present, the document is not overtly an account of the Shoah as a particularly Jewish tragedy. But it is certainly a universal condemnation of genocide as much an anti-militarist, anti-fascist and anti-racist tirade. He was criticized because it turns the Holocaust into an abstract cultural process, and is not specific in terms of ethnicity and victimhood, as is Lanzmann's subsequent film *Shoah*.[21] The genocide is presented in a detached almost cynical style: a visual archetype of industrialized mass murder depicting modern impersonal killing as routinized, as well as evil (more so than does *Shoah*) – it is a powerful paradigm for a new audience. Resnais never aimed at a prurient or commercial appeal: he portrayed the camps as they were, on behalf of his version of a cosmopolitan sensibility and a plea for renewed remembrance, and resistance.

Whilst enabling us to differentiate the European genocide from previous events (such as Armenia) and those still in the future (Cambodia/Kampuchea), both Resnais and Lanzmann also help to locate the Shoah sociologically. Their narrative of memory retrieval, 'revisiting' the past, is set within the organizational culture of totalitarian obfuscation and denial (e.g. the Saurer vans, the SS letter read in Shoah, the camps 'architectural styles') in Resnais's film. The use of a colour, and black and white distinction between representing the tourist present (*colour*), and the victims past (*black and white*), in particular, was an inspired contribution to cinematic memory work, stressing time and contemporary relevance (Figure 6.1).

By the 1950s, the increasingly transnational peace movement had become equally focused on nuclear weapons, which were also now spreading to bases in Europe – even to Germany. It feared the dangers involved in the rearming of the two German states; *Night and Fog*, was a metaphoric warning that both Germanies, so soon after 1945, were being re-militarized. Sensing a resurgence of the Far Right, fears of an undiminished German militarism or revanchist ambitions were resurfacing: it spurred remembrance of the Holocaust, taken up as an

FIGURE 6.1 Alain Resnais, *Night and Fog* (*Nuit et Brouillard*), 1956. Revisiting the territory of 'present day' (1955) Birkenau is filmed in colour; the camp in 1940–45 conversely is presented in black and white, using the contrast for past and present.

issue in both East and West German communities, especially by a new generation, but for their own separate political agendas.[22] In the late 1940s in Germany, as in Austria, Poland and at other sites of genocide, immediate acknowledgement of atrocities remained rare. This silence fostered fears amongst an anti-Nazi Left in Europe of a resurgent militarism in Germany. This largely ignored the analogous problems of suppressed memory in Austria, Poland and indeed in France itself.

When young German radicals became proactive in memory work, it was linked to a revised history. Their role was in encouraging a range of post-Holocaust memory projects, and visits to sites that uncovered forgotten experiences. Those re-examined sites included desecrated cemeteries, and began the archaeological explorations of the hidden or ruined Nazi-era structures, especially in Berlin. Between 1953 and 1962, the Left, the German youth (SDS) movement, took up such issues of Holocaust memory. Alongside its anti-Nazi campaigning, and whilst opposing German rearmament, anti-fascist groups revived the political narrative of resistance to war and militarism at execution sites such as Plötzensee prison in Berlin. Such German political sites, especially Buchenwald, Ravensbruck, Sachsenhausen and Dachau, were the initial focus. Later, in the 1980s and 1990s, German 'reconciliation' volunteers also worked at most of the Polish camps and later established a centre outside the formerly half-Jewish town of Oswiecim near the Auschwitz Museum, and an Anne Frank Centre near the synagogue in Berlin.

Lieux de Memoire: Auschwitz, Yad Vashem and Anne Frank's Amsterdam

Estimates still vary, but up to 1.3–1.6 million deaths occurred at the Auschwitz/Birkenau camp, of whom at least 80–90% were Jews, and 75,000 were non-Jewish Poles, and though estimates vary, many tens of thousands of Soviet prisoners.[23]

National and if not postnational, at least internationalist or transnational frames of understanding of 'Auschwitz' existed from the start with the arrival of the Red Army,[24] first at Majdanek (July 1944) then Auschwitz/Birkenau, largely emptied. (Later the Allies arrived at Belsen and other camps – finally Mauthausen in spring 1945.) The first structure at Oswiecim was Polish (Auschwitz was the German name from 1940); it was the former barracks, a state memorial and designated as a Polish site of martyrdom. The memorial site ('state museum') would be next to the Polish, and formerly half Jewish, town of Oswiecim that gave it its name, rather than Birkenau. The second template was Soviet, to fit the ideological needs of the expanded Soviet hegemony and its anti-fascist narrative. The third, and fourth, were the religious demands, first of varieties of Catholicism (imbricated with national martyrology) and later Judaism. Beyond that, other ethnic, gender and political groups claimed their space. The 1952 oversight committee was both international and socialist, including Jews. Auschwitz was chosen as the symbolic site rather than Majdanek, partly since Auschwitz had a more substantial surviving fabric for a museum (the reception centre and army barracks) and it had held many more victims. It was therefore a natural base for holocaust memory from that moment, as the other four death camps or sites were completely in ruins.

Enacted by the Polish government in 1947, and framed around Polish national trauma, it had a Catholic subtext. With a Polish committee, which included Polish survivors/former inmates (and initially with Jewish-Polish representatives), its designation has also to be seen in a context of Soviet geo-political expansion and legitimation. These emphasized the crimes, from an anti-Nazi, anti-Hitlerite perspective, and stressed the role of the Soviet Union in the European liberation. The site was created a year before the Israeli state was formed; the much later role of Israel as a national state actor in the memorials process in the 1980s, served especially in confirming Auschwitz's already iconic role.

After 1947, the key issue of presenting of Jews as victims was gradually and controversially dealt with – by 'nationalizing' the Shoah, but initially without designating Israel, as nation state. Rather Auschwitz presented its history (eventually in over twenty *national* exhibits) classified by countries of deportation. In this way the Museum side-stepped the issue of how many national transports were in fact entirely Jewish; as a result there was no link made with the *exodus*. Even the two generic 'Jewish exhibit' blocks were suppressed for eleven years (1967–78).[25] The Museum's framing evolved uneasily; for example, Catholicization in the 1970s and 1980s and beyond, Judaism and the first Israeli March for Life (1988), the post-Communist amendments after 1989 (erasure of Soviet text) and the Carmelite convent controversies at both sites were all part of this contested evolution. After the end of Communism in 1989–90, the Museum and displays were again revised, and some replaced, including the Soviet-era inscriptions erased on the Birkenau memorial.

The role of Holocaust memories in the foundational mythology of Israel is complex, contradictory and successively changes over the course of many decades, especially between 1967 and the 1980s (when the Jewish displays at Auschwitz were suspended). In public terms, the image of Jews as victims was anathema to the self-identification of the heroic Jewish warrior, the emancipatory fighter and liberator of Israel in 1947. This is the image of Nathan Rapoport's defiant memorial sculpture to the ghetto rising in Warsaw (1946–48) symbolizing resistance, but not of millions of 'lambs to the slaughter'.[26] Nevertheless international committees between 1945 and 1948 found almost universal support amongst surviving Jews in Europe for a Jewish homeland, and state. *In legal terms the nexus* was clear even if the public myth, religious or secular differed; and if Israeli identity remained contested and diffuse, it was because the ambivalent images reflected social division, continued prejudice and cultural change.

The shocking example of how Israel's 'liberating' heroic nationalism influenced the treatment of post-Holocaust migrants to Israel – some seen as 'losers' – is a sobering one. They were subject to racist contempt and abuse as 'inauthentic' non-Hebrew-speaking victims, leftovers from the European Shoah – discrimination was rampant.[27] There has been some debate over the degree of Israeli state involvement in Yad Vashem and its national significance at the time, and the debate on the law of Remembrance in the Knesset, 1947–49.[28] The subsequent development took many decades (such a memorial was first mentioned in 1942). Many examples exist of the role of groups of survivors, but in Poland itself, they created unofficial or informal local memorials at various sites including synagogues and destroyed cemeteries (some desecrated). Unlike the religious site at Mount Zion, Yad Vashem started as such a small memorial in a physical sense, and slowly expanded years later.[29] But key sources such as James Young see it as significant even in the 1940s for Jewish memory of the Shoah. It is true that the role of Israel as a protagonist in the process of holocaust memory in Europe itself only occurred much later, especially in the 1980s (1988). But its claims to a special memorializing role around the Shoah and its sites were always contentious issues.

In the same years, through the successive publications of various editions of the *Anne Frank Diary*, and other works, accompanying bookshops, guides, postcards, film, eventually videos, posters and various mementoes appeared, not only in Amsterdam, but also worldwide. The small remains of the Annex in which Anne hid, survives: simple, moving and essentially authentic. But since 1947, the story has changed,[30] as discussed below and in Chapter 9.

The extraordinarily large crowds that wait in Amsterdam, on along Prinsengracht, and into the next street, stand in all weathers to visit the small museum and tiny rooms where Anne had been hidden. They hope perhaps to gain an imagined impression, a prosthesis, reliving her final year or so of 'freedom' in that constrained space. This urge to experience memory explains perhaps in part the lines waiting, not only in Amsterdam, but also at Auschwitz I, or the Hiroshima Peace Museum.

The numbers of such holocaust pilgrimages have grown rapidly, especially since the 1980s. Amongst symbolic instances of such 'virtual re-enactments', endlessly repeated in worldwide sites, the Anne Frank icon is readily identifiable, but her myth is complex. Given her status as a universal holocaust victim, she is a personalization of the holocaust experience. But there were multiple Annes in hiding, during and after the diary years. There was Dutch Anne; a Jewish (assimilated) Anne; and a very much 'Western' Anne – as witnessed by her Hollywood pin-ups. There was also an 'Auschwitz' Anne, as well, most horrifically the Belsen one, barely known in the West.[31]There was an intelligent, inspiring Anne and a moody teenager. But there was no happy ending, and the final image of Anne is too shocking and desolate to promote. And almost always it is censored. In the last account of her dying of typhus in Belsen, a month before liberation, reported by a surviving friend, she was naked, shorn and covered with lice – she said she had no one left in the world. But such an image is not a publicly acceptable one. Nor is it, arguably, even 'the real Holocaust', since such mythology is both confused, contested and often problematic. But at least Anne's diary as a document was saved, with the story of her hiding. But like many other such narratives, it is not an image of the Shoah.

From Nuremberg to Jerusalem

The debate over what to do with captured Nazi 'leaders' was considerable. Multiple suicides were the most convenient form of closure.[32] Dead enemies were sooner forgotten. Too many trials might be provocative, or misleading with narratives in which so much was omitted. Like the famous German trials, Israel's Jerusalem trial was always likely to have an ambiguous legacy. But whilst vengeful attitudes existed they did not predominate. Best known were Simon Wiesenthal's searches for culprits, but in the main, as a lone operation: anti-Nazi groups organized to attest their losses, and where official initiatives failed, some did begin to hunt down perpetrators – for them revenge was a motive.[33]

After the event the relationship of such processes as war crime tribunals to constructing, or reconstructing either a more enlightened public history or a more truthful collective 'memory' is both contradictory and highly political. In most cases the reconstruction of crimes is first and foremost intended by the victors not as conciliation, but as giving 'history lessons'.[34] This, as at Nuremberg, and the subsequent German trials or in the Eichmann trial, was an ambiguous process.

Although she did not directly talk about comparable memories of genocide and military excess, Hannah Arendt understood and described much of this process.[35] In Israel, as at Nuremburg it was rather the state, or states, not 'the people', who chose to pursue collective crimes in court, and often selected token criminals. It *was* the conceptual basis of her specific and controversial critique, and her status, as an involuntary political exile, rather than as a Jew – of the Eichmann Trial that was criticized.[36] Whilst of course exhibitionary trials, such as Eichmann's, cannot be compared with those of the third Reich, they still serve modern memory poorly. In 1961 news of the revelations of the final solution had real impact on public consciousness worldwide. But for many at the time, the procedure was counter-productive in terms of Israel's public image, even amongst those previously sympathetic. It was also arguably problematic in terms of confronting anti-Semitism, intolerance and prejudice generally; its decision-making was not clearly 'truth-seeking', and it certainly did not represent 'reconciliation'. It had been argued that the Eichmann Trial would give an opportunity to victims of the Shoah to confront their tormentors, which Nuremburg and the other post-war trials had not, but this was not to be the reality.[37]

What was being confronted was not the perpetrator but the Holocaust itself, seen by a larger international audience through multiple victim witness accounts. Eichmann faced not his 'victims', but the Israeli state. But these statements were not presented as evidence of Eichmann's guilt – his role was already well documented and established. It revealed the scale and the barbarity of the atrocity which he helped administer. The trial showed no animus by the defendant against Jews, nor evidence that Eichmann was anti-semitic. Instead of confronting the pathological sadists who did the tormenting (some of whom, as *kapos*, or camp guards may have fled to Israel despite their crimes), it confronted one individual who facilitated the machinery of lethal totalism.[38] Decades later, Lanzmann's film *Shoah* stands out as the document of modern memory that truly gave voice to the victims. In making his film *Shoah*, it has been suggested that Lanzmann felt the need to compensate for this failing. The 1961 trial, like the German trials, had failed to give the victims suffering, an adequate personal voice or ability to confront the physical perpetrators. Yet even this could not be directly achieved, despite some interaction with camp officials – these were no longer processes of Truth and Reconciliation, but at best of acknowledgement.

Former US Secretary of Defence Robert McNamara's later admission in the Errol Morris documentary *The Fog of War* concedes that in such processes the judge and the jury are the victors. Those judged usually emerge as merely passive objects of the process of vengeance, or as symbolic ones;[39] a desk-killer like Eichmann could be portrayed as an iconic puppet. Some of their evidence may prove of value to researchers on facts, but rarely authenticates memory, or enhances truth-telling about war or genocide. As Buruma in *Wages of Guilt* concludes, the trials for war crimes and genocide, by their very nature, limit responsibility to a few individuals such as Eichmann, and thus may not be the best history, politics (nor sociology) lessons.[40] "This was the one history lesson of Nuremberg that stuck". It is not a system that is judged at trials, just individual perpetrators. Indeed, there is a real danger that such trials may represent a kind of closure, an opportunity to "close the books that enables repression of further memory, once the criminals are punished".[41]

Eichmann had been a middle-range functionary despite his prominent role at the Wannsee Villa conference (1942) that planned to implement the 'final solution'. Nevertheless he was a criminal figure and also symbolically needed as a scapegoat. Whilst some at the time saw him as being publicly humiliated and bullied by the court, it was never intended to be a good advertisement for 'the rule of law'. Eichmann's fate was to be the exemplar. But the image of him as a banal human cog in a genocidal bureaucratic machine was the one controversially promoted by Arendt, to draw unusual lessons from the process.[42]

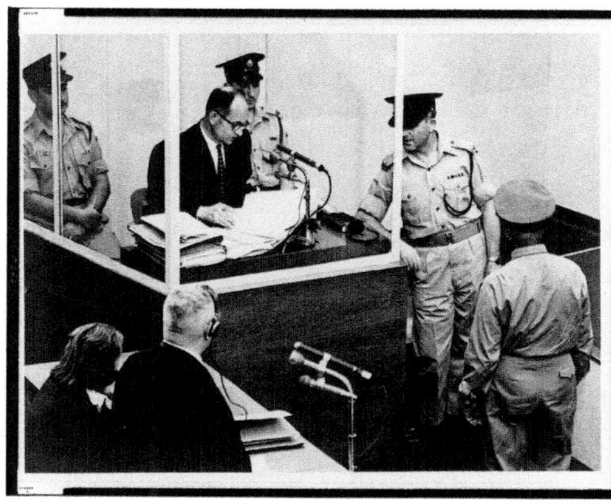

IMAGE 6.2 Eichmann and Servatius, lawyer. Jerusalem, 1961. A key event in the evolution of holocaust memory, not least because of Hannah Arendt recording it in her account. Photo: Library of Congress.

For those, like myself, who witnessed the trial on film at the time, the event was mesmerizing, but for the wrong reasons. It portrayed not 'victims confronting their tormentors', but rather a pathetic German bureaucrat facing relentless state prosecutions in Hebrew. Yet this was not an evidential trial of Eichmann, and Arendt rightly calls such elements as 'K. Zetnick's' testimony 'theatrical' (and created doubts about his authenticity). Overall these procedures were a distraction from comprehending mass tragedy itself, and from the traumas of European Jews, which continued long after 1945. The trial did draw attention to the fact of the Holocaust; indeed, it was the Shoah that was on trial. But even more, it advertised the theatre of the event, and the new state of Israel, and its agendas. It was as much the banality of the trial as well as the banality of mass death by industrial production, that Arendt famously exposed in her critique. Arendt's report was not published in Hebrew, and despite the widely hostile reviews of her book in the USA, at times evoking over-reactions, partly based on misunderstandings of her concept of the 'banality of evil', Arendt's views confirmed the reaction of many elsewhere who saw, or read about, the trial.

Even more than Nuremberg, the asymmetric, and apparently one-sided nature of Israel's court process showed neither clear equity, nor transparent fairness. Eichmann's situation elicited a perverse sympathy amongst critics of Israeli or Zionist policy and rhetoric. More seriously the focus of the trial on one accused may have deflected attention from the appalling crimes, the moving individual testimonies of a number of holocaust victims, and also screening an understanding of the real nature of the totalitarian machine which carried them out (see Image 6.2).

Lanzmann's *Shoah*

I have devoted a significant part of this chapter on post-holocaust memory to what I judge to be one of the major postnational texts of the twentieth century: the film *Shoah*. The genius of Lanzmann's masterpiece is multi-dimensional. It exemplifies, like *The Journey*, a universal methodology, beyond states. It takes the particular (a Jewish tragedy) and universalizes it; it links modern genocide to the fate of nations (Poland, Israel, Germany) but transnationalizes it. It abounds with religious reference, Judaic, but also Catholic; but is fundamentally universalistic and humanist – not particularist. It returns on an obligatory, but not obeisant pilgrimage to Israel: but it does not remain there, because it is of all places, and times – past, present and future – and many images intentionally transcend specificity.

More than providing a 'prosthetic' memory, a substitute experience, I have suggested how a film, a play, or a series of texts can become 'memory' in its own right. Actors talk of scripts, even screen-plays as 'the book'. When the printed text of Lanzmann's documentary *Shoah* appeared, it presented over nine hours of gripping testimonies documenting the realities. By reinstating the filmed text as a 'book', it is constantly throwing light into forgotten shadows.[43] By sustaining its mnemonic level throughout,[44] *Shoah*'s *mise en scene* and editing of film encourages a unique reflexive recall of memory, giving full space to witnesses, to eliciting testimonies and using a patient, multi-layered and intertextual methodology.[45] These language, images, interviews and commentary go far beyond most previous memory narration.[46]

And *Shoah* is no familiar form of cinematic re-enactment. Instead, an impeccable essay in postnational memory representation, it involved much prior historical or remembrance research, helped not least by Hilberg's authoritative history of the genocide (1961). It emphasizes the process of discovery in what is an almost positivistic approach to the past. The enquirer – usually Lanzmann himself – asks 'what?', 'why?', 'where?' and 'when?' Yet it is also a multi-lingual team production. The creative skill of the filmmaker, and collective documentary team – combine the voice – of the intermediary (Lanzmann and his interpreter or interrogator of the text) – scriptwriter, interpreters and the camera crew. Imaginative, permissive direction of interviews allows uninterrupted dialogue, including silences and pauses, amongst witnesses, bystanders, even with some perpetrators. But central is the witness, some of them chance survivors, not least from Chelmno. Simon Srebnik is a one-time boy singer who Lanzmann and his collaborators brought back from Israel, even to the obliterated site of the killings, both to recall the past and to sing, even a Nazi marching song and a Polish folk tune.

As this suggests, *Shoah* can be read and experienced at several levels, not only as memory work, but equally about individuals and locations. As Shoshana Felman observes, in her exposition it is the re-engaged memory as 'time and place', temporally and spatially researched, yet as 'present reality'.[47] The process is demystified as a result. The impact relies on immediacy. Through witnesses of the events, even in 'second hand' re-visits to sites, it shows the power of being there. Through Lanzmann's lens we return to a 'moment', a represented present accumulated, as film. This cannot be faked. Whilst at Treblinka, Lanzmann asks "how many miles from the station to the camp?", "How long?", "What was the weather?"[48]

Film memory, a process of recall of the time/space, represents the past/present of immersion in Lanzmann's revelations. Where this develops as history, on a site, or at the places of atrocity, or in the movement of the rivers, the railways, traffic on the roads, these are journeys in time. They are representations of present past(s), to be engaged in, even if not re-visited, but they also represent a contemporary 'memory': that of the 1980s. It presents recall in the manner of W. G. Sebald's later invocatory prose, or Anselm Kiefer's art of material collage: it crosses imagistic boundaries. Similarly, despite the film's nexus with Israel and Lanzmann's inspirational visits there, *Shoah* in the end completely transcends its Jewishness to create a work of universal art, a template of memorized modern genocide.

As Terrence des Pres argues of the ambivalence of the survivor, in the compulsion to testify about public events as a way to recover truth, the memory of the witness lies somewhere between truth and fiction, art and remembering, each testimony adopts a different perspective. Like the camera angles, neither real, nor false, but a contribution to a collective vision, lighting up the past in a historical whole. And, in that the complementary role of the scholar and historian is acknowledged; in this case, the voice of Hilberg, whose research authorized revelations of witnesses.

As in *The Journey*, *Shoah* provides us with such methodologies of memory work where paradoxes in the narratives of victims and witnesses are well portrayed in the faces, body language and voices of those interviewed. The role of the secondary testimony or witness becomes more central over time, as victims and survivors of atrocity die or remain silent. It is narrative, the power of storytelling in *Shoah* that particularly resides in the staging of returns to the sites and witnesses of the Holocaust.

Absorbed into a Polish crowd, at times defensive, even shrill, outside the Catholic church in Chelmno, Lanzmann stands with Srebnik. Some do recognize him, as the sole Chelmno survivor, of the 'second period'. They hear that the church organist, 'Mr Kantarowski gave them bread and cucumbers'.[49] At the time of filming, Mr Kantarowski was still the church organist, and keen to talk. The cucumbers are remembered by several women as ways Poles 'helped Jews' (one also mentions the latter's 'gold' in their suitcases).

An impassive Srebnik quietly listens as the Chelmno locals, Polish residents recall him singing for the SS in 1942. The scene reflects the defensive, ambivalent yet, sceptical attitude of Poles towards Jews at the time. Interwoven in the dialogue, this uncovers a collective, shared, part-concealed, hesitant and often selective recall.[50] Resentment of Jews, and even at times some collaboration with the feared Nazis, clearly existed; such quiescence or connivance happened all over Europe. The scenes also recall the banality of memory,[51] these dialogues in the church square and in Grabow bring out the repressed memories of both victims and witnesses. Mr Kantarowski's includes repetition of the myth of Christ-killers which inevitably remained strongest in Catholic Europe, now retold as a story of a local rabbi from Lodz.

Similarly sites can be authenticated (like the road from Chelmno), not so much by the filmmaker, commentator, interlocutor or editor, but by revisiting. To interact with a re-awakened memory of decades earlier as victims, witnesses, or chance bystanders as at Chelmno Church is to enable us not only to authenticate, but also to prosthetically share absence – to recapture a sense of the loss of a community, and of the sad ambiguity of a repressed or forgotten past, even if we cannot physically visit there.

From Henri Bergson's writing on time, to late modernist critics of temporality such as Huyssen, Koselleck or La Capra, it has been frequently noted how memory compresses time. What takes hours in fact is recalled as a flash. Proust noted this elision of events, yet the longevity of actual time passing, and he attempted to stretch it by narrative prose. Lanzmann, like Peter Watkins, self-consciously uses film to similarly return temporality to a past recalled: to slow the ever-pressing rush of events.

As an example of such film documentary as memory research, there is the extraordinary passage at the end of Part 1 of *Shoah,* when Lanzmann and his crew return again to the Chelmno killing grounds, the site which had opened the film. He asks local witnesses how long it took the gas-vans to drive from the town (the castle, or the church) to the place where the bodies were unloaded and the corpses burnt – whether victims were dead or not. He interviews a Polish forester and several other local witnesses, and as with the questions asked of Simon Srebnik himself, they are precise and impersonal: "At what speed did the Saurer vans travel?", "How many kilometres?" His film team then retrace or re-enact that drive – at the estimated pace and time of the Saurer vans of the 1940s.

To remind us of the asphyxiation in real-time evocation, there could be few more powerful representations to the reality of past trauma than the simulated van journey from Chelmno Church to the forest clearing where the bodies were unloaded by Srebnik and others. Lanzmann's retraced journey to the 'funeral pyre' site seems to be an exactly calculated one. Part 1 of *Shoah* ends at that moment, when the duration of killing in these journeys concludes: it includes the sounds of the vans' engines. One can see, if not reinvent in imagination, the smell of the fumes of the exhaust, simulating the carbon monoxide from the vans which killed the 'load' in the Saurer companies vans. Srebnik describes his regular work, stacking the bodies at the end of the journey, some still moving, then burning them.[52]

Much of the photography is of the road itself, which becomes a forest track; incidents on the journeys are recorded as voice over, and include witness by the former forester. He recounts how at one wooded corner he watched an accident to one of the transports. When it occurred the van doors opened, and the half dead were flung out. Some were reloaded, some shot.

But film of the journey ends not on the forest track, but on a 1980s autobahn, and in the industrial Ruhr. A 'modern' Saurer van is driving. A letter, a cold, depersonalized, Nazi 'business' letter from the SS to the Saurer company is intoned. It is a letter regarding 'improvements' to the van. It is read out by Lanzmann in French (subtitled in English). The German text of the letter scrolls on the screen during these final moments. Only one word inadvertently humanizes it. In the event, the object in the van 'screams' ('cries'); otherwise there is no mention of killing people.[53] They are described as 'the load', and in other situations 'transports', 'consignments'.

Simulation is not the intention, but as the SS letter signs off, the final shot of the van driving through its homeland indicates the maker's name, 'Saurer'. The factory landscape reminds us, as do Resnais's references in *Nuit et Brouillard* (*Night and Fog*), of a continuity – with contemporaneity. The chilling final images and sounds of the engine, and the fact that the same company, that in 1942 made the gas vans, not only still exists, but also has kept the name is no aberration. For many contemporary Europeans, the reminder was recognizable. As in Japan, one part of the modernities of genocide is a corporate political economy of manufacturing mass death that continues, not only from 1944, but also in the depersonalized, technologized postnational slaughters of the present – and an arms production for the future. For example, in the worldwide manufacture of arsenals of weapons of mass destruction and their delivery systems, it includes Israel's 'deterrents' near Dimona in the Negev.

This raises the question of whether *Shoah*, any more than other mnemonic representations, enables us to imagine more of the unimaginable? An attempt to deny the deniers is perhaps one attainable task, but another serves to apportion some 'blame' beyond any nation, or the SS, or racism, but to the long-term role of modern industrial capitalism, and its collaboration and participation not only in holocaust, but also all the global killing fields. In other words, a shared guilt with corporate power and its excesses. Does Lanzmann succeed through such a device, to force us to reflect on our own sites and moments of collective guilt? Beyond the focus on culpable action, in *Shoah* there is the existential paralysis in the face of surviving totalism. Can we discriminate between implicit collaboration in further genocide, urbicide or potentially omnicide or ponder our own inaction? Such memory of past denial reminds us how repressive erasure works; most choose to live, and simply not to confront that reality at all: and like so many survivors, it is one option.

Like two other major examples of film text used in this book, *Hiroshima mon Amour*, and *The Journey*, *Shoah* does not use archive film.[54] In Resnais's drama of Japan, the Hiroshima Atomic Bomb Museum's film of the bombing appears, but is not real footage, but dramatized representation. *Shoah's* nine and a half hours contains no historical footage but, it does, like *The Journey*'s nuclear war re-enactments, mimic reality. Lanzmann, for example, chose to simulate: in the barber shop sequence in Tel Aviv, the survivor Abraham Bomba recalls his work. He vividly recounts the original experience of cutting the hair of Jewish women outside the gas chamber at Treblinka. He describes trying to give them a 'nice haircut', trying to reassure them before they walked to their deaths. Whilst enacting his present hairdresser's role in Israel, he stops and breaks down into tears as he remembers the short time he had for preparing and calming the victims, moments before they went into the gas chambers (Image 6.3).[55]

In *Shoah,* as in *The Journey*, selected individuals also revisit actual places of memory and trauma. Such witnesses engage in a new kind of experience in the course of interviews. Some react emotionally, some passively. At Chelmno, Srebnik, mostly silent, audibly sighs as he recalls the trauma. Thanks to the directors' intervention, we as audience can interact with the testimonies: Srebnik, Bomba, Mrs Fuchs, and the tear-filled silent language of Mr Podchelbnik (through his daughter). Even perpetrators are persuaded to recall (at times through subterfuge). Like so much modern memory work, what it tells us is of course as much about the 1980s as about the 1940s: about feelings about revisiting the past. Pasts and presents have changed during that time, even in the decade that filming is completed. *Shoah* took eleven years (1974–85) to make – testimonies, imagined scenes, and stories break the ongoing silences. Beyond the shocking film of the original camps (1945), sich as Belsen, Buchenwald and Auschwitz, there are silences and

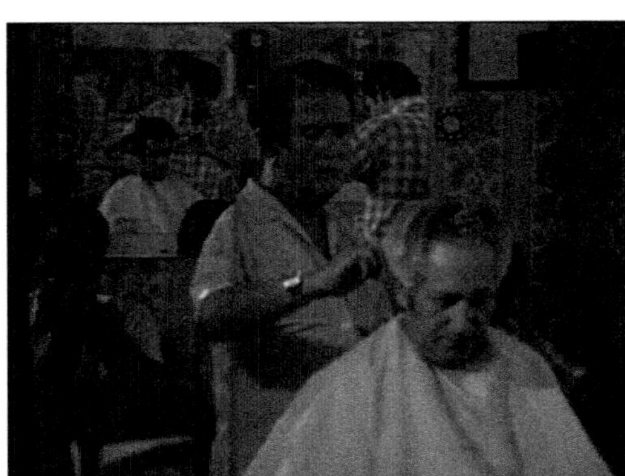

IMAGE 6.3 Claude Lanzmann, Shoah, 1985. Abraham Bomba, interviewed by Lanzmann at his barber shop in Tel Aviv, describes cutting the women's hair before they were gassed in Treblinka, and breaks down in tears as he does so.

deaths, both of the victims and of the witness, which must be further historically broken, and before they are lost. In order to further revive holocaust memory, Lanzmann and the feminist author Susan Griffin use oral testimony to do this. Their interviews serve to give back a 'voice', (Shoshana Felman's term), even to the bystanders, and some of the perpetrators.[56] To that extent the narrative resumes and amplifies the unfinished project of the Eichmann Trial of 1961; either through victims (of bombings and of Nazi crimes) or as perpetrators, and there are always unwitting bystanders of atrocity, some indeed numbed by it. Such 'accidental witnesses' exist, some suppressing memory. This is exemplified in Poland, as at Chelmno and Treblinka; Lanzmann found them living near the camps and killing fields, these accidental witnesses also became part of the overall holocaust testimony,[57] and teach us more about memory. But it is the perpetrators of such crimes who most easily forget. It is for the survivors, the victims that forgetting is hardest.[58]

We make assumptions when we examine the memory of genocide, as with war. In both cases 'retrospective formulations' appear: subsequent narratives; new, constructed, memory, and new memorials; and new facts are used to assess guilt and responsibility. Yet these may remain ambiguous as evidence; as in analysis, it is only in the testimony of the witness that memories are both reflective and potentially reflexive, giving us a past that can be reassessed. In that potentially critical self-examination, a certain revisionism or reconsideration, of contradiction and ambiguity in the story, is given space and possible explanatory power: 'It wasn't quite like that!'[59] That is another powerful contribution of *Shoah:* to update memory, to fill in spaces, silences; to probe ambivalence.

Nevertheless, Lanzmann's truth-seeking has been criticized – for example, by Martin Gilbert – for what is seen as manipulation, and inaccurate reconstructions of the Holocaust.[60] It is clear that overall as a creative work, even such projects as *Shoah* may become a distortion, an invention, an exhibitionary *mise en scene* – where the onlooker becomes voyeur. This is also a continual problem in museumology. But whilst in strict historical terms the dangers of cinematic license is real, in both *Shoah* as in *The Journey*, it also represents the power of narrative recreation based on fact. Whether some fiction or 'faction' is included or not, it is a constituted reinvention, in order to restore memory, rather than created as entertainment. Such projects are inevitably selective and involve artifice. However, neither of these films use fictional characters.

As shown by Pat Barker's exemplary novels of the Great War, one can weave fact and fiction together successfully. But the central ethical principle remains of using only authentic oral testimony – enabling a witness to revisit the past to testify. Reawakening the memory of those once involved is presented at face value: a revelation even for bystanders. Recall of memory is best challenged in an actual participatory experience of re-engaging with historical sites and scenes – remembered, sometimes collectively, with other witnesses.

The Shoah industry: stewarding atrocity and the past as commodity

From the 1970s in the West, first in Germany, and later Poland, the 'Memory Business' had already seen a gradual popularization of 'the past as commodity', with war and genocide displays, especially for visitors to the camps. But as official endorsement of such visitation from the West to the sites grew, the expansion of memory tours, new textbooks, special anniversary exhibitions, added incremental value to later memory tourism in the 1980s.[61] Many began to exploit sites' relationship to 'heritage' business opportunities. Worldwide commodification made 'some corners of foreign fields' prize properties. As such venues continued to proliferate, they became confused with other contingent but distinct cultural genres. For example, popular heritage, and semi-official memory entrepreneurship, together with the 'official' memory of the archive thrived, and by 2014 the anniversaries of the Great War[62] revived a more conventional memorializing of a public version of the past on a mass scale.[63]

In the case of the Holocaust, however, the veracity and postnational character of holocaust and trauma studies became compromised by a growing popular appeal. When the remembrance boom came to be channelled into memory study, museumology, or touristic voyeurism, 'exhibitionism' often predominated. I have argued that a documentary such as *Shoah* is a truth-seeking and universalistic project and it may assist 'prosthetic' memorizing. On the other hand, and despite its technical skills, many critics, including memory scholars, dismiss Spielberg's film *Schindler's List* as escapist popular entertainment. Its narrative provides a 'screen memory' that appears widely misleading as fact, and unreliable as prosthetics: as a sentimental, manipulative drama (as is also true of *Sophie's Choice*) it diverts from the historical evidence, and obfuscates genuine memory.[64]

But the long catalogue of contested holocaust memories especially at sites has continued for many decades. In Berlin, whilst Libeskind's highly original Jewish Museum has been praised as authentic, inspirational and appropriate,[65] it contrasts sharply with both the competition and the controversy over the much criticized memorial to the 'Murdered Jews of Europe', now near the Potzdamer Platz and Brandenburg Gate.[66] To many the latter is void of symbolic power, and wrongly sited (I discuss it in Chapter 9).[67] Many later holocaust museums, including the US museum in Washington, are riven with such contradictions: some identified in survivor literature.[68]

As for the camps, many had been levelled, appropriated for other uses, and sanitized after 1945. But this allowed an active visitation without too much visual horror; for example, at Belsen and Dachau.[69] Birkenau and several other Polish spaces in particular have been under threat. A Nazi headquarters in East Prussia is now popularized as a tourist destination. Reconstruction in bombed cities such as the restaurants and discos around the Potsdamer Platz (Berlin) make too great a demand on the historical imagination. One Chinese restaurant sits nearly above the site of Hitler's bunker, another bar, popular with young people, looks down on the newest holocaust 'memorial', whose stones devour an incompletely resurrected memory space. As one critic observed, it would have perhaps been better left as a children's playground, which at times, de facto, it becomes – a skateboarders' maze.[70]

If holocaust memory was not always mismanaged or sold, it was certainly often misappropriated. Too often memorial sites were demeaned, or commercially exploited and misrepresented; these makeovers and aberrations must have provided grist for deniers. If Shoah is remembered as 'heritage' or 'kitsch', it may help sustain some deeply troubling claims and counter-claims, exaggerations and denials. Many were the result of distortion, even graft.[71] The other source of contest is the politicization (or specification) of sites and competitive national or religious claims, and manipulations of them.

Later, I will describe the moment when organized Israeli groups began to visit the Auschwitz camp I, from 1988, with an annual pilgrimage: a 'March of the Living'. These events were often marked by speeches, visits at the museums, use of touristic amenities and, while there, photo opportunities. Similar tours started to operate in the area, not only to Birkenau and Krakow, but also to the Warsaw Ghetto memorial, attracting visitors in large numbers. Some Jews had already returned to nearby Krakow, to open businesses as visitation expanded after the book of *Schindler's Ark* was published, then filmed (in Krakow). Steven Spielberg's film was a commercial success, and by the 1990s, there were *Schindler's List* memory tours in Krakow and Plaszow (the local camp). These were described to me by the organizer of his own 'Stephen Spielberg tour' by Spielberg's local driver during the making of the film. There was at least some identification by non-Jewish Poles, with this largely suppressed or forgotten past, some converted to Judaism, like the young rabbi in the renovated synagogue at Oswiecim.

Discussion of '*Shoah business*' remained common in the 1990s, especially during the various media controversies and competitions. But the phrase had been used decades earlier, albeit in a different context.[72] Awareness of the financial aspects of victimhood and compensation claims raised ethical concerns about reparations, as much as did the later entrepreneurial exploitation of memory. In the 1950s, this had elicited the infamous quip, which was widely attributed to the Israeli diplomat and though claimed by others (see previous footnote), Abba Eban's 'There is no business like Shoah business', was typical of his aphorisms. The phrase was frequently quoted and used beyond Israel, with and without attribution and with new connotations which developed in the 1970s, and 1980s, in relation to memorial projects such as the US Holocaust Museum, and competition for major Berlin Holocaust memorials, especially to the 'Murdered Jews of Europe'. These (and 9/11) are analysed and compared by James Young.[73]

This museumization of the Shoah also presents a problematic history of manipulated memory documents and artefacts, especially of the uncensored diary that the real Anne Frank wrote, which has its own mythology, discussed earlier.[74] The dissembling narrative of the diary's discovery, its control, production, editing, and publication reveals distortion and censorship over decades and in many editions. It is both a troubling but also a revelatory history. The Frank Foundation's work to combat prejudice and discrimination is rightly widely admired. In a media-focused narrative, the censorships relate to the role of Otto Frank senior (the lone survivor). It has been criticized as part of this convoluted entrepreneurial 'memory' narrative, and the various texts are widely debated. Yet the return to the site in reality was inspired by just such voices of testimony and witness, including the Anne Frank story, provoking a range of public reactions.

Again in the 1980s, and encouraged by civil society groups, a new generation of young Germans especially focused on Auschwitz (and many more sites in Poland) and expanded their work at Dachau and some other German camps. But there was also censorship, and the two Jewish displays at Auschwitz were closed in 1967 until 1978.[75] These reflected the Polish anti-Jewish purges. Between 1947 and 1953, with competitions for designs for memorials, and in the 1970s, and after 1989, the Museum at Auschwitz has been given successive, sometimes problematic makeovers, though often only minor revisions, but including a post-war, shoddily reconstructed gas chamber (mostly fake). Fifty years after the closures of displays in 1967, in the Polish history museum in Gdansk, complete with Catholic martyrs, the events are once again being 'nationalized'.[76]

Yad Vashem, between 1953 and 2005, had several incarnations, as it expanded, tending in many critics' view to become more Zionist in the process.[77] Yet by the 1980s, a renewed forgetting had paradoxically also become part of the rebuilding and healing process. Once again, for many it was time to move on. For instance, among those who lived locally, the commandant's house outside Oswiecim (not far from the barracks and first controversial Catholic convent) had been deemed a perfectly sound house in a country of ruins after 1945. The new occupants could hardly be sentimental – it was one of the best houses in the district, even if it was close to the wall of the infamous 'Auschwitz' barracks, the prison execution bloc – a martyrs' site and the place of Father Kolbes's death. The area resumed its silence for decades after the liberation by the Red Army, broken only or mainly by the groups of Polish school children on mandatory school visits. And the washing, drying on the clothes line stretching from the house, still reached to the perimeter wall of the camp: laundry still hung there in the 1980s and 1990s.

Some of these sites screen and/or 'enclose' the past – as most museums do – other sites open up the spaces. This stark contrast is well revealed in the different role of the Auschwitz I Museum (the army barracks originally Polish) and the later German construction of the Birkenau camps, or the 'territory', as it is sometimes called locally (Auschwitz II), built on the site of a demolished Polish village.[78]

Among those who lived at sites of urbicide or of genocide, such as the Polish inhabitants of Oswiecim, few would *want* the debris of atrocious events to remain. The territory of Birkenau (Auschwitz II) is several kilometres away from Auschwitz I (Museum), and despite one or two offensive or inaccurate elements – some removed or revised or changed – the site still speaks for itself: as the ruins of 1945: it remains largely authentic as a site of mass murder, and retains, like Majdanek, some partially surviving structures (huts, walls of gas chambers and crematoria).[79] To make contact with the past through such places as these, however grassed over, rusty or decrepit, remains possible because its spaces are kept in a semblance of past times, rather than through a token reproduction or reconstruction. Away from the tour buses, Birkenau retains its silences.

Les lieux des memoire

Vignette:
Being there – Poland 1988–1996

Arriving at Birkenau early on a February morning, the frost and light snow covered the grass. The various ponds were frozen except the one near Crematorium V, one in which they placed the ashes. That one, green and opaque, apparently does not freeze like the other ponds, perhaps because of the spoil dropped there. A rabbit scuttled across the foundations of the camp huts, and a white-tailed deer leapt over a high, wired-fence near the perimeter.

The fear of 'grassing over' this past contributes to a strong desire to experience such a place, before all traces are gone – however drastically transformed, or almost obliterated, the site may have become. Just a scratch (now a criminal act) beneath the barely grassed surface at Birkenau, specifically at the 'Canada' storage zone, reveals bone fragments or small personal objects. Domestic remnants of a death camp; a spoon in the sandy soil.

Visiting here with survivors, witnesses and relatives of victims, there was always that sense of looking for "where might Aunt Lili have been; where might they have died?" And on one of our many subsequent visits to Birkenau in the 1990s, there was the shock of finding the photographs taken surreptitiously by an SS man, newly fixed to the birch trees near Crematorium V, of the recently transported Hungarian women waiting amongst these trees for a space in the overfilled gas chambers, huddled, naked (Image 6.4).

IMAGE 6.4 Hungarian women having been made to undress to await death under birch trees in Auschwitz-Birkenau concentration camp, near crematorium 5, likely 1944. The women had to wait as the gas chamber was already full. A few photos taken clandestinely at the death camp survive. The photograph is displayed at the site. Photo courtesy of Auschwitz-Birkenau State Museum.

A prevalent compulsion to experience the sense of 'being there' is not just to view the ruins but to reconstruct the event in our imagination: to personalize the experience, as if it is our own; as if we are transported to the moment; and yet, at the same time, to engage with it as social ritual, a shared mood of remembering, however horrifying. Against such collective cultivation of return remembrance, it has been argued that sites destroyed or abandoned lose their sacral quality; such was a Jewish cemetery: it had over-grown weeds and broken tombstones, desecrated tablets, where no one had been buried since 1938 or a little earlier, or later. It has lost, it is said, its 'sacred' meaning because it is no longer used. Perhaps some sociologists misunderstand how its sacred quality can be re-imparted by remembering, by my being there, or survivors rebuilding a small memorial, at the site.

Such modes of revisiting the past takes many forms, some described in this book,[80] including the now familiar scholarly 'study tours'. Many academic memory workers or historians such as Martin Gilbert, organized and led these visits to encourage educational engagement with memorializing in general. These trips may overlap with new rituals at Birkenau/Auschwitz, Warsaw, Verdun, Ieper/Ypres, or participation in longer-term memorializing volunteer projects such as those developed in Flanders, or Arras (Nord), or in Oswiecim or at the Gestapo Gelande (Topography of Terror) in Berlin.[81] A variety of mnemonics are both sought and provided in such spaces, because otherwise they would each be by now anonymous, faceless *lieux,* without clues or signposts.

I have observed how civil society groups, especially from Germany, played a key role in encouraging a range of such Holocaust memory projects and visits that uncover forgotten sites. Some have become major secular memorial places, and now tourist destinations. I have referred to placing the deeply moving photographs placed at Birkenau (Crematorium V), they were not present in the 1980s and indeed not until the late 1990s. They gave terrible added meaning to the place. It was by illustrating, as the Hungarian women's transports do, a 'hidden past' (see clandestine photograph in image 6.4), that moved later memory travellers. A student on Gilbert's 1997 *Holocaust Journey* remarked on this memorable juxtaposition, images of a represented place at the site and a past visual record of the Shoah.[82] This process can be criticized at many levels as illusory and over self-indulgent or 'prosthetic memory', but as a mnemonic, it has perhaps more force than any other display at the sites

Through such signs, these encounters with sites of memory, similarly experienced by other independent visitors and witnesses, offer prosthetic moments. When proxy memory or empathetic remembrances are shared, they often prove deeply disturbing ones – and sometimes elicit an enduring, numbing silencing.

In the imagination of past events it can be argued that *place* is, in itself, void of intrinsic meaning, but through ritual and re-invention it becomes a central trope of modern memory. Visiting Holocaust sites with curators, witnesses, relatives of victims, museum staff and student study groups, the question remained: does such proxy memory appropriately reclaim or restore, or reconstruct the memory and give such meaning? And if so, how? The argument for leaving it to the grass (nature's business) 'to do its work' is always in the background. Compromises were sought, and the issue of authentic preservation has provided the roots of many ongoing, passionate, controversies, public and private.[83]

One such group visit, which included Auschwitz-Birkenau, in 1988, raised other issues of postnational framing: it coincided with the first 'March of the Living' (see 1996 photograph in image 6.5), organized mostly for Israeli youth; there was an element in it of re-claiming the site, of a new assertiveness, and of course overcoming the problem of persuading any group (both groups were mostly teenagers) to avoid touristic voyeurism and holidaymaking misbehaviour at a site of silence.[84] On one of my subsequent visits, eight years later, I witnessed the same annual assembly, once more, a deeply ambiguous event. Respectful sincerity, mingled with prurience and proxy-memorizing, and the cult of privileging some victims; an identification with 'victimhood' overlapped with the normal celebratory pride of ethnicity and nationhood, the agenda was secular, political, more nationalist than religious, but still ambivalent.

The ruins of Warsaw, Berlin, Hiroshima or the US World Trade Center area were never to be retained perpetually in situ, even if some buildings (such as Coventry Cathedral's shell, the Gedächtniskirche in Berlin, or Japan's Atomic Dome) had been made safe. This was major real estate, and in some cases

IMAGE 6.5 Annually each spring since 1988 many hundreds of young Jews, mostly from Israel, march from Auschwitz museum to the Birkenau death camps in Poland three kilometres away. Photo: Alik Keplic/PA Images.

quickly purchased after 1945. Much the same is true of sites of the Shoah. Some debris has been imaginatively recycled as memorials or counter-monuments. But at Birkenau, the real 'warning' space is the 'absence of the past'. At sites of atrocity, replacements, or 'footprints' of atrocity, however tasteful in design, are in danger of being pseudo ruins. As in Berlin, Hamburg, Dresden and other German cities, and also in Coventry and Hiroshima, they remain tokens: a footnote to, as much as a footprint of, history and the result may contribute to an obliteration of the significance of place.

As in Poland, Austria is also open for business. Tourism developed sooner there after 1945, and money can just as easily be made from other things than recollections of atrocity and trauma. I return to the case of Austrian amnesia in Chapter 8. It is still claimed, as at the end of the War, that as the allies concurred, Austria was a 'victim' of Nazi oppression, not a perpetrator. The camp museum at Mauthausen, renewed after 2010, though an Austrian memorial, is barely advertised beyond the site. It is not commercialized. As at Dachau, only a McDonald's exists, and it is a mile away from the slave labour camps.[85] Mauthausen near Linz, one of several camps like Melk and Ebensee, is where alongside several tens of thousands of international victims and equal numbers of

Soviet prisoners died, many executed.[86] But Austria prefers its tourists to recall the *Sound of Music* or indulge in Mozart-mania than contemplate such crimes committed nearby. Such holocaust sites do not traditionally fit the tourist image of a holiday destination, and very much the same has been true of sites in Spain after Franco, where the ghosts of the civil war are avoided, similarly censored from the tourist brochures.[87]

None of this analysis or commentary should in any way serve to diminish or demean the unique horror of the Shoah. However, it is imperative to discern how we best remember the seriousness and implications of holocaust mnemonics in postnational terms: how genocide fits into the larger picture of our memory of global catastrophe, by connecting totalistic war and holocaust to the threat of human destruction on a universal scale. I continue this argument in the next chapter. I suggest fusing these atrocities into one human narrative. Far from de-valuing them, this may enhance our appreciation of the overall meaning and significance of the European Holocaust, and Jewish Shoah, as a cypher. By such contextualization, a sensitive procedure to be sure, it may be possible to compare or contrast Holocaust memories with those memories of total war, and other genocides which can only deepen a serious analysis of them. The logic of seeing memories of total war, and memory of modern genocide, as overlapping and contiguous appears to me undisputable. These connectivities serve through collective memory to help understand our present and future threats, rather than mystify them.

The reawakening of German memory of the European/Jewish Holocaust of the 1940s, touched on here, is clearly not an unproblematic one. But such responses as Jürgen Habermas's invocation of history, representations such as Anselm Kiefer's major art (especially 'Margarethe' (see image 7.5) and 'Shulamith'), and Sebald's writing – for example, on *Theresienstadt* in Auschwitz[88] – are symptomatic of a major post-war shift in culture, and by the later 1980s, a postnational German reaction to the Shoah. I have chosen to deal with these writers and artists in that context – a context of post-war, post-urbicide and post-totalism – and a renewal of a more European era in Germany and beyond.

Notes

1 On the actions of the Einsatzgruppen, see Martin Gilbert, *The Holocaust: The Jewish Tragedy* (New York, 1986), dealt with country by country in chapters 12–37.

2 Daniel Levy and Natan Sznaider, *Holocaust and Memory in a Global Age*, trans. Assenka Oksiloff (Philadelphia, 2006). Perhaps this framework can be seen as a reaction to Israeli or 'Zionist' efforts to 'nationalize' the Holocaust in Europe and the USA, co-opting it as part of its nation-making myth. For critical commentary on aspects of this, particularly the treatment of Holocaust's immigrant survivors, see Keith Lowe, *The Fear and the Freedom: How the Second World War Changed Us* (London, 2017), pp. 324–42. See also Astrid Erll, *Memory in Culture* (Basingstoke, UK, 2011), pp. 62–63.

3 On cosmopolitan memory of the Holocaust and war, see excerpts in Jeffrey K. Olick, V. Vinitzky-Seroussi and D. Levy, eds, *Collective Memory Reader* (Oxford,

2011), pp. 462–67. Amongst other theorists raising these issues were Jürgen Habermas, Zygmunt Bauman and Reinhart Koselleck (see also note 9).

4 A. Rosenbaum, ed., *Was the Holocaust Unique? Perspectives on Comparative Genocide* (Oxford, 1996).

5 J. Sartre, *Réflexions sur la Question Juive* (trans. as *Anti-Semite and Jew*) (New York, 1946).

6 Like the Roma, Sinti and Gays who were equally transnational, and with a history of persecution, they were each a poor fit with nationalist fascist identities, despite integration into host 'nations'.

7 See, for example, Jay Winter, *War Beyond Words: Languages of Remembrance from the Great War to the Present* (New Haven, CT, 2017), Introduction and pp. 9–17.

8 This was summarized in Terrence Des Pres's landmark critique, see T. Des Pres, *The Survivor: An Anatomy of Life in the Death Camps* (New York, 1976).

9 Des Pres (1976), p. 36, commenting on Wiesel's writing, he describes the witness as a necessary connection between past and future. See also Reinhart Koselleck, *Futures Past: On the Semantics of Historical Time*, trans. Keith Tribe (New York, 2004).

10 Hannah Arendt, *Eichmann in Jerusalem: A Report on the Banality of Evil* (London, 1963) and H. Arednt, *Origins of Totalitarianism* (New York, 1951); Keith Lowe (2017), pp. 59–63, 328–32 and 335–38.

11 In her major work, Arendt refers to Marx and Marxism multiple times, but to the German sociologist Max Weber only once, in a perfunctory and dismissive footnote on Hans Gerths's important essay, combining 'bureaucratic' and 'charismatic' dimensions of Nazi power. Her class analysis remains, even when she describes 'massification' after 1914.

12 Such a view omits all the other sociological factors contributing to 'massification' that were already powerful in the pre-1914 years, for example, mass literacy and mass media. The more conscious, and to some extent political, reconstruction of the past in the late 1920s was to be repeated in the 1950s. Both long predate the more recent modern memory boom, since the mid-1980s, but the sense of political-sociological continuities which analysts such as Arendt describe, amplified by sociologists such as C. W. Mills, complements historians such as Eric Hobsbawm in his later work, and the perspectives of Bauman, Habermas and others. The generational memories of 1945 were civilianized by the impact of total war, and the business of memory was deepened and broadened to create a challenge to existing hegemonies. On this see Koselleck (2004).

13 'Totalitarianism' is used to some extent polemically to describe an ideology, and the state structures which underpin it, and the physical and cultural violence associated with these. It is not a 'more' or 'less' for Arendt: Stalin's Soviet Union during the 'war Communism 40–45′ either suspended 'totalitarianism' in favour of conducting 'total war', or it did not: it is not clear.

14 See Tim Cole's *Selling the Holocaust* (New York and London, 2000), which brings together most of these topics in a discursive overview.

15 On the origins of Yad Vashem, see James E. Young, *Texture of Memory: Holocaust Memorials and Meaning* (New Haven, 1994), ch. 9, especially pp. 243–47 and 249–52; and see also Cole (2000) ch. 5, especially pp. 122–23.

16 See later authoritative editions of Raul Hilberg, *The Destruction of European Jews* (New York, 1985), originally published in 1961.

17 Lowe (2017), on Ferencz at Nuremberg, see pp. 205–07.

18 Another corpus of film and literature on Holocaust memory that I do not cover here on collaboration, and acquiescence in denial (Ophuls's films, *Sorrow and the Pity*, and *Hotel Terminus*, and the work of Rousso). See Henry Rousso, *The Vichy Syndrome: History and Memory in France since 1944*, trans. Arthur Goldhammer (Cambridge and London, 1991).

19 As with Armenia, Spain and Argentina, after revelation, denialism is re-cycled politically. More than four decades later, politicians dispute numbers of the victims of

repression. Elie Wiesel argued that such constructed denial not only blocks healing, but also enables further such crimes to occur. Peter Balakian makes similar points on Armenia in Peter Balakian, *Black Dog of Fate* (New York, 1997).

20 Resnais raises these problematic issues that Arendt also delineates in her writing, and which can be linked to the subsequent treatment by Lanzmann.

21 Although awareness of the fate of millions of Jews was becoming more widespread by the late 1950s, Resnais's film was criticized for not naming them as the principal victims of the death camps.

22 The French, often Jewish Left, took the issue as priority, and this tradition was much later exemplified by Claude Lanzmann's work in *Shoah* which, though it took decades to make, came from the same roots.

23 I have noted elsewhere Reinhart Koselleck's commentary on the lack of memorializing of the millions of Soviet prisoners who died in Nazi custody (see Chapter 10).

24 On 'Auschwitz', see Teresa Swiebocka, Jonathan Webber and Connie Wilsack, eds, *Auschwitz: A History in Photographs* (Oswięcim, Bloomington, Indianapolis and Warsaw, 1995), esp. Webber's useful chapter 'Auschwitz: A History in Photographs'; see also J. E. Young (1994), ch. 5, pp. 128–33; Cole (2000), pp. 110–18 and ch. 4 *passim;* see also Ian Buruma, *Wages of Guilt* (New York, 1994), pp. 69–91.

25 The two blocks were in effect 'residual'. Logically perhaps these could have been devoted to Polish Jews (who were internal deportees), but this was not specified, and between 1967 and 1978 these were closed. See Young (1994), pp. 130–31 and Cole (2000), pp. 100 and 124–51.

26 J. E. Young (1994), pp. 95–96 (on Rapoport) Warsaw Ghetto Memorial and ch. 6; and see also Lowe (2017), pp. 328–32; Cole (2000), pp. 14–25 and 148–49; and see image in Winter (2017).

27 See Lowe (2017), ch. 19 on Israel's foundation myths.

28 Young (1994), ch. 9, especially pp. 244–46; Cole (2000), pp. 122–25.

29 Young (1994), pp. 242–49, 250 and 260.

30 Cole (2000), p. 9, ch. 1 *passim* and pp. 27–29.

31 See Otto Frank in Cole (2000), pp. 23–30, 33–36, 38, 43 and 98. Cole downplays Frank's role to stress others' who sought to exploit the diary's economic potential.

32 See Lowe (2017) and Buruma (1994) on the post-War trials 'History on trial'.

33 On Wiesenthal, see Cole (2000), ch. 2, especially pp. 51–54.

34 The Dutch historian Ian Buruma comments in his *Wages of Guilt* (New York, 1994), on the post-1945 War Trials, pp. 137–58 (especially p. 157), and pp. 160–77. See also in Lowe (2017) and Cole (2000), ch. 2.

35 On Eichmann Trial, see Arendt (1963); and as background, her *Origins of Totalitarianism* (New York, 1951) and note also the debate between her, Shoshana Felman and Cathy Caruth, summarized in Caruth, ch. 11 in Richard Crownshaw, Jane Kilby and Antony Rowland, eds, *The Future of Memory* (Oxford and New York, 2010), pp. 207–25.

36 Arendt (1963, 1951).

37 See Shoshana Felman, *Judicial Unconcious* (Cambridge, MA, 2002) and critiques of her by LaCapra, Caruth and others. See Dominick LaCapra, *Representing the Holocaust: History, Theory, Trauma* (New York, 1996) and *History and Memory after Auschwitz* (New York and London, 1998).

38 See Lowe (2017) pp. 332–39 on the reception of European Jews in Israel.

39 Robert McNamara, on Iran, quoted in the film *The Fog of War: Eleven Lessons from the Life of Robert S. McNamara* (dir. Errol Morris, 2003).

40 As Buruma (1994) points out, pp. 148–51.

41 Buruma (1994), 'History on Trial', pp. 156–58.

42 Arendt (1963, 1951). Far from a 'genocidal monster', the pathetic figure of the captured Eichmann seemed for many to embody Arendt's phrase 'banality of evil'. See comments in recent edition of *Eichmann in Jerusalem: A Report on the Banality*

of Evil (London, 2006), with Preface by Amos Elon. Arendt added a postscript to later editions to respond to her critics.

43 See Shoshana Felman, 'Return of the Voice', in Shoshana Felman and Dori Laub, *Testimony: Crisis of Witnessing in Literature, Psychoanalysis and History* (New York, 1992).

44 Resnais's *Hiroshima mon Amour* is another key exemplar of modern memory work, which I will deal with, along with several other documentaries concerned with memory, especially malleable ones, but none have this same quality. But Marguerite Duras's script for *Hiroshima mon Amour* and some classic comic scripts, such as *Dr. Strangelove* on nuclear war, sustain a creative level throughout, unlike *The Journey*.

45 Jay Winter's Great War TV series for PBS/BBC had this quality succeeding beyond most memory documentaries; see accompanying text, Jay Winter and Blaine Baggett, *The Great War and the Shaping of the 20th Century* (New York, 1996).

46 It is significant that Martin Gilbert's book *Holocaust: A History of the Jews of Europe during the Second World War* (New York, 1986) should also include witness testimony and survivors' accounts – unlike previous academic histories (such as Hilberg's) it involves recall: experienced events.

47 Shoshana Felman's often-quoted analysis of *Shoah* does not directly focus on memory or even sites of memory. Her focus on Lanzmann's film is rather on witness and testimony and 'the voice'. See Felman, 'The Return of the Voice', in Felman and Laub (1992).

48 Claude Lanzmann, *Shoah* (New York, 1985), English edition, script, pp. 11, 33–34.

49 *Shoah*, script p. 89 (church sequence, pp. 85–90), and in Felman (1992).

50 The church where the dialogue took place had been used by the Nazis to hold Jews on their arrival in Chelmno, before a larger space was required; the Jews were then moved to the larger castle.

51 This attitude is betrayed by the remarks of some local women: they tell Lanzmann they had been jealous of Jewish girls who were 'too pretty', whilst they were still unmarried; see script of Shoah, references to Garlow, especially pp. 77–81.

52 *Shoah*, script, p. 91.

53 *Shoah*, script, p. 92. Like Lanzmann, Susan Griffin, *Chorus of Stones* (New York, 1992), rewrites events-without-a-witness into a witnessing, and then into a history that fuses traumas personal and public. The participants' memory, even its deadness, is precisely what must be challenged and transgressed.

54 Later, Peter Watkins in *The Journey* does use contemporary newsreel footage for media-critique, and some historical photographs of Hamburg and Hiroshima. This fourteen and a half hour film includes interspersed archival footage, enactment of events, interviews, textual and visual quotations relating to contemporary events. Whilst as a text the whole does not maintain the unity, quality or continuity of the other works I cite, it is an exemplary document of modern memory work, and comparable in the survivor witnesses from Leningrad, Hiroshima and Pacific testing; (note Emma Bierman's tearful testimony from Hamburg).

55 *Shoah*, script, pp. 103–08.

56 Felman (1992), Testimony.

57 Buruma's *Wages of Guilt* (1994), as in Lanzmann's film, deals with these three categories of participation in remembering the Shoah. Also Felman and Laub (1992).

58 Lanzmann, like the poet Peter Balakian (1997) writing about the Armenian genocide, concludes that blaming the victim is bound up with the culture of the perpetrators. The pathology of denial accompanies an attempt to achieve impunity or rehabilitation, as well as erasing traces of the event. Denial continues long after an initial shock. See also T. Garton-Ash, *A History of the Present: Essays, Sketches and Despatches from Europe in the 1990s* (London, 2000) on the Stasi.

59 In Chapater 14 I give an example from Khaldei's famous photograph of the Red Army in Berlin.

60 Martin Gilbert, for example (personal conversations).
61 See Cole (2000), pp. 110–20.
62 See James Young (1994). Similar 'sculptural' events on a mass, semi-official scale occurred elsewhere whilst some were bordering on the kitsch, some as extraordinary inventive 'counter-monuments'.
Languages of Remembrance from the Great War to the Present
63 See Winter (2017), pp. 152–53 and the mass poppy displays in images 6.15 and 6.16. He returns to comparing and integrating Holocaust images and memories within a larger frame of iconic representations of mass violence.
64 Much post-Holocaust fiction or faction has been justified as equally prosthetic, though equally problematic or banal. Before Spielberg, the *Schindler's Ark* story had become misappropriated, it was not only Hollywood film that commodified memory and created fake narratives. In 'Prosthetic memory', Alison Landsberg's *Prosthetic Memory: The Transformation of American Remembrance in the Age of Mass Culture* (New York, 2004) uses Spielberg's widely viewed commodity as an example of this type of representation uncritically, despite its inauthenticity. See Cole (2000), ch. 3, especially pp. 74–79. Whether as amplification or justification, Spielberg's Holocaust archive was created subsequently, complementing those in Washington and at Yad Vashem.
65 See Andreas Huyssen, *Present Pasts: Urban Palimpsests and the Future of Memory* (Stanford, 2003), pp. 65–71; Young in Crownshaw et al. (2010) ch.4, who compares the Berlin and New York competitions, pp. 81–85. I return to the plethora of memorial competitions below.
66 Cole (2000), ch.6.
67 Huyssen (2003), pp. 66–71; Young in Crownshaw et al. (2010), pp. 81–85.
68 See Cole (2000), Preface and *passim*.
69 Tim Ryback, 'Report from Dachau', *New Yorker* (3 August 1992).
70 See J. Young article in Crownshaw et al. (2010), pp. 81–85.
71 See Cole, 2006.
72 This infamous quip has been widely attributed (without specifics) to the Israeli diplomat and foreign minister, Abba Eban (it is claimed from the 1950s). However, in 1997, Edward Linenthal referenced this aphorism (nd) to an unpublished 'Reflection' (from Linenthal's text, nd, assumed date 1979) on the 1978 *President's Report on the Holocaust* and brought to his attention (see p. 277) by an Israeli historian, Yaffa Eliach. It is in a closed Yad Vashem private archive, so could not be accessed. In Linenthal's text, Eliach puts the phrase in quotation marks. E. T. Linenthal, *Recovering Memory: The Struggle to Establish the US Holocaust Museum* (New York, 1997), see p. 13. I have been unable to corroborate this alternative citation as the original usage of the quoted phrase. See also Jonathan Freedland, 'Finkelstein: The Row Rumbles on', *The Guardian* (19 July 2000), who still repeats the attribution of the aphorism to Eban, in his review article on Norman Finkelstein's book, though still without a date.
73 See James Young's article on the Berlin memorial competition 'Memory and the Monument', in Crownshaw et al., eds (2010), pp. 81–85; also Jane Kramer, *The Politics of Memory: Looking for German in the New Germany* (New York, 1996) on Lea Rosh and the Berlin competition, pp. 260–92. See Cole, (2000), section on Anne Frank. Cole plays down the role of Frank senior and focuses instead on those who saw the commercial potentialities of the diary.
74 See Cole, 2006.
75 Tim Ryback, 'Report from Dachau', *New Yorker* (3 August 1992). See my earlier discussion of the nationalization of exhibits at Auschwitz and the rationale.
76 See sections on Yad Vashem in Young (1994) and Cole (2000).
77 On the original construction, see Webber's essay in Swiebocka et al. (1993), and in Young (1994). See Cole's (2000) section on Auschwitz.
78 Yet here even the remains of the original barracks have been an arena of contest, some allowed to rot, some repaired or reconstructed for film sets.

79 I discuss these in a later chapter. Martin Gilbert, *Holocaust Journey* (New York, 1997).
80 Gilbert (1997), 'Introduction' and 'Epilogue', especially pp. 401–02.
81 See Young (1994), pp.81–89 and Reinhard Rűrup, ed., *Topography of Terror: Gestapo, SS* and *Reichssicherheitshauptamt on the 'Prinz-Albrecht-Terrain' A Documentation* (Berlin, 1987).
82 Gilbert (1997), especially pp. 401–02. Student Ros Morris's quote: "An image stays with me of a photograph of Hungarian Jews made to undress at the entrance in the wooded area leading to the gas chambers. Nothing has changed. The Hungarian deportation made its way, naked and defenceless, to death one hundred metres away. The trees stand still, taller and leafier, but the Hungarians have vanished".
83 More recently, should Guantanamo's camp X-Ray, scheduled in 2018 to be demolished by the US war department – be retained as a physical memorial to 'unusual and inhumane' treatment of those incarcerated, interrogated and imprisoned without trial there?
84 On Auschwitz tourism, see Cole (2000), pp. 74–79.
85 See Tim Ryback (1992). In Germany the plan for a McDonald's next to Dachau camp was prohibited – or at least distanced from it by several kilometres. See Young's discussion of the Mauthausen memorial (1994), pp. 92–100.
86 See Young (1994), pp. 92–100.
87 Ironically a similar controversy arose when the 1940s wooden barracks at Birkenau were reconstructed on site for a feature film (not Spielberg's, but an earlier venture). Spielberg's later construction of a gas chamber near the camp perimeter was widely criticized.
88 In W. G. Sebald, *Austerlitz* (London, 2002).

7

AIRWAR AND MEMORY

IMAGE 7.1 Iri and Toshi Maruki, *Hiroshima Panels 'II Fire'*, 1950. The poem written to accompany this panel describes the abysmal moment right after the explosion of the atomic bomb, when the world seemed to burst into an all-consuming sea of flames. Maruki Gallery for the Hiroshima Panels.

Vignette:
A Silence

Despite the victory parades, East and West, the spring and summer 1945 is a period of overwhelming silences. There is numbing denial, muted grieving and loss, silent starvation and wordless flight. In England, VJ Day arrived in August, but as a damp squib, an anti-climax after the relief of May.

I grew up in that age of forgetting – my grandfather, and later my father-in-law, did not want to recall or talk about their 1914–18 horrors, dreams that still plagued their sleep. And my father never talked about the top secret blueprints and the designs for new bombers he had handled, the same bombers used to mass bomb German cities in the mid-1940s; nor, till decades later, did my aunt talk about my uncle who had died returning, crashing in flames after flying one of them over Germany. My childhood home was totally destroyed by an incendiary bomb during the Blitz. It seemed quite unremarkable, and it was rarely mentioned. No one talked about it even long after the war. But I did hear the hushed tales of the refugees.

IMAGE 7.2 John Boorman, *Hope and Glory*, 1988. "Pauline ... Pauline, do you want some shrapnel?" The child is trying to comfort the girl who has just lost her mother and home after a night of bombing in the London Blitz.

It took twenty years before Kurt Vonnegut felt he could write about Dresden. Nor did the German prisoners of war we befriended after 1945 want to talk about the war – or the camps. My parents shielded me from images. As for the pictures of Bergen-Belsen, 'starvation' in Germany was, it was said, the problem. And there were the whispered stories from those fleeing. As in 1918, there was the phenomenon of mass corpselessness. There was a new kind of silent wilderness, not typically rural battlefields but rather the remnants of death and slave labour camps especially in Poland. Nothing left to bury. The silences were this time as much in soundless cities as in rural killing fields. But the voiceless sites of atrocity still existed, now largely undisturbed in the countryside in 1945, and in the ruins of the towns, such as the desert of central Birmingham I visited that spring.

The vast majority of the mass graves of 1945 were large city plots, like those in Leningrad or outside Berlin.[1] Existing cemeteries were greatly expanded, or in the Soviet cemetery in Berlin, newly created. Memorializing dead soldiers of the 'Thirty-one-year War' from Austria, to France, Belgium and Britain, to Canada and the Commonwealth becomes a continuous one. In a number of countries such as these the military war dead of 1939–45 are typically added to the local war memorials for 1914–18. The 'two wars' are symbolically merged into one. But almost always, and for a variety of reasons, the list of 'combatant' dead and missing on these memorials of 1945 is far smaller than after the Great War. There are some memorials to partisans and local massacres, especially in the Balkans, but there are very few civilian ones, and these are usually political – but even fewer for war resisters, conscientious objectors – or deserters. The civilian casualties in Japan, in Yugoslavia or the Soviet Union and even in parts of continental Europe were up to ten times higher in number than military dead. Russian, Polish and Yugoslav losses, both military and civilian, were immense: but any memorials to *collateral* in World War Two would, in effect, be counter-monuments. Whilst formal memorials to World War Two non-combatants are few, their 'requiems' were written by musicians, poets and artists – by Dmitri Shostakovich and Anna Akhmatova in the Soviet Union and by Benjamin Britten in England, whose music and poetry weaves the two wars together in a protest against totalism and atrocity, into a single cry of anger.[2]

As for the tens of millions of the disappeared, they rarely and only slowly acquire monuments, or even names, at the death camps and the other memorials. And even those memorialized names change: Russian, Polish, Roma, Slav, Jewish, German. Given the extensive politicization and revision of death statistics, and of the wording on monuments and memorials, there was as much mass self-censorship and denial as state repression of memory.

These fragmented memories were also the result of World War Two becoming constituted as mobile war. From a global perspective, highly mechanized military action was just as much in the air and on or under the sea as in the huge roving land-battles. In such key tank battles, in the desert or deep in Russia – in the region around Kursk, Belgorod or Stalingrad – the scale of operations was vast, and, as a result, the silence of memory represented a different wasteland of experience. Simultaneously, whilst whole cities were affected, the losses were either at a far distance from home, or else on an often static 'civilian front'. It was one which had become the new combat zone and where, among other things, the war was conducted and fought metaphorically, and actually, across or over civilian bodies, not least in rape. In the industrialized genocides, beyond civilian deaths from starvation and epidemics, there was widespread targeted mass killing on both sides. The Nazis began with interning or executing political opponents in Plotzensee and Buchenwald. In Stalin's Russia, there were strong parallels in gulags or in military excesses such as the massacre of Polish officers in Katyn. Bombardments, vast sieges (e.g. Leningrad) and battles fought on the ground, through the city streets, or from the air, meant that the imagery of military action, embedded in memory, was no longer static as it had been, at least on the Western Front between 1914 and 1918.

In many target areas by 1945 war would be remembered as urbicide: city death, and not just from the air. The civilian experience in World War Two was dominated by intrusion – flight or fear: of Blitz and '*katastrophe*'; of deportation, the camps or imprisonment; of being trapped, in cellars or sewers (e.g. Warsaw, Hamburg, Dresden, Berlin); or sheltering in the underground railway stations in London. There are Henry Moore's sombre sarcophagi depicted in his prophetic drawings of sleepers in the subway: they doze between life and death; all are mummy-like images.

But there is also East and West, this sense of being politically trapped, waiting in terror for the air-raid sirens; the visit at dawn, the arrest of the informer, and the transports from the *Umschlagplatz* or other assembly places such as Drancy or to Westerbork. The victims (even in transit) to Chelmno, Sobibor, Birkenau, Treblinka, Belzec or Maidanek were already trapped. Others were enslaved in brutal forced labour camps, such as Mauthausen in Austria, with its vast network of grim prisons, mines and factories around Linz – still juxtaposed, then as now, with pastoral 'normality'. The escapees, mostly Russian prisoners of war, were hunted down and shot 'like rabbits' in the fields around the camps.

Here too the memories of such horrors, including those replicated in the camps of the Pacific (China, Malaysia, Korea, Burma and Japan), were repressed. These were the new 'memories' of 'post-war' Europe and Asia, memories silenced once more, delayed, repressed or forgotten.

In the war booms and pre-war memory-booms of the 1930s and 1940s, the truths of 1914–18 had, not least through veteran narratives, gradually begun to educate the European 'home front' about modern war. But in 1945, repression of memory represents more a mass civilian response than a military one. After 1940, such self-suppression of war experiences is almost reversed. In Hemingway's story of *Soldier's Home* in 1919, it was the veteran unable to deal with his own war experiences. Now it is the surviving soldier who returns to the silence and unexpected horrors of the home.[3] It is their plight, that of the civilian families, that has become almost unimaginable and impossible to deal with – it represents a kind of traumatization of return. As in 1618–48 or Goya's Spain, the civilian has become a veteran of war; but in 1945 the form is entirely new.

An ability to mourn

As I have argued, it was especially women's bodies that became a battleground in this war: this continued as a psychological contest; in Berlin, for example, the experience and the individual and collective denial of the trauma, also revealed the power and extent of official censorship and repression in occupied Europe. It silenced hundreds of thousands of true accounts, especially from April/May 1945. This can only partly be explained by an inability not only to mourn, but also to mourn others. It continued in the Pacific. The pressure of denial was so strong that even fifty years later only an ambiguous sympathy for the German civilian victims rose to the surface in some among the populations of the former Allies.

These mass rapes remain one of the largest 'untold stories' of war: not only in central and eastern Europe, but also in Korea, China and other parts of Asia and across the Pacific. Even in Germany itself, that memory was suppressed. As with the Holocaust, a personal numbing of experience induced by trauma or brutalization was seen as a sign of one's own partly or wholly lost humanity. Perhaps as was widely said, it was 'better to forget', as the daughter said of a survivor of Chelmno, Simon Podchelbnik, when interviewed by Lanzmann.

But state memory-suppression systematically collaborated with this painful process, and produced self-censorship. This was often a collective silence of ostensible convenience: mourning was now irrelevant. Some even accepted suffering as post-hoc justifications for the catastrophe, even articulated as a self-admonishing justification that 'we deserved it'. Other survivors of these traumas could, and often, did choose death.

Part of the revival of cultural resistance in Europe was rooted in intentional memory projects that worked to confront such silences and to overcome 'psychic numbing'. One response to urbicide, or the Shoah, was a refusal to allow or accept such emotional paralysis and an erasure of memory. That erasure was a social fact not only in Germany, but also in a global diaspora of refugees, exiles and survivors, and challenged the memorializing project. The syndrome was similar to the 'death in life' responses to trauma described in Robert Jay Lifton's several studies of survivors. It took decades to develop acknowledgement of the depth of this repression. Both in and beyond continental Europe of the 1940s silence was the default, if not normal, response to the shocks and emotional scarring. In much of Asia enforced forgetting, censorship and collaborative denial were the norm for decades. Inevitably, in such deeply traumatized societies, forgetting and memory co-exist in these unresolved tensions, over several generations.

Central to much memory work in Germany was the thesis that the pain of such mourning was not sublimated but repressed. The syndrome first propounded by Alexander and Margarethe Mitscherlich in the 1960s focuses on the ability or 'inability to mourn'. This included both the Shoah and the deaths of the war years, especially in the bombed cities. Their thesis suggested that before society's acknowledgement of, for example, the city destruction of those years came the need for personal grieving, and an individual's coming to terms with the past: 'a permission to mourn'. They argue that reasons to forget are multiple and complex and are not confined to psychic numbing.

The Mitscherlichs' post-Freudian concept of an 'inability to mourn' was important because it gave larger meaning to the blocking off of remembered trauma, and it was a theme returned to at the end of the twentieth century by the critic W. G. Sebald. To talk of a generalized collective repression may be inappropriate,[4] but whilst an 'inability to mourn' may be the wrong term to describe much of this, it is true that there was no public debate on the bombing experience in Germany until the 1980s, or even the 1990s, and that even this belated response was muted. But it is also clear in line with Mitscherlich that some Germans refused to remember the raids or were unable to mourn their civilian dead, numbed by the sheer horror, intensity and scale of the experience.[5] But for others this was a self-repression, either a socially imposed silence or a determination to move on, to live with an unconscious forgetting. For many Germans, for example, it was deemed politically inappropriate to share a common 'victimhood' as a nation. To that extent postnational realignment offered a healing space.

Metamorphosen was a remarkable piece of music gestated by the ageing Austro-German Richard Strauss after hearing of the destruction of Dresden, in the final months of World War Two, and finished in the aftermath, before his death. He confronts the cultural impasse, caught between the weight of the past (3,000 years of 'German' culture) and memories of the achievements in music – as against, in particular, the privileging the present ('Twelve years of criminal rule'; The Third Reich), and the new forces shaping the future. Far more than the destruction of '*Kultur*' his creation poses the question: is there an end to cultural memory? Is this a music for the ruins? The culture of shock expressed in the German term *Betroffen*: astonishment, comprehended war and environmental crisis, consumerist culture from North America and also weapons of mass destruction. It led some to moods of terminal despair and to a debate of an end, not only to history, but also to a wider civilizational memory.

For those beyond the victim/perpetrator syndrome, a lack of interest in such German narratives outside that country indicate both an ambivalence and a saturation point of second-hand witnessing after the Holocaust and other represented catastrophes.[6] After Rotterdam, Coventry and Warsaw, research and testimony confirm that there *were* indeed widespread public doubts, but their articulation was repressed or largely silenced. Unlike in 1915–18, moral accounts, even condemnation, of aerial bombings were rare in the 1940s. After 1945, the amoral or non-judgemental character of the accounts persisted on all sides, even where some freedom of discourse existed. Outside Germany, ethical debate about aerial bombardments of cities is sparse – even at the outset the literature of air war between 1940 and 1945 was largely lacking. Even Virginia Woolf in her acutely postnational transatlantic 'Thoughts on Peace in an Air-raid' (1940), her humanist witness to the Blitz, is notably non-judgemental. Though in the UK, public figures such as Bishop Bell and Vera Brittain were free to express moral outrage at British indiscriminate terror bombing of civilians, first in Germany then in Japan, they were exceptional. The memorialization of Bomber Command in Britain has remained ambivalent and contested: its Hyde Park monument sober and non-triumphalist.

In the Third Reich, it would have been (and was) an act of extreme political courage to raise similar doubts about German *Luftwaffe*'s bombings of London, Rotterdam, Warsaw or anywhere else.[7] The German experience of civilian losses of the 1943–45 raids, although vast, were only widely discussed in domestic settings rather than in public.[8] Nevertheless there was much talk of the city bombings privately in German homes, especially within families after 1945; some of these stories I heard in the 1950s.

Bambi to Belsen 1943–45

Vignette:
'Bambi' and Belsen: Memories from the Camps

The Disneyfication of Europe was significantly delayed by World War Two. I had to wait until 1944 for my most memorable Christmas present. Although fear of gas attacks had subsided after 1940, the rocket attacks of 1944 revived them, and to replace my standard issue, I was given a Mickey Mouse gas mask. There was still the terrible smell of rubber, and when trying to breathe, an oppressing sense of asphyxiation, but at least it looked like a toy.

Yanks, as well as gum, comics, nylons, had arrived in the UK by 1943 – when kids like me met them and were called 'smarty pants'. But Walt Disney's Bambi, in colour, did not arrive in Europe with them – it took two more years of convoys before it arrived and immediately after, it was shown in local cinemas. Mine not until early June 1945. A group of us, with mums, were taken to see it. But parents were concerned: would children panic during the forest fire (image 7.3)? Or get upset at the death of Bambi's mother? We were marched out at that point, by mum's, in hats, into the foyer – for me as I was almost eight – very reluctantly. We were then allowed back in for the film's ending. And then – more film: newsreel, not in colour, followed.

IMAGE 7.3 Walt Disney Studios, *Bambi*, 1942. The fire images of Bambi's ordeal were deemed too worrisome for European audiences before 1945, with cities in flames and heavy censorship. It went on general release after May 1945 with huge success, having had limited success in the USA.

It was black and white pictures of a fence. Cows in a field, a laconic commentary, and a familiar voice. There was barbed wire, emaciated figures, tattered striped pyjamas, skeletal forms in caps – and many corpses – bulldozed piles of dead into a vast ditch (Image 7.4). Bodies stretched like marble forms. I had never seen anything like this despite the Blitz.

IMAGE 7.4 A Hitchcock and S. Bernstein, *Memory of the Camps*, 1985. (Film footage from 1945.) These scenes, filmed on the liberation of the Belsen death camps, were seen in shorter segments in Britain and elsewhere after May 1945, with official authorization. In *Shoah*, a survivor comments that such corpses appeared 'like basalt'.

As I later discovered this footage was of the first 'liberated' camp by the British and Canadians in the West, part directed by Hitchcock; it was at Bergen-Belsen (Anne Frank's death place). Filmed in May 1945, it was shown in all British cinemas, but without prior notice. So parents of young children had no warning. Once back at home, I asked my parents: "Who were all those very thin people and why?" "Well people have no food in Germany at the moment", was the reply, which was a true, but partial answer. Starvation, typhus, maltreatment was not the whole answer!

I rediscovered these scenes of the Holocaust as a student, with a shock of recognition. In 1959 the first feature documentary about the camps was shown. We used it in a film series organized at Oxford. It was Alain Resnais's *Nuit et Brouillard* (*Night and Fog*). The phrase 'Nacht und Nebel' was painted on the cattle cars. The mass burials for example were among those I had seen in a Gaumont cinema in the summer of 1945.

Decades later, I met and heard firsthand Sir Brian Urquart's personal account of being the first senior armed officer to arrive there (accidentally). At Bergen-Belsen camp, he arrested the Commandant, Kramer. Urquart was already behind the lines and in advance of the allied forces; their mission was to find a German atomic research lab in Celle nearby. They found some laboratories. But they only found the site of Belsen by chance, because of the stench of death.

In 1985, I watched a much longer PBS Frontline version (Bernstein) of Alfred Hitchcock's original complete, scripted and directed film of the extensive 1945 Belsen footage, 'Memory of the Camps', it was an edited version produced for American TV. It included over a further hour of horror beyond the 20 minutes approved for screening by the British government in May 1945. Was the delay in showing *Bambi* a political decision, as was that to publicly and widely show the film of Belsen? The scenes of the camp were introduced with a commentary that was also, effectively, a retrospective justification of the war. But whether *Bambi* was a case of censorship is a question related to how appropriate the film would have been with Europe's cities on fire. As an initially unsuccessful US film of 1942, it was hardly a morale booster. It might not have made it to Britain on the Atlantic convoys anyway; there were more essential cargo to avoid the U-boats. Modern memorists might discover whether Bambi's fire images were indeed considered inappropriate for a Europe in flames.

German guilt: remembering the bombing and Nazi crimes

If bombing memories were both politically repressed and collaboratively silenced in the 1940s and 1950s, it risked ignoring the very real emotional scars of the 1940s. If it took far too long, in public life, to enable any acknowledgement of trauma in a 'civic' sense, the repercussions were unclear. Even if depicted by some Germans as being 'punishment deserved', the problem remained. Urbicide had been justified, before and after 1945, as an allied retribution for German (or Nazi) crimes. But at what point were the limits of Just War transgressed? It took almost fifty years for the widespread acknowledgement of the problematics of strategic bombing: a recognition that saturation bombing as a weapon of terror was cruel, and in some views criminal, in both domestic and international law. It was often even militarily counter-productive as some critical research evidence suggested. The morality of an indiscriminate destruction of a population that as a clear majority had not actively supported the Nazi rise to power, or voted for Hitler a decade earlier, was questionable.

I have suggested that one context for this debate was the concerns about German re-armament after 1950, and in the nuclear Cold War, that was a key political factor. This background is essential for any understanding and critique of memory, and long silences, in West Germany about the Nazi period, and of the role of official 'memory' in East Germany. This suppression not only concerned the Shoah, but also the overall cataclysmic of character of World War Two itself. Memory of allied bombings was a latent issue in the cultural memory that continued long beyond the 1960s. One reccurring problem was a fear of, and a risk of, encouraging a German victimology.

Later, decades after the 1960s, in an 'enlightened' Germany this ambivalence still engendered an understandable reluctance of many Germans to claim or assert 'victimhood'. It was feared that the appearance of such a claim to victimhood was one that might be taken up by extremists, neo-Nazi deniers, or apologists, and could suggest a moral equivalence in acknowledging both urbicide and holocaust memory. But fears that this would be claimed as having an equivalence, in German experiences, with the memory of the Shoah, or replace any responsibility for genocide was exaggerated. Rather than the view that the guilt, or a German collective acquiescence in genocide, was largely consensual ('willing executioners'): another version was needed. But given the paucity and fragmentation of resistance to Nazi rule after 1936, and especially after 1940, a selective relativization in remembering would be a more acceptable path for wider society.

This was a political and ethical minefield; charting it worried Germans, especially on the Left, but also external onlookers. For the Liberal or Social Democrats the elision of war and genocide in totalism was made theoretically legitimate by political and social analysts. Nevertheless it remained politically dangerous in national terms. But the alternative risk foreseen by the oppositional German Left, both old and new in the 1950s, 1960s and later, was that there would be a popular counter-reaction to the suppression of realities of a very real German suffering. The memories of the mass bombings of the civil population and the atrocities of the last months of the war, not least those committed by the Red Army on German soil, and the forced evacuation of many millions of Germans from the east of both the Oder and Elbe were established history. To deny this, history could be exploited to support a new national victim myth, as it had in the 1920s and 1930s. In any case if not actively supported, others argued, the '*normalization*' of the suffering of people's experience of urbicide in Germany was equally unhealthy and dangerous.

However shocking any calculated blockage of public memory appears, it is explicable given this political bind – and may even be existentially necessary; it enables victims to survive mentally and emotionally in a transformed national context, further complicated by the post-1990 reunification. As in other societies, forgetting is chosen as a lesser evil; the guilt which would be entailed by a 'self' or collective confrontation with the ghosts of past would involve too high psychological and personal costs, as well as political risks. Such repression of events, in any case, may have totally different meanings for different families, communities and individuals – and societies.

In France this insight was utilized by Rousso's *Vichy Syndrome* and by Marcel Ophuls's film of French collaboration and denial, *The Sorrow and the Pity* (1969). Both documents focus on a shared forgetting or distortion of the past, of the France of the 1940s.[9] The external source of such silencing, qualitatively distinguishes it from the psychological repression of the Mitscherlichs' study. But in the light of the interactions between personal and social amnesia, this enforced forgetting becomes all the more predictable, even understandable. French collaboration and Vichy illustrate the fact that it is not only individuals who 'forget'. Whole communities forget, or deny the events they have witnessed or acquiesced in: they close ranks against the 'whistleblowers' whose refusal to forget is a public act of resistance. Such individuals, often acted alone, as courageous witnesses to atrocity: civil society actors driven by a moral imperative to reveal a past suppressed. The Dutch journalist and historian Ian Buruma sought several such witnesses of the 1940s in both Germany and Japan – in ostensibly 'normal' towns. In Bavaria, the 'naughty girl', Anja Rosmus, revealed the unspoken guilt of her whole community in Regensburg. She obstinately and bravely challenged the media, the collaborators and the corporate suppressors of memory.[10]

In Chapter 8, I return to examples of modern amnesia in Austria, Spain and Japan. Such examples of the public and private manipulation or censorship of memory are nothing new in descriptions of twentieth-century history. But, as in France and Spain, consensual repression – for example, in Japan – is a subject only recently and partly analysed. Continuing in East Germany until and after reunification in the 1990s and other parts of the Eastern bloc, since 1945, such blocking out of the past was only in part an enforced response under totalism. But both Nazi and Stalinist state repression had also fostered a shared self-suppression of memory: silencing of experience of the past accompanied intentional and voluntary forgetting that was highly personal. This model can be applied to many other amnesiac societies, including liberal democracies in the West, fostered by both state elites and public media, and then endorsed by social pressure.

It is clear that remembering the Shoah and the Nazi period in the two Germanies has been continually evolving over the long term, with a nuanced narrative; it had a wide range of different inflections and themes, often uncovering new dimensions, and is highly politicized and contested. Emerging over many decades, such revelations are often detached from war memories. The complex recovery of memories can teach a great deal by studying their evolution. Their cultural importance lies particularly in their relationship to the regaining of both moral stature and political identity amongst Germans in the half century after the war. This recovery was crucial for both Germans themselves, and in the eyes of the wider world, and especially for the society of Europe as a whole, in which the German-speaking parts played such a key role.

Much German literature after 1950 deals with this 'working through' of these memories of wartime – Boll, Bochert, Grass and Sebald are just a few examples that signify the existence of a much broader genre – and I focus here on only one, a writer for whom remembering is such a central theme. A major attempt to deal with such 'coming to terms' with these unresolved issues is W. G. Sebald, in his Zurich lecture, *Airwar and Literature*.[11] He stresses a huge imbalance in public discourse on the Holocaust, and the air war in Germany the half century after 1945; it was one which was perhaps influenced by the 'inability to mourn'. Sebald accuses the literary elites of refusing to discuss the Allied bombing – thereby blocking adequate remembrance and acknowledgement by all sides in and beyond Germany. Although Sebald was born in 1944, and was not of the generation that witnessed and/or experienced the catastrophe directly, his reflections are of a German 'in exile', and far from victimology.

After amnesia: Sebald and Kiefer

Like the art of Anselm Kiefer, W. G. Sebald's life and work is symptomatic of the long-term effects of an acute crisis of a post-war sensibility across Europe already described, especially in Germany and France. This is invoked both in his prose (*Rings of Saturn, Austerlitz*),[12] and his magnetic critical writing such as his lectures (*On the Natural History of Human Destruction*).[13] These essays deal with acknowledging Germany's civilian catastrophes. Sebald's work notoriously brings together two vast traumas, and at the same time two sites of modern mass killing – *the camps* and *the destroyed cities*. One example is his visit to the camp at Theresienstadt (Terezin) north of Prague and another is the return to bombed sites, especially Frankfurt-am-Main. It was one I witnessed when still in ruins in the 1950s.

To rebuild German cities was to cover those traces, and Sebald uses photographs to suggest there are lacunae, absences, spaces in the German psyche of the ruins.[14] Later in this chapter, and in Chapter 14, I will return to the issue of memory images and photographs: Examining the mass bombing of German cities was represented in much of German *Trümmer* (ruins) literature of the 1950s, the start of 'coming to terms' with the 1940s. The authors who wrote of these incinerated cities were mostly returnees, they wrote after the fact. It was not a literature of those living through the bombings themselves. For those rarer accounts which document direct narratives, testimonies of the bombs, we must turn elsewhere. Forty years after the events, as an example, Peter Watkins filmed moving interviews with survivors of the Hamburg raids for his film *The Journey*. Even in the 1980s these memories still seem scattered and private – and not easily accessible.[15]

When Sebald returns to the topic of aerial bombardment, his ethical stance is clear.[16] His argument is to bring the re-memorializing of these events into the same conceptual and territorial space as other atrocities. Regardless of statistics, urbicide and modern genocide are one of a piece, part of the process of total war being turned inwards against civilians, both by external combatants and the state attacking, enslaving or conscripting its citizens. Civilians in prisons and camps were as much targets as were people bombed in cities elsewhere, and Sebald like Watkins, Lanzmann and Griffin, personalizes the process. Defying the technological rationality of mass death planned by using the railway timetables from 1914 to 1945, Sebald images as memories, such mechanical methods of separation, deportation, exile and death, and not least the personal goodbyes – the last glimpses, the attempts to contact again. Sebald constructs and deconstructs such places of loss: a railway station, a torture chamber, a barracks at Theresienstadt (Terezin), a prison cell, a shop. As well as the act of remembering itself, as with *Shoah*, we re-visit the past. In acknowledging trauma, the Holocaust and die Katastrophe are melded in the reciprocal process of totalism and political intrusion. However problematic politically, and difficult to apply practically, Sebald's moral position, even if couched in fatalist and existential terms, is hardly a hidden one. These are metaphors for a memory that was terminated at the ramp or railhead at Birkenau, in actuality, or later in the killing fields in Cambodia, Rwanda or Srebrenica, or in prophesy – in the skies over New York – or at a nuclear submarine base in Bangor, Maine.

These are the concealed narratives of modern remembering that authors such as Susan Griffin explore in prose. We can re-make the story or, as she suggests, re-assemble our own 'journey'. Through our own scrapbook of faded images the past can be re-interpreted, re-enlarged, placed in our wallet, shown – or not shown – at the border, and revealed, or not, to grandchildren or others. Through murky photographs, or concealed as cosmetic items or the dusty objects left in the shop window that Sebald found on his return to the 'city' at Theresienstadt (Terezin), he creates a phantom world that sits between the future and experienced life, between purposeful invention and studied recollection, between knowledge and guess-work – or dreams. It also challenges many of the conventions of previous autobiographic sensibility – as if experiencing was in itself a pretence, a chimera, an illusion. Any failure to re-make the past is our own failure; a failure of moral imagination and political responsibility, and one that is unable to acknowledge a past – our past. It is the unhappy burden of memory work to re-constitute it.

In his aspiration to use such depictions of the same totalistic past, Anselm Kiefer is the pre-eminent artist of German memory, indeed perhaps of all European memory for the later twentieth century. Deeply marked by growing up, like Sebald, in Germany after the Third Reich, his painting focuses on the historic complications of Nazism and the German civilizational past. As expressions of modern memorizing, Anselm Kiefer's Holocaust art is deeply felt, and also, as in his Hitler salutes, in scenes in photographs and printed self-portraits (1967–72), they express a unique personal angle on Fascism. Unsurprisingly, his pseudo-identifications were ones that at times created public discomfort and outcry, not least in Germany.

As in Sebald's return to Theresienstadt, or in the use of mnemonic objects, in Kiefer's art the everyday becomes the exceptional and memorable. His paintings are remarkable for their use of physical materials: debris, detritus, broken pots and shards of glass, matting, straw, metal, wire, ashes, soil, burnt trees, charcoal, sand – this is the mnemonic wasteland, the battlefield, the ruins, the remnants of a death camp. In the tangible physicality of Kiefer's images, to use Des Pres's phrase, he represents 'an excremental assault' on the viewer. Kiefer's allegories rewrite the primordial landscapes of destruction as well as the specifics of a German disaster. No anodyne collage of objects – the elements that stand out are inanimate – constituted memory: ash, hair, domestic items and lead. Occasionally a poppy, a cornflower, sheaves of wheat or sunflowers give some relief from trauma, and the Margarethe's Aryan golden hair is symbolized by straw in the series created around the theme of Paul Celan's (1944) holocaust poem, *Death Fugue*. In his anti-militarist pieces the icons of the burnt books, or the 'battleships in the bath tub', are juxtaposed with empty 'spaces'.[17] Some of Kiefer's major works, and his installations are, like Sebald's, reconstructed sites of camps, torture chambers and other structures littered with battlefield objects, but also haunted by absences and by memories – fragments of that German or 'Modern' past. As it is in the post-Hitler time, it focuses on disconnecting and reassembling the cultural idioms of Nazism, so that Albert Speers' concepts of triumphalist Nazi architecture become designs for mausoleums, or crematoria – 'great ruins' for posterity – or a charnel house framed by Shulamith's black and ashened hair (Celan's '*Death Fugue*').

Yet, as I have suggested, there is one odd caesura in this extraordinary memorializing oeuvre. His work marks a somewhat odd historical leap from the nineteenth-century 'Kultur' and the major German intellectuals before 1914 seamlessly straight to 1933 and the catastrophe of the Nazi era. Much of Anselm Kiefer's art retains the critical bite of a Grosz or a Dix – but in his apocalyptic vision we move from the nineteenth century of Bismark, Hegel, Wagner and Götterdämmerung direct to the rise of the Third Reich and the new Valhalla of Speer after 1930. It presents a seamless evolution, as if neither the catastrophic Great War, nor the creative space of the Weimar Republic intervened. Perhaps they do not quite fit Kiefer's intellectual or aesthetic scheme of continuity. This is especially odd as one can clearly link his work to the oppositional masterpieces of German Expressionism; indeed, it seems clear that there is in Kiefer, a precise, if unexplained 'memory gap'.

Those events – the Shoah, the appalling destruction of cities, the obscene slaughter and immense suffering on the Eastern Front – that dominate so much

IMAGE 7.5 Anselm Kiefer, *Margarethe*, 1981. Kiefer's series based on Paul Celans' poem, *Death Fugue*, (1945) describes the inter-relationships of Margarethe, an Aryan, mistress of a camp commandant, Shulamith, a Jewess, and 'death' (a "Meister aus Deutschland"). It depicts a landscape of war, with ashes, the ashen colour of Shulamith's burnt hair, the wheatlike corn blonde of Margarethe's hair, also now burning. The wheat (or straw) hair, as the bars across the picture, could denote both the imprisonment (Celan was himself a concentration camp survivor) and division, but also regeneration (of wheat's re-growth) out of Germany's post-Holocaust war-torn bloodied soil. Doris and Donald Fisher Collection at the San Francisco Museum of Art. Copyright: Anselm Kiefer Photograph: Katherine Du Tel.

of his work are alarmingly decontextualized. A shaping event, '*a rehearsal*', the gestation, in and after 1914–18, is blotted out in his seamless German nightmare. By erasing the radical innovative and progressive culture that arose out of war – the carnage of 1914–18 – one that continued oppositionally, even after 1933, until it was crushed by the Nazis 1934–38, Kiefer bypasses immensely important and intrinsically German work.

It is this critical output which I have linked precisely to *the birth of a modern, more transcendent memory*: if this is omitted from Kiefer's own expressionist narrative, the culture and critical genius of Weimar Germany and its intellectual courage and creativity, not least in the Annales and Frankfurt schools, the outrage and innovation of early German expressionism, is bypassed. Given its continuity with the deeply expressionist character of Kiefer's own art, this presents a continuing puzzle that still needs to be critically unravelled, not least because of the importance of Kiefer's own role in the tradition's continuity.

'The Hiroshima Panels'

With the unexpected scale of the vast bombings of Japanese and German and other cities, art, poetry and writing after 1940 was forced to address a new set of war imageries, and memory of trauma. The start of the nuclear arms race, despite a prevailing public silence, was also a setting for the conscious artistic construction beyond Picasso's *Guernica* (1937) of new and classic memory pieces about war. The so-called *Hiroshima Panels* of the 1950s–1970s are the prime example. The Left-wing painters Iri and Toshi Maruki are foremost amongst nuclear memory recorders, their ambitious work falling across boundaries and between genres – the panels are neither highbrow nor lowbrow, not categorically popular art or fine art, nor of East alone or of West. Symbolically such pluralist, cross-cultural, certainly postnational art of the Marukis, by touching on so many modern tragedies, including the Holocaust, encapsulates that painful and controversial birth of a new 'modern' Japanese memory work: it was one that challenged denial.

Iri being at the epicentre within the first twenty-four hours to search, and Toshi a few days later, were both deeply traumatized by the atomic bomb. They were so numbed that they could not paint or draw 'what they saw' immediately. Theirs was truly a memorial art out of atrocity, re-representing the scenes when Iri had gone to the sites in the week after. He was looking for relatives, dead or alive. Then with Toshi, he helped bring out the wounded (there is a self-portrait with sketches of this). Seeing the horror at first hand, the Marukis prepared after 1945 to paint their 'truth': what they had seen of the Hiroshima bombings, and could then eventually recall. In their own words they had seen 'tens of thousands of bodies, human forms, alive and dead and dying' – 'ghosts'. The Marukis obsessively sketched each other for months before starting the panels. For long periods after the bomb they continued to draw each other nude to help continue to recapture the experience of both whole and broken human forms after the atomic holocaust, as they prepared the larger work of the huge panel paintings.[18]

Initially part of the Communist wing of the Japanese peace movement, they had abandoned that affiliation by the 1960s. But the stigma of the earlier association always remained, even though their work clearly transcended the political and ideological division of Left and Right. Whilst also combining East and West stylistically (both artists' training was cosmopolitan), they continued different traditions; European fine art, and Japanese brush painting. In the fusion they found a universally accessible popular language.

From Hiroshima, they moved artistically to other sites of Japanese 'forgetting', including Nagasaki, Okinawa and then to many more over the decades and later beyond Japan. These included Japan's own nuclear radiation catastrophes and the irradiated *Lucky Dragon* voyage,[19] and victims of US testing. The Marukis in search of remembered events knowingly painted clearly controversial themes as part of the historic sequences of the *Hiroshima Panels*. Going far beyond national, cultural traditions, the *Panels* warn of global apocalypse, whilst still facing particular ghosts in the Japanese past. By provoking public outrage, the Hiroshima panels represent part of a critical alternate trend also expressed in several Japanese novels, that is in ethical forms essentially pacifist and profoundly critical of collective violence. They depict maltreatment of victims, Americans, Koreans and Chinese, and not least those of the massacres in China. In *Crows*, they controversially depicted Korean unburied dead, or left for dead, in the wasteland of the destroyed city

For over four decades, their work linked transnational memories of Okinawa, occupied China and the Pacific testing to other crimes including the Nazi camps. In the context of memory of trauma, even those Japanese artists and novelists who had not directly experienced the effects of the bomb at Hiroshima or at close quarters were numbed by shock. But it was those Japanese, such as the Marukis, who were able to convert the trauma of an atomic experience, through images beyond national identity, and who could, to some degree, universalize its reality.

Atomic silencing: after Pikadon

As for representing the Atomic initiation worldwide, especially in the USA, public reaction to these first uses of the bombs on 6 and 9 August was extraordinarily muted. Official responses were carefully orchestrated: the media remained largely dependent on limited official information about the effects. This was long delayed from public availability and heavily censored, as exemplified by the fact that film footage and scientific information of Hiroshima and Nagasaki eventually released to Columbia University, was delayed for fifteen, twenty or even twenty-five years (1970).[20] Initial Western figures often wildly underestimated the extent of the casualties and radiation effects, though independent bodies such as the International Red Cross, as well as Japanese physicists, attempted to redress the balance. But the full impact of the nuclear arms race was only gradually understood, and acknowledged. After 1953, the physical implications and symptoms of the H-bomb tests and increasing global radiation levels were beginning to be publicized. But before that John Hersey's *Hiroshima*[21] account of the, by later standards, relatively tiny atomic bomb of 6 August was the main popular publication about the bomb. Its powerful eye-witness accounts had more long-term public impact than perfunctory news reports. In the aftermath, US authorities only slowly released segments of documentary footage previously suppressed, and gave heavily censored accounts of the effects, and the research role of the non-therapeutic A-bomb 'hospital'.

Even photography as evidence was limited, much of it without showing human physical damage. Some survivors' drawings appeared later, and a series of photo books were published in Japan.[22] Only later did such imagery emerge, more widely in art, as did the *Hiroshima Panels* (not on canvas). These first went on tour outside Japan in the 1960s, when the documentary '*Hiroshima 1945*' was made available. This was followed by the research of Robert Jay Lifton, the work of Robert Jungk (*Brighter than a Thousand Suns*) and Resnais's major international feature film, *Hiroshima mon Amour* (1959) with Marguerite Duras's script. The heroine reminds her Japanese lover:

> Listen to me. I know something else. It will begin all over again. Two hundred thousand dead. Eighty thousand wounded. In nine seconds. These figures are official. It will begin all over again. It will be ten thousand degrees on the earth. Ten thousand suns, they will say. The asphalt will burn. Chaos will prevail. A whole city will be raised from the earth and fall back in ashes.[23]

These works helped provide a critical context in the 1950s, which stimulated other productions. The first films refer directly to the initial images and photographs of atomic death. In the opening of *Hiroshima mon Amour*, there are long slow scenes which provide metaphors of the bomb's effects: beads of sweat on the lovers' backs that imitate photographs of the keloid scars on the skin of the atomic victims (Image 7.6).

Such images of effects were first seen in the photographic collections, and in the atomic film stills, made public in the late 1940s, followed by film of the tests. By 1952, some of these were being displayed in the new visitors' museum at Hiroshima, but it took a decade for their distribution and the Marukis' art, the oral accounts and Hershey's book to become widespread.

At Hiroshima and later at Nagasaki, and other non-atomic sites, oral testimonies from individual survivors were collected and published, as well as accounts describing

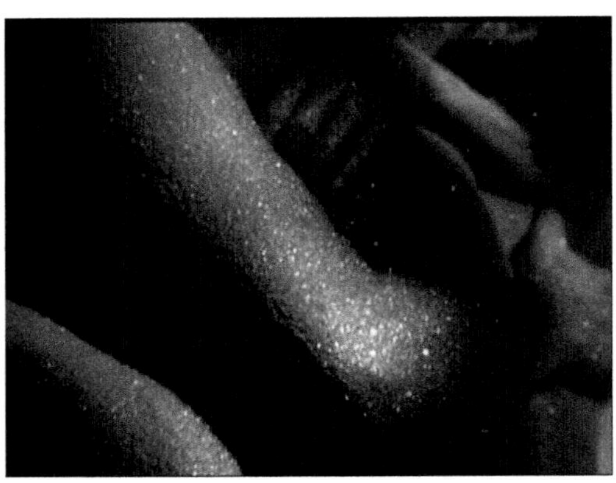

IMAGE 7.6 Alain Resnais, *Hiroshima mon Amour*, 1959. Are these lovers or victims? The lovers' bodies, the beads of sweat as metaphor, seem to imitate the bodies in pain of the atomic bomb victims, as they discuss the reality of the event revisited.

the lives of atomic survivors, the *Hibakusha*. Individual stories of victims such as Sadako and her paper cranes became publicized. Scientific documents were slowly released in Japan about both the bomb and some medical accounts of the physical suffering. Subsequently these multiple sources were analysed by Lifton, so that the psychic effects of the bomb could be independently assessed. The concept of atomic 'psychic numbing' was comparative, linking survivors 'death in life' – after the Bombs – to other collective trauma, including the European Holocaust.[24]

Such as it was, the critical public response in Japan, the USA and Europe was notably influenced by these individual testimonies. The psychoanalytic studies of the *Hibakusha* portrayed not only the silencing of memory, associated with this inevitable trauma after mass death in August 1945, but also the collective repression of memory. These social psychological revelations, combined with mutual denial and political manipulation in Japan, indicated that it was not just official (state) repression that silenced memory of the atomic bombs. Perhaps with the Hiroshima victims' numbing, trauma was sufficient in itself to reduce survivors to silence. But Japanese self-censorship of memory also coincided with the USA's officially imposed blackout. General MacArthur's occupation authority, which initially decreed the 'atomic silence', and enforced political inactivity, accompanied an already widespread suppression of information. This official 'amnesia' together with the self-imposed voluntary repression of the past, complemented a more covert victimology, about the bomb, and later US nuclear testing and basing. Each dimension needs to be seen in a context of a *national* forgetting, characteristic of modern Japanese history in general.[25]

Beyond oral history, images, testimonies and cultural production, academic revisionism of the history of the 1940s confirmed the problematic nature of the bombing and testing itself – and of deterrence theory. After the post-Hiroshima silences there was growing public acknowledgement by the late 1950s of the mass bombing of civilians in Japan and in Germany. In Europe, publications showing images of what future nuclear annihilation might look like became more widespread, disseminated by emerging peace groups. In the USA and continental Europe, this threat was represented not only in film, photography and art, but also as described in futuristic novels and poetry. Yet atomic war was not only censored, but also presented through trivializing or distorted images, the clichés: of mushroom clouds. As the enormity of nuclear tests was witnessed – for example, the vast Crossroads tests at Bikini Atoll – they intensified an atmosphere of Cold War paranoia, and the response was often silence.

In the 1960s, Bruce Conner's radically innovative masterpiece *Crossroads* involved recycling film of the tests, but was seen only by minority audiences. An American exceptionalism of the 1950s created its own bizarre popular 'atomic cult', depicted in the film *Atomic Café*.[26] This sardonic nuclear entertainment collage was also a clear example of 'screen memory' – a representation of how to block both the past and the present, and turn threat into pastiche and trivia, as opposed to the satirical wit of Kubrick's *Dr Strangelove*.

Other accounts focusing on nuclear witness of the testing, generated critical scientific evidence that atomic physicists such as Joseph Rotblat used for political lobbying. But since such testimonies – for example, by the Marshall Islanders – were often promoted and sponsored by the politically organized peace movements with their differing Cold War agendas, they were treated with widespread scepticism. In McCarthyite USA, those physicists who raised doubts, such as Oppenheimer and the Pugwash group, were often targeted as disloyal. The anti-nuclear peace movement in Japan became deeply divided by 1960; it broke into two main 'communist' and 'socialist' wings. Both had a substantial mass base and municipal power, and neither were strictly pacifist. Each wing had several million supporters, and real political influence (1956–63). Their campaigns had an effective international outreach, and were an important, if not vital, stimulus generating Western peace activism after 1956, and sustaining an atomic memory.[27] In part this campaign stimulated by the Municipality of Hiroshima focused on commemorating the August anniversary on a large scale – and so, to a lesser extent, did Nagasaki. The ceremonies of the 6th and 9th of August played a special role in communicating an understanding to the West. The movement helped sponsor trips by the atomic survivors to the USA and Europe and included the 'Hiroshima maidens', women physically scarred by the bomb.

But memory work in the decade following was eventually shadowed by the more apocalyptic notion of 'omnicide' by the creation of the far more destructive hydrogen bomb. Despite the Cold War and its mutual justifications for the need for deterrence through armed strength, this future-oriented 'prophetic memorizing' became more global and precipitated growing awareness. This 'No nuclear weapons' mood spread particularly to Scandinavia, and to Canada, and the English-speaking world of the South, where testing was an issue, and was informed by the heightened concerns in the scientific community. But the crises of the early 1960s threatened to paralyse the imagination, and disempower concerned civilians as much as activate them. In the Cuban Missile Crisis, those nuclear fears became embodied in popular culture.

The mood of alarm was unprecedented, and as the later banning of the film *The War Game* (1965) showed, it was *prophesied* nightmares of global war rather than past events that were being politically repressed in nuclear states. They were not merely reproductions of images of direct experiences of the past, but predictions of the future. I will return to Peter Watkins's BBC-sponsored nuclear war film in Chapter 10. *The War Game* was prevented from being screened by the British Home Office because it was deemed too frightening. Unlike the images in the Maruki panels of the atomic destruction, the slave labour camps, the persecution of Koreans, or military massacres, Watkins's images were not a regrettable part of 'history'. Established facts could be managed, suppressed, or denied by the states involved. But now imagined future holocausts, constructed from previous events, scientific prediction, and near misses, were to be censored!

Breaking nuclear silences

The evolution of postnational memory is marked by recurrent silences about nuclear weapons. Since their first use in 1945, it parallels other censored or silenced experiences and memories of war and genocide discussed in this book. These had prevailed both before and after 1960 and the hydrogen bomb. References to the terminal character of modern weapons appeared in cinema during the 1950s, though often obliquely. In Georges Franju's savagely critical anti-militarist documentary *Hotel des Invalides* set in Paris in the Army/veteran's Museum (near Napoleon's tomb) during the visitors' tour, the lugubrious voice of Franju's 'guide' to the military exhibits wryly warns about the bomb:

> Some of those machines can by their aspect amuse visitors and yet, when we measure the dangerous rise of an industry that springs up like poisonous mushrooms, you must recognise that this is no laughing matter![28]

Direct and actual references to the use of the atomic bomb in mainstream cinema were surprisingly rare and even less explicit than in *Hiroshima Mon Amour*. In Resnais's *Night and Fog*, the oblique prophecy of war is also *implicit*, as is the reference to it as 'genocide'. As the camera pauses, viewing the destroyed crematoria at Birkenau, the commentary warns us of new, impending holocausts in Europe. It talks of 'monsters with one eye open'.

The two Japanese atomic sites and monuments, and their memorial museums, first built in the 1950s, opened for visitors, at first on a small scale. With the annual commemorative displays and events, growing in size, and especially Hiroshima, in reputation, they became iconic venues of remembrance rituals. The cover art, used for this book, is part of the Marukis' representations of the annual ceremony of the floating of lanterns on 6 August on the rivers of Hiroshima. The ceremony was replicated worldwide, often annually, typically by local peace groups.[29] The episodic construction of an anti-nuclear culture through such rituals and symbols competed with more bellicose anniversaries in the memory booms of the 1960s and 1980s.

Like the place names of the Great War, and the camps of the Shoah, such atomic sites became markers, and new memory places were added: the H-Bomb Pacific test zones, such as Bikini or the destroyed atolls by the Marshall Islands and Christmas Island, new seascapes and maritime sites of nuclear memory and prophesy. Warning of global disasters ahead, they also became venues for protest. Partly influenced by images of irradiated Japanese fishermen caught in atomic dust on the *Lucky Dragon* fishing boat, which had fatally strayed into the radioactive areas of Pacific testing, a spectacular series of volunteer anti-nuclear, trans-oceanic voyages into testing zones were undertaken in the next twenty years. These included *The Golden Rule*, *Everyman* 1 and 2, and most notably culminated in the Greenpeace voyages to the same areas. These continued from the mid-1950s to the late 1970s. Best remembered is the later Greenpeace boat the *Rainbow Warrior*, about to head from New Zealand for Mururoa. Its destruction in 1985, bombed by France in Auckland harbour, became an iconic reminder of the role of pacific resistance to international atomic testing. Although the scale of continuing nuclear irradiation globally had declined by the 1980s, the testing and the threat remained. A localized series of resistance movements in the Pacific multiplied and stimulated the move to a Pacific Nuclear Free Zone. At that time, Almagordo and the first US testing sites such as Trinity in New Mexico were also still among many 'closed zones'. Most of Los Alamos was off-limits. Yet these too became sites of visitation; tourists could ride on the 'Atomic bus', but saw little.[30] All attempts to create a memorial at Los Alamos were blocked. These memory places were portrayed in the 1980s in Robert Del Tredici's photographic essay *At Work in the Fields of the Bomb.*[31] From this survey of the landscapes of an Atomic USA images were used in the film *The Journey* (1985). Vast atomic landscapes worldwide provide the backdrop for much of Peter Watkins's epic, focused on exploring the global nuclear war machine.[32]

Des Pres: denial and memory on the nuclear grid

Nuclear denial brings parallels with the fears of total war in Europe in the 1930s; the threat of a terminal arms race leading to catastrophe was comparable with screening out potential nuclear wipeout. Moreover, denying the actual reality of atomic carnage

IMAGE 7.7 Robert Del Tredici, Pantex Nuclear Weapons Final-Assembly Plant, 1982. Pantex, America's only nuclear final-assembly plant, receives parts from facilities throughout the USA, in some 120 subassemblies made up of about 2,000 separate pieces. Pantex provides 2,700 jobs. It is Amarillo's largest employer. In *At Work in the Fields of the Bomb*, image 12. © Robert Del Tredici.

has echoes of subsequent Holocaust denial. For the American poet and critic Terrence Des Pres this threat paralyses us – it:

> [E]ngenders cynicism, despair, allegiance to a mystique of physical force, and to say 'No' to such destructive powers requires an enormously vehement 'Yes' to life and human values.[33]
>
> Nuclear wipe-out is possible, perhaps probable, and every day I talk with people who are convinced it will happen. No soul is free of that terror, nor of that knowledge: and simply as a state of mind or way of knowing, it dramatically alters how we received and value our experience. Birth, for example, of one's own death; surely having children troubles us in a way not known before, and we need to feel that each of us shall have a death of his or her own, simply in order to feel fully possessed of our lives.[34]

In writing about the nuclear age, Terrence Des Pres managed to create out of his local pastoral idyll, a future landscape of threat. He urges us to share again the nuclear fears of 1979–85 keenly felt in the hills of Upstate New York. In his writing they become an imaginary killingfield of the future – a future Birkenau, or Hiroshima, or Verdun:

> The military state of mind becomes an alien element in the landscape as we behold it, the B-52s, the proximity of the missile site, the grid and its planners. These forces have broken into our world, they have defiled its integrity, and the new points of correspondence between ourselves and the landscape are the condition of vulnerability and the threat of terminal defacement. Self and world, nature and landscape, everything exists in itself and as acceptable loss on the nuclear grid.[35]

The poet also introduces air war into these images of pastoral as a setting for modern memory; the juxtapositions of time and place are the memory of home contrasted with the banal present of service life. The pilot and soldier are 'brothers-in-arms', who grasp at natural scenes to maintain a non-militarized self. But Des Pres reminds us of the danger of this divide, of self and nature by military intrusion:

> Every person has his or her own place …'The kinds of personal vision to which a landscape corresponds must … be fairly limitless. But all vision converges in the fact that every landscape is part of the nuclear grid. I have the air base in Rome to remind me of this'. (Author's note: Rome is a town in upstate New York)[36]

Des Pres considers the distanced view, from above, by the bored bomber crews:

> We and the landscape are expendable; to think this way, after all, is their job. We cannot say, there, that the landscape corresponds to their minds and to ours in the same way.

Like the Marukis, Watkins, Griffin and Resnais, such contemplation of omnicide also involves uncovering concealed memory of the past. That memory for poetry especially, serves as a template for representing an apocalyptic future. In the poetry of Richard Wilbur's *Advice to a Prophet*, the past is used to introduce a sombre preparation for nuclear Armageddon.[37] The poet asks the prophet to "spare us all thought of the weapons, their force and range" and not "scare us with talk of death of the race" but instead, "speak of the worlds' own change", the impact of nuclear catastrophe on the natural landscape, '*a nuclear winter*'.

For Des Pres's memory work is about creating presence in face of omnicide:

> the prospect I share with my neighbors, our part of the nuclear grid. Not a landscape of the mind, no inner weather sort of scene, its just life's natural place for those who live here.

I have chosen, besides Des Pres and Resnais, also lesser known memory workers, such as Watkins, Del Tredici, Griffin and the Marukis, since they helped us construct or reconstruct an alternative memory for the nuclear age, and one which accepts acknowledgement of what Des Pres calls nuclear intrusion into everyone's memory space: one that knows no national borders. Whilst Des Pres wrote about such threatened nuclear landscapes in Upstate New York in *Landscape, Self and Grid*, its reflection is at the same time both prophetic and retrospective: he quotes a Russian, Osip Mandelstam, killed by Stalin's regime. Although Des Pres was best known in his lifetime for work on witness of the European and Jewish holocaust, he created perceptive witness pieces on our own nuclear existence – on sites of a potential political holocaust.

Our fear of future horrors gives a significance to almost anywhere on that worldwide atomic grid.[38] In the flux of experience, past, present, future, the sites he located were very personal, in or near his arcadian college hometown of Hamilton. With bombers overhead, maintaining MAD (Mutual Assured Destruction) promotes a new sensibility beyond continents. In the early 1960s the B-49s could be seen being refuelled in mid-air above the Cotswolds hills, near Adlestrop in Oxfordshire, England, in a context of spreading concerns about the real threat of nuclear war. By the early 1980s, the Soviet Union and America were in a renewed missile race. There was widespread evidence that children felt deep anxieties and experienced nuclear nightmares. It was an issue about which Des Pres felt passionately and spoke particularly about, not least as a parent. Des Pres makes few explicit links between his nuclear 'Landscape' and the territories of the Shoah, but the confluence of *place* and *memory* is unmistakeable,[39] as is the prevalence of denial.[40]

Postscript: missile gaps and memory gaps; 1994–1995 and the *Enola Gay* affair

The post-war omission from American collective memory of nuclear weapons, their history, and their use, was to be clearly illustrated in the *Enola Gay* controversy in 1994. It involved an exhibition at the Smithsonian Museum, Washington DC, related to the 50th anniversary of the bombing of Hiroshima, including the symbolic fuselage of the bomber (all at the Air and Space Museum), and artefacts from the city itself. The plane was named after the pilot's mother, Enola Gay, and the name was painted on the plane (see image 7.8). In this confrontation, the role of veterans associations, mostly aligned with conservatism and denial, was conspicuous in a campaign led by the Speaker of the US House of Representatives, Newt Gingrich. Their lobbies were largely supported by established authorities in government. In the public sphere, amnesia and silencing had enveloped the very names of the incinerated cities after 1945. But by the 1990s, the destruction of 'Hiroshima' and the use of the atomic bomb had started to have a more ambiguous meaning for US national memory. The prevailing mood in a conservative government was opposed to dangers of evolving 'counter-memories' of 1945, especially since these were emerging outside the USA. Signifying Hiroshima and Nagasaki as a truly universal events, it could both remind the world of the US

IMAGE 7.8 B-29 Superfortress *Enola Gay* and the crew. The plane was used to drop the first-ever nuclear bomb. The name *Enola Gay* was derived from the pilot Paul Tibbet's (who is in the middle) mother's name and was painted on the fuselage. Photo: US Air Force.

role as the first user of weapons of mass destruction, and of the start of an inevitably more postnational nuclear age. Or even worse, such a display could raise again the ethical issue of the dropping of the bombs on civilians, as morally as well as particularly militarily, questionable.

But for the majority of US citizens in 1945, the atomic bombings had been framed as the victorious *end* of the Pacific War – and an act of vengeance for Japan's attack on Pearl Harbour (1942). Over the following decades there were few major dissensions. But fifty years later, and after two global cold wars, the Cuban Missile Crisis, Reagan's nuclear rhetoric, nuclear proliferation, and not least the divisive and protracted Vietnam War, perceptions had changed decisively. A well-documented revisionist history of the end of the war now existed. Even in America, especially after 1990, the debate was much more evenly poised. This was because over the decades, the changing demographics and politics of modern memory, together with the impact of anti-nuclear movements such as the 'Freeze', the large protest organization in the USA, calling for a cessation of the nuclear arms race, had contributed to altered public perceptions of nuclear weapons.

Yet though the veterans of 1945 were a declining generation, their voice remained a strident one. Even if their response was by no means uniformly triumphalist, their sympathies were with US achievements, not Japanese victims. The curator of the museum, Martin Harwit, was impossibly cross-pressured about the revised scripts of the exhibition, and forced to resign. After considerable changes in the texts, it proved an exercise in ultimate denial. Having eliminated all reference to the victims of the bomb, 'Little Boy', was now apparently a weapon with 'no impact'; and the human effects, not only on 6 August, but also over time, such as radiation did not exist. The results on the ground were to be ignored.

In the event, the *'Final Act'* exhibition was cancelled and Harwit left. The artefacts supplied from Japan to the Smithsonian for the display included remnants of the bombing, such as a clock stopped at 8.15 a.m. Sent from the Hiroshima Museum, they were returned unceremoniously to the donors, a discourtesy causing consternation and distress there. Only one timeless iconic object, part of the fuselage of the bomber, remained on display, with a few photographs.

This controversy exemplified a signal chapter in America's contests over national and postnational memory. Newt Gingrich became known all over Japan as a figure of infamy. The state view of history was endorsed by the revisions; the omission of the Japanese targets were an acceptable editorializing for millions of Americans. But not for Japan. For others worldwide, it simply represented further denial of hegemonic amnesia. But even before the *Enola Gay* went on display in Washington in 1995, the atomic bombs ('Fat Man' and 'Little Boy') and Claude Eatherly, the pilot of the reconnaissance plane, had created dramatic controversy.

This chapter of memorial history was controversial because it divided the post-Vietnam US 'national' memory. The divisions were attached to two different

'Americas', and two national versions of America's wars. The multiple, contested scripts presented competing 'truths' (though few memories) about the first use of nuclear weapons, moral and strategic perceptions of it, and of its necessity. But rewriting the script of national collective memory demands a resistant mode of interaction with existing cultural life, and with national history and political elites. Through selective accentuation of memories and through artistic representations of them, oppositional, non-official memories can be privileged as 'counter memory'. Yet most of the scripts of the Smithsonian Museum Exhibition told only one side, and there were no witness stories.

These events illustrate a conflict in both academic (historical) and public, popular, narratives that revealed a cultural lacuna: the gulf was in part a generational one.[41] Whether in London, Manchester or at the Washington Smithsonian Museum, the postnational framework of memory, as the controversy showed, remains a subordinate one to the demands of patriotic framing of myth. Whether or not states are nuclear powers, modern, national governments of all persuasions judge the issue of nuclear war as a topic best to be avoided. In general, the less we, the public know, the better. But the memory workers – writers, filmmakers, poets and photographers: Griffin and Des Pres, the Marukis, Del Tredici, Wilbur and Watkins – chose, prophetically, to confront this denial: their warnings of catastrophe are as relevant now as they were then, not least because the threat, like climate change, remains a planetary one.

Notes

1 In this case mostly Soviet or Russian.

2 Except for the Arlington cemeteries and other DC monuments, for the USA, the major memorials of 1917–18 and1943–45 are on site in Europe – and later in Asia.

3 Ernest Hemingway, 'Soldier's Home', *The Short Stories of Ernest Hemingway*, 2nd edition (New York, 1925), p. 78.

4 As Sebald in his lectures implies. This was confirmed in my own conversations in the early 1950s, where the destruction of nearby German towns was discussed around the family dinner table.

5 One syndrome central to much memory work in Germany, was based on the thesis that the pain of all such mourning was repressed. It was propounded in the 1960s. Alexander Mitscherlich and Margarete Mitscherlich, *The Inability to Mourn* (New York, 1975).

6 Public repression of the events may have totally different meanings for different families, communities and individuals. This separates such silencing from the psychological repression of the Mitscherlich's study (1975). See Ian Buruma, *Wages of Guilt* (New York, 1994). See also W. G. Sebalds's *On the Natural History of Destruction* (New York, 2003), UK edition. Originally *Luftkrieg und Literatur*, it was published in German in 1999.

7 Certain pastors and bishops (including Bonhoeffer) took such risks. Others such as Niemoller opposed the policy after the war.

8 The Mitscherlichs' thesis focuses on the ability or 'inability to mourn' – both the Shoah and the deaths of the war years, especially in the bombed cities. They argue that the reasons to forget are multiple and complex and are not confined to 'psychic numbing' after trauma.

9 On the Vichy Syndrome, see Roussos and Ophuls' film, Henry Rousso, *The Vichy Syndrome: History and Memory in France since 1944*, trans. A. Goldhammer (Cambridge and London, 1991).
10 Buruma (1994).
11 W. G. Sebald (Zurich lectures, 1994), published in 2003 as *On the Natural History of Destruction* (New York).
12 W. G. Sebald, *Austerlitz* (London, 2002).
13 W. G. Sebald (2003); and in Andreas Huyssen, *Present Pasts: Urban Palimpsests and the Future of Memory* (Stanford, 2003), ch. 9.
14 Sebald's Zurich Lectures, especially his remarks on Frankfurt am Main.
15 Peter Watkins, *The Journey*, Part 8, note interviews with Mrs Biermann and others in Hamburg.
16 Sebald (2002, 2003), Zurich lectures.
17 Perhaps he is experimenting with memory as Benjamin described 'memory play' – ***trauerspiel*** rather than mourning work – ***trauerarbeit*** (see references in Arendt's introduction to *Illuminations* (London, 1999) by Benjamin on this).
18 Elaine Scarry, *The Body in Pain* (New York, 1985).
19 They also draw attention to environmental disasters as at Minamata.
20 The project Hiroshima Nagasaki August, 1945 launched by Japan Film Company and filmed by a previously jailed anti-war cameraman, was cancelled and the footage confiscated.
21 John Hersey, *Hiroshima* (New York, 1946).
22 See books of Photos in *Conflict, Time, Photography*, curated by Simon Baker at the London Tate Modern, 2015.
23 Voice of Emmanuelle Riva speaking, Marguerite Duras's script (trs.) for Alain Resnais's, *Hiroshima mon Amour*.
24 Robert Lifton, *Death in Life: Survivors of Hiroshima* (New York, 1968).
25 On collaborative amnesia see Chapter 8.
26 This is identified in a collage documentary of film from the 1940s and 1950s, a symptom of the atmosphere of denial. *Atomic Café* (1982), directed by Jayne Loader, Kevin Rafferty and Pierce Rafferty.
27 See Lawrence Wittner, *The Struggle against the Bomb. Volume 1, One World or None: A History of the World Nuclear Disarmament Movement through 1953* (Stanford, 1993), and Lawrence Wittner, *The Struggle against the Bomb. Vol. 2: Resisting the Bomb: A History of the World Nuclear Disarmament Movement, 1954–1970* (Stanford, 1997).
28 Translated from sound track of Georges Franju, *Hôtel des Invalides*, trans. Melanie Rohse.
29 See the cover artwork and caption, Iri and Toshi Maruki, *The Hiroshima Panels: XII Floating Lanterns*.
30 Fay Godwin made similar photographic journeys in Britain, though not focused on weapons.
31 Robert Del Tredici, *At Work in the Fields of the Bomb* (London, 1987).
32 Scenes in *The Journey* are filmed at these locations with local residents and witnesses. Like Watkins's other experimental projects, and despite its ambitions and eccentricities, it won critical acclaim not least for its documentation of a hidden history of nuclear denial (see discussion on *The Journey* in Chapter 10).
33 Terence Des Pres, *Landscape/Self/Grid*, in *Writing into the World* (New York 1991), p. 175.
34 Ibid.
35 Ibid., p. 10. Jim Schley, ed., *Writing in a Nuclear Age* (Hannover and New England, 1984).
36 Des Pres (1991), p. 175.
37 Richard Wilbur, 'Advice to a Prophet', in Jon Stallworthy, ed., *Oxford Book of War Poetry* (Oxford, 1987), pp. 336–37.

38 Des Pres (1991).

39 His experimental and experiential attitude to trauma may have contributed to an untimely death. But it also led to timeless writing about apocalypse, poetry and the banal continuous flights from the local (Rome) Griffiths Airforce base, armed with weapons of mass destruction. The Arcadian campus in Hamilton was his potential epicentre – his '*Oswiecim*' – but a killing field of the future waiting for its 'transports' on the horizon.

40 The various modes of silencing of atomic survivors has inevitably evoked parallels with the European Holocaust.

41 The exhibit was framed as an end, not a nuclear beginning, and the official title was instructive: '*The Last Act: The Atomic Bomb and the End of World War II*'. On the Smithsonian Museum script and article, see A. M. Winkler, 'Mushrooming Anger', *Times Higher Education Supplement*, Barton Bernstein, *New York Times* (31 January 1995), and in *Foreign Affairs* (January 1995); Gar Alperovitz, *Washington Post* (16 October 1994); 'Murdering Anger' *Times Higher Education Supplement* (December 1994); Charles Krauthammer in *Time* (February 1995); Martin Harwit, *Washington Post* (7 August 1994); Eugene Mejer, *Washington Post* (21 October and 18 November 1995 and 31 January 1996); John P. Dick, 'The Chronology of the Smithsonian's Last Act', in *Organization of American History Newsletter*, November 1994. Harwit was the curator of the exhibition.

PART 3

Re-writing memory

8

BEYOND AMNESIA

Breaking silences

> The path toward sanity will require memory work: the task of recuperating what has been supressed, so we can live honestly in an open world.[1]
>
> Peter Dale Scott

Amnesia and the national frame

The main task of postnational memory work has been to break a wide range of silences, not least denial about the effects and dangers of nuclear weapons and nuclear war but also to record testimony of atrocity; to name the nameless, the victims of total war and genocide; and, where possible, to give them voice. But beyond that, modern memory also has the longer-term responsibility to reframe, re-contextualize and demythologize representations of the past.

Far from exhaustive,[2] this chapter specifically deals with brief cases from Austria, Japan and Spain, and stories of their national silencing and forgetting since the 1930s. These examples are where I have myself experienced the suppression of memory first hand. Personal research has revealed disparate patterns, and each has different implications for postnational memory more widely. These cases involve traumas which modern memory began to confront after 1940. This perspective now, however, appears increasingly anachronistic in any postnational interpretation. Globally in dozens of other societies historical amnesia has played a major political role, where for different reasons the past has been forcibly repressed or denied.

I have already discussed the repression of memory in West Germany(1940s–80s). I will briefly discuss a differing case – that of East Germany (1945–90) and revelations after unification.

The range of collective amnesia is complex and evolves in historical phases. This is most obvious in Germany before unification in the 1990s – a process which brought new forgetting with it, even after the Cold War was officially over.

In the unique case of the GDR, in formerly Stalinist, East Germany, the collaborative forgetting of the whole post-Nazi period was re-enacted differently, and was revealed after 1996. After reunification, members of the Stasi were confronted with evidence of their complicity in repression. Despite its attempts to cover tracks when the Communist Secret Service was disbanded, their files were opened. In his books *The File* and *The History of the Present*, Timothy Garton-Ash, as historian and reporter, writes about his personal experience of the malleability of (individual) memory in the context of post-1989, the end of the Cold War, and the unification of Germany. He had befriended officials and others in the East, and later confronted their denial of informing on him. In the convenient amnesia of a number of these Stasi informer friends, he approached them directly with evidence of their guilt.[3] In such cases the interaction of the victim and the perpetrator becomes mutual, if not collaborative, and is metaphoric for a larger syndrome: the victim remembers, the informer forgets. The interaction of systematic denial and deception includes self-deception: the apparent intellectual complicity of even notable dissident figures, such as Christa Wolf is revelatory of how corrosive collective silencing is. In this example there are a wide range of overlapping phenomena: state denial, consensual forgetting, and pacts of 'oblivion'. There is also the switching of the blame in 'victim' nations to other sources. East Germany, as Austria, was victim of the Nazi dictatorship. In Japan it was the 'enemies', especially the USA. Mechanisms of an organized forgetfulness are reinforced by media; this process spreads systemic disinformation,[4] and is even more pronounced in war time, and permeates civil society.

Through collecting individual stories or other research, modern remembering across the globe continues to involve recovering lost narratives: of civil atrocities covered up, witness of civilian bombings silenced, or the effects of nuclear testing. In the case of collaborative silencing, the role of investigative journalists and whistle-blowers has been crucial in the task of finding lost testimony, and in attempting to reverse this amnesia.

Trials and commissions as formal processes often involve testimony and recall, whether voluntary or required: their overall importance to a public remembrance of events remains questionable, at times acting as a screen: the closure of a chapter, or an occasion for collective forgetting, rather than lasting revelation. Memory work involves piecing together lost narratives – pasts silenced or experiences repressed – and in different contexts, a range of patterns emerge. Comparisons can reveal not only how collective suppression of memory and denial of trauma and atrocity varies in specific states and societies, but also how each civic memory can be revived and re-constructed. Some major traumas are even dis-interred, after decades of silence, when a regime change occurs; for example, after a civil war or dictatorship. The rush to cover up past crimes, even after such autocracies fell, as in Spain between 1936 and 1975, in central

Europe after 1945 (and again in 1990), in Indonesia in 1965; in Chile in the 1970s, and in Argentina in the 1980s, a sinister process of erasure ensues.

There is an omnipresent tension between truth-seeking and processes of reconciliation: that of 'raising' ghosts. This dilemma became part of the ex-Yugoslav story of the 1990s, given the unresolved and unacknowledged legacies of bloodletting of 1940–45 and after. Ideally such a memory work is sensitive to a past of civil atrocity and uses revelatory narratives to universalize them. In this way postnational remembering tries to counter the malign, vengeful memorializing of the past that may otherwise re-emerge. It also acknowledges the accompanying paradox: the continuing personal need, at times to forget, and yet the civic imperative to remember.

A World of Forgetting

These understandable reasons for *forgetting* and the ambiguous aspects of creating, even of sustaining a post-conflict memory, suggest to some that re-starting with a *tabula rasa*, free of phantoms of past horrors, is preferable. Political justifications for doing that have been presented in recent post-war situations. Blotting out the past, or 'not remembering', has also been advocated as therapeutic, especially for individual cases. Others argued that recalling distressful conflictual and provocative memories can be potentially as socially and personally destructive as silencing. Part of the inner dialectic of modern memory work therefore is to resolve this key tension between the pain and risks of individual and collective remembering, and the dangers of continued amnesia. These dilemmas facing modern memory still bedevil contemporary conflicts, and are often a direct result of the political revival of many national or cultural of myths, and enemy stereotypes.

In the twentieth century, the virtual silencing of memory of whole societies took place – not only in Spain, Germany, Austria and Japan, but also, for example, in post-1920 Russia, and in Turkey, Indonesia, China, Chile, Argentina and parts of Central America such as Guatemala. Attempts at truth-telling or truth-seeking about war or trauma transformed the memory-maker into the troublemaker. If not as comprehensive, silencing was as excessive in open societies such as France, as in Eastern Europe after 1945.

Facing these uncomfortable challenges, memory work inevitably continues to involve uncovering hidden history, unarticulated lost or silenced narratives of atrocity and betrayal. But encountering these suppressed pasts does not make either for good public relations or easy reconciliations. Before all living bearers of first-hand accounts are gone, and before memory workers are forced to rely only on diaries, memoirs and reports of past interviews, the role of the outsider becomes crucial. The international memory workers, researchers, visionaries, investigative journalists or those supporting the local whistle-blowers may help provide missing links and (sometimes crudely sensationalist) breakthroughs. There is often time pressure if revelation is to be achieved whilst first-hand accounts of witnesses are still available, or before written or visual evidence is destroyed. This occurred in Spain, Japan, Rwanda and many other such sites of memory. Evidence of atrocity has continued to be shredded or buried, and as examples of truth-seeking these investigations pose ethical and political problems. This is especially true as exhumation of the past (such as the Franco reburial – to be discussed later in this chapter) takes place after civil wars. Unlike those following interventionist wars, such memory often reflects the aftermath of societies already divided. As in Spain, in Central and Latin America, in Africa, and in former Yugoslavia (Bosnia and Kosovo) reawakening memory is not – or not only – about wars between states. Each situation has proven fraught with dangers of provoking recrimination and revenge. Pasts remembered even threaten to rekindle conflict itself by re-starting the cycle of blame, guilt and violent retaliation, as occurred after Tito's death in Yugoslavia.

As his reaction to the denial and cover-ups of the 1965–66 Indonesian genocide (in *Coming to Jakarta*), in his Brandeis essay Peter Dale Scott[5] appeals for memory work, rather than transitional justice or reconciliation. But the question remains as to what formal shape can or should such projects take? Sensitive to this issue, one significant form that was eventually institutionalized globally was the Truth and Reconciliation process. It developed most notably in post-apartheid South Africa, supported by Nelson Mandela, but was subsequently applied in at least eighteen countries, including Ireland, Rwanda, Chile, Bosnia and Argentina, in some form.

Civic initiatives outside the state structures have contributed more examples, sometimes at local level, but these have usually revisited past crimes individually. When Truth and Reconciliation processes were inaugurated decades later in South Africa, an alternative collective path for a whole society was sought. Any purely national construction of public memory, or a state's self-justification for its current actions, often has much more to do with the political nature of the past and immediate policy goals than peace or acknowledgement. The purpose of many post-conflict trials is not usually equity or justice – nor healing. Whilst war crimes trials and tribunals maintain political order, and the dominance of the victors, the continued methodology of Truth and Reconciliation processes focus on alleviating individual and communal pain, even obtaining mutual resolution, or pre-emption, of remaining conflicts. Responding to the need for remembering, acknowledging and testifying, the Truth and Reconciliation process can be cathartic, potentially healing, even redemptive. Its main political virtue is to alleviate some pressure for vengeance and of a residual sense of injustice. Rather than blame and guilt what a community seeks is truth and reconciliation,[6] but this it can also act as a means of civic closure. Sadly however, contribution to a transnational collective remembering beyond particular intra-national conflicts, these exercises remain questionable; in terms of globalizing memory and remembering the bigger picture, they may even prove counter-productive.

'Justice' after violent conflict is at best 'transitional', as illustrated by the dishearteningly limited revelations of Spain's covered past, and Argentina's 'disappeared' in civil war atrocities. As in Chile, it was an issue of first obtaining a simple acknowledgement of events – of facts as facts – a priority in Northern Ireland and, not only in South Africa since the end of Apartheid. Truth and Reconciliation processes to bring forward varied, often incomplete, narratives and ambivalent representations of unresolved inequities, and are framed within a territorial, if not national context. Setting up a wide range of trials and commissions has often exemplified an ambiguity about amnesia and denial, about war and violence as a crime. At best it is a means to civic accommodation.

Globally, more than twenty countries each lost more than a million dead in twentieth-century wars – some of them lost tens of millions. There was widespread public revulsion and war was even formally named a crime. Yet despite Nuremberg, war remained legally represented in a context in which a victor's 'national' justice prevailed. War crimes trials, tribunals and courts after 1945 were created and operated both multilaterally internationally and independently by major states. These were even publicly and widely welcomed in the defeated societies. At Nuremberg, though war (of aggression) was declared the crime, War itself was not put on trial – only the war 'criminals' from one side. Despite this, the implication of the Nuremberg principle itself holds for all belligerents: the principle of '*obedience being no defence*' (of war crimes) was enshrined in law despite scepticism and opposition.

Most trials were nevertheless ritual events, a minor appendage to memory of unimaginable atrocity: the Tokyo trials in particular were a problematic, often ambiguous and formalistic afterthought to the war itself. Both official and public reactions to the horror of war and genocide was an unexplained, unanticipated (and unjustified) suppression or silencing of collective memory. In traumatic experiences, which could not be faced or admitted in the immediate aftermath: the scale of atrocity went far beyond the few crimes specified, indicted, and prosecuted in the courts, or tribunals.

In terms of a postnationalist interpretation of the past, the retrospective responsibility to recall such crimes continues into the twenty-first century and stretches back beyond the twentieth. It is arguable that trials may serve to shield the guilty and become a part of the denial and forgetting process, since such modes of control of public history including trials of war criminals are set alongside rituals of commemoration these. In retrospect many appear at best inadequate and remote, at worst they are myopic and obstructive. By compromising memory, these processes create a 'screen' memory rather than a source of the truth-telling or truth-seeking that is needed.

The various state trials after wars and genocides since 1945 have reflected a deeply defensive, and politically and temporally limited official framing of events. Even many post-conflict initiatives, embedded in international treaties, pacts and laws, have had little, if anything, to contribute either to an altered sensibility or a stable peace or the construction of a more cosmopolitan, collective acknowledgement. How far a more global remembering of the past can, or has started to, provide a cultural counterweight to the constraints of state memory remains questionable. If, on the whole, formal initiatives by states have done relatively little to help, and much more to obstruct acknowledgement of modern catastrophe, then the task of postnational memory work still remains vast.

In relation to the denials of state-sponsored crimes, and the attempted repression of a society's memory of atrocity, modern memory's role, truth-seeking and truth-speaking are effectively counter-memorializing. It has at the same time a postnational role. The limited number of cases where 'Truth and Reconciliation' commissions, even if problematic, have played a role include post-apartheid South Africa, Ireland, Spain, and to a lesser degree in the Balkans, Rwanda or Palestine.

Popular 'patriotic' motives for silencing the past are no longer as acceptable in civil society. The global catalogue of such denials is too voluminous to be fully detailed here: China over Tiananmen and the Cultural Revolution; Russia over Katyn and the Gulags; Turkey over the Armenians and the Kurds; Indonesia and the massacres of 1965; Chile during and after Pinochet and its purges and reprisals – and until recently, Argentina and the disappeared. Like Britain and the USA on the reality of the slave-trade, most slave-owning and -trading nations still avoid much of their brutal past. In some cases, after international conflicts, such as those in Latin America, suppressed memory has emerged, but only decades later. These memorial lacunae are well observed in public spheres; in the major national museums worldwide these reveal major omissions, even absence of whole historical periods.

For example, in Brussels, Belgium's role in the Congo: Adam Hochschild has documented how most Belgian institutions omit or ignore King Leopold and the crimes in Congo. This lack of revision of decades of history is not an atypical response to an unwanted past.[7] Long afer his death, Stalin's national myth-construction remains highly successful, not only on the Patriotic War, but also in constantly re-texting the Soviet historical narrative. In totalitarianism, by definition, denial is comprehensive, and often covers an inconvenient memory by lies. But mythical representations and an invention of history leaves some gaps. In many societies, collaborative amnesia of absence allows major events to go 'unnoticed' and people to be 'disappeared'; the coincidence of personal 'closing-out' of the past, with an officially accepted, even if limited, censorship from public memory allows selection for official displays of an appropriate national past. In the USA, cancellation of the *Enola Gay* exhibition at the Smithsonian in 1995 is an obvious example.

Curating memorial museums, choosing amongst contested symbols, facts, agendas, interpretations and artefacts, represents an effort to walk a tightrope. Caught between conflicting forces, narratives and unacknowledged pasts, such ventures demand both diplomacy and courage. Like Martin Harwit, most historians feel pressure to make some accommodation to, if not compromises with, historical truth, in the name of 'balance' or moderation. Curators also feel pressure of events, to adjudicate between claims and grievances in divided or diverse communities. These are described in Paul Williams's extensive global catalogue of politically controversial memorial museums, which are often perpetrators of national myths, as in Japan's Kamikaze 'peace' pilots museum.[8] Such myths can survive because of confluence of the forces working on behalf of voluntary amnesia, together with state or group denial, and the repression of inconvenient 'facts'. Some of these exclusions of unwanted narratives are ongoing, and represent conventional opinion. Small truth-telling museums in Japan, such a Kyoto or Osaka, are embattled. This suggests, in Japan in particular, how fierce an area of contest a 'memory' museum can represent.[9] If mere selectivity fails to sustain the narrative, then, as some museums have shown, by adding a memorable atrocity tale or other symbol-laden image it may succeed to persuade. By tapping deep reservoirs of collective belief and symbolism, such patriotic legends achieve considerable power: they can exclude the victims, the slaves, the indigenous peoples, and smaller embattled communities, and, in many societies, women especially. Memorial exhibits that expose the excesses of the colonial legacy remain rare and are controversial: no British apology for Amritsar and still no noticeable rush to commemorate slavery in France, Spain or Portugal. In the past, the few slavery memorials and museums were mainly in Africa.

Belatedly, new significant slavery memorials and museums have developed in the USA, during or since the Obama presidency; America's homegrown holocausts have neither the communities nor the diasporas with necessary political influence, nor the resources. Both Native America and African America are notably rich in memory, and culture: yet neither have major national or memorial museums to mark domestic atrocity, only the Shoah.[10]

As a result the task of confronting chauvinistic imperial myopias remains an immense, postnational memory project. But such commemoration represents a global counter-remembering, internationally, and in nation-states.

Victimology and denial: Austria

At the level of 'national' societies, the Austrian case of collective forgetting is both one of the best-documented but least acknowledged or understood examples. Austria's exemplary self-silencing has an astonishing quality of 'innocence'. The shadow of this past is still ignored, even amongst liberal elites. Often forgotten is that Austria was given a free pardon (a collaborative public relations 'let out card' internationally). After the Anschluss, a poor, and widely anti-Semitic Austria had already, in the 1930s, accrued its own dark memories, especially those of the Austro-fascist government from 1934 to 1935. Yet the far more ominous ghosts of Austria's Nazi past survived afterwards in the political discourse into the twenty-first century, it was almost as if Austria had not fought as fully part of the Reich and Nazi Germany in World War Two. A third denier generation has emerged in recent decades: whilst the ghosts became harder to ignore in international public media, at home they were extraordinarily veiled. These include associations with the Nazi past, as the Kurt Waldheim cover-up of his World War Two record famously illustrates. The provincial hubris that imagined the wartime military biography of a public (UN) figure could remain concealed from the world for ever, given the revelations of his involvement in the Salonika deportations and the available photographic evidence was revelatory. It seemed that Austria remained blanketed in denial and banal political collusion, unaware that 'the world was watching'. More locally, one could not ignore such regular celebrations by SS veterans; for example, near one of their memorials at a small town in Eastern Austria, on the Hungarian border. It was where the majority population of Jews had left 'voluntarily' in 1936; it was, we heard, because they could 'make more money elsewhere'.

Much was made of the 1943 Moscow declaration, in which the Allies effectively handed a blank cheque to Austria: 'the first free country to fall victim to Hitlerite aggression'. Yet over half the concentration camp guards and three-quarters of death camp commanders were Austrians, as were a high proportion of the SS. In truth, the Anschluss annexation of a right-wing province in 1938 had merely appended a political vacuum to German militarism: Nazism filled that space, one of post-imperial identity, of an imperial history and of rural folk memory, or it implied a radical amplification of the *volkish* popular memory of peasant rebels.[11]

The pattern of Austrian denial after 1945, in which the world was complicit, is therefore quite unlike both West German mass self-censorship, encouraged by occupying powers, and the East German state-sponsored 'victimology' and the tacit repression with which the Soviet Union collaborated. Mythical narratives of World War Two were helped and funded by the 'culture campaign', subsidized by Marshall Aid and fostered during the US occupation – the international tourism was a distraction from pasts better forgotten. A romantic fantasy of an Austria of classical Kitsch and sentimental muzak, helped drown out social protest. Sustaining a collaborative illusion, the economics of tourism in a bankrupt rural society needed such an absence of recrimination or even mourning. Winter sports or culture filled the memory spaces with performances: in places such as Salzburg and Vienna, consumers sought a past of Mozart or Strauss, not Braunau-am-Inn, or worse, slave labour camps, Holocaust memories. A historical memory gap about both atrocity and resistance was purposefully cultivated. Already politically 'neutral' space provided by the internal settlement, led by the established majority Social Democrats, allowed conniving in the revised victim self-image. Like the tourist brochures, the national museum largely omits World War Two, the 1930s and the 1940s and the Shoah; neglects the shadowy history of Austria's cultural elites, anti-Semitism: even ignores Austria's own local traumas of poverty, and the failed risings of the left before 1936.

In his important analyses of Austrian memory, James Young describes in his *Texture of Memory* dramatic counter-'memory' events in the 1980s; a challenging anti-fascist memorial installation (imitating a Nazi rally construction of 1938) in conservative Graz, was firebombed by followers of Jörg Haider's right-wing extremists, who had become a major political force there. Fifty years after *Kristallnacht*, the artist Hans Haacke's *Point of Reference, A Memory of Nazi Propaganda* was destroyed on 2 November 1988, with its reference to the November 1938 attacks on synagogues in Austria. The provocation of such memory 'construction' caused immense communal controversy; memory debates about sites of persecution and forgotten crimes of the 1930s and 1940s – not only in Graz – re-emerged.[12] It also awakened a more liberal response to the past, and spurred a new generation's readiness to re-examine history. Not intended as a 'counter-monument', its dramatic destruction by fire made it exactly that.

Even before liberation, a generation of Austrian politicians, mainly those Social Democrats and some others released from Mauthausen concentration camp near Linz in 1945, had planned a political settlement involving a compromise to achieve reconciliation – a post-war internal peace of a liberal-pluralist, if bureaucratic, kind. But this accommodation was at the cost of adopting a distorted, palliative myth of the past, and therefore of a delusional self-image. Like Spain's 'pact of forgetting' (discussed later in this chapter), there was a collaboration in an Austrian myth that rewrote the years of the Anschluss and in the Reich, and omitted the war and their traumas, and role in the SS. It took over half a century to publicly acknowledge another horrific part of Austrian war memory and to mourn the losses. The memory of the Eastern campaigns of the early 1940s was also repressed. It was a narrative of an Austrian catastrophe, not only at Stalingrad and the appalling Austrian losses there, but also on the 'Ost front', generally, memories still not mentioned in Austria's National Museum in Vienna, except in one special 1990s exhibition.

It is a sobering fact that the banale tourist image of *Sound of Music*, skiing and Tyrolean bands could, within decades of the war, become a credible new national identity for a traumatized, brutalized and what continues to be a politically contradictory and divided society. Not only was it politically the far right that endorsed it, but also the moderate centre which negotiated it for social 'peace'. It adopted a culturally 'happy self-image' even with its lederhosen, beer halls, hunting traditions (and for some, even swastikas). This accommodation, it was said, was in order to 'move on'; but that inconclusion brings its own dangers.

Japan: shrouds of amnesia

In one sense, of the several cases of national or postnational amnesia dealt with here, Japan should be the simplest to dissect: it is a relatively homogenous society in which memory culture has changed least. Despite political change, there is a continuity and stability in peace and war memory. Beyond the various political divisions over seventy-five years, certain strands remain constant.

Part of the reason for this is the strength of traditionalism. This in turn, can be related both to Japan's history, a sense of victimhood, and to the sense of honour, and also therefore dishonour and shame, about the past. In acknowledging aspects of history, this is also multi-layered formation of memory, and these layers need to be separated; for example, victimhood, from shame.

A major example is the 'atomic silence'. This comprises memory of both the nuclear and conventional bombing and the repression of the trauma and numbing that followed; indeed, denial by the victims with direct memories. But also it spread as proxy memory to other Japanese with only indirect association. The second aspect of nuclear amnesia was the suppression, imposed by censorship by the US occupying authorities, both about nuclear weapons and the conduct of the war in general. This then contributed to a third collective amnesia:

self-censorship, not only about the bombings, but also about Japanese military action abroad. Related to this closure was Tokyo's War Crimes Tribunal, which failed to provide any analysis or acknowledgement of Japan's role and crimes in the thirty-one-year Pacific War. To some extent the US occupation, the trials and alliance was complicit in this denial. These events and self-justifications (as victim) for them became symbolized at the Yasukuni Shrine to War Dead. The fourth and final dimension of denial, was silencing and amnesia about domestic internal repression, in both war and peace time; the crimes in Japan itself were an extensive aspect of the suppression of the past.

All of these aspects of amnesia can be linked in some way to the issue of national honour and cultural shame. Beyond this critique is the need to summarize the counter-memorizing: the real attempts at public acknowledgement of, and atonement for, the past, not least the role of the substantial Japanese peace and human rights movement. This movement played a role in memory construction, but was itself divided and ambivalent about some aspects of that collective memory. Given Japanese traditional culture, values and attitudes, the blanket victimology, the denials of atrocity and a systematic censorship of history, comprehensive amnesia was perhaps inevitable. But the voluntary popular suppression of memory and self-censorship reflected deeply conservative attitudes, and an ingrained fear of being dishonoured. As a result, research on past deeds remains taboo – evidence is shredded, and discussion still blocked in the twenty-first century.

Censorship of historical memory by the Japanese State throughout the twentieth century is a narrative less known.[13] It was reinforced by the US imposed atomic silences of 1945, and continued the censorship of Imperial repression, long after the war ended. Endorsed by the emperor and the 'diktat' of the US occupation generals, such as Douglas MacArthur, this silencing coincided with widespread, self-imposed cultural repression I have described. It even included denial about the effect of 'Pika-don's' (atomic bombs) radiation. This suited America's interests in several ways. Whilst repression of memory and denial of atrocities were deeply rooted in Japan's culture, the US presence had crucially reinforced a subtle political mystification and, at least in political terms, it continues to do so. The suppressed atomic experience, its post-war silencing, the promotion of victimhood, self-suppression of trauma, and personal and collective denial, gradually came together as a single story in which Japan's 'pacifist' constitution played a role.

But it is also clear that over the generations many Japanese, with no direct experience of war, positively embraced their own myths of suffering: the bombs, the war and even the plight of its suicide pilots, and sustained their own collective victimology. It was considered politically acceptable to select what was appropriate, and inappropriate to comment on, and also what was proper to have visitors or tourists comment upon. In any 'other' narrative of Japan's past,[14] anything which raised memories of the actions during military expansionism in China and the Pacific, especially the assault on Nanjing and the large-scale massacre, or the attack on Pearl Harbour, was taboo. In many historical accounts, Japan's expansionist war, the excesses of the Imperial armies after 1931 (including Manchuria) are ignored;[15] history has been 'corrected'.

In school textbooks, the suppression of accounts of the Japanese Army's rampage in other parts of the Pacific was systematic: there was no official acknowledgement of the massacres, the mass rapes, and summary executions of the war, or the treatment of Korea, and Koreans. For example, the failure to react to the sufferings, and continuous organized rapes of the Korean and other Asian 'comfort women', were typical. It took over fifty years to even acknowledge them, publicly and officially. In the West, where it was largely the Burma railroad and similar experiences endured by allied prisoners of war that were remembered, the other unpublicized mass crimes were largely unknown until the 1990s and beyond.

Since 1962, the traditional Yasukuni Shrine to the war dead and Yushukan War Memorial Museum[16] are the most notable examples of the regressive politicization of overtly revanchist and supremacist memorials. Yushukan has also become a national museum with tacit official blessing; it has been revived and newly reconstructed, and is now a venue for millions of visitors, including Japanese prime ministers. This represents both an exoneration and a legitimation: it is both a shrine (with memorials to war criminals) and also a revisionist history museum. Since 1986, it serves in part, at least symbolically, to undermine the verdicts of the 1940s Tokyo War Crime Trials. Its displays also revive the narrative of a Japanese 'progressive', 'anti-colonial' imperialism against an offensive, mostly Western, threat. The museum's role and the significance for a Japanese national memory is now perhaps greater than its importance as a national place of mourning for dead soldiers. It is a hub for a conservative, chauvinist ideology. In strong contrast to Germany, the retrospective denial of atrocity has made inroads into Japanese peace culture and to a democratic narrative, thus representing a serious reversal.[17] Whilst the Kyoto Peace Museum at Ritsumeikan University, which describes these truths, is vilified by the nationalist right, Yushukan is officially legitimated by the cult of this notorious shrine. Despite the Tokyo War Crimes trial, the museum continues to include, without apology, previously suppressed justifications of the criminals themselves.

The domestic exploitation or death of hundreds of thousands of non-Japanese, especially Chinese and Korean, slave workers – the story of conscripted labourers – was denied, silenced or forgotten. So was the cruel and degrading treatment of millions of Filipinos, Koreans and Chinese in camps located in the Philippines, Korea and mainland Japan. Multiple massacres occurred at the mainland camps which were hardly publicized. Individuals who were the whistle-blowers on local atrocities were threatened, as were those who uncovered mass crimes against the Chinese slave labourers or others.[18] For example, in Hanaoka, Yachita Tsuneo, who like other heroic memory workers such as Nozoe Kenji had witnessed the massacre of these labourers, campaigned at great risk to expose the atrocities.

There is a cruel irony also revealed in a moment of Watkins's film *The Journey*, when a witness in Hiroshima describes how the 'victims' of the bomb turned on their own oppressed 'non-people' after 6 August 1945. Koreans were not even included in lists of atomic fatalities; their bodies left unburied, even desecrated. This event, depicted by the Marukis in their *Crows*, is part of the historic sequences of the *Hiroshima Panels*. Amongst these self-critical images, one panel shows Korean dead, or left for dead, in the wasteland of the destroyed city. In addition, Japan's domestic minorities, including the Buraku caste, the Ainu, and several ethnic groups, such as the Okinawans, during and after the war, lacked any acknowledgement or public memory of their period of acute suffering. Even local atrocities were denied including those in Okinawa in 1945.

Yet despite this daunting record of denial, as an Asian example of collective memory the Japanese attempt to transcend victimhood has been a significant project. However incomplete or embattled, this work continues to evolve in and from Japan. For many citizens it remains a selective and political – and an often unpopular – 'truth-seeking'. But even as a minority movement, memory work continues its anti-nationalist campaigns into a new generation, impacted by global social media.

These contests over Japanese memory, the unfinished work of redemption and acknowledgement continues, and the war is still recent enough to be confronted by living witnesses, such as the surviving children of Nanjing, elderly comfort women, and child victims of nuclear radiation sickness from 1945. But what is clear is that, in the main, it is still a heroic minority of groups and isolated citizens, artists and journalists who awaken such silenced memories. They are typically ostracized and harassed by their 'normal' communities.[19] In Asia, as in Europe, this reveals how 'forgetting' also involves the suppression of the memories of opposition, of how Japanese pacifists were persecuted and many killed (1931–45), and then ostracized later. But thanks largely to the Japanese peace movement and non-violent demonstrations, the Hiroshima and Nagasaki victims' experiences were voiced and the personal numbing that reduced most survivors to silence was breached and became widely publicized outside Japan.[20] It helped, despite a consensual bias against any alternative voices or images, to promote counter-memory, especially the Marukis and their heroically critical witness, but marginalized art; I return to them in Chapter 10.

Japan's non-nuclear, misnamed, but nevertheless importantly 'pacifist' constitution – and its public anti-militarist commitments – have been praised, but continuously compromised, and challenged by the work of conservatives and nationalists alike. A contest about memory has also evolved over Japanese public education, and even over the school textbooks, which censored basic evidence of atrocity in national history. Amongst those foremost in combatting public and official forgetting have been Japan's Peace Institutions such as the Human Rights museum at Osaka, and some institutions linked to private universities, such as Ritsumeikan University and Peace Museum in Kyoto. They have met obstruction and criticism, official and unofficial. But the range of still incomplete memorializing is vast, and Japanese peace scholars remark on the urgency of the timetable of acknowledgement. Much work is unfinished and, internationally, denial remains a political issue in relations with China, Korea and other victims of nationalist expansionism.

Complicit amnesia: confronting Spain's memoried ghosts

My last example is also predominantly of civic denial: Spanish memory work exemplifies the silencing of traumatic experience in a society which occurs after a nationalist dictatorship wins a brutal civil war (1936–39). This consensual avoidance of the 'Ghosts of the Civil War' in post-Franco Spain is a potent illustration of how, even where political liberalization occurs (as in Japan, West Germany or Austria after 1945), it does not automatically bring the emancipation of a society's remembered (and suppressed) past. Long-term traumas, previously repressed, remain silenced for decades after the end of state censorship. Not only does such a regime rewrite the past on a grand scale, but it also celebrates that revision. It is symbolized by Madrid's vast 'Valley of the Fallen', and Franco's mausoleum behind the Escorial. The monument commemorates the victors (*Muertos para Dios y España/Valle de los Caídos*), but blocks much of society's recall. Some Republicans had been added to the list of 'the fallen' in the 1970s as a token gesture, but by the millennium they were being removed in turn – many were disinterred by relatives, to dissociate them from the Fascist movement and Franco's monument.

A lesson George Orwell learnt as writer and protagonist in Spain in the 1930s was that people experiencing conflict voluntarily subscribe to lies or choose to forget and bury the truth: 'Lies are on sale and we choose to consume them: immunity from the past makes life easier'. Forgetting is the placebo that allows us to escape from the real. If it is the truth of a memory that creates discomfort, and if, as Huxley and Orwell argue, 'Big Brother' has already invaded our consciousness, then creating a desire to repress, to deny, to 'rephrase' memory and to believe what is convenient – the 'brainwashing' of our memories – is not only possible, but also likely. Even though Francisco Franco, Spain's authoritarian, nationalist and pro-fascist '*Generalissimo*', had died in 1975, decades of transitions followed. Between 1978 and 1986 something called 'the pact of forgetting' was established. It was almost a pact of oblivion: a semi-formalized collaborative (and near consensual) agreement about blotting out the past. It aimed to keep a social peace by excluding especially memories of the worst horrors of the Civil War (1936–39): the repressive police actions, and the tens of thousands of executions of captives that followed victory.[21]

The Civil War had been a complex tragedy: it was never a simple divide, and preceding World War Two, it also evolved into an international proxy war. This added - with vicious internal feuds and repressions - to the conflict. Not only was memory of civil war atrocity silenced and repressed, so were the personal stories of loss on all sides, and of the massacres and barbarity that typically characterize all civil wars. Even the sense of it as a shared tragedy, an immense national trauma was denied. Opening the mass graves of victims and tracing the disappeared took over fifty years to even start. In an increasingly fragmented society and even before the war ended in 1939, people's overt memories in the various militarily occupied areas, on both sides of the front lines (controlled by Nationalists and Republicans) had already been silenced. Even amongst those fleeing abroad – for example, in occupied France – narratives were still repressed, and decades afterwards. Like East Germany, Spain in the 1950s and 1960s was effectively a police state. There was a palpable fear of open discussion: to travellers who cared to look, it appeared as an occupied country where armed Falangist Guardia Civil rode on buses and trains.

Long after 'freedom of speech' was formally restored in the 1980s, the agreement about mutually suppressing the past included a clause that Franco was not to be mentioned. Such an amnesia, shared by a whole society, confronted those visitors, including former refugees from the diaspora, who tried personally to revisit or revive the past after the 1980s. Those political groups attempting to exorcise the ghosts of the 1930s included some who were surviving Anarchists or their heirs. The tradition in Spain had been strong. Some in that tradition tried to revive memory, both as a matter of principle and as political activism or propaganda. They were ostracized or punished as a result.

Such suppression may initially be 'collaborative' as in the Spanish case, by means of an informal 'civic agreement' initiated between citizens, politicians, and the state. To collaborate in suppressing endangered memories in the name of 'peace' is inevitably transitory. As it became more formal and accepted, such a 'pact of forgetting' meant that discussion of the past often represented a return to the private, politically neutral realm of the home. Nevertheless, as Andrew Rigby observed, this proved a corrosive, even regressive factor in political reform, and in the long term it was unsustainable.

For over two decades, those from both 'sides', and from none, accepted such a 'normality of silence'. Locally visitors found bizarre omissions: examples of leaving the key events of the years of conflicts (1931–39) and Franco's regime (1939–75) out of local tourist brochures and histories of each area. It was as if 'nothing happened' from 1931–75, and even beyond! The eventual liberation of repressed, complex and muddled memories is never a smooth process. Nor was acknowledgement certain even when the dictator finally died and his regime failed.[22] Only by the early twenty-first century was that pact weakening. On 24 August 2018 it was decided to exhume Franco's body and divisions reopened.

By then, finding first-hand witnesses of the horrors and internecine atrocities of the war and post-war was becoming hard. But as political liberalization grew, inhibitions also faded: the mass graves were opened. By then many of the records of the informers and collaborators, the victims and torturers, the accused and accusers had been lost or destroyed. The records had more or less effectively been 'cleansed'. Like the Nazis, the Falangists (*Moviemento Nacional*) had been keen to cover up and clear the records, and this continued long after Franco died.[23] In many places, records of local interrogation, execution, even imprisonment, were systematically destroyed by police, army or officials. In each region where they survived, most police files were kept locked. Opening the Patio Civil at San Rafael in Malaga, and searches for exhumed remains of Republican prisoners, whether innocent or guilty, killed there by firing squads was a gesture of re-balancing memories. It reminded public opinion that this was a war in which, whilst a whole society suffered, only one set of perpetrators were punished.

Internationally, Spain holds another special place in the cultural history of modern memory since the 1930s. Its transition to political totalism was recorded by multiple modern poets, artists, critics, novelists, photographers and journalists, on all sides. The majority were Republican sympathizing internationalists and volunteers: not only George Orwell, but also Martha Gellhorn, Ernest Hemingway, and writers such as André Malraux, Arthur Koestler, W. H. Auden, Franz Borkenau and Gerald Brenan; and poets such as Townsend-Warner and of course Lorca. Picasso and Dali painted passionate images of Spain's agony. In particular, Orwell and Hemingway focused on transnational memories of relationships: they personalized moments in the war, as did Capra's photographs. In the many veterans' or journalists' stories, such recall includes much spontaneous truth-telling, others included sometimes ironic comment on the contradictions of a society at war. Hemingway chatted to his iconic 'old man', abandoned by the refugees and fighters alike at the Ebro Bridge. Such mnemonic accounts, by outsiders, humanize 'great' events by the recognition of individual civilians caught up in them. It reminds us that not only were Republican volunteers themselves civilians alongside others, but they were also amongst thousands of civilian conscript soldiers. They shared a common destiny or plight with those without 'politics'. Many involved were both potential victims and perpetrators of atrocity. A semblance of shared suffering is at the core of the depiction of Republican and International brigades' wounded, lying on a hot beach since the hospitals were full and the nurses over-occupied. Those placed there were recalled in Sylvia Townsend Warner's testimony: her poem *Benicàssim* represents an image outside a Republican hospitals near the front (see image 8.1 and vignette 'Benicàssim'). Her verses recall humanity *in extremis*: but scenes were omitted from the Spain of tourist advertisement.

The move towards accommodation, if not healing, which had started in the 1970s, was indicated by shifts in the Catholic Church, which had been Franco's ally in the war and after. Following the papal *Pacem in Terris* (Peace) Encyclical of 1963, the Spanish Assembly of Bishops and Priests issued an Apology in 1971 for its complicity in past crimes. Although Franco's monuments were gradually removed or de-legitimized after 1980, political prisoners were still not released for many years after his death.[24] It had been a murderous and reactionary conflict. Nor did selective forgetting allow a new history to emerge. Even fifty years after a bitterly cruel and divisive civil war, at the Valley of the Fallen near Madrid, the huge triumphalist Franco memorial remained as a monstrous affront to reconciliation. Temporary political justifications for some forgetting in Spain were to be expected. But the past, like the monument, was neglected, rather than reinterpreted. But an asymmetric apportionment of guilt and justice, with a one-sided exoneration, was 'accepted' only by an inertial public amnesia. An official 'year of historical memory' was announced for 2007. It had been long awaited. Unlocking parts of the past, open up not only stories, but anger, remorse, buried resentments and sentiments of a denied past, symbolized by monuments to Nationalist dead.

Spain shared with Russia and China, beyond these memories, a vast unwritten modern history. Five decades of a society rich in culture and intellectual tradition had been consigned to the abyss. The project of postnational memory is immense, and for some, because of emotional and political costs, it is not worth pursuing.

The coup of 1936 was a symbolic, though often unacknowledged, setback for democratic governance internationally. In 1989, fifty years after Franco's putsch, the return of memory began slowly. The silence of the Franco years remained and remains a sensitive issue. It was difficult for strangers or visitors to enter that memory – the cleansing and forgetting of atrocity survived into a third generation. After 1985, in a context of building a fragile democracy, still threatened as in 1981 by a thwarted military coup, such selective forgetting was still deemed necessary. But with unacknowledged atrocities on all sides, it seemed the Republican victims who were, after all, defending a democratic polity would never be atoned for. With many of the perpetrators now dead, no full reconciliation, no healing process was ever fully allowed.

In his 'Postlude' to his book *Pyramids of Sacrifice* in 1972, the sociologist, Peter Berger described his visit to 'The Valley of the Fallen'.[25] He sees an anachronistic space that has nothing to do with what either side fought and died for. It was those military forces, obedient to Franco, who were a crucial factor in that catastrophe, including the most brutalized elements of the Foreign Legion. This is their memorial, and with it is Franco's mausoleum. The human costs of the war were enormous, because the Republic organized civil society – and its movements and unions, against a highly armed and funded Nationalist elite, and its powerful allies: the Church, and the large landowners. Tarnished as it was, the resistance to the Francoist army coup was a defence of civil society and of an elected democracy against a small clerical fascist clique, whilst internationally the liberal democracies kept aloof. Nevertheless it is a tribute to the maturity of Spanish and regional civil society that at last after eighty years, it can finally fill a void about these dark forty years and foster some increasingly balanced narratives.

Vignette:
Benicàssim – raising the ghosts of Castillon de la Plana

I was invited to teach a short graduate course on 'Memory and Peace' in Spain, about twenty-five years after Franco's death. I had not returned to Spain since being arrested, briefly imprisoned and then deported (to Gibraltar) when I was nineteen and a student. I had not intended the course (in Peace Studies) to focus on Spain, and the only Spanish historical period I had studied in any detail at university level had been the 1930s and 1940s. However, whilst there I was interested in personally exploring the nearby sites associated with the Civil War – including Benicàssim, where many of the beautiful villas had been commandeered as Republican hospitals (Image 8.1). I knew that Sylvia Townsend Warner wrote her well-known poem there, when the front line came near to Castillon de la Plana, about the wounded and dying on the beach outside the hospital. I wanted to visit it. The 'rest homes' and Republican hospitals at Benicàssim stood at the northern end of the broad bay, surrounded by trees. It was there that Warner saw the wounded, many in pyjamas, lain out in hot sun on the sandy beach near the Spanish Medical Aid Hospital; other convalescent homes were not large and were already full with the worst cases.

IMAGE 8.1 Spanish Civil War Republican Hospital in Benicassim, Spain, ca. 1990. The hospital is described in poem by Sylvia Townsend-Warner, 'Benicàssim', which portrays the wounded lying on this beach. The villa is one of the hospital buildings. International Brigade wounded were also taken here. Photo: Nigel Young.

Visiting that area again, sixty years after the trauma of the war itself; hours after driving from Barcelona, in the Catalan north, across the new bridge, south over the Ebro, I began reflecting on the carnage in the nearby orange groves. These near Castillon and Benicàssim were on the northern edge of the southern front in the war, after the Falangist (nationalist) forces broke through to the sea, dividing the government forces to the south (Valencia) from those in the north (Catalonia). Castillon finally fell in June 1938, after being bombed by the Italians, and I soon learnt that it was followed by dreadful local reprisals.

In the lecturer's room I had been assigned, and in the University Centre's reading room, were piles of tourist brochures – they contained a history of the area, up to the late 1920s, resuming in the mid-1980s. Perhaps unusually, and unwisely, I took these to the first class I gave, simply to illustrate a case of collective amnesia, or the blocking out of historical periods. Had I done more research on the Spain of 1980s and beyond, I would have perhaps been more aware then of the 1986 'pact of forgetting', the sensitivities that remained even in the late 1990s, and the potential charge of stirring dormant ghosts!

But, as an example, it had a surprising and powerful impact on the class, they were a group of international students (only one was from Spain, and was quickly alienated), but many were from Latin America, and from the USA. In the next class there was a consensus (the Spanish student was absent) that we should, as a class, pursue a 'memory work' project on the area Benicàssim/Castillon, during the Civil War (1936–39). Students then started to interview locals, including the old veterans (from both sides) who played dominoes in a nearby canteen. A retired local professor showed archival slides and an extraordinary film from the time. Another academic gave a lecture on the politics of the struggle. A local antiquarian and enthusiast helped us find documents, and a private museum in Benicàssim was specially opened up to us by its owner, with a store of extraordinary photographs, letters and other documents. The International Brigade hospital was now one of several boutique hotels nearby, and could not be visited as a group. The Spanish student expressed her disquiet about the project and came to few classes, and did not submit final work.

The denouement was when some of the students created a large mural – a collage of photocopied photographs, newspaper cuttings and quotes about the research. The centrepieces were the local tourist brochures which had been daubed with blood where the historical gaps existed. This was placed in the foyer of our study centre, and several administrators and secretaries expressed alarm! Then I was carpeted by the Dean, who reminded me of the divided families still living, and their descendants: the revenge killings, the betrayals, the ongoing vendettas, and how the ghosts of the 1930s and 1940s still remained a presence. It was not for me, he said, 'from outside', to encourage such research, even though at least sixty years had passed. The 'pact of forgetting', he said, was still in force for some. But not for all. Several younger professors came to my defence and supported the project. One invited me to write about cultural amnesia in an academic journal (which I did)! But I was not invited to teach at the Center ever again! But one day I might try to stay at that hotel on the beach. I remained in touch with several of the 'guilty' students over the years. The pact of forgetting has subsided now, and memory work has returned to intervene in the oblivion. But I should have researched the Spain of the 1990s with more diligence before raising these very present ghosts, and prepared my hosts for the intrusion, and not least to have considered how best the work of reconciliation should be pursued.

As I drove back north again from Castillon to Barcelona, on the new highway, I was crossing the land that the Nationalists had captured after the 'betrayal of Teruel' in 1936. This had included Castillon's active municipal participation. After the Fascists reached the coast between Valencia and Catalonia, they later attacked south through the orange and olive groves near Castillon. As I re-crossed the new modern concrete replacement over the River Ebro, I wondered once again where Hemingway's 'Old man's bridge' was now. I headed north towards Walter Benjamin's two post-1939 memorials on the border of France, at Port Bou. There was irony in the fact that he had been heading south that year, via Franco's Spain, hoping to escape from what was to be Vichy France. At that time Basque and Republican refugees were still seeking escape in the other direction, north towards France. It was there that Benjamin killed himself.

Comparing national amnesias

In Japan as in Austria, and Spain – and for long in Germany, East and West – salient memory, a segment of the recent past (especially of 'war' memory) has been politically erased or self-suppressed. Of these three cases, two, Austria and Japan, were occupied countries, which adopted two different forms of victimhood – Austria's as guilt-free exoneration. As in Austria and Germany the American occupation of Japan reinforced and even legitimated this suppression of experience. It shows how, though 'Victimology' has been a key part of Austrian denial, we are complicit in the amnesia. Despite different trajectories, Spain's 'self-repression' bears some resemblances to Austria's 'agreement'. By the 1970s, both countries were major tourist destinations, and both self-image and public image needed to match, even producing collaborative false-consciousness. It was an absence of the past that for decades almost all tourists connived with. As consumers we collaborate in the erasure and the myths of victimhood. My examples of erasure of the past, used in this chapter, have as well as Spain, included Austria's tourism: its music and its natural beauty has been celebrated, whilst avoiding scrutiny of its abandoned rabbi's houses, the SS memorials, or the former slave labour camps. To some extent tourism operated to provide a functional screen memory in all three, except that in Japan, Hiroshima and Nagasaki became in themselves venues of international visitation, a memory tourism that compounds erasure of the past. Uncovering such lost narratives and sites of trauma has proved laborious and slow. State censorship played a more crucial role in Spain and Japan, and collaborative forgetting occurred in all three. This was most formalized in Spain.

Enforced 'amnesia' is accompanied by self-imposed and voluntary repression of memories of the past: Japan's denial has not only comprehended the atomic bomb and US nuclear testing and basing, but modern Japanese history in general. Civilian experience, especially atomic radiation, was unique. Japan suffered air war in other ways that parallel, for example, European cities bombed from the air and with the same numbing effects. But perhaps the denial of national atrocity and oppression that has remained in Japan is even more obdurately resistant than in Europe.

Victimology has been a key aspect that still formalizes Austrian denial. Like Austria, but unlike Germany or Spain, Japan sees itself as a victim, sharing a preference to forget its own behaviour. Its special significance in terms of memory is in its closing ranks as a national society, on behalf of its country's honour. This is assisted by the existence of an only partly dismantled semi-feudal order, and it reflects a structure of deference that contradictorily also underlies its rapid modernization. This paradoxically may now point towards a more global future.

Spain is a significant case because, however long delayed, its collective recall was built on an already pre-existing transnational memory. The savage Civil War had created an internal and external memory culture, even before World War Two. Spain's ghosts derive from an intra-national conflict, but it was already fixed as a symbolic internationalist memory by a range of oppositional movements by 1938. It was a European memory that, in the end, Francoism could not suppress.

But the importance of this is that the recovery of memory and the return of democracy were politically linked. It is therefore significant as both a postnational, European and a decentralist regional memory: Spanish, Catalan, Andalusian and Basque. It was one also inspired as much by Internationalist and Socialist ideas of transformation as by Liberal pluralism. It was sustained for over half a century, even as a suppressed memory, by heroic civil society groups and movements under constant threat of persecution.

Notes

1 Peter Dale Scott, *Coming to Jakarta: A Poem about Terror* (New York, 1988).

2 In a longer book, consideration of the Turkish and Indonesian cases of repression of memory would be essential. If Japan remains, with Austria, one of the greatest denier *societies*, Turkey, like Indonesia (and to some extent, Japan), remains one of the greatest denier *states*. A Turkish government continues to silence Armenians' century-long

memories, and Indonesia blocks serious acknowledgement of the vast massacres of the 1960s. There has been Western complicity in both denials.

3 Timothy Garton-Ash, 'Bad Memories', in *A History of the Present: Essays, Sketches and Despatches from Europe in the 1990s* (London, 2000), pp. 286–91, and Timothy Garton-Ash, *The File: A Personal History* (London, 1998).

4 Philip Knightley, *The First Casualty* (New York and London, 1975).

5 P. D. Scott, *The Sleep of Reason: Denial, Memory Work, and the Reconstruction of Social Order. In Literary Responses to Mass Violence.* Report of the symposium held at Brandeis University (Waltham, MA, September 2003).

6 Ian Buruma, *Wages of Guilt* (New York, 1994).

7 Adam Hochschild, *King Leopold's Ghost* (Boston and New York, 1999).

8 P. Williams, *Memorial Museums: The Global Rush to Commemorate Atrocities* (Oxford and New York, 2007); see reference in Joyce Apsel, *Introducing Peace Museums* (London, 2015), on peace museums.

9 On topics such as slavery and the slave trade, it is obvious that national acknowledgement of such collective critiques of slave owning and trading is extremely rare.

10 The Legacy museum in Montgomery in Alabama, opened in 2018, is an ambitious attempt to redress the balance.

11 Since the sudden dismantling of Austro-Hungary, and the emergence of a provincial, largely rural and inward-looking Austria, the end of Vienna as a cultural capital, bereft of its Jewry, the instability, parochialism and lack of reality in its national self-perception was perhaps inevitable after 1970, but Europeanism was a counterweight to this.

12 James E. Young, *Texture of Memory* (New Haven, 1994), p. 102.

13 Laura Hein and Mark Selden, eds, *Censoring History: Citizenship and Memory in Japan, Germany and the United States* (New York, 2000). Several authors deal with issues of censorship and history, textbooks and nationalist revisionism in Japan.

14 On the Yasukuni Shrine, see Buruma (1994), and in Paul Williams, *Memorial Museums: The Global Rush to Commemorate Atrocities* (Oxford, 2007), p. 68.

15 Since these were painted by the controversial 'Left-wing/pacifists' and internationalists, Iri and Toshi Maruki.

16 In 1962, Okinori Kaya, a member of the Liberal Democratic Party, a convicted class-A war criminal who later served as justice minister, was appointed chairman of the organization.

17 Buruma (1994), pp. 219–13; 'Yasukuni Shrine', pp. 63–64; Apsel (2015); on Koizami's visits, see Eric Langenbacher and Yossi Shain, eds, *Power and the Past: Collective Memory and International Relations* (Washington, DC, 2010), pp. 195–97.

18 Buruma (1994), see section on 'Two Normal Towns'.

19 One reaction to this art when it raises an uncomfortable past (Okinawa, the Koreans, the 'lynching of prisoners', even the bomb) is to ensure that the panels are publicly marginalized: their motives misrepresented.

20 This syndrome is described in Robert Lifton, *Death in Life: Survivors of Hiroshima* (New York, 1968), and became known, globally not least, through Robert Lifton's work. But it is also clear that many Japanese, with no such direct experiences, positively embraced their own myths of suffering the bombs and the war, even the plight of the suicide pilots, for half a century.

21 See Jay Winter's latest book *War Beyond Words: Languages of Remembrance from the Great War to the Present* (New Haven, CT, 2017), p. 23, footnote 32 quotes very high casualty figures from Helen Graham, *The Spanish Civil War: A Very Short Introduction* (New York, 2005).

22 As James Young (1994) shows us (see section on Graz, pp. 100–04.)

23 Unlike the Stasi files in East Germany, which Garton-Ash studied. See endnote 4.

24 In the context of the 'process of truth and reconciliation', I have been inspired by a useful, short account of Spain and these years, and a discussion of the issues raised,

by Andrew Rigby, *Justice and Reconciliation: After the Violence* (London, 2001). See also Giles Tremlett, *Ghosts of Spain* (New York, 2006), and Paloma Agilar, 'Agents of Memory: Spanish Civil War Veterans and Disabled Soldiers', in Jay Winter and Emmanuel Sivan, *War and Remembrance in the Twentieth Century* (Cambridge, UK and New York, 2000), p. 84.

25 See Peter Berger, *Pyramids of Sacrifice: Political Ethics and Social Change* (London, 1976), Postlude *In the Valley of the Fallen*, pp. 261–64.

9

A TESTIMONY OF PLACE

Vignette:

Walking the fields of memory: Germany 1994; France and Flanders, 1988 and 1992

Rounding a summer corner, coming into the village of Fromelles in Picardy and seeing a mass of glorious red poppies, we had to stop, get out, and walk to them, and touch them. In scores of visits in Flanders, probably because of herbicides over the decades, I have never seen a live poppy in the Salient itself, but here on the Somme, they still thrived en masse. Days later back in Flanders, in the Tourist office at Ieper (Ypres), there was a large poster of poppies! 'Oh, where are those?' we asked 'Scotland, I think' the helper advised.

Visiting such places and spaces of memory, it is often the unexpected, or unanticipated, that becomes the memorable: the deer at Birkenau, and the rabbits. Sometimes at such places, figures of re-enactments intrude, and whilst both are predictable and improbable, even bizarre, they still have the ability to shock. Encountering two 'World War One soldiers' in khaki and full 1916 pack, stumbling along the side of a remote sunlit cornfield on the Somme in the 1990s was still surprising, and, unlike the typical re-enactment, humbling.

Whereas at Bergen-Belsen, we heard the unexpected boom of real guns from a nearby NATO exercise, while we – and uniformed soldiers visiting from the Bundeswehr – dutifully walked around the grim memorial tablets. This interrupted a sullen moment at a desolate concreted site. It seemed a fatefully numbing combination, lacking even the inspiration from the house on Prinsengracht, to at least remind us of Anne Frank's incarceration in Belsen, if not her appalling death.

Early in 1945, I visited with relatives the bombed ruins of central Birmingham in England. It was soon enough to see the destruction, the debris and ruins of bombed streets and the broken tramlines. The physicality of such memory places experienced by direct personal presence – by touch and by the weather – has been explored by a succession of modern writers and artists: memory workers, who not as tourists, or voyeurs, but as virtual time-travellers situated moments in space before their physicality is replaced, covered over.

The framework of location, as Halbwachs observes, is maybe in Freud's sense the *screen memory*; it survives and substitutes for the trauma, the absences and the disappeared. But it is cultural memory that re-imparts the traumatic interpretation, the images of lives and relationships damaged or destroyed. Like Anne Frank's hiding place, some will be saved, and perhaps portrayed as representations, especially in the graphic images of them in novels, films or memorable photographs.[1] Such representation also lends meaning to a place now otherwise devoid of signature or index. That is the role of memory work. The creative memory worker is as likely to be a painter, poet or filmmaker, as an historian, archaeologist or scholastic researcher because the point of such work is to impart life to those *lieux des memoires* (places of memory) through *representation*, and to give meaning through an imagined and prosthetically re-experienced past.

In France, Pierre Nora's development of the concept of such sites of remembering, in his historical series of volumes on *Les lieux des Memoires* (1984–1996),[2] was an important contribution to the recent re-conceptualizations of collective memory. However, his extremely broad categorization of potential 'places' or 'sites' of memory leave us with somewhat a passive or static set of 'objects' or events, which will remain essentially lifeless without active interpretation. My own usage of *lieux* is narrower, more specific and more constructionist than Nora's. This focus is on physical sites and spaces that can be, or already have been, given meaning by, for example, creative and critical visitation and re-memorialization. This constructiveness is in contrast to archiving or museumization or simply presentation. These examples of memory sites, places of mourning or commemoration, are ones actively re-represented, sought out and memorialized – and not only by scholars. The localist activity of memory work is crucial. Invented memory rituals and counter-monuments are within that scope of any sense of such *lieux*, and innovations in popular community culture are integral to their representation

But this growing focus of modern memory work on the testimony of place, or 'landscapes of remembrance', is rarely without its contradictions. Generally its representation is not 'postnational'. I have described how in France and Belgium national cemeteries are the norm, juxtaposed with German and British, or 'Commonwealth', sites.

These graves sit illogically along a line of battle on the Western Fronts, reflecting advances and retreats. They are the mnemonic place names on a map: villages destroyed, villages rebuilt, villages abandoned;, villages moved, or like Fleuris, near Verdun, now disappeared. One I will discuss in detail in this chapter is Craonne, on the Chemin des Dames, first devastated and then rebuilt next to its ruins. Such *lieux* are our special sites of an imagined past. Often we have only a glimpse, a remnant, an image – prompted by a letter, a poem, a painting – or just the name itself: 'Passchendaele' – the name has nothing to do with the fact that farmers place crucifixes in the fields. But with Birkenau/Brzinka, the name does refer to the birch trees, which still grow there: and Kiefer's painting revisits a present, past the real *Wald* or 'territory' of Buchen – and its woods.

In discussing the sites of holocaust memory, it was clear that their fate and of each new killing field everywhere – many of which have yet to become established as memory sites – remains in question. Major examples of 'concreting over' pasts include the Hiroshima bomb's epicentre, the Potsdamer Platz memorial area and the Twin Towers footprints. Some of the sanitized German concentration camps (including Dachau, Buchenwald and Belsen) remain the norm. Halbwachs asserts that it is the *space* that endures, and that is true, but not if it is obliterated as a parking lot,[3] a supermarket or a housing development, or in Modris Eksteins's telling image, a dump for wrecked automobiles near the Voie Sacreé near Verdun.[4] The imagination is stretched when so little remains at Nagasaki or Belzec. In these examples, the space is not *destroyed*, as much as covered; even sacred spaces are filled in.

Neglect in fact makes some sites unique: rarely visited memory places, remote sites remain that have a capacity to reduce visitors to silence, protected by isolation, as at Sobibor or Treblinka. At these and other sites less visited, it is much easier for the imagination to make contact with the past. Despite a few intrusive monuments, however grassed over, rusty, or decrepit the remnants of such sites are, they retain a semblance of pasts. Some reconstructions at death camps have been meticulous, using original plans, but at sites such as Birkenau, its territories are preserved, giving an authenticity rather than token reproduction. In other places this is precluded in a 'memorial site', fabricated or built over with token 'memorials', such as Majdanek, with its reconstructed crematorium, or at Mauthausen, however well museumalized; and not least at the sanitized tourist venue of Dachau near Munich. But at Chelmno, the site must be rediscovered: 'Yes, this was the place!' (Simon Srebnik declares to Claude Lanzmann at the field where corpses were burnt.)

The 'Chemin des Dames' and the remnants of Craonne

The fear of grassing over the past often generates a strong desire to experience such a place, before all traces are gone – however drastically transformed, or almost obliterated the site may be. After 2017 some of these remnants of conflict have been revisited in the work of a Bradford artist John Allcock, who developed a project on 'the past in the present' in Friuli in northeast Italy. There both in the Alpine landscapes and in the village communities, an area is still marked by the physical scars, ossuaries and memorials of the Great War campaigns. As a mountain climber, he discovered these 'battlefields', even as military metal fixtures in the rock still now used as aids in climbing by the contemporary mountaineers. Old and new memorials were discovered when he returned again. He imagined and painted scenes from the sites and from experience, referring to Eliot's lines in *Burnt Norton* about the 'redeemability' of memory, where the present continues to embody and represent the future and the past, and the sacral character of such inscribed pasts. But that 'memory-as-experience' seeks to recreate a nexus with events and represent it in new ways. The older memorials created in the proto-fascist nationalist atmosphere of 1918–22 have symbolic references to laurel wreaths and, ironically, Imperial Roman 'victories'. Given the bizarre and catastrophic setting and circumstances of the killing on the slopes of these once un-peaceful Alpine terrains, so far from the Western Front, the monuments seem inappropriate to the local communities of memory, then and now.

Uncovering such remnants worldwide continue to pose questions about the future, indeed the past realities. The soil of the whole Western Front – from Langemarck to Verdun – and equally no doubt on the less memorized 1940s Eastern front around Kursk, Belgorod and Stalingrad, still yields an annual harvest of shells, bones and barbed wire. In France the farmers pile the detritus by the roadside, along with the other wrecked machines and ordnance of war; still many hundreds of tons of it every year. Whilst domestic remnants of death camps may contrast to the rusted metal objects in the grassy mounds on the battlefields such as Chemins des Dames, these were also domestic places, where men (and women) lived. These *objets trouvés* are not only rusted metal military objects, but also grog bottles, cutlery, buttons and belt buckles. In France the grassy 'Chemins' runs along a hilly ridge, now reforested. More remote than Verdun, it has fewer memorials and little habitation; the armies on both sides lost heavily there – but there is a narrative in the soil.

These sites of battles are far less accessible, known, or visited than Verdun, the Somme, the Argonne or Flanders, but the traumas of this ridge deserve equal attention. For the French army, in 1916–18 they represented a time of deep discontent, bad conditions and vast casualties, resulting eventually in a massive mutiny in 1917. It occurred during and after the fruitless offensives of General Nivelle. One name, Craonne, was remembered as symbolic of that desperate, but insurgent mood, and images of French *poilus* trudging to the Front bleating as '*lambs to the slaughter*'. It presaged the first major mutiny on the Western Front (Image 9.1).

The words of the soldiers' song, '*Adieu la vie, Adieu l'amour*' ('Goodbye to life, Goodbye to love'), were from the so-called *Chanson de Craonne*. Local versions of the song had evolved from previous verses, first sung at the Battle of the Marne (1914). In France it was perhaps the most popular soldiers' song of the war, and it is likely it was sung during the mutiny itself. But for the military hierarchy, it was seen as anti-authority and deeply subversive. From 1918 onwards the French radio banned it, as did subsequent

IMAGE 9.1 C. R. W. Nevinson, *Returning to the Trenches*, 1914–15. The body language signals the grim resignation of those going to the Front 'as lambs to the slaughter'. The uniform (horizon bleu) was modified later. Nevinson's picture can be compared with Kennington's and Williamson's pieces. Nevinson, earlier than most, turned to modernism and towards a more honest view of war in his 1914/1915 pieces, which deconstruct the patriotism of the French army in a brilliant, almost expressionist version of the futurist style. It captures the already sullen, determined but almost resigned postures of the French troops as they trudge back again to battle. National Gallery of Canada, Ottawa/Bridgeman Images.

political authorities for six decades: In fact the ban was, remarkably, enforced in France at least until 1974.

The chorus ran:

Adieu le vie, adieu l'amour, Adieu toutes les femmes
C'est bien fini, c'est pour toujours De cette guerre infâme
C'est à Craonne sur le plateau Qu'on doit laisser sa peau
Car nous sommes tous condamnés C'est nous les sacrifiés.

(Goodbye to love, Goodbye to all the women, It's all over now we've had it for good
With this awful war. It's in Craonne up on the plateau that we're leaving our skins,
'Cause we've all been sentenced to die. We're the ones that they're sacrificing.)

In the mood of 1917, in the revolutionary period when events between February and November were reported from Russia, many soldiers also started singing the socialist anthem – the 'Internationale', *en masse*.

Gibeau and the Presbytère a Roucy

Given its neglect in the 1920s and again in the 1970s, a mercenary and destructive pillaging from sites ensued in these regions. It reflected little care or public interest in maintaining the ridge as a major memorial place. The vandalism and looting, which included the destruction of soldiers' art and sculpture in the quarries of the Aisne and in Picardy, went on without any restriction from local authorities. In contrast to such commodification and abuse, and recognizing its historic significance, in the 1980s and 1990s, a handful of dedicated memory workers showed how to re-memorize such a site. One was a British artist Steven Hurst. Collecting remnants of catastrophe, he based his anti-militarist wooden sculptures on countless visits to the Somme and the Ypres salient, and pursued much research on the sites themselves as he did so. Other memory workers let the wood and metal, 'found-objects', speak for themselves; of these perhaps the most notable was Yves Gibeau on the *Chemin des Dames*. His dedication to the region near Reims reveals Gibeau as the archetypal memory worker. On the Chemin, his inspired, non-professional work illustrates the pull of a place and a past – to be revisited and reclaimed at first hand. After 1945, Gibeau combed the whole tragic ridge of suffering from the Marne valley as far as Laon to the north. He recovered the past by dwelling among the 'phantoms'; 'the remnants', which haunted the villages, many destroyed totally by the fighting and bombardments, gave the sites a special meaning – especially around the historic village of Craonne.[5] This was where the 1917 mutineers had gathered. From the 1970s to his death in Roucy in 1994, these were the sites Gibeau scavenged.

Gibeau (1906–94) was a French writer, anti-clerical anarchist and anti-militarist. He had spent ten years (1913–23) as a performer in a uniformed child troupe. He was imprisoned in Germany after 1940, and then returned to be involved in the Resistance and its newspaper *Combat*. Reflecting his own childhood, he wrote the partly autobiographical, well-known *Allons z'enfants!* (*Arise Children!*) (1952). Widely read, the narrative reflected on the role of children in war propaganda. In 1981 he moved to Roucy in the Chemins area, northwest of Reims, not far from the village of Craonne. Some of the most terrible fighting of 1914–18 had taken place here. He bought the 'Presbytere', a priest's house or vicarage. Completely destroyed (1915–18), like many such villages, Craonne was later rebuilt near, but not on, the site of the original community of 1914. Gibeau was to be buried in its original old cemetery.

He aimed to create in his *Presbytère*, a memorial home for his collections of all the *objets trouvés* and remnants of atrocities found on the killing sites, not only from around the old (disappearing) traces of Craonne but also from many other destroyed villages, and tunnels and caves used for shelters on the now wooded *champs de bataille*. He saw these not as museum objects, but as mute testimonies. They were stacked, and stewarded, but not 'museumized'; nor were they separated by category, like the piles of suitcases, spectacles, crutches and women's hair at Auschwitz or Majdanek. He was interviewed and photographed from 1981 by his photographer and filmmaker friend Gerard Rondeau. Rondeau documented his life, recorded his collections and

IMAGE 9.2 Yves Gibeau in his *Presbytére* at Roucy. Photographed by Gérard Rondeau sometime between 1981 and 1994 with some of the found objects he recovered from the sites on the Chemin des Dames. © Gerard Rondeau.

promoted his work. This continued long after Gibeau's death to include photos, a book and film of Gibeau and of the legendary 'collection'.[6]

These were presented in exhibitions from 2003 to 2004, and many of the objects remain in Peronne (at the Musée Historial de la Grande Guerre[7] and exhibited at the Caverne du Dragon museum in 2010). Promoted by Rondeau, and assisted by the curators, the purpose of Gibeau's work and philosophy was made plain: in contrast to memory business, it was not to pillage or to sell mementoes, or to create another voyeuristic 'exhibition', but to present a memorial collection in silent witness, a testimony – not even for research, or curiosity, but as a time-capsule – a 'memoire' of day-to-day life in a modern war zone (Image 9.2). His responsibility to that memory showed a new but enduring aspect of global memory work, its respect for authenticity, in a search for a time and place: the objects rescued as testimony rather than as commodity, and as a trace of lives lived there. Gibeau was in some ways a traditionalist, but this exhibitionary project was, in essence, postmodern and postnational. Such 'memorials' add temporality to our sense of place: to describe time at a site, entails retaining an element that *was* there at the moment of departure, however small or reduced; an element that has not significantly been *altered* or *re-presented* and that can signify continuity with our own witness.

This story of Gibeau reminds us that leaving a site as bare and raw as the territory of Birkenau, only a few kilometres from the Auschwitz Barracks (museum) and the town of Oswiecim, is quite rare – and the site is always threatened by collectors. A scratch beneath the barely grassed surface at Birkenau at the 'Canada' storage zone, reveals bone fragments or small personal objects; for example, a spoon in the sandy soil. It raises current issues: it may be still possible for some sites in present disasters to be preserved; questions remain for the mass graves of Aleppo and all the other destroyed cities of the Middle East, and in the early twenty-first century, the very nature of monuments and memorials is challenged by the excesses of modern violence.

Given nature's recovery of such sites, the vision of planting hundreds of thousands of birch trees in Berlin as memorial for Brzinka (Birkenau) was an inspired and appropriate reference to it. Counter-monuments raise questions about sites: beyond all the lifeless granite, basalt, marble and cold rock memorials and monuments, using natural mnemonics, from poppies to birch trees, are intentional but less anonymous signifiers than Carl Sandburg's uncaring grass that conceals the past. Giving roots to memories, nature can retrieve these spaces, and with them, a glimpse of renewal, a desire for transformation.

Such camps, like that of Mauthausen (near Linz in Austria), were liberated so very late in the war, many buildings remained virtually intact; almost half the camp survived physically much the same as in 1945. Whilst a majority of the wooden buildings and the death barracks have been demolished, its small gas chambers labelled *ausser betrieb* ('out of use') are still there; sobering places, now made exhibitionary and experiential. On the other hand, the clutter of national and political memorials next to the prison, above the quarry and on the site of demolished buildings are unsightly and distracting. Bombastic competing claims and agendas from the 1940s and 1950s avert the gaze from the terrible quarry and the 'staircase of death', where so many, regardless of ethnic or political affiliation, died as slave labourers, killed themselves or were murdered.[8] The quarry itself is neither 'museum' nor 'memorial', it is the affective site of Mauthausen – the place of warnings, the *mahnmal*.

Counter-memory, commodity, or 'museumification'?

Remembering the two world wars has been the main stimulus to many of the memorial museums in Europe. For many of them, the Great War seems to have been the founding, if not, the watershed event. They were a key part of memorial museum revival, even if some were not created until after 1980. At the outset, encouraged by local entrepreneurs, the Michelin battlefield illustrated guides of 1919 (Chapter 1, image 1.1) did not signal innovation: these were not the first such enterprises organized around memory ventures of collective mourning. Since the Paris Commune in the 1870s, Thomas Cook had catered for those looking for touristic voyeurism. Despite difficulties, and dangers, visits to battlefields even preceded November 1918[9] and included post-war services to mourners looking for personal sites of loss. Though a major marker for what has developed as modern mass memory visitation, the first Michelin project was initially a business failure (Image 9.3).[10]

IMAGE 9.3 'Liberated Belgium: Visit its battlefields' (*La Belgique Libérée: Visitez ses champs de bataille*). Belgian post-World War One tourist postcard, 1919. Hardly indicative of the horror and devastation of the Western Front, but tourism was a way of surviving for the returning population. © Imperial War Museums (Art. IWM PST 3951).

Now, visits to such sites appear in global holiday brochures alongside Amsterdam, Ypres or Krakow, even Saigon (Ho-Chi-Minh City) or Hanoi. They indicate the topographical commercialization of commemoration sites and anniversaries. Memory is diluted; turned into official, public – and typically 'national' – 'heritage cults' and rituals.

Since the 1980s and 1990s, popular participatory re-enactments, with media coverage and opportunities recruited large numbers to centenaries lacking any political or ethical implication. But in dozens of countries, these conflations overlapped with more serious educational projects, school trips and teaching packs. In the late 1980s more didactic museums in Ieper (Ypres), Caen, London, Manchester, Peronne (Somme) and Osaka developed, some with small visitor centres, such as those at Thiepval, Passchendaele and several in Berlin. Holocaust museums such as Mauthausen and the Anne Frank House, discussed earlier, were regularly revised and changed. At Guernica (the 1936 memorial museum), as elsewhere new curatorial demands were met, for example, after the pact of silence. Visitor numbers grew everywhere. Yet a reappraisal of these projects by critics was often negative: new 'memory cults' implied greater press scrutiny, TV programmes and links to biographical films. It was a mood of consumerism that generated and encouraged the memory 'business' and museums met touristic and popular demands. But this commodification of the past created issues of dubious judgement and taste. It explains the scepticism and ambivalence with which scholars approach the ethics and aesthetics of the 'museumification' of memory.[11]

The contest over what exploring 'the realms of memory' means raises dilemmas of preservation, development and what might compromise the 'sanctity of remembrance'. As early as 1920, the abundance of kitsch and shoddy souvenirs was a complaint by numerous visitors (many mourners) to Ypres/Ieper in Flanders. New memory entrepreneurs have transformed scores more local and lesser-known unofficial venues. Some sites are carefully preserved and enhanced, collecting and storing memorial artefacts, reviving memory traditions and re-enacting events. Some even created new 'concepts' for museums, public and private, to commemorate issues of human rights, slavery and genocide. For example, the 'Africa Museum' in Brussels is being transformed to acknowledge the atrocities of King Leopold II in the Congo, despite its triumphalist architecture. In addition memorials are created to resistance and to social movements: in the USA, civil rights, in South Africa the anti-apartheid struggle, and in many places the women's movement, and such specifics as the AIDS quilt. A number of small, inspired peace museums have flourished, as in Bradford, England. Other more spectacular projects as in Lisbon became beset by controversy over presenting the imperial past.

The operations of the memory business reveal that, if a semblance of a past remains, once such sites are restored and opened for visits then many became eminently exploitable. To encourage visitation for commercial gain, not just a souvenir shop, a restaurant, but also potentially a theme park, or at least a film, an 'entertainment' dimension or an 'experience' can be created. Even if short of Disneyfication, this ambiguous and problematic development risks unhealthy voyeurism even if it claims educational aims. In such displays, the danger of mystification is never entirely absent. Deep ambiguities of purpose attend visits to sites of prosthesis; a memory remains there of past pain and depravity. To celebrate past martyrs or heroes, new ideologues, as one commentator observed, risk cultivating resurgent hagiographies and personality cults. The international controversy over the Polish priest Father Kolbe's 'martyrdom' at Auschwitz is a clear instance of clashing agendas and manipulation of memory.

Some 'time capsule' preservations produce a bizarre effect of a past frozen in time that has its own strange authenticity. Visited by British war tourists since the 1920s, the muddy 'Hill 60' Museum at Sanctuary Wood near Ypres (Ieper) is one of the best examples of such a commercialization of 'remnants'. *The Tranchées/Loopgraven* (trenches) stand in complete contrast to Gibeau's work at Craonne. There a site survives, rusting in the Flanders mud, except for new saplings growing, it is virtually unaltered since 1918. The trenches and a museum are on a small family farm, and little has changed since the Armistice. The owners patched up the remains, and they annually repair or re-dig some muddy 'saps'. These saps are the small front line attack trenches used by the British and Canadians. Nearby, in a converted farm building, an archaic exhibit of found objects from the area includes battlefield bric-a-brac. The *pieces de resistance* of the place, however, are rare glass plate slides: raw and shocking contemporaneous photographs (Belgian and French) of atrocity. They are presented in machines, almost constituting a peepshow, like an amusement arcade. To view these, visitors enter the 'museum' through a bar and a dusty café. Many coach tours arrive and pay the ticket at the turnstile. They gaze at the dilapidated trenches, and the stark, horrific, if not obscene, photographs of slaughter. The exhibit has no age restriction. The images are as disturbing and as atrocious as anything at Auschwitz, Mauthausen or Hiroshima. Yet visitors cannot avoid a childlike or sensationalist gaze. Such raw paraphernalia, on the edge of a small Belgian wood, in a corner of fields in Flanders, nevertheless in one sense also remains, in Rupert Brooke's cliché, a place that is 'forever England'. I wrote to the local museum that "Perhaps the British National Trust should have acquired this as one genuine 'corner of a foreign field?'" But if so, then the world might have lost a piece of time-warp memorabilia, for it too might have been tidied up, 'museumalized, censored, presentized', and even 'nationalized'.

'Museums for peace'

This new generation of 'memorial' museums, as I have noted, includes several describing themselves as 'peace museums'. Other new, alternative examples of 'exhibiting the past' reflect a more internationalist and public 'peace' ethos, if not using the epithet peace. A mile from the Hill 60 museum, the civilian-oriented *In Flanders Fields Museum* (IFF), Ieper, defies the archetype, of a purely militarized memory, of war museums. It states that it is *not* a peace museum, but curated by a memory worker with wider vision, it focuses on following human stories, many electronically recorded.[12] With new sophisticated digital technology in many new museums, these displays are more easily revised, translated and copied. Each tell an individual story, even using the 'identity' card as a guide.

Nevertheless such exhibits remain fraught with contradictions of purpose. Curators are asked, 'For whom are they created, to display what, and why? To argue what?' To focus on the horror of war and militarism? A vision of a transformed world? To illustrate genocide as a moral lesson? To seek to empower and transcend racism and prejudice?

I have discussed the Ann Frank House Foundation and its attempts to do the latter, to promote tolerance, to create empathy with victims, and yet still not paralyse with horror as Ernst Friedrich's Horrors of War Museum in Berlin had.[13] Is it possible to balance in an exhibitionary setting, the humanity in the soldier, or detainee, as well as the civilian, with the compromises of real life, the ambiguities of 'heroism' and the problematics of conflict in pursuit of national advantage? To respect suffering without necessarily validating such overall contexts of 'victimhood' or 'sacrifice'? In displaying a more civilian than military memory, the mnemonic device of 'recognition' of multiple actors involved in conflict is an obvious one. Innovative aspects of 'truth-telling about war' institutionalize changes in site visitation, and confront these questions conceptually.

A seriously motivated *International Network of Peace Museums* (INPM) was established in the 1980s. It was led by Peter van den Dungen, a Dutch peace scholar based at Bradford in the UK. He recognized that there was a wider urge for peace history to capitalize on the boom in 'memory tourism'. Yet there was a need to change the culture of visitation and raise moral concerns: to ensure, for example, that buying Hiroshima's tourist t-shirts could no longer accompany ignorance of the facts of the 'atomic' past. Tourist publications needed to be supplemented with peace history, and not only in Japan. Peace Museums implied a contestation with the manufacturing of memory as myths. It challenged an ambiguous trend towards burgeoning 'battlefield' and 'heritage' tours, as newly 'sited' foci of remembrance, promoted by popular press and film coverage, proliferated.

Large redesigned memorials and museums also fostered public architectural competitions for the buildings and monuments. Major examples were at Caen (Normandy), the Jewish Museum extensions and several other sites in central Berlin, also the Imperial War Museum (IWM) North at Manchester (Salford), the Holocaust Museum in Washington DC and the Ground Zero memorial in Manhattan. In the main, these were conventional, mainstream projects. But a more transnational, pacifist, even postnational approach to memory, such as that of the peace museums network, formerly appeared at Verdun (the 'Mondiale' in the renovated Bishop Palace), and in the 'Historial de la Grande Guerre' at Peronne' in a former fort on the Somme.[14]

Indeed the In Flanders Fields museum (IFF) shared some of the INPM's perspectives. Such projects represent attempts to universalize and compare the experiences of specific sites and aspects of wars, previously ignored within the different national societies and groups involved. For example, as Winter has argued, at Peronne: in a postnational comparison, uniforms and equipment from each protagonist lie separately, flat on the ground, each is set as anonymous as its neighbour. The first three galleries depict the global background to the World Wars comparatively, perhaps addressing the increasingly international character of its visitors.[15] But Dix's *Krieg* (War) series is given its own key space in the initial transition gallery. Some late galleries, especially the memorials, are more specifically French in concept, approach and application perhaps in the spirit of Pierre Nora.

The IFF also has a local flavour: it exists in an area of Belgium where Flemish and Walloon/French culture was always in tension. The presence of many international troops, not only the Belgian, but also the British and French armies contributes a unique transnational element. Whilst the German army was at a distance from Ypres, on the perimeter of the Salient, marked by the new Paschendaele exhibit, newly revised displays provide a growing counterweight to a segregated Allied/German memorializing. Aspiring to a more transnational and European approach, even if less self-consciously demystifying than at Peronne, the (IFF) is significant as a Belgian site: it is close to both the French border and the Channel coast. The Belgian curator, Piet Chielens, himself an internationalist memory worker, is a local doctor's son. A Fleming and a folk-music enthusiast, a key figure in the work of the museum, he has been able to transcend some local and larger conflicts, by promoting interest in such themes as Irish, Chinese, Flemish and, overall, particularly local, civilian memories. He also innovated by integrating contemporary issues and global conflicts together with media and world music, transcending purely military aspects of events in the locality of Flanders.

If not yet a fully postnational museum, the IFF 'crosses borders' and is multinational: it is 'populated' by both civilians and soldiers, 'officers' and 'men', women and children; its sound narratives are in French, German, British, Irish and Dutch, including local Belgian civilians. Such local voices, French and Dutch speakers, also remind us of key ethnic divisions, reflected in the Belgian forces: Flemings were mainly conscripts, and Walloons were mainly the officers. Overall protagonists and onlookers, local and foreign, including non-Europeans, find an equality in collective memory. The nationalities who from 1914–18 lived, fought or died in the salient: African and Indian troops and even Chinese labourers are placed alongside local civilians, refugees, nurses. Even those 'shot at dawn', as deserters, spies, or objectors[16] are included.

Interestingly, the Ieper region is now more Belgian (Flemish), and is also more Anglophile than before, with the French-speaking community now a minority. Moreover being very close to the Channel ports and importantly to the British exam syllabi, there is always a significant proportion of English children and their teachers throughout the school year, visiting the museum and the area. It is accessible for descendants, relatives, veterans and the curious tourists – increasingly Germans, as well as thousands of Commonwealth visitors. The IFF museum is experientially a more approachable and popular venue, with its universalistic perspectives.[17] As the exhibits are represented in an accessible, less stylized way than at the *Mondiale* at Verdun or in the Historiale at Peronne,[18] it is ideal for educational groups. Its directorship is more cosmopolitan, both committedly European and locally rooted. Chielens' role as a director has been to steward the traumas of the Salient into a remarkable museum of permanent and temporary exhibits, accompanied by continued research. Its depth of personal identification contrasts with the oblique, almost academic approach, of many similar or more traditional memorial museums across Europe.

Memorial City: Berlin

Testifying to its success in coming to terms with the past, the vocabulary of German memorial sites is the most diverse and sophisticated of any modern culture. As a city Berlin is not a 'memorial' in itself, but it is so full of sites that make it itself a *Mahnmal*, a place of warning, as well as a *Denkmal*, a place of contemplation. In the context of confused and contested memory spaces, Berlin as a city stands out. This is symbolized by Norman Foster's renovated Reichstag, with all the ambiguities that surround it. The absence of the Berlin Wall after three decades of existence illustrates the importance of spaces in depicting an urban past. There is no lasting marker of the idiosyncratic, visionary and independent 'Checkpoint Charlie Museum'. It was at heart a trans-European, even postnational project and crossed boundaries in art and politics. Focused on nonviolence and human rights; escape from the GDR was framed as transnational civic emancipation.

Other sites are amended to give new meaning; the *avant-garde* extension of the otherwise modestly traditional Jewish Museum could have been a risk, but the recreated modernist memorial space of Daniel Libeskind makes it an exceptional building. Its genius lies in its open-endedness; it is not an anti-enlightenment statement, but suggests the initial failure of the humanized cosmopolitan project in its first embodiment. As intended, the experience of a journey though the conservative museum and radical memorial is extraordinarily disorienting: the transition represents a disconnect from the conventional, even comfortable, significantly integrated Jewish (bourgeois) history of the old building. Since it is an addition of a wing to the original city museum buildings, this juxtaposition represents the symbolic structuring of cultural discontinuity and a traumatic rupture,[19] in which memory may be lost, confused, ill-remembered. But it does not become part of the 'screen' that conceals the 'murdered Jews of Europe', now memorialized elsewhere nearer the site of the Berlin Wall, with its own maze of multiple stone blocks. In each case the metaphor of a maze is that of a disorientation: a dislocation. Libeskind's monument gives the Shoah this sense, where others have failed.

The parallel or reference may be unintentional in Berlin, but something similar to the new Holocaust memorial at the Potsdamer Platz exists in the monument at Treblinka in Poland. But there the stone monoliths retain ugly power, because they stand alone at an authentic site of mass death. But at the Potsdamer Platz, at a new hub of commerce and high-rise offices, with no trees, no grass, such effect is lost. The memorial installation was a result of a widely media-promoted popular and controversial competition; the result appears, as it is, a committee compromise. Critics have judged the design a sterile product, in an inappropriate place – at worst banal and mediocre rather than offensive, it is too easy to ignore. In the German lexicon, it is not a 'think place' or 'warning place', like Plotzensee, nor is it revelatory like the Gestapo Gelande interrogation centre (uncovered as the 'Topography of Terror' near Prinz Albrecht Strasse, at either side of the former Wall).

These sites (*Geländer*) were revealed step-by-step by local volunteers in a post-1989 non-governmental archaeology project. Like the protected remains of several ruined crematoria in Poland, or civil war graves in Spain, these initially unpopular projects serve the same end: they are modes of authentication and counter-denial. These revealed topographies, worldwide, are local sites which both represent and break a silence that still exists. In and very near the city of Berlin and Plotzensee are Ravensbrűck, Sachsenhausen, even Buchenwald; they were promoted by German volunteers since the 1950s, but have not been as visited. Since they are linked to German opposition and resistance, they are 'political'. The 1940s sites are retained and now their reference and meaning are revived, for example, in Kiefers art. They become clearly evidential – not only of the initial trauma (and some miraculous individual survivals), but also as testament to where the Nazi assault on democracy and human rights first accelerated. So far these sites have been less sanitized by fake reconstructions, grand token monuments or extensive visitor centres and museums. As examples of notable memory places which easily could have been erased, they represent memories of acts of early resistance – perhaps more significant than the museum at the Bendlerblock, where the Stauffenberg conspirators were arrested and executed when news of the failed plot against Hitler arrived in Berlin.

The Reichstag has been re-invented with an appropriate new dome. But also now acknowledged is another of Berlin's significant places of decision-making: the handsome suburban Wannsee Conference House stands as testimony to evil. It retains its table, around which Eichmann, Heydrich and the other organizers of the Final Solution sat in 1942, to plan the Holocaust. Memory sites of this kind are perhaps needed as much, or more, than further sites of loss. The lakeside Wannsee Villa also belongs to the victims of 1943–45. Though most such sites are destroyed, or not open to scrutiny, wherever totalism has been defeated they locate decisions of technical rationality – their survival testifies acts of political will by national states. To restore that memory in Berlin, the Conference House was eventually in 1992 established as a museum to commemorate the fiftieth anniversary of the catastrophic decision. Across the globe many similar sites exist: far from Cold War Europe in South Africa, Chile and Argentina, or for example in cities such as Madrid, Rome or Vichy, which would prove equally as revelatory as Wannsee.

The Neue Wache memorial

Another monument at the memorial crossroads of Europe, on the Unter den Linden, in what was once East Berlin, stands one of the oddest, most contradictory, yet perhaps surprisingly effective, juxtapositions of *contested symbols*, denoting human loss in war and totalism. The monument is about a European, not merely German, mourning of 'war *and* genocide'. Despite many twists and turns in its history, it survives as a postnational icon, an enduring memorial and a *Gedenkstatte*. In1960, it was dedicated by the GDR government to the 'victims of fascism and militarism'. Sited in the classical 1815 Neue Wache building it was a military site, a former a Prussian guardhouse. It has an open roof, so the weather, sun, rain and snow enters the space and transforms the monument. After 1920, it was a war memorial, and it housed the 'Unknown Soldier' placed there in a democratic Weimar Germany. The sculpture now inside is anti-war, a so-called 'Pieta'. It is an enlarged version of one of Käthe Kollwitz's existing smaller figures: a sculptured mother cradling a dead son (Image 9.4). Despite the religious references or attribution, it is not particularly 'Christian', but more a universal cypher than Michelangelo's Pieta, and stylistically quite different.

IMAGE 9.4 The interior of Neue Wache in Berlin, with Käthe Kollwitz's sculpture, an enlargement of a Pieta. Once a Prussian Guardhouse, an unknown soldier was placed here in the 1920s. After 1945 it served as a memorial to victims of fascism and militarism, and in the 1990s to victims of war and dictatorship. Kollwitz's sculpture was added after World War Two. Photo: JHA.

This adaptation and fusion of elements – secular and religious, military and civilian, memorializing and critical – was widely criticized as incongruous. Even though the sculpture reproduced is of a larger figure than the original – not of a size envisaged by the artist herself – the evidence is that visitors view it as one of the most powerful and memorable sites in Berlin. Neue Wache is certainly politically contestational: it counters both its Prussian militarist original surroundings and, in a sense now also, retrospectively, the Stalinist East German communist authorities. It was they who commissioned the figure and inscription, and first put it there in 1960. Even the West was challenged by its existence, since Germany's allied occupation authorities had banned all war memorials after the war. The communist-influenced Left in both East and West Germany, which had already used Kollwitz's compassionate images for its own political protest, now endorsed her work.[20] Yet Kollwitz had become a pacifist in the 1920s, and her art was strong enough to resist co-optation by any ideology. After the reunification of the two Germanies, the previous 1960s dedication of the memorial was changed to 'Victims of war and dictatorship'. This represented a more inclusive list, to allow also for the victims of communism (before 1990). But adaptations of Kollwitz's work and its meaning, like the Neue Wache itself, was controversial, perhaps ambiguous, but undeniably powerful.[21]

Another physical space linked more personally to Kollwitz's tragic life is at Vladslo and her *Grieving Parents* (*Eltern*) monument there. The sculpture finally fulfilled her eighteen-year promise to her dead son Peter. After its placement near her son's grave, originally in Roggevelde, it is now in a quiet tree-lined German graveyard. Enhancing the ambience of a site of memory, and described as her greatest achievement, it expresses an alternative way of mourning. The *Parents* memorial in Flanders is both personal and universal. It represents Kollwitz herself as a self-portrait, a sculpted kneeling figure next to that of her husband, Karl; her head is bowed over Peter's grave (Image 9.5). Her husband's statue (depicted in the 1932 photograph) stares out over the cemetery, as if over all the mass graves, and all the killing fields of all the wars, grim if not resigned. Many who view it, interpret it as an anti-war statement as well as a personal plea: asking forgiveness, not indeed just from Peter and from Karl (who opposed his son's decision to go fight in the war), but also from all the victims of modern war and genocide. But not least from their son, for allowing him, if not encouraging him, to go to fight.

Since the millennium, the role of major public monuments and new museums has become ever more controversial. I have alluded to a major example, 'the murdered Jews' memorial in Berlin, situated near the Potsdamer Platz and Brandenburg Gate. Its siting is purely artificial. Unlike Kollwitz's memorial, it has little connectedness to an irrelevant and, to many, an inappropriate place. In sharp comparison, for example, in a neglected industrialized area a few miles away, is the depressing (and often bypassed) Plotzensee Prison with its harrowing history. It is small, often forgotten, but intensely moving; hundreds of opponents of Hitler, mainly civilians, were tortured and hung there, one for listening to the BBC.

IMAGE 9.5 Käthe Kollwitz, *The Grieving Parents*, 1932. Vladslo German War Cemetery, West Flanders, Belgium. The sculptures were moved to this large collective cemetery (see also Image 1.3 of the Kollwitzs at the Roggevelde site in 1932). The grave of their son Peter is one of those in front of the parents, amongst many 'unbekannte deutscher soldaten' (unknown dead). By permission of IFF.

Sites for monuments, or spaces for memories?

Plotzensee and Vladslo, as opposed to monumental places of 'history' and large ambitious memorials, are physical *lieux*. Most of these are validated by being *personalized* in terms of the lives of the individual actors: victims, such as Anne Frank in Amsterdam, activists and war resisters, such as Sophie Scholl and the White Rose students in Munich, or Rosa Luxemburg with her tiny memorial plaque by the Landwehrkanal in Berlin; Walter Benjamin's two memorials in Portbou, or in the USA, memorials to murdered civil rights activists, including Medgar Evers in Jackson, Mississippi.

In Munich, the memorial plates for the Scholl siblings are set in the pavements of the Scholl Platz at the university, where the Munich students defied Fascism (Image 9.6). These simple sidewalk markers, commemorating acts of resistance on 18 February 1943, sadly so often vandalized or in disrepair, speak for themselves: 'it happened here – remember these acts'. Sophie Scholl was rushing to distribute her pile of clandestine anti-Nazi leaflets; she carried them in a suitcase to place on the seats of the large lecture auditorium (Aula)

IMAGE 9.6 Memorial outside the main campus of Munich University for Hans and Sophie Scholl and the 'White Rose' resistance movement against the Nazi regime. The memorial depicts the anti-war leaflets Sophie dropped as she ran away from the lecture hall. This led to her arrest and execution with others of her group and Professor Huber. These sculptural reproductions are set into the paving stones outside the 'Aula'. Ludwig Maximilian University of Munich, Germany. Photo: Martin Siepmann/Nordpool.

upstairs at the Ludwig Maximilian University. Hurrying before the next class of students arrived, she dashed down from the hall, dropping her remaining leaflets. She was seen by a janitor who informed the Gestapo. More leaflets fell on the sidewalk outside the building. There they still 'lie', now reproduced, as engravings, embedded in the cobble stones as a permanent memorial to that moment, and to her and her courageous fellow students. This was the 'White Rose' (Weisse Rose) group, formed in 1942; and six of the Munich group, including Sophie, her brother Hans, and Christoph Probst, and later her professor, Dr Huber, and the two other students, Alexander Schmorell and Willi Graf, were arrested, interrogated and all six executed, as were others in

Hamburg. Four days after her arrest, on 22 February 1943, Sophie was guillotined, with Hans, and the others followed. The concept of the 'Geschwister Scholl Platz' (the Scholl Siblings' Square) and the 'Huber Platz' opposite has an immediacy and simplicity, made more powerful by the fact that what now is the law faculty has the same appearance that it had in February 1943. Place and presence give spatial and temporal meaning to an event with the simplest of memorials; today's students' walk across them or picnic nearby at lunchtime. As a 'monument', the White Rose memorial brings resistance to atrocity together with a story of collaboration and witness – the perpetration of historic crimes into an everyday working environment.

Names and places

In discussing both the Great War and the Shoah, I noted how remembering can be linked to images triggered by the names of sites – such as the Umschlagplatz in Warsaw. These mantras bring back a 'shared past'. It suggests that memory and identity can become linked by places even in a global culture, the mnemonic name summons an image of a traumatic sites shared across borders. A postnational imagination in the arts is offered huge scope for such twinned representations.

Since classical antiquity, control over the place, form and meaning of public rituals of mourning, the framing and imaging of remembrance, has always been highly political. This is especially true of war monuments such as Madrid's Valley of the Fallen, and major military cemeteries, in the USA and Russia, which enable the public design of icons of mourning for the dead. Even if there are names, sculpted in stone at the Menin Gate and similar monuments, they are mostly out of reach. But it appears new generations seek a more individualized, tactile memorial, a name in stone for survivors or relatives to find, a personal mnemonic presence, at the Vietnam Wall, for example, as a ritualized prosthesis. This is symbolically completed by touching one or more of the Wall's names, physically (Image 9.7).[22] This is symptomatic of what Reinhard Koselleck sees as a democratization and in some ways civilianization of memory that emerged with drafted mass armies and modern war. Increasingly memorials individualized loss in the twentieth century by listing the dead by name, especially in the Commonwealth, Europe and the USA. Since 1918, these inscriptions of relatives attract visitors, mourners and veterans from around the world.

To feel the engraved names of the mostly conscripted victims in Washington is perhaps a key to the controversy stirred by the Vietnam Wall's symbolism. It identified the individual draftees among the American dead, not as representatives of a victorious nation or state, but as a lost son, brother, daughter, sister or friend. The physicality of names of the individual 59,000 US dead engraved on marble was the essence of the experience of being there. One could not touch the body – it might not have survived – only the name. But the nationalization of an asymmetric loss in such a distinctive way is also made tangible too. A million Vietnamese names would require a very long wall indeed, and

IMAGE 9.7 Student searching for names at the Menin Gate in Ypres, Belgium, 1994. The gate lists the names of the missing soldiers in Belgian Flanders. Photo: Nigel Young.

It would take a lot more time to find a relative's inscription. However, with over 600,000, names a new large-scale postnational memorial at Notre Dame de Lorette in Picardy aspires to this. But it asks different questions – 'Read all the names', it asks us, '***They are all there; all victims of war itself***'.

Thiepval too has its names, and whilst I have interpreted it as critical, it is not self-consciously a 'counter-monument' any more than the all American presentation of the dead on May Lin's Vietnam War Veterans Wall Memorial. Despite Washington's less war-related setting, both memorials defy conventional thought on what such a structure should be. They counter our expectations of such sites, and both have become sites of mass visitation and a dimension of a contest over images of loss. As James Young argues: "The aim of memorials is *not* to call attention to *their own* presence", so much as to 'past events' (the Somme), because they have gone and the viewer needs to be steered towards a focus on *imagining* the past.[23] Normally, that seems the case. Whilst May Lin's Wall sinks beneath the ground, Thiepval rears skywards. Lutyens is saying something different: 'view this space', Thiepval demands, as it rises above the ridge overlooking the Somme, the position that the armies tried to reach in July 1916.

The Vietnam memorial, several European memorials and monuments to World War One dead, such as Thiepval and even the Menin Gate in Ieper, were widely controversial at the time, and contested in different ways since. None exist as simple 'ideological statements'.[24] Far from being an obvious critic, the genius of Lutyens's Thiepval potentially engages us in a dialogue about *war* and of absences after war, which I discussed in Chapter 2. The more simple, conventional Menin Gate on the other hand engages in a narrative about power and collaboration in war, and individual loss. The power over commemoration and the control of political contest reflect long-term struggles over the possession of historical memory, which is unlikely to end soon. Grandchildren have visited, and formed their opinions, and memories in generational cycles continue, and increasingly that will relate to either national or postnational identification.

If memorials should not draw attention to themselves,[25] covert counter-memorializing is perhaps the only 'closure' that a memorial such as Thiepval could offer. For the post-modern imagination that would involve its own symbolic demolition, the ultimate deconstruction in a counter-monumental event. Thiepval has been, perhaps aptly, described by Samuel Hynes as 'a pile of bricks and stones' – *and it is exactly that.* Unlike the Reichstag, Christo has not draped it yet, but Thiepval decidedly repels more than attracts – it even shocks. Mocking many other more traditional memorials, including Lutyens's own Imperial 'epics', such as his Delhi Gate in India, and Blomfield's more modest, but locally and internationally admired Menin Gate, it also stands in contrast to the large, stark Canadian sculptured monument dominating the Vimy Ridge. But Thiepval is different. It obtrudes into the scene – drawing attention to itself and to the spaces in or around it. Over the years and in terms of modern, if not postnational, memory, Thiepval arguably survives as a brutal, truth-seeking, counter-intrusion both into our historical present and into our presence in a now pastoral landscape. Yet it also defies Sandburg's 'grass' and the cosmetic of farmed land and serves to deny closure or cultural acceptance – to mock the grass – to say 'something else happened here!' Like the preserved Guard Towers at Birkenau, this part of the Somme is an awkward, conflicted site, and at each visit it poses new questions.

Less personalized ruins, such as the Hiroshima's atomic dome, warn of omnicide, but the remains of the ruined memorial church, the Gedächtniskirche in the Kurfurstendam in Berlin, or the ruined chapel left alongside the new Coventry Cathedral, serve different purposes as mnemonics of city death. Each reminds us that the project of urbicide continues in modern cities such as Aleppo, Damascus and Mosul. Ruins will be left to mark the 'death' of these or in Gaza, Lebanon, Iraq, Syria and perhaps in Yemen.

As such a reminder of urban death in Berlin, in an area at the ruins of the former Anhalter Bahnhof station, a counter-memory has been creatively installed and enacted. The noises from a rebuilt, populated station in Cologne (as it is now) were broadcast over the empty spaces of a no-man's land in Berlin from 1945. At such memory places, imaginaries, the sounds of past and present, can be potentially transported to other memory sites, even worldwide.[26]

Places past remembered: Nevers and Hiroshima

Alain Resnais's film *Hiroshima Mon Amour* is not an easily accessible work of art, but with Marguerite Duras's script it remains one of the most innovative classic transnational texts of modern memory: a highly discursive meditation involves a return to two specific physical sites of memory in two continents. The main site is the city of Hiroshima, with its then 'new' (1954) Atomic Museum. Quite close to the Atomic Bomb's epicentre and the so-called Hiroshima Dome, the story represents a return both physically and mnemonically. Another secondary site is returned to in the film in flashbacks: Nevers, in France, the home of a French actress' buried memory of an occupied small provincial town on the Loire. In her Japanese self-dialogue she is forced to confront her own silenced traumas: as a branded and shorn 'collaborator'. After the German occupiers left in 1945, it was the death of one young German soldier, her wartime lover, that marked that moment. If her memory of this is not a dream of her 'collaboration' with 'the other' (the enemy), but, as critics have suggested, a real loss, then it matches some of the reality of her new Japanese lover's memory of war.

But the film is also centrally concerned with the two places, and in Duras's text, the two lovers emphasize their salience. But he tells her, "You were never there!"[27] She is a French actress visiting Hiroshima, making a 'peace film', and although also a 'survivor' of war, she could never re-experience such events from museums or artefacts. The Japanese survivor from the outset dismisses any second-hand remembrance of the 6th of August events from the museum. Only by implication – by remembering her own memories of humiliation and love – could she understand this past. The present, the flashing neon city, busy erasing real memories of the past, is the backdrop to this dialogue about alienated memory. Their recall is linked to sites of trauma, and whilst it includes acknowledgement, this is a very different kind of 'recognition' scene. But the tortured dialogue of the lovers does eventually take the woman (played by Emmanuelle Riva) beyond her predominantly proxy, tourist 'memory' of the atomic bombing, to engage with an *experienced memory*. Through her lover, the Japanese architect, and his own experience of 1945, she reaches her own memory of that year: shamed, shaved and punished – not for having a French, but a German lover. The stark symbolism of this transnational recognition – Japanese, French *and* German – metaphorically but powerfully transcends 'wartime' national identities: these evolve into potential post-nation, civilian ones, with a recognition scene of the 'time and place' of twinned traumas.

Through the couple's discussion of the museum as atomic tourism, the text also implicitly criticizes the superficiality of a naïve 'international' 'peace movement' and its 'peace culture', then sustained in a Cold War context. Resnais's political awareness of such manipulation of peace by politics, both municipal and national, enables this to be contrasted with authentic individual experiences: two lovers in a chance encounter. The man from Hiroshima, and the woman from Nevers, meet but in a special yet manufactured and desecrated site of universal memory. A key moment, near the end of the film, is when the lovers underline how important *place* is:

> 'Hi-ro-shi-ma. That's your name.'
> 'That's my name...
> Yes. Your name is Nevers. Ne-vers in France.'

Again the names of two places, Hiroshima – his family was there in 1945 – and Nevers, "by the river, just as it was": time overshadowed it, even screened it from memory for years – a doomed love affair with an 'enemy'.

One can imagine in another version of this moment, her saying 'Don't forget me' to her soldier lover as he lay dying, even having written in French an equivalent message to that in Keith Douglas's poetry: a scribbled note like Steffi's left on another German corpse. In the scripts and filming of *Hiroshima Mon Amour*, Duras and Resnais propose that we cannot relive someone else's experience. However, revisiting the past, and returning to these sites, the places in memory may be crucial in any achievement of empathy in recall:

> 'You are Nevers' ... 'You are Hiroshima.'

The Japanese images later used in Watkins's film *The Journey* also remind us how little this part of modern Hiroshima has changed in the many decades since its reconstruction in the 1950s. There is the mound where ashes and human remains were and are placed, that is surrounded by memorials, and little else: it has been tidied up, the survivors grow old or have died, fewer relatives visit. The witnesses themselves are now few. Even the well-tended garden and sculptures, like those at Nagasaki, now seem contrived, manicured, even cosmetic. Displayed near the Atomic dome they help screen out the past, yet this ruin, once scheduled for destruction, was saved; at least it is an authentic part of a site.

In summer, the dome is sometimes floodlit for the tourists; it watches over the headlights and the snarl of downtown Hiroshima traffic, whose fumes still clouds the modern city, hiding the epicentre. A city that was once lit by the 'pika-don', a 'thousand suns', seventy-five years later is lit by thousands of flashing neon signs as in the postcards, just as the city of the early 1950s. In the film it is already a tawdry celebration of modernity that still challenges remembrance.

Seeking landscapes of memory in literature

At its best, mnemonic writing, like Duras's script, including inspirational journalism, is able to summon up a visual landscape. Both Orwell and Hemingway were able to impart such a vision to conflict, not least in Spain. They create images of place that remain long after the details are forgotten about. Here Hemingway describes a scene in dusty northeast Spain:

> I was watching the bridge and the African looking country of the Ebro Delta ... It was Easter Sunday and the Fascists were advancing towards the Ebro. It was a gray overcast day with a low ceiling so their planes were not up.[28]

Hemingway's coverage of the Spanish Civil War for a New York newspaper includes this famous moment when he was retreating, with the refugees to the north, from the Teruel Front. The Fascists were advancing to the River Ebro. The Republican forces, already weakened, were moving back to defend Barcelona. Hemingway met an old man there with his animals. Hemingway interviewed him as he rested by the bridge over the river; he wrote it first as a newspaper article, but he then transformed it into a now familiar vignette, and an iconic memory piece. The brilliant terse short story, *The Old Man at the Bridge* (1937), preserves that moment, long beyond the life of any newspaper story. And that was presumably why Hemingway chose to write about it as 'faction': to turn 'fact' to narrative memory, literature. Perhaps he hoped the image would last longer, be read more deeply, and returned to more often than any faded newspaper clipping (or possibly saved in today's digital archive).

Moments of recollection in such scenes recall civilian and domestic peace. Although this episode at the bridge was one largely of *non*-communication, it was a dialogue between 'equals'. As such it can be seen as one of the more honest interchanges in modern literature. It was effectively constructed because it was also a reproduction of an observed event, of an experience, of a refugee in the context of war. Hemingway's actual discussion with the 'Old Man' is particularly ironic. An American war reporter is trying to give an elderly Spanish civilian refugee, who cares for animals, some sound advice. And thankfully for the history, for memory and for literature about war, he reported it – not as a journalist, but as a creative writer:

> 'This not a good place to stop,' I said. 'If you can make it, there are trucks up the road where it forks to Tortosa.'
>
> 'I will wait a while, he said, and then I will go. Where do the trucks go?'
>
> 'Towards Barcelona', I told him. 'I know no one in that direction,' he said 'but thank you very much. Thank you again very much.'
>
> He looked at me very blankly and tiredly, then said, having to share his worry with someone, 'The cat will be all right, I am sure ...'
>
> 'If you are rested I would go,' I urged. 'Get up and try to walk now.'
>
> 'Thank you' he said and got to his feet, swayed from side to side and then sat down backwards in the dust.
>
> But at least their planes were not yet up, and the cat could look after itself.[29]

Just as I was prompted to visit and revisit a bus shelter at Adlestrop, or a graveyard at Vladslo, the impulse and fascination of modern memory work prompts some of us to seek such places. What place was it? Twelve miles from San Carlos? Hemingway's village is probably one of those nearby; south of Tortosa, one of which was then called Ribarroya, or another Ampota. Such sites remain elusive – and no doubt local researchers, other equally obsessive memory workers, can and will tell us more. It is a site which I twice tried to re-visit and confirm the memory, as much to question the settings and to date this actual moment. Credibly it *was* on Easter Sunday 17 April 1938. But certainly there was nothing that could be done for the old man, or the cat – or the goats and pigeons he also had to abandon.

Six months later on 16 November 1938, Hemingway and the other journalists on the Republican side were amongst the last people to retreat north across the same river, possibly at the same place, after the disastrous second battle of the Ebro. This retreat preceded the beginning of the Nationalist advance into Catalonia in December 1938 and January 1939 that presaged the final act and bloody defeat of the already fragmented Republic.

The takeover by Franco's authoritarian nationalists – essentially fascists but with a deep catholic base in society – and then their brutal reprisals, was a rehearsal for World War Two. It is not hard to see how many who had been genuine pacifists, felt a need – not only a heart-felt compassion, but also an intellectual imperative – to compromise their anti-militarist principles, however painful. It was also in the hope of perhaps averting the greater catastrophe of a wider war. Perhaps that is why the images of 1936–39, even Capra's sometimes staged photographs remain amongst the most poignant and jarring reminders in modern memory of the historical junctures and places that still haunt us in the twenty-first century. My own return to the beach at Benicassim or the bridge over the Ebro, and several other sites of the conflict in Spain, was because of a poem, a short story, a photograph or a novel. Such *a site of memory* once captured in prose or poetry, is one to be re-visited. Such sites invite questions – about our past, present and future – far more than they provide answers.

Notes

1 Maurice Halbwachs, *On Collective Memory* (New York, 1980).
2 Pierre Nora, *Realms of Memory: The Construction of the French Past* (New York, 1996).
3 Halbwachs (1980).
4 Modris Eksteins, *Rites of Spring: The Great War and the Birth of the Modern Age* (Boston, 1989), Preface to book.
5 Gèrard Rondeau, *Les Fantômes du Chemin des Dames, Le Presbytère d'Yves Gibeau* (Paris, 2003).
6 Rondeau (2003).
7 Like the Historial at Peronne, the In Flanders Fields museum (IFF) also offers a more sensitive resting place for objects from the battlefield.
8 Such memorials could be easily moved to another less obstructive site near the camp, and give back dignity to the sites of murder.

9 Paris after the Commune, even the American Civil War battlefields, provided precedents for the tours.
10 Writers on the Great War, such as Robert Graves admitted he cashed in on the memory boom after 1929, having noted the impact of Remarque's best-seller.
11 See Joyce Apsel and Amy Sodaro, *Museums and Sites of Persuasion: Politics, Memory and Human Rights* (Abingdon, UK, 2019).
12 Some outstanding peace and human rights museums in Japan do the same.
13 See Chapter 4: in general, 'war horrors' proved poor peace education or propaganda.
14 This involved professional historians such as Jay Winter and the Annette and Jean-Jacques Becker in key roles.
15 Except for an impassioned, one-sided and British film, it is European insofar as it includes German and British exhibits. The pre-1914 and 1914–18 gallery is especially successful in transcending a purely national perspective.
16 British, Germans, Canadians and Belgian alike are among the deserters, the shell shocked and the resisters memorialized in Ieper.
17 Contradictorily, however, Flemish opinion was in both wars more pro-German than pro-French. The unsightly Yser Tower memorial ten miles away stands as a symbolic 'peace' monument, but radically oriented towards Flemish nationalism.
18 Surprisingly the In Flanders Fields Museum is not mentioned in Paul Williams's *Memorial Museums: The Global Rush to Commemorate Atrocities* (Oxford and New York, 2007). Presumably this is because the slaughter in Flanders does not count as 'atrocity' in Williams's vocabulary.
19 See Andreas Huyssen, *Present Pasts: Urban Palimpsests and the Future of Memory* (Stanford, 2003).
20 For other references to Kollwitz and her memorials, see Jay Winter, *Sites of Memory, Sites of Mourning* (Cambridge, 1995), and Richard Cork, *A Bitter Truth: Avant Garde Art and the Great War* (New Haven, 1994).
21 This was the first time I remember seeing the work of Kollwitz, this rare collage poster was produced in about 1957, by the German anti-nuclear movement, but I was unable to find a copy as an illustration for this book. See also G. Mosse, *Fallen Soldiers: Reshaping the Memory of the Great War* (Oxford, 1990), pp. 97–98 and 113.
22 This 'touching the Wall' is part portrayed in the film *In Country* (1989), where veterans seek comrades who died. Also note the scene in *Memorial Day* (2012).
23 In Winter (1995). Also James E. Young, *Texture of Memory* (New Haven, 1994), 'Introduction'; see also Allyson Booth, *Postcards from the Trenches* (Oxford and New York, 1996) on Thiepval.
24 As Winter puts it.
25 See James E. Young, 'Memory and the Monument after 9/11', in R. Crownshaw, Jane Kilby and Antony Rowland, eds, *The Future of Memory* (New York and Oxford, 2010).
26 The Anhalter Bahnhof installation (Bill Fontana, *Distant Trains*, 1984), see Joan Gibbons, *Contemporary Art and Memory* (London, 2007), p. 50.
27 Marguerite Duras, *Hiroshima mon Amour* [script] (1959).
28 Ernest Hemingway, 'The Old Man at the Bridge', *The Short Stories of Ernest Hemingway*, 2nd edition (New York, 1953), p. 78.
29 Hemingway (1953), pp. 78–79.

10

BEYOND MILITARISM?

Peace and war in civil memory

Imperial War Museum

Here, let us say, all war is sanitised –
The question of the *product* isn't raised.
It's like a factory where clean machines
Hint at well-ordered past production lines.
The guns stand silent in their lovely paint
And it is innocent air at which they point.
There are no shells scream witchlike as they ride
Or charred black corpses on the Basra road.
There's camouflage, and razor wire, and scrim –
But not the wounded or the dying scream.
War was imperial, even now it's royal.
Some bodies here would make it much more real!
Some glorious wounds, to frighten or amaze
(some mustard gas would not come much amiss),
Some arms and legs, perhaps a severed head?
To reconstruct what History likes hid,
Waxworks could re-create the grievous harms
That are not seen in television homes.
This is the War that time cannot corrode,
The Fly-Past and the Victory Parade.
Sadness and Pride, of course, are in the cast –
But no true indication of the cost.
Bring on the war-struck, dazed, the dim civilians!
They should be here, the mild maltreated millions.

Gavin Ewart[1]

Public life in many parts of the world responded to a cultural imperative that met a need to recapture lost pasts. With travel tours to memory sites, and new museums proliferating, fresh generations of children and young people started pursuing such 'memory' projects as a family tree. Similar activities are now part of normal school experience in most industrial societies. It is one with, arguably, considerably more appeal than a traditional history lesson.

As a small example of this educational outreach, a week after Armistice Day in November 1994, a group of British secondary school students (Years 10 and 11) from Crestwood Community School in Eastleigh, Hampshire, England, visited the brilliantly conceived exhibition at the Barbican (London): 'A Bitter Truth, Avant Garde Art and the Great War'. It was a show ambitiously curated by Richard Cork, the then art critic of *The Times*. The Gallery's Educational Department worked with Andrew Snow, Head of English at the school, to produce an anthology of some of the students' work – mostly poetry – responding to the exhibition: 'Remembrance' and 'Memory' are common themes. One piece is entitled "I'm war, remember me" and of course, being November, the inevitable poppies. The cross-generational impact of that visit was potentially profound. It enabled an encounter with great twentieth-century and modernist art, images and quotations from those such as Paul Nash, who talks of a 'bitter truth', and other soldier artists who had confronted war as witnesses in the depth of trauma. Their work was presented in accessible, semi-representational ways. Subsequently, the popularity of Michael Morpurgo's memory-orientated children's stories and the National Theatre's unique Australian puppetry production of his *War Horse* story attracted a new generation of school children to theatres and to books that gave contact with such experienced memory of the Great War.

A more pronounced demilitarization of culture and society was predicted, and might have been expected, after two world wars, given the scale of twentieth-century violence. But with superpower rivalry and the often bloody process of decolonization, this hope was perhaps naïve. The sheer immensity and impact of modern mass conflict, coupled with the weakness or inadequacy of most political peace projects made this alternative unlikely. The one possible exception was the transnational formation of the European community of states, a region of co-operation and shared sovereignty, which has retained a fragile and threatened peace. Structured in a wider region of insecurity, demilitarization on the margins of this integrating Europe remained minimal. But the cultural, peace-creating aspect of memory that combined active representation of the negative results of twentieth-century war with new human aspirations and pragmatic proposals to transform conflicts became the central imperative of conflict analysis. Peace study acknowledged the necessary civic transformation to a less militarized culture. At times such an idea was little more than an existential 'lighting of candles' in an otherwise hostile institutional context. But even given the successive setbacks for peace movements, such as the end of illusions about the UN, a striving for grassroots reconciliation continued in many post-conflict societies, with new methodologies and projects.

Opposing the divisiveness of enemy images in culture, such utopian constructions of social action nevertheless showed how they can involve a positive depiction of conflict; for example, as potentially non-violent engagement. Such representation of change allows for the recognition scenes of the self-in-the-other/the-other-in-the-self that I have described in art, literature and cinema; these occur even in extreme moments of engagement such as in genocide or military combat. Pessimist theologians such as Niebuhr have dismissed such earthly dreams as idealistic. Yet such sites of acknowledgement and constructive engagement are a key element in demilitarizing and de-territorializing memory. Such moments can be interpreted as essential elements in transforming highly militarized cultures in the direction of less violent narratives. But they require a change of sensibility to a more empathetic consciousness and new forms of remembering. This explains the salience of sustaining a postnational, cross-boundary identity in the institutional preservation of the past, in museums, symbols and rituals.

The Imperial War Museum in London, which had opened in an abandoned mental asylum in 1921, was said, in the words of King George V in a speech at the opening, to exist 'in order to remind us of war' (1914–18), and to 'prevent us from repeating it'. When the project of war prevention failed in 1939, the museum became an arena of more intense public contestation. How could such an exhibit be both pacific and imperial, victim and perpetrator? The result – ambivalence and confusion of purpose, competing myths, randomly displayed – is a clear indication of the maelstrom besetting the postnational contest: anti-imperialist or anti-militarist projects sitting uncomfortably in an 'imperial' space of mainly national artefacts.

Inevitably by opening up such objects as museums, memorials and commemorative occasions to scrutiny – to a more critical memory of war and atrocity – we unleash a welter of competing images, agendas and ambivalent recollection: clashing interpretations and contrasting statistics. But who is to mediate military and civilian agendas, to arbitrate between religious and secular orientations, to care for the needs of personal mourners, as well as acknowledge those of school teachers, politicians, tour organizers, community 'morale boosters' and chiefs of staff? Each audience has different priorities and needs, as well as ethical and national agendas. Critiques of any public remembrance ceremony – such as the Armistice Day rituals, the Poppy Day events, or the Last Post ceremony at Ypres – range from pacifist to militarist, Christian to atheist, national to postnational. But what, if any, are the roles in this dialogue for social movements – including the non-governmental 'peace' movements? These not only seek a place at such ceremonies, but also at times attempts to change them, or create their own.

Representations of modern memory, the statues of historic figures and the displays that relate to war and atrocity, can be a *civilian* memory, and often a cross-frontier one. But an anti-militarist tendency did not simply counterpose 'Peace' museums with 'War' museums; indeed, these co-exist, sometimes uneasily. Both the British 'Imperial War Museums', in London and Manchester, now have clear peace references, quite unlike the traditional museums, such as the Napoleonic Musèe des Invalides in Paris. This time-warped display, which includes Napoleon's horse, is lampooned in *Hôtel des Invalides*, Franju's' ironic, anti-militarist film of the Army Veterans' Museum in the domes edifice and its adjoining hospital – a Parisian landmark (Image 10.1). In the film made in the 1950s, reacting to such archaic exhibits, George Franju follows tourists round these sites. The film ends with a buoyantly sardonic scene of a gaggle of children, army orphans from the school attached to the military 'Ecole'. Filmed leaving the Invalides, and marching along together, they are singing the former soldiers' song 'Auprés de Ma Blonde'. This seventeenth-century song was still sung by soldiers in 1914, and is now sung everywhere, especially by children, and almost as a nursery song.[2] In this mordant critique Franju suggests the layered incongruities of such re-visitations to patriotic military life; where army bric-à-brac is encountered with such a civilian presence, including tourists and army orphans. In constructing a demilitarized culture personified in this film, the hidden agenda of the whole corpus of postnational memory work is revealed. It is to displace, as Franju does, the language and imagery of nationalized militarism, to satirize it, and to start to civilianize and humanize it.

In contrast to this anachronistic '*musealization*', the IWM as an institution remains an impressive contradiction. It is a major site of memory, a priority in any visit to a city that seriously engages with its memorializing and its monumental militarization. Despite the finest collection of critical war art anywhere – an unrivalled library of war and anti-war posters, and probably the largest

IMAGE 10.1 Georges Franju's *Hôtel des Invalides*, 1952. In this ironic anti-militarist documentary Franju follows the tourists around the exhibits in the Army Veterans' Museum located in the historic Hôtel des Invalides in Paris. Here a wounded veteran is wheeled past an artillery piece.

archive on conscientious objection in the world – the museum, if not the city, remains a shrine to the military experience. The entrance hall ('the largest boy's bedroom in London'[3]) is full of iron and steel objects: weapons, including tanks, aeroplanes and missiles. This paraphernalia is part of the contested experience of military London, and by extension military Britain and its arms industry. The IWM's basic character is not much concealed by often excellent, but temporary, sometimes token, exhibitions. In general, peace and pacifism are subtly censored, even in the bookshop.[4] Exceptionally though in 2017, a 'People Power: Fighting for Peace' exhibition was thoughtfully curated, representing several breakthroughs in museum policy, and covering over a century of anti-war memories. As that exhibition illustrated, for some communities in the twentieth century, the negative focus on collective loss and a burial of the past was being transformed by social movements into a political, utopian goal: 'the abolition of war'. In societies worldwide, successive waves of mass anti-militarist sentiment in civil society arose: in the 1890s, in the 1930s, in the 1960s and also from 1979-86. Each sustained or revived a peace or anti-war memory: they united for example, many of those survivors who had fraternized, resisted, refused, objected even deserted or mutinied after 1914, and some from even before the Great War.

When soldiers 'voted with their feet' in Russia in their millions in 1917, in the USA, a vigorous militant mass anti-war struggle was already underway, based on socialist and labour union opposition to war and conscription. In 1917, resistance also spread in the French army, on the Chemin des Dames, and Verdun; it occurred in Italy after the battle of Caporetto, and had spread to Germany by September 1918. By the end of the war even Britain 1918–19 saw mutinies and riots. The early 1920s saw the growth of organizations such as the War Resisters International (WRI), and the 'No More War' movement inspired by anti-militarist resistance, and the refusal of conscripts to fight. Branches of WRI flourished in dozens of countries. In addition, after the unofficial Women's Hague Conference in 1915, an international anti-war women's movement and the Women's International League for Peace and Freedom also grew. Moreover, in the context of the rise of fascism, and remembrance of its victims, there were those whose compassion drove them to notable, extreme acts of selflessness in resistance both to the war of 1939 and to the excesses of totalitarianism. The memory of Pastor André Trocmé and the villagers of Le Chambon in protecting thousands of Jews is just one such testimony to a pacifists' role in extreme circumstances.

The democratization of public memorials

Reshaping society's memory after the Great War required a much more active involvement of local communities in the public construction of war memorials, creating consciously postnational sites and events, as well as engagement from cultural production, film and theatre. This process varied across national societies, and prioritized remembrance in different ways. Notably there was a deep and growing divergence between nationalist–militarist memorializing, symbolized by statues of generals and other military leaders, on the one hand, and a more universalistic, or pacifist orientation, on the other. Such postnational orientations in the 1980s were expressed both in peace culture and in institution building (such as museums, libraries and university centres). In film, theatre and art, a creative genre was adopted and publicized: it was work that condemned all war. Certainly in the cases of Käthe Kollwitz and the two Marukis, it endorsed without reservation a humanist and de-territorialized compassion for humanity. This was popularized and stretching beyond kin, ethnicity or homeland, such cultural product represents a species' search for a more redemptive response to modern violence.

Such rewriting of the script of collective memory in response to global catastrophes, actual and potential, cultural and political, demanded a resistant mode of interaction both with existing social life and with the conventional telling of history. Selective accentuation of an anti-militarist and resistant past, through oppositional counter-memories, were conveyed by counter-images, painting, music and literature. This process privileged other stories to challenge the hegemony of a public and national history filled with militaristic icons, such as Picasso's 1937 painting, *Guernica*.[5] Since it contained shadows of urbicide, the image became 'dangerous'. It later had to be veiled from view at the UN in New York, as an unsuitable background to General Colin Powell's 2003 speech justifying the Iraq Bombing campaign.

By the millennium this opposition, in poetry, art and counter-memorializing events, also reflects the social crisis engendered by new media-technology and organizational change. It was now not only the '31 years of war' (1914–45), but a longer span before and after these cataclysms that prioritized the need for this counter-memory. The opposition had responded to post-colonialism, Vietnam, and the Middle-East, and developed in popular culture, even soldiers' songs, an iconoclastic view of the military, its codes and practises.[6] Since 1945 the bellicose rhetoric of domestic militarism has been deconstructed in new theatre and fiction: classic sardonic novels, such as *Catch-22*; later the TV series MASH; the more bitter *Slaughterhouse 5*;[7] the film of *Dr Strangelove* or even *The Goon Show* exemplify interpretations of this new mood. Later the imagery was dissected in comedy such as *Blackadder*, in which the culture of hierarchy, the army as a military and bureaucratic setting, became once more the object of satire and irony. Metaphorically, civilianism organizes from within war itself: at some stage, though victims, they resist in spirit, creatively and personally, as do Reed, Douglas, Heller and Vonnegut (even perversely perhaps Fussell), who exemplified this consciousness in World War Two.[8]

This political and fundamentally anti-militarist project had emerged particularly in the West by 1960. It was directly related to the social movements with which this creativity interacts: an embryonic postnational attitude is linked in its opposition, globally, not only to racism, colonialism and misogyny, but also to the indiscriminate strategies of weapons of mass destruction. An extensive picture of how this way of remembering was 'made' includes radical memorial architecture, new exhibitionary art, installations, 'happenings' and counter-monuments (Image 10.2). It was combined with a renaissance of popular memory in music which has continued beyond the twentieth century. What so much of this cultural output reminded the world was that those who work in military environments are in fact often 'civilians', both men and women, in uniform. Alongside these impulses, the women's movement also represented in essence a non-national, often transnational response.

Few of the major twentieth-century memory workers were strictly speaking pacifists though they had contact with anti-war groups and individuals: few were active in the 1920s and 1930s peace movements. Nor were they, with a few exceptions, involved in the pre-1960 peace action. However, from the 1960s, a wider peace 'milieu' became increasingly a context for popular memory construction, even if pacifists remained a prophetic minority within that frame. Lew Ayres, a Hollywood actor who played Paul Baumer in the film of *All Quiet on the Western Front* (1930), had become a conscientious objector and pacifist.

IMAGE 10.2 Josefina de Vasconcellos, Reconciliation statue, 1977. Note the barbed wire between the reunited figures, which was twice removed, and the original name changed, to emphasize peace. By permission of J.B. Priestley Library, University of Bradford.

Earlier both Virginia Woolf and Käthe Kollwitz were on the fringes of a principled pacifist milieu, as was Siegfried Sassoon. Walter Benjamin in Berlin, who like Kollwitz, and Rosa Luxemburg, endorsed an internationalist socialist anti-war, though not pacifist, position. In Kollwitz this was exemplified in her memorial tribute to Karl Liebknecht after his murder: the *Gedenkblatter* graphic.[9] However, in Britain, after the war, Vera Brittain did become a leading pacifist; in the 1930s, amongst composers, Vaughan Williams, who had been an ambulance driver and whose work was shadowed by war, and Benjamin Britten (*War Requiem*) clearly identified with absolute pacifism publicly; as did Michael Tippett who composed *Child of our Time*, and Henry Moore, the sculptor.

As we have seen, in Japan Ira and Toshi Maruki were linked to anti-nuclear peace work throughout their working lives. The pacific orientation – or anti-militarism – of many key memory-makers was more covert and implicit, rather than public. Subsequently a number of British revisionist and radical historians, including Edward Thompson and A. J. P. Taylor, neither pacifists, became actively involved in anti-war protests and the unilateralist anti-nuclear weapons campaigns. Hundreds of British writers, artists and musicians joined them in the protests, as well as actors and filmmakers. A wide range of musicians, poets, playwrights, painters and architects publicly supported the CND, and the non-violent 'Committee of 100' (both part of the Nuclear Disarmament Movement, in the years 1958–65). Having directed *Oh! What a Lovely War!* and *Gandhi*, Richard Attenborough became president of the pacifist British Gandhi Foundation. Prominent filmmakers in the 1960s, such as Lindsay Anderson and Peter Watkins, and those in the free cinema movement, were also strongly associated with the international peace movement. This continued in the 1980s – Ken Loach focused on radical memory in his later films.

However, some influential figures in Britain, George Orwell for example, and Robert Graves, were contemptuous of the naïve pacifism of the 1930s. Yet despite this, Orwell's work has an internationalist and at times anti-militarist inflection. Manifested symbolically in Henry Moore's or more latent in Stanley Spencer's art, this anti-war critique is implied. Transitions towards pacifism such as Vera Brittain's emotional journey, or Kollwitz's evolution towards radical anti-militarist after 1914, or Sassoon's ambivalent casting away of his Military Cross, and later the Marukis' move from communism in Japan to a humanist universalism in their post-Hiroshima art, all represent such changes of direction. Each represents a unique creative response to moral crisis and human atrocity. Contrarily, Paul Nash moved away from his anti-war stance of 1918, to endorse World War Two.

The portents for Auschwitz, Dresden and Hiroshima had already been very clear from the first years of the Great War, with the mass technologized slaughter of often very young 'civilian' soldiers. By then the war in the West had reached a haemorrhaging stalemate. This could have been the occasion certainly for a shift in European cultural history. The warning had been there during the pre-war arms race; but whilst individuals reacted to the end of any illusions about modern war - populist politics, and traditional militarist attitudes, conspired to both confuse and subordinate internationalist traditions and pacifist counter-narratives. In a century of total war, the impact of this catastrophe on public rituals, even sensibilities, has been slow moving and radically limited, not least by the survival and populist resurgence of residual and aggressive nationalisms, to frame public memory.

Out of atrocity: Kollwitz, Dix, the Marukis

Nevertheless, an evolving anti-militarist sensibility symbolized by the work of many of the 'memory' artists that I focus on in this book has come to occupy a global niche. For example, four of them created enduringly powerful cycles or series about twentieth-century war: Otto Dix, Käthe Kollwitz, and Iri and Toshi Maruki. These are in a tradition of established classic artists such as Jacques Callot and Francisco Goya before them, who had, with extraordinary power, documented two previous periods of continuous savagery in Europe (1618–49) and (1789–1815). The new work, just as Goya's and Callot's, was from the start creatively individual, and not integral to any anti-war internationalist movement or its propaganda. It was created as fine art and was rarely promoted and borrowed by political movements. Two exceptions are Dix and Kollwitz in the 1920s and 1930s, and once again from the late 1950s and 1960s in Germany. In those latter years the work of the Marukis also began to gain a peace audience, some in Japan, and more in the West, but not a mainstream one.

As an example of the use of Kollwitz's work in anti-militarist context, her *Seed Corn Must Not be Ground* (*Saatfrüchte sollen nicht vermahlen werden*) from 1941 was transformed and recycled in a 1957 poster by the German leftist, anti-militarist, anti-nuclear weapons movement Kampf dem Atomtod (Image 10.3). Kollwitz's image of an androgynous adult protecting three children from threat originally implied a protest against conscription of young boys by the Nazis. This image, later dramatically superimposed on a mushroom cloud in the nuclear protest poster, symbolized protection against atomic holocaust and nuclear radiation.

For the Fascists, part of the degeneracy of radical expressionist of art, of those such as Dix and Kollwitz for the Fascists was its encouragement of a postnational empathy. The genre was, for example, supportive of identifications portrayed in 'recognition scenes' as in *All Quiet on the Western Front*, or *Kameradschaft*. All four artists are in actuality, and symbolically, reaching out to the 'other' – to the 'enemy'. In their art there is no human enemy; the only enemy is the crime and insanity of war and genocide. As a result they were predictably accused of making pacifist propaganda in their art – and harassed as supporters of the international Left: of 'peace', of socialism, of communism, or all three. Even by the 1930s the word 'peace' had become a pejorative, 'dirty' word. Kollwitz and Dix were both banned by the Nazis as 'degenerate artists'. Kollwitz because of her

IMAGE 10.3 Käthe Kollwitz, Seed Corn Must Not be Ground (*Saatfrüchte sollen nicht vermahlen werden*), end of 1941. Originally a protest against Nazi conscription of young boys, it was one of Kollwitz's last works. Käthe Kollwitz Museum Berlin. Photo: Studio Bartsch Berlin.

Left-socialist links lost her job. Rather than for his anarchist associations, Otto Dix was fired for his 'pacifism': for "sapping the will of the German people to defend themselves".[10] Some of their finest work, like that of Grosz and Barlach, was destroyed in the Third Reich. The Marukis, whilst not actually banned in Japan, were marginalized when in 1947 they joined the Communists, though they left the Party some years later. It is also significant for work on a postnational memory that these artists were 'victims': they represent creations from the 'vanquished'. Both as citizens of nations and political marginals – as well as victims of war – these are the official 'losers'. Their work predictably lacks any triumphalism, but it also signally lacks any of the self-pity of much 'victimhood'.

Marked by an at times explicit global identification with humanity, their icons of contemporary memorializing also stand as epitaphs for, as yet, our most violent century. Invoking a transnational community of mourning but with an anti-militarist core, their art represents a temporary suspension of understanding, in favour of experience: an interruption of analysis by an attempt to find personal peace. This is often also part of a poetry of witness, and emerges in social-psychological biography or autobiography. Far from irrationalism, such passion, as is also expressed in Munch's and Kiefer's painting, shows an attempt to represent the scarred and the scarring, the 'burning in' of memory in individual life stories. Whilst the idea that a specifically humanist, but sceptical and debunking form of representation emerged – and is part of a trend stemming from World War One, and underlined by World War Two – is accepted, it has rarely been seen and analysed as a whole corpus.

Ignored at the outset, even over the longer term, their painting was generally little appreciated in Japan; this was partly because it went far beyond victimhood, and discomforted conventional mainstream feelings. In both East and West their work was little known outside specific groups in Japan until the 1960s. Then the fragile panels were taken on world tours, and were more widely appreciated after 1980, though the work remained largely unknown, and often neglected in Japan itself. The Marukis went beyond victimhood to a universalism in their creative statements (Image 10.4); they painted honestly about Auschwitz, the rape of Nanjing, lynched American prisoners of war, the maltreatment of Koreans (*Crows*) and environmental themes, such as Chernobyl, the effects of radiation, and the Minamata pollution scandal.

Nevertheless in Japan's conservative climate, a lingering stigma surrounded their work. It probably explains why a major gallery has never been built in Tokyo for displaying their memorial masterpieces, giving access for a wider international audience. Much of their work is still housed in a less than palatial gallery, relatively inaccessible, in a remote suburb of Tokyo. As some of their work is very fragile, it cannot travel safely; it is not represented in Western galleries, rarely appears in the Western press, and was even censored from Japanese textbooks.

Each of these artists have personal stories which accompany their images. The differences in the style of these artists (even between Ira and Toshi) mirror their direct experience of war. The Marukis and Kollwitz lost loved ones in war; Dix was a machine gunner, he survived the dank hell of the trenches. Dix's complex personal odyssey was from an early naivety about the war, through numbness amidst mass death, nihilism and then flirtations with the far Left in 1919–22. He was helped in recovery from personal crisis by recreating – therapeutically – the horror and trauma in his work. Dix's specific memories of both being at, and even beyond the Front, are used to portray men – and women – as fragile victims of an obscene crime.[11] All of these are timeless references beyond specific events to a common humanity. There is a smell of death in his paint and ink: like the trench poets, his personal 'bitter truth' was portrayed with bitter skill and irony. But only in his late masterpieces, such as the stunning and defiant *Flanders 1917* (1934–36) does a deeper compassion and a universalism for these 'remnants' of his fellow soldiers, 'beggars under sacks', emerge. What he portrays is not just a depiction of suffering humans, but also an environmental catastrophe. It was one of the few of Dix's 1930s paintings that survived the Nazis, and

IMAGE 10.4 Iri and Toshi Maruki, *Hiroshima Panels 'IV Rainbow'*, 1951. The poem attached to this panel talks of the indiscriminate killing of friends and foes by the atomic bomb. It describes the grim destiny of the enemy soldiers taken as prisoners of war. The bodies of two American soldiers, still wearing shackles, were found lying on the side of the road near the Dome. The story then describes a brilliant, toxic rainbow appearing in the smoke and dust darkened sky, above the destruction and death. Maruki Gallery for the Hiroshima Panels.

it is one that consciously reaches out to the enemy (France), and to the anti-war sentiment of a potential enemy, and of many serving soldiers who had opposed war. In his title, Dix directly alludes to the 1916 anti-war novel of Henri Barbusse, *Le Feu*, included as part of the painting's description, and dedicated to those "who had been through the worst of the war" … [they] "cry out together against its repetition".[12] It is a shared image of hell.

Dix's courageous response to the Nazi attacks on his art was to produce several large and dramatic works such as a great triptych, which was destroyed, and his astonishing painting *The Trench*. Like *Flanders*, these were painted in the period 1930–36. Like Kollwitz and the Marukis, these were images of personal testament, yet also images that de-romanticized war:

> a lot of books in the Weimar Republic, once again peddling the notions of the hero and heroism which had long been rendered absurd in the trenches of the First World War. People were already beginning to forget what horrible suffering the war had brought them ... I did not want to cause fear and panic; but to let people know how dreadful war is and so to stimulate people's powers to resistance.[13]

Challenging the Nazi cult of memory, politically, and therefore deemed subversive, Dix explained that his triptych had been painted precisely as a response to this myth. In 1934 Dix was forbidden to exhibit altogether.[14]

Dix's savage imagery is not simply pacifist: it is not only militarism that he is dismembering, but also the very idea of the warrior and the image of war. He unravels the idea of the enemy and the cultural system that produces them. He dissolves the mythical distinction between victor and vanquished, victim and executioner, even the civilian and the soldier. Like other critical artists he reveals how, after 1918, a construct of 'war' as a homogenous entity becomes difficult to sustain. The meaning of the frontiers, the uniforms, the triumphalism of the winners and the symmetric atrocity tales is lost. All become in themselves an anachronistic backdrop to a theatre of war. But Dix avoids a sordid peepshow where 'museal' objects of the worst and most egregious kind are displayed. Ernst Friedrichs's museum of grotesque horrors, discussed in Chapter 4 had threatened to become just that, but instead Dix used such photographs to enhance the power of his lithographs.

The warriors' return

Returning veterans such as Dix and other 'survivors' of atrocity face an uncertain welcome on return home. How and why did *they* survive? It was a question asked of holocaust survivors, and one they posed themselves. Some realize they have PTSD; they are an embarrassment, an outcast. It is not only the guilt felt by the survivors of atrocity and trauma, but also hostility and stigma. Survivors of the camps were met by suspicion even in Israel.

Through the sociological analysis of return, one aspect of demilitarization is revealed: a gradual demolition of the idea of the warrior. In Koselleck's work the figure of the conscripted soldier is universalized as victim, rather than just perpetrator- and potentially witness: Koselleck's own biography included all three experiences.[15] Part of the mythology is the warrior's narrative, and now it slowly erodes the idea of 'the heroic individual'. In face of arbitrary and depersonalized modern technological war, this steady deconstruction is already implied as in Koselleck's concept of soldier as victim. Koselleck's postnational framing of the conscript includes empathy for example for three and a half million Soviet prisoners who died in Nazi custody and have, as he points out, no memorial in Germany, Russia or anywhere else. This dismantling of imagery is an aspect of Fussell's commentary on the Great War ironies. The process is also exemplified in Hemingway's short story *Soldier's Home*:[16] Harold Krebs's silence suggests all the veterans' numbing and denial, and the unreality of both civilian views of war and the scepticism of drafted conscripts on return. A graphic image is H. S. Williamson's honest painting of his own wound (see Image 10.5): it captures and personalizes a recalled moment of pain.

Warriors in modern war frequently present such accounts: the contemporary memoirs of veterans of real-life combat, such as Broyle's Vietnam stories, often make almost unbearable reading. Sassoon, Dix, Grosz or Barbusse all suffered the graphic return of such memories; it is an anti-heroic process. Contemporary with Broyle are the reflections of Ron Kovic, the Vietnam veteran actively protesting against the war, and portrayed in the film *Born on the Fourth of July*, revealing much of the stress of modern, mental and emotional odysseys. Like Dix, Broyles and Kovic carry memories not just of combat, trauma and injury, but also of revelation. A popular song 'Brothers In Arms'[17] in the post-Vietnam years expresses some of this ambivalence about comradeship and the other.

Typical of this memory is an inability to adjust to a world where military prowess is functionless. It carves out a new sensibility that is both political and personal survival: military necessity becomes a mechanical reaction. As recent

IMAGE 10.5 Harold Sandys Williamson, *A German Attack on a Wet Morning April 1918*, 1918. The artist himself is the retreating figure (wounded) on the right side of the picture, it was his second wound in action. Its honesty and authenticity, as well as unromantic simplicity, makes it a memorable personal record of war. By permission of the artist's son, Paul Williamson.

theory argues, the soldier is trapped within the machine, sensitivity blunted, producing an emotional damage that never fades. The symbolic lessons of the Homeric ballads seem lost to us now. Insufficient to reflect such modern narratives, the over-inflated Odyssean memory of war seems over time to become irrelevant to our recent experiences. In the saga, Homer's warrior displays a reversion to soldiery: this revives the functional virtues, which restore him to his unrecognizing wife. He 'shoots' his weapon, but, what next? Like many veterans, the truth is far from Homeric. In Hemingway's tale, once back in Texas, Harold Krebs is changed, not as in an Odyssean myth, but, like many, emotionally reduced, scarred psychologically. Through much twentieth-century research we now know a great deal more about that silence, psychosis or 'madness' of the veteran. Unable to deal with war experience and its brutalization, the veteran's inability to escape a recurring memory and nightmares like Sassoon's 'dreams from the pit' result in melancholy and depression. A neurasthenia, or what has been renamed post-traumatic stress disorder, it takes many forms. Despite the medical knowledge, public culture has not yet been able to dislodge the disturbing and politically corrosive mythology of warriorship. Even a veteran social activist and war reporter Chris Hedges (*War That Gives Us Meaning*) cannot avoid the classic myth.[18]

I heard an utterly credible account of a German Wehrmacht officer, 'a gentle man', confirmed by his son, who is a pacifist German pastor. He described how his father, despite four years of front-line combat on the bloody Eastern front only consciously killed one man, who was coming at him with a flame-thrower. After the war he struggled to recover from his trauma and horrifying wounds; he created an aviary and tended birds.

Demilitarizing images

In the context of postnational discourse, are there differences in the memorializing experiences of World Wars One and Two? Was the first war remembrance, as has been argued at the extremes, both more *national* and more myth-laden, less critical and less 'European', or 'universal' than the post-1945 remembering? An impressive case has been made for this, but it has been greatly overstated. The legend of 1914 does not change the fact that the transformed character of remembrance 'attitudes' started in the 1920s. They occurred with the represented experience of the Great War. It is true that Sassoon's 'ideal image' of a world before the war was a prevalent myth, but it was not a world of which he is uncritical. As often previously in the history of literature, a contrast-concept to conflict or militarism is developed. For example, Edmund Blunden, Edward Thomas, Ivor Gurney and Sassoon all use pastoral memories and rural scenes: the civilian-soldier grasps natural images to maintain a non-militarized self.

But a mythical England, which even Orwell echoes in 1938, was in fact a widely shared 'collective memory' like Germany's 'heimat'. For all its selectivity and even sentimentality, it was an image created before Britain's commitment to the 1914 war had been determined. It is a reference to a loss of the past, an arcadian memory. Many ordinary people, including serving soldiers responded to it. But for the conservative historian Samuel Hynes, and possibly in Raphael Samuel's socialist critique, it is an aspect of the genre that sustains a romantic, misleading – even reactionary – view.[19]

But pastoral in counter-memory can be defended. In a gently chiding piece from World War Two, Henry Reed, a civilian conscript, contrasts the military life in which he serves, to home; in particular 'basic-training' provides a context for poems in a trilogy: *'Naming of parts'* (weapons) and *'Judging distances'* are set in scenes of English countryside – not in 1914, the year of Reed's birth, but 1940. The sheep are grazing in fields, whilst 'Japonica glistens' in the neighbor's garden. At the same time Reed cleans his rifle.[20] The poet introduces these bland images as a setting for recalling military moments before combat; juxtapositions of time and place occurs as domestic memory is contrasted with the 'present' of army life. Reed, like Terrence Des Pres, reminds us of the danger of this divide of self and nature, bred by military intrusion into our mental landscape.

I have already described many allusions to, and recreations of, this sense of a social and historical divide that occurs between 1918 and 1939; it is reflected in a recurrent imagery in film and fiction. The corpus of representations of the watershed is immense: from Renoir's *Grande Illusion* and Remarque's *All Quiet on the Western Front*, to Humphrey Cobb's book which became the basis for the film *Paths of Glory*. Each depicts the end of an old order. Memoirs of war in many languages, and translations of these and other Great War literature for non-English readers, including Owen's poems, the reproductions of German expressionist art, and the vast stores of graphic images, posters, photographs, the work of Dix and Grosz and Ernst Friedrich were distributed worldwide. Mining these resources were powerful influences on deterritorializing modern memory. They were enhanced by the further wave of Great War representations a decade after 1945, which became overtly anti-militarist. The irony and absurdity of war embedded in memory, and enshrined in art, passes into the bitter sarcasm of 1960s works such as *Oh! What a Lovely War!* or the surrealist theatre of the film *King of Hearts*.

De Broca's parody *King of Hearts* (1966) represented the absurdity and caricatured military mentality of attrition – whether by bomb, Maxim gun or rifle. This mind-set is observed by the occupants of the local mental institution in a small and otherwise abandoned French town. With their minders having left the inmates to their fate (in fact a very *real* situation in some cities both in 1914 and in 1941) the 'lunatics' have emerged from the hospital to resume their 'roles' in society. As the returning German and British battalions proceed to annihilate each other in the evacuated town square, one of the escapees ironically observes 'They are over-acting!' and as the film ends, the inmates return to the sanity of their 'asylum'.

Vignette:
Oh! What a Lovely War!

In Britain the most innovative and conscious demilitarizing projects of the 1960s sustained a life and impact long beyond their first appearance. Not surprisingly this was in the popular and symbolic tradition of musical theatre. *Oh! What a Lovely War!* evolved from Charles Chilton's BBC radio programme, *No-Man's Land*. It was first transported to the stage and then eventually into a large-scale film production (Attenborough). Its resonance was due to its focus on early twentieth-century popular songs, many from the music hall. When it was initially conceived in 1960 as a BBC production, it was a light-hearted, popular, although anti-militarist 'musical' programme. It was a send-up of World War One with songs and skits; it included quotations from leading figures (such as Sir Edward Grey's prophetic "The lamps are going out all over Europe" (spoken from the foreign office in August 1914 in London)[21] and General Haig's 'We will walk through the enemy lines' (at the Somme)). In both play and film the master of ceremonies or compère acts as both a fool and a 'chorus'.

But when it was transferred to the stage at the Theatre Royal in East London directed by Joan Littlewood, it proved a major success. Yet this was a more savage, and satirical, cabaret-style version. Littlewood's more political direction had been strongly influenced by 1920s and 1930s German theatre, by the bitter anti-militarist musical theatre of Bertold Brecht, typified by the Threepenny Opera. Brecht as an anti-Nazi, socialist writer, poet and playwright seminally used irony as a political wrap and this darker version chimed with the increasingly radical mood of early 1960s 'angry' Britain. Revived many times later on stage, often locally, it was transformed for the cinema on the grand scale by Richard Attenborough. His ambitious film appeared in 1969. Though by the end of the radical 1960s, active concern about nuclear war had been largely replaced by anti-Vietnam War opposition, in each case World War One was seen as metaphoric for contemporary 'theatres' of war and their threats of escalation. Each medium gave a different inflection on the material. As a memory document, Attenborough's production was both more surreal and poignant than Littlewood's. Less raw, but more sentimental, it used many of the same sketches, quotes and songs of the era, as had Chilton's original. Its symbolic setting was the Brighton Pier, an Edwardian seaside structure. In order to give it a more civilian context and social critique of the home front, a 'family' was to occupy centre stage. The film introduces the mythical Smith clan who appear throughout the film. Each one is doing her or his 'bit' for the war effort. The songs were accurate re-enactments of authentic popular ballads of the period, mostly in English, many from music hall/vaudeville. Such songs sung there were transported by men returning to the Front. At the same time, those sung, even composed in the trenches found their way back home, with snippets of trench verse even to the stage. 'Chanson de Craonne', the popular subversive lament of the French soldiers at the Chemin des Dames internationalized the repertoire, as well as Australian, and after 1917, American songs.

As a largely British memory document of World War One, however selective, *Oh! What a Lovely War!* is an influential and mnemonic piece of entertainment. Memorable graphic scenes, with major actors including Maggie Smith as a music hall diva, enticing men to their fate, with a recruiting sergeant present on stage. She sings "I'll make a man of any one of you", a reminder that burlesque shows in 1914–18, as well as soccer matches, were used to recruit men or boys to fight from audiences; eventually on both sides of the Atlantic. In a post-Armistice sequence at the end of the film version, the denial of the war experience is included: "And if they ask us – and they are certainly going to ask us [how dangerous it was] we'll never tell them". Enveloped in emblematic crosses and poppies (see Image 10.6) the surviving members of the Smith family enact a post-war reticence, a silencing of memory; each of the dead is handed a poppy.

IMAGE 10.6 Richard Attenborough, *Oh! What a Lovely War*, 1969. The poppy thread leads the last of the Smith's to his end. Not a symbol of triumph, but of suffering.

In 2014, at the centennial anniversary events of the war, such sentiments of anti-militarism were confronted again by a traditional militarized view of the Great War. A media campaign was consciously mobilized by government and popular press to thwart any offensive of 'peace memories', and post-1918 doubts. The revisionist images of *Oh! What a Lovely War!* were again under challenge from conservatives and patriots. Some of the military historians of the London Imperial War Museum shared with critics such as Samuel Hynes a particular animus against the soldier poets, such as Owen and Sassoon, and the meaning they had given to dissent. Students studying Great War literature were aghast, when one British military expert, in a public talk, described one of the British army's less glorious, but well-publicized moments at the end of the war. "*The only good thing about the battle*" (of the Sambre Canal in 1918) "*was that it got rid of one of those darn trench poets!*" The poet referred to was, of course, Wilfred Owen. The moment and event was real, but had recently been re-captured in popular fiction by Pat Barker's character, Billy Prior, at the end of her novel *Ghost Road*,[22] and was well known by the 1990s.

This nationalist mood re-emerged in British media as a prevalent military and patriotic perspective with its own priorities and criteria. The poetry of compassion irks many other military buffs: Hynes's typical disapproval of Sassoon is not so much as a writer – he does not mention his poetry in one significant critical article[23] – but rather he dismisses him not least because he was an inadequate patriot and an ineffective *soldier*. Sassoon's exploits may have been brave, but in Hynes's view, they are invalidated since they contributed nothing to the British war effort (he says nothing about his creative art).[24] This distaste is also for Sassoon's nostalgia for the English past, and implicitly his lifestyle and his politics, and not least his exceptionalism and his stand on the war.[25] The 2014 anniversary responses to war in Britain reflected a very familiar militarist attitude to a 'constructed' anti-hegemonistic or counter-memory of war which emphasizes alternative narratives. Hynes denies this *is* 'memory' at all, but merely an invention sustained through the popularization of these historical narratives in such best-selling Great War fiction as Pat Barker's *Regeneration* trilogy or Sebastian Faulks's *Birdsong* (both filmed). These showed how accessible personal stories can be in affirming the enduring power of 'the memorable War' as an archetype. They illustrate 'the pity' of such disasters, but are set alongside serious research on true experiences, such as the vivid depiction of tunnel warfare in Faulks's novel.

Vignette:
A mass of memoried flowers – poppies and ploughboys

At Hiroshima, it was cornflowers that flourished, possibly affected by the radiation; in the debris of London after the air raids, it was London Pride. In France and in Flanders (as Americans find it harder to imagine) it was bright, scarlet poppies. Part of the contest over the 1914–18 memory related to this flower. They were Flanders poppies, not the vapid pale orange, Californian variety, but a blood red, which contrasts more dramatically with the white dust of the Somme or in Artois. This was the crimsoned flower that an East End Londoner, Rosenberg, plucked from the parapet and put behind his ear. The Ordnance of the Western Front had smashed the drainage systems, soaking the already partly inundated lowland swamps of Flanders, and also the Somme in the lower areas (Les Etangs de la Somme). It churned the mud better than any team's head brass; indeed, so deep that some horses sank in it.

These were the 'red wet things', the weed flowers that preceded pesticides and weedkillers; they were the bright red souvenirs that, even uniformed ploughboys, dried and sent home, uncensored, with letters to their loved ones. And Flanders, intentionally half flooded by Belgians in 1914, was by the time of Paschendaele an ever more a well-watered habitat for them by 1917.

It may have been the Canadian medic, MacRae's words with his Flanders' poppy, as he scribbled in a dugout medical aid station beside the canal at Ypres that inspired the movement of 1918 to inscribe the flower. But ordinary soldiers had adopted it long before, and long before the two remarkable ladies Moïna Michael and Anna Guérin promoted them. The two met again in the YWCA in New York in spring 1918, and started the campaign for its adoption (one had been promoting them already, for France). Though neither had visited France during the war, like others, they were moved by John MacRae's opening lines.

The "parapets poppy" of Rosenberg's poem *Break of Day in the Trenches* belonged to the troops and their loved ones at home. But it was co-opted in name by a General, Lord Douglas Haig, and the British Legion to raise money for veterans; then generations of jingoists and the patriots also claimed it. The meanings given are multiple. It was the symbol later copied by the lads who re-created the ceramic souvenirs. This veterans' symbol was not Oscar Wilde's poppy, or the Taliban's earner, or of militarism. It was a mark of a bullet wound, of a sudden death that could be anyone's; Attenborough uses the device as a prediction of death from the Archduke Ferdinand in 1914 to the last Tommy on 11 November– each were handed one before they were killed. Such a blood flower is hinted at in both Williamson's *German Attack* and Kennington's paintings. These blooms were far removed from the sentimental Picardy roses of the song worn behind the lines, or sung about at home. These are the obstinate growth of 125 miles of 'no-man's land', out of soil churned by heavy modern guns, shells and high explosives. The sacrificial association with blood is ambiguous, not heroic or futile, tragic or uplifting. A poet's symbolism of blood fertilized soil from where the plants spring – Rosenberg's "where its roots are in men's veins, drop and are ever dropping". For it is more passion than pastoral, more blood than sacrifice, more abandonment, pity – than 'honourable' triumph.

In 1934, the pacifist movement in Britain and the Peace Pledge Union (PPU) started to distribute the Women's Coop Guild's alternative, a white poppy. But the white poppy did not serve as well to represent death, tragedy, or symbolize the obscenities of the trenches. In the longer term, the generals were to be denied monopoly on the best popular symbol of 1914–18, it would eventually no longer be Haig's poppy.

But for the poet, the poppy is still the scarlet flower that rests *"In my ear where it is safe. Just for a little while, white with the dust"* (of the Somme chalk), or wet with the *"jolly old rain"* of Ypres. It is the poppy of memory. In the autumn every year 'as the nights draw in', the poppies of November, thrive again. And not only in England, but with the ice-hockey players in Canada or local firemen trumpeters in Belgium, worn at memorials from Australia and New Zealand to Ulster or South Africa, and in the mixed throngs at the Menin Gate in Ieper and on the Somme: the power of a red flower is annually, actively repossessed. They are not the plastic replicas sold at the Tower; they represent, not a token, but a hope. An emotive political sign of modern remembrance, not just as a pastoral reminder of the past or a part of its poetry, but about "the pity of war", and the universal sense of loss it distils. In spite of the contests over the colour and naming, it represents for many a yearning for peace, and for some a marker of a pledge to resist war: an awareness of a struggle unfinished. In that sense it is the red poppy that remains a timeless symbol of Owen's "pity of war" and his invocation to acknowledge its futility.

Poppy wars

The transformations of post-1918 Armistice Day events and of Poppy Day symbolism, and Remembrance Sunday rituals as national events, not only in Britain, illustrates well how our judgements about modern memory are constantly in need of revision. Adrian Gregory's account of the process records a decline in these commemorations by 1990, both in the substance of the 11 November events and the size of Remembrance Day ceremonies. They were, he believed, losing their salience and appeal.[26] Yet now, not only because of the 1914–1918 centenary, this judgement seems premature. Even whilst Gregory's book was being published in 1994, the later stages of the memory boom since the 1990s were evolving, and this included a 'Poppy Day revival'. Demographics, and cultural change, helped in a confused reinvention of the rituals and a renewal of meaning in the November events. It made poppy wearing fashionable again, and, for a variety of reasons, that was even more widespread in the period of Tony Blair's government and the Iraq war. The British Legion changed the fund's name. Its ritual, and iconic meaning has revived since then: the Poppy's symbolic resonance, given the military deaths in Afghanistan and Iraq, marked not only 11 November itself and Remembrance Sunday, but enjoyed a popular renaissance that was international. In the context of the latest and more general memory boom, Poppy Days and events have certainly not been demilitarized, but did acquire a new poignancy and relevance in a context of wider war memories.[27]

The deep red scarlet Flanders poppy and its complicated career as a symbol, especially in contests around and after 1918, after which the British Legion adopted it, must make it the most politically 'contested' and later reconfigured flower anywhere on earth. Individuals, not only pacifists, had from the 1920s opposed the British Legion's handling of the image (by the Haig Fund, after 1920). Nevertheless they still became wearers of paper poppies. Millions more did so once General Douglas Haig's name was significantly removed in 1994. Those millions who wore it before that, did so often with a sense of scepticism and ambivalence. Such contradictions surfaced publicly first in the war-boom of early 1930s when the Flanders poppy was worn by many veterans with their medals – but sometimes with white poppies too. These varieties only became sharp alternatives in the 1970s, but the debates continue.

In contrast to this split in the 1980s the notable weaver and feminist artist Thalia Campbell understood this potency of the poppy. She included poppies in both colours in many peace tapestries, including several banners for the Greenham Common Airbase women's protests that focused on memory (1981 onwards). One of her best-known banners "Remembrance is not enough" and its red and white poppies is frequently reproduced, and is now displayed in the Bradford Peace Museum (Image 10.7).[28]

IMAGE 10.7 '*Remembrance is not enough*' textile banner by Thalia Campbell, 1981. Campbell was the most notable of the banner artists of the Greenham Common women's peace movement. Photo: © The Peace Museum Bradford.

As poppies as symbols returned (and remained) into the twenty-first century, one notorious culmination (2014) was a vast commemorative display of them in London. In its decorous, ceramic proxy for public memorializing, it fitted well with the successful co-optation of much Great War remembrance – including the icon itself. The revisionist right's 'history' campaign had been to demolish the myth of catastrophe. Those returning from the more traditional killing fields ceremonies in Flanders and on the Somme were forced to re-assess what was the meaning of the puzzling, but a vastly popular pottery display – an installation around the Tower of London. Critics acknowledged that the vast crowds, and the almost 900,000 objects were impressive.

Whilst the Norman 'Tower' had little to do with 1914–18, it still represented a symbol of millennia of oppressive militarism, and filling the moat surrounding such a military structure with blood-red 'flowers' seemed in principle appropriate. The problem was not only that these mementoes were more pink than scarlet, but the actual poppies (on sale) looked like souvenirs from a tourist boutique. Echoing Gavin Ewarts remarks on the IWM (see previous epigraph), for peace critics the display demeaned the icon and the experience, as did its staging, establishment co-optation and the inevitable militarization of several events there.

But were the over five million people who visited the display, too gullible, too easily moved by a cosmetic display? Its very meaning was being questioned: was it representing mass death or each individual memory? One journalist was bold enough to argue that, beside Otto Dix's stark representation of war and the trench experience, these souvenirs were bland, if not banal.[29] But many others argued that the lack of horror is exactly what made them 'accessible and appropriate' to a mass of ordinary 'prosthetic' mourners. The pottery emblems in various special arrangements continued on display in various sites for years even after the dispersal and sale of many of the 888,246 accumulated symbols – each marked one of 'our dead' (British and Commonwealth). Clearly this was no 'postnational' staging of war memory, but a nationalist, or rather 'imperial' event.

Like Ewart's poem, the objection of some anti-militarists was that the installation sanitized and re-militarized the 1914–18 experience in popular minds. Through the efforts of a London-centred media that was plausible. Through such public extravaganzas perhaps the truth of a pitiable war could be safely shelved, and the nation's memory of it could blandly move on. Locally, however, even in small villages, schools and churches, a more personal revival of community history of 1914–18 produced authentic displays of regret, moving sincerity, – and poppies.

Nuclearism and postnational memory

Both in the 1950s and 1960s, and later in the 1980s, a peace activism clearly associated with anti-nuclearism played a significant role making and popularizing aspects of memory culture in Europe and the USA. This remembrance work and internationalist movement helped, if intermittently, breach silences, not only about Hiroshima and Nagasaki and the nuclear state, but also about the World Wars and modern genocides from Armenia to the Shoah. I have earlier analysed the unlikely revival of interest in Great War culture that occurred in the context of the Cold War. It sustained, in the late 1950s, a nuclear war metaphor of mutual attrition: 'Mutual Assured Destruction' had been rehearsed in the trenches; it linked the lunacy of that slaughter to a new vision of 'MAD'.[30] A potential failure of 'deterrence', nuclear strikes, would mimic the anachronistic and suicidal tactics of direct assault on mechanized defences: a memory of 1914 in the 1960s is imagined as a prophecy of war to come.

Representations of the carnage in film and photographs appeared in mass campaigns, exhibitions, meetings, film shows, manifestations and blockades. Nuclear armed rockets, some with names such as 'Honest Johns', had replaced machine guns; trench mortars were superseded by 'small' tactical warheads, some ten times the power of the Hiroshima bomb. Later in the 1980s, worldwide opposition to this re-militarization revived movements in Japan. As in the 1960s this renewal coincided with an innovative autonomous popular culture. In the 1960s, 'hipster' poetry had been especially linked to rock, jazz and blues music; Bob Dylan, Joan Baez and John Lennon are perhaps the best-known representatives, mediated by Pete Seeger but it drew on a much broader trend in protest songs that dated back to Woody Guthrie, Bessie Smith and much folk and protest music of the 1930s. In the 1960s, this aspect of 'peace memory' is 'made' more self-consciously, and critically and is more globally inflected. Post-1945 generations blended in the transnational youth culture, in protesting an 'Eve of destruction' (the title of Barry MacGuire's popular song). With nuclear testing occurring globally in the Cold War context, radioactive dust actually did blow 'in the wind'. As well as accessible mass expressions of this counter-hegemonic project in memory arts, avant-garde pieces appeared, especially in film: Bruce Conner's 1976 film *Crossroads*, of the 1946 Bikini nuclear tests wove together shots of the explosions into a cinematic masterpiece.

But such populist transnational politics needed to be self-reflective and self-critical: if there was a construction – or rather reinvention – of peace 'memory', it entailed not only a peace myth or Utopia, but also needed a conscious re-awakening of an international peace history, of a tradition of dissent. The spread of television as a popular medium was an opportunity for new media, which explains the significance of banning critical TV films about nuclear war. Early in the nuclear disarmament campaigns in Britain the use of self-reflecting, if not self-critical, media represented the creation of its own identity. The movement was also able to capture the first major 'ban the bomb' event on film. The *March to Aldermaston* documentary was made by the Free Cinema 'movement' (associated with the New Left, especially with Lindsay Anderson, and Karel Reisz, but also Tony Richardson, and others). It was non-commercial, and it was shown mainly to campaigners and students, in churches, universities, film clubs and political groups. This initial 'identity creating' film, made in Easter 1958, was low-key and small budget, a sober document of the first significant

British nuclear disarmament demonstration of the 1950s. The four days' Easter anti-bomb march, first sponsored by Direct Actionists, from London to the British A-Bomb factory at Aldermaston in Berkshire, became an increasingly sizeable annual ritual of the Campaign for Nuclear Disarmament (CND). For six or seven years it involved many hundreds of thousands of people (1958–64), and was replicated internationally. The *March to Aldermaston* and other films and photography, preserved these images in peace memory.

Compared with Kevin Rafferty's popular compilation of mostly satirical clips in *Atomic Café* or Stanley Kubrick's *Dr Strangelove*, where the brilliant script is brash, sceptical, even a cynical, a 'gallows humour', *the Aldermaston* film is sombre: it is in complete contrast to those who chose to ridicule nuclear war. Indeed, initially CND's tone was even seen as unpopularly moralistic and in tension with the cultural hipster revolt of Ginsberg and the iconoclastic beat poetry of the 1950s. Films such as *March to Aldermaston*, despite its jazz accompaniment, was often shown together with various documentary footage, especially Japanese, that revealed a peace campaign that is reacting to a conspiracy of silence and the same public cynicism, arrogance and paranoia, even apathy, portrayed in *Atomic Café*. CND was supported by a growing social movement, with ethical and political argument. This was an alternative cinematic response to the scepticism and silence of establishment media. Seen by critics as self-righteous, the movement was not consistently serious, but celebratory, musical and coincidentally associated with a New Orleans Jazz revival, skiffle and folk music clubs. Such contested memories of the 1960s over the nuclear threat have become part of a wider public memory, even internationally. One symbol became globally 'mnemonic': even that was controversial at first. Within a decade it was widely recognized as the so-called 'peace sign'. The symbol was the iconic 'N/D' logo, but the fact that it contained the semaphore flag signals for 'N' (nuclear) and 'D' (disarmament) was not much understood outside the context of the British nuclear disarmament movement.[31]

The work of Peter Watkins

The War Game

In 1962 the Cuban missile crisis brought the fantasies of *Dr Strangelove*, *Failsafe* and the surrealism of *Atomic Café* into the cold, hard print of newspaper headlines and TV news announcements. The unusual interruption of news broadcasts several times between 1960 and 1963 suggested to a mass audience that normal life might at any moment be on hold, to await Armageddon. A film for such an audience was made to depict that moment.

In 1964, the British BBC commissioned this for TV, then, under pressure from government, subsequently decided not to show it. Peter Watkins's 40-minute film *The War Game* graphically portrayed a nuclear attack on Britain. It was considered shocking, and politically risky in 1965. In terms of memory methodology, Watkins's 'factional' documentary and re-enactment work was always 'witness' oriented; like Pontecorvo in *'Battle of Algiers'*, it used local people from the specific site, some survivors or descendants of historic participants in events, and rarely professional actors. Subsequently similar techniques were deployed in Barry Hines's 1980s film, *Threads*, using local councillors in Sheffield. These 'witnesses' of *The War Game* report on a fictional but realistic limited nuclear attack near Chatham, and Gravesend in Kent. Non-professionals, local parents, a fire-chief, a nurse, a child, a pensioner and a police superintendent – and victims and food 'rioters': they each speak to camera as witnesses of the missile strikes, and the after effects, such as a simulated fire storm in Rochester. These are presented as part of an escalating European exchange of intermediate range nuclear missiles, and bombs. As in all Watkins's films, his own voice and critiques loom large in the commentary and editing.

A public protest campaign in Britain grew calling for the film to be released publicly, at least in some form – for informational viewing – even if not allowed on general release. But the BBC, pressured by the Home Office, and the government of the day, continued to block it. It was believed, probably correctly, that it would stimulate a massive response not only against the pathetically inadequate, indeed mendacious, 'Civil Defence' (nuclear protections) programme, but also against nuclear weapons as such, and the then British threat to use their 'deterrent' even in a conventional war.[32] The banning of *The War Game* remains one of the clearest instances of public British political censorship in the twentieth century. Seen as a gross political intrusion in a democracy and 'free' media, it certainly succeeded in curtailing political dialogue in the interests of a military status quo. The experience confirmed Watkins's own sense of isolation, and indeed persecution, by the nuclear state, and even of conspiracy: an attitude that overshadows all his work since the early 1970s.[33] By the time the film, still powerful, but by then dated, was finally shown on TV, twenty years later, it could do less damage. But by then, Watkins's next project, *The Journey*, was evolving.[34]

The Journey

Starting in the 1970s and maturing by the early 1980s, a much more informed, engaged public reaction and less severe censorship of the nuclear topic emerged: it was assisted by a broadening of the academic study of critical issues relating to war and peace. In the 'Second Cold War' in both the US and Europe, in fiction and films, post-nuclear scenarios were revived. Depicted in such 1980s films as *The Day After*, *Threads*[35] and *Testament*, numerous nuclear war 'aftermaths' and re-enactments were created. Few achieved more immediate impact or realism than had Watkins's *The War Game*, though reaching far wider audiences. Some were based on popular novels, which also dealt with post-apocalyptic memories. The collage artist Peter Kennard used these images to create his own nuclear landscape in Britain after 1979. For example, he superimposed mobile

Cruise Missiles quite aptly on a farm cart in John Constable's classic painting of a pastoral scene.[36]

At the same time, Del Tredici's photo-essay on America's atomic–industrial complex, *At Work in the Fields of the Bomb*,[37] constituted a key piece of memory work. These images of the USA and Japan were subsequently used by Peter Watkins as stills in his global film *The Journey*. Together with photographs of the atomic dead, wounded and devastation from 1945, they were used to prompt reactions from families in dozens of countries worldwide. They elicited parallel memories with past events, from other survivors, victims and witnesses – and political critics. Remembered traumas, including World War Two, created links across time and physical space. Whilst Watkins's previous nuclear documentary, *The War Game*, acquired notoriety, *The Journey*, on the other hand did not: it avoided the *The War Games* more direct graphic methods, and as a result was largely ignored.

Mentioned earlier, Bruce Conners's silent sequence of mushroom clouds in *Crossroads* illustrates the multiple memory triggers, images and icons that competed for attention in the first decades of the atomic Cold War. By the late 1950s, the world felt assured of a humanly achievable atomic Armageddon. Paradoxically this was affirmed by the transnational protest movements. Through the strategy of nuclear attrition, total collaborative global devastation would, it was claimed, deter war. The spread of atmospheric radiation made the extra-territorial aspect of nuclear testing physically obvious.

But public anti-militarist and anti-nuclear sentiment contrasted with simultaneous widespread nuclear numbing and denial; this even marked the escapist counter-cultural responses of the late 1960s Woodstock generation. Though the more specific political opposition to the war in Indo-China (1965–75) modified rather than enlarged an imagery of global destruction, I have argued previously that it sustained a style of counter-hegemonic action representing a more universal and accessible perspective on modern 'war'.[38]

From 1966 to 1975, transnational peace projects involved media symbols and images as well as news of active global resistance and rebellion, including the events of 1968. Critically involved approaches to visual memory in style and creativity and in arts and design became popular and salient in the counter-culture. A popular revisionist history developed simultaneously that suggested a more self-conscious and autonomous relationship with the past. By 1970, not only internationalist, but also most importantly feminist protest and consciousness enhanced a more gendered remembering focused on the 'personal as political'.

However, images of past disasters, recalled in an everyday present, failed to undermine public acceptance of concepts of nuclear deterrence. Even prefiguring future disasters in film and prose merely induced fatalism and paralysis imagined in nightmares of nuclear holocaust. As research in the USA in the 1980s showed, these began to haunt childhood dreams on a mass scale. As witness to such an imagined future, Peter Watkins had been under pressure in the later 1960s and again in the early 1980s to make a new, expanded, updated and even more graphic version of an anti-nuclear film after *The War Game*. Initially he considered that. But as he travelled and canvassed support and funds, in a round the world peace 'journey', seeking local and international help for the new project, his concept evolved from 1981 to 1986 into a more global, multi-layered, film. This postnational project was unified by this sense of a continuing nuclear threat with further missile deployments in Europe in the early 1980s. *The Journey* was to be a 'world' peace project, positive as well as negative, with global activism fused into its production.[39]

Postnational film

Quite unlike, for example, Lanzmann's *Shoah*, Watkins's fourteen and a half-hour film was from the outset almost self-consciously marginalized. In the event, given its unusual style, pace and length, the film was destined for an avant-garde oblivion. It also suffered from some of the inevitable flaws relating to low-budget and amateur performance, as well as the use of soon to be dated 'news' materials which illustrated his media critiques. Over several decades, *The Journey* had extremely limited exposure and appeal: it was only to be shown intermittently, or in parts and mainly, as with *The War Game*, by local peace or specialist film groups.[40] Some avant-garde film critics lauded the film as a work of modern genius but generally it was ignored and *The Journey* became a 'collector's' item. Yet it has deserved more, and still does. As a detailed commentary on postnational memory, despite all its lacunae, it constitutes a major document of recollection. By discovering and recording worldwide witnesses and uncovering censorship, it documents the infrastructure of looming nuclear disasters, and its world themes unite these issues as few other memory texts do. It moves us towards new concepts for postnational filmmaking.

At different levels and layers these perspectives demonstrate how Watkins connects and references his key themes of 'War', 'Peace', 'Remembering', 'Modernity' and 'Economic development'. By using the self-reflexive methodologies and techniques he had previously developed in films including *The War Game*, *Culloden* and *Edvard Munch*, his art pressed beyond 'documentary' or re-enactment. His directorial self-commentary on the film is used to critique both itself, TV film and all modern media: it aims to alert the viewer to the role of excessive 'edits' of news reportage, the technical manipulation by directors and camera crews, the exploitation of news locations and editorial intrusion. Watkins's film aims to make the viewer conscious of distortion of the present: of the construction of the images/sounds/text, including Watkins' own – for many intrusive and self-conscious – interventions.

At root Peter Watkins is a global organizer. On shooting the film he renewed his extraordinary tours of five continents. After five years of this filming and documentation, his topics spanned in time over almost a half century of evolution from the 1940s to 1980s.[41] His final cut of 870-minutes of film aspires to represent 'models' of a transnational reality. It interviews dozens of families and many individuals in over twenty languages, often on site. It involves local communities, movements and individuals in Tahiti, Norway, Mozambique, Angola, USA, Scotland and Mexico. It includes much oral history, and survivor testimonies of World War Two. Witnesses combine with the voices of current activists and critics, French Algerian teachers of language and cultures are juxtaposed with Polynesian radiation victims. It reviews subjects of gender, racism, language hegemony and identity. Nuclear war preparations are juxtaposed to those of literacy. The development of environmental hazards are linked to political resistance to them and to its suppression. It relates current global conflicts to gender and development in Africa. It re-enacts nuclear 'civil defence' exercises and the nuclear scenarios in Hamburg, Norway and New York; existing German underground nuclear shelters are referenced back to the 1940s bombings; Norwegian schoolchildren and teachers in Stjørdal village school re-enact a nuclear alert (Image 10.8); communities from Utica in upstate New York re-enact a nuclear drill.

The vast atomic landscapes of the USA are real not imagined; this becomes a backdrop for many scenes in Watkins's film, exploring the nuclear war machine in the paralleled images from Del Tredici's *Fields of the Bomb*. The narrative moves from such sites as Hanford, Washington, to the Savannah River Plant, to Oak Ridge, Tennessee and to Bangor Maine. Then from the bomb assembly centre at the Pantex Plant (Amarillo)[42] to Los Alamos, and follows the journey of the 'White Train' across America.[43] Each site has its memories. Like Watkins's other experimental projects, and despite its ambitions and eccentricities, the film retains critical acclaim not least for this documentation of the hidden atomic history, which Susan Griffin touches on in her writing about the nuclear Americas. In the next section, I will return to these topics which she visited and interrogated in *A Chorus of Stones*.

IMAGE 10.8 Peter Watkins, *The Journey*, 1987. Re-enactment of a nuclear drill at Sturdahl in Norway. There is no room in the first school basement for all the children, and a sister and brother are running to an alternative shelter as the sirens wail.

Cinema in a global frame

The project starts with an explanation of the ambition of *The Journey*: to create through multiple sounds and texts (and Watkins's own ever-present commentary and voiceover) with maps and verbal prompts, a multi-layered temporal/spatial scheme of the militarization of the planet. This larger context is a daunting reality – as is the ever-increasing global arms race, which is watched from Scotland to Tahiti. The quest commences with the steady journey of a truck across a Hebridean island (South Uist). It has been marked for the construction of a new military airbase, linked to the nuclear grid; this is the Cold War's Atlantic response perimeter. As the vehicle travels, a Gaelic psalm is sung by a lone young chorister, unaccompanied. The singer is a boy from the Island. Simultaneously the use of indicated time for each journey of the truck, for example, is marked by sound. In reminding us of timing, it parallels Lanzmann's use of temporality in the Chelmno gas van journey in *Shoah*. Simultaneous statistics, such as the accumulating costs of the arms race, or world deaths from hunger, convey the expense – time and money, marked by the device of 'beeps', and subtitled figures for social and military spending and deprivation.

Similarly, as the 'White train' makes its journey, timed across America, it is collecting nuclear components from Tennessee to Washington State throughout the film's fourteen hours. As it is accumulating its load of nuclear weapons materials, another set of warheads can be completed. The Journey continues, interspersed with memories of previous air wars – testimony from Hamburg (1944), from Hiroshima (1945), from the bombed refugee trains leaving the besieged Leningrad (1943). Watkins's images of trains again remind us of the 'journeys' of 'the final solution' by train, and by road. In *Shoah*, the train tracks are symbolic of these 'transports of mass-destruction': death by railway timetable and technological rationality.[44]

In this way, Watkins's multi-layered concept of peace is imaged globally, without any anti-war or anti-militaristic rhetoric but constant questions: "Did you know that?" Though postnational framing remains fundamental to the project's overall organization, the concept of 'human security' and positive peace is a broad one, including – as has been seen – development, education, environmental concerns and the emancipation of women globally, as well as anti-war issues, are implicated in the role of local peace activism and the community.

But, at a deeply personal level and at the heart of the project such as Lanzmann's *Shoah* are the individual stories of the victims: it is the survivors and activists' narratives and recollections that give *The Journey* its postnational memorializing potency. Occasionally these individual memories are heard from one family member such as the childhood memory of a Russian evacuee from Leningrad in 1943. By the 1980s, she had become a Communist Party wife, but in 1942 she was a traumatized refugee child. Re-telling that story is hard for her. In Hanford, Washington a conventional American middle-class woman, a church-goer, a wife, who resigned from a military corporation, Honeywell, in the USA, after a pang of nuclear conscience, modestly relates the family's evolution after that. Others include a father, working on munitions at Lockheed, and a worker on a military base. A dignified Pacific Islander, and his family in Tahiti, tells his story: he was a test-site contract worker who had suffered serious illness from radiation sickness as a result of atomic testing on Mururoa atoll. First-hand survivor interviews relate to the bombings in Japan and Germany. Mr Hamada's collection of Buddhas have been saved near the epi-centre in Hiroshima. In Germany, Mrs Biermans' graphic and tearful testimony is of the firestorms in Hamburg (1942): the vivid hell of those three days of bombing, which she lived through, described by her and others, are testimonies which provide terrifying, sobering documents of our modern memory of air war. Mrs Biermans's trembling voice reminds us of all the long untold stories of the urbicide; not least those we might not find easy to hear now because of our own selective listening.[45]

Memory and counter-memory

Circumscribed by harassment, misrepresentation and at times extreme repression, this century-long de-militarizing project has included much resistant creativity. Its work can now be treated as a corpus, and one especially relevant to the postnational twenty-first century. The peace dimension of this disconnected memory-making has often been both censored and over-neglected. This is partly explained as the construction of a modern memory from the bottom-up has been an essentially civilian, grassroots and idealistically motivated effort; it is by definition at times 'amateurish', anarchic or naive. This characterization stretches far beyond sectarian peace groups, since the evolution of memory has often interacted with a growing, particular community's political or cultural agenda. Acknowledgement of such issues such as the physical effects of nuclear testing and of previous mass bombing of civilian targets after the 1940s was marginal and slow; modern governments, of all persuasions, judged these topics best avoided. Susan Griffin stresses and documents these cover-ups in her interviews and reports.

But for Watkins and the Marukis, and the writers, poets and photographers who prophetically confronted and described them, such issues cannot so easily be ignored. One literary parallel to Watkins's anti-nuclear films, the Marukis' post-atomic art and Del Tredici's photography of nuclear weapons production is represented by Griffin's idiosyncratic work, especially her *Chorus of Stones*. Partly autobiographical, semi-fictional, but based on multiple individual interviews, it is a profoundly personal, feminist survey of nuclear America in the 1980s and before. As she touches on the history and the hazards of the nuclear age from the 1940s, her narratives illustrate the dangers of radioactive materials and their mass usage, civil and military. Her family stories and historical references reveal the cultural and political implications: censorship, systemic manipulation and the official distortion and silencing of memory. Like Des Pres, Watkins and Wilbur, Griffin also reflects the prophetic implications of memory in an age of potential omnicide. As an illustration of multi-layered, multi-genre memory work drawing from worldwide examples, it has a unique place in 1980s American literature, not just women's literature.

In considering memory and militarization in this chapter I have included several under-celebrated, but uniquely creative individuals working in the arts and in communities: Watkins, Del Tredici, Griffin and the Marukis (and previously Des Pres). They are crucial to this project because they helped construct or reconstruct an alternative memory for the nuclear age, and did so from below. This is especially true of those who focused on nuclear weapons between 1958 and 1965, and continuing again in 1979 into the 1980s, but as I have tried to show, its roots lie even earlier in a pre-atomic transnational ethos.

Linked to social action and alternative media by the 1980s, and not least within the women's movement, the demilitarization project above all confronts patriarchy. This was well illustrated in the woven banner art of the various International Women's Peace Camps, such as at Greenham Common (nuclear missile base) in Berkshire, UK. Such icons provided an imagery to empower a new 1980s opposition. Similar women's action groups, by using music, photography, banners and films (such as Beeban Kidron's), engaged with a revived movement, networking transnationally, as well as through independent media. This autonomous creativity also presaged a recurrent resonance of feminist themes in popular music, writing and cinema through the mid-1980s.

Nevertheless, re-engagement with the past remained central to that project, even a 'remembering' of the 1960s or more recent past, as well as previous historic oppositional struggles. These transgenerational stories and traditions of involvement became part of a continuous 'movement culture', if not 'cult'. Whilst some of this has proved ephemeral, and whilst such 'new social movements' were certainly cyclical, much continues into the present. Nuclear awareness has episodically dwindled and the Cold War 'thaw' after the 1980s at first made such threats seem less globally imminent. But a contingent movement memory and the cultural productions described here survived into the nuclear crises of the Trump era. In response to modern militarism, and mass violence, this memorizing process epitomizes the difficult and often political struggles needed to make and sustain a de-militarizing, truth-speaking culture in the face of the current global threats, in Asia (North Korea, India and Pakistan) and the Middle East (Iran). By influencing both social myth and popular culture, often from the political margins, these contests influence postnational sensibilities and potential. However small, this is sustained not least through the medium of the civil society groups who promote them, and the major memory-makers they celebrate.

Notes

1 Gavin Ewart, Imperial War Museum. By permission of the Estate of Gavin Ewart.
2 Originally derived from the Dutch/French wars of the 1700s.
3 See *Guide to the Imperial War Museum*, which exemplifies this mix.

4 "*People Power: Fighting for Peace*", IWM London, 2017.
5 When Picasso's *Guernica* image of bombing was covered up at the UN in New York during an Iraq war escalation, it underlined the power of iconic visual representations of urban destruction. Memorable images of violent intrusion from the air – Nagasaki, Coventry, Dresden, Warsaw, Hiroshima, Berlin then New York city's twin towers (9/11) – have become cultural markers since 1936 (see multiple examples in Simon Baker and Shoair Mavlian, eds, *Conflict. Time. Photography* (London, 2015).
6 Such genres of production, in film and literature, evolved from the writings of Hemingway, Woolf, Rosenberg and Sassoon and art of Grosz, Kollwitz and Dix, and in his earlier work Paul Nash, as a corpus all implicitly sceptical of war.
7 Joseph Heller, *Catch 22* (London, 1962); Kurt Vonnegut, *Slaughterhouse Five* (London, 1970).
8 *The Goon Show* emerged from serving soldiers.
9 Even before the movement grew in the UK. Jay Winter, *Sites of Memory, Sites of Mourning* (Cambridge, 1995) and with Blaine Baggett, *The Great War and the Shaping of the 20th Century* (New York, 1996).
10 Otto Dix, cited in Cork (1994).
11 Richard Cork, *A Bitter Truth: Avant Garde Art and the Great War* (New Haven, 1994), pp. 305–06.
12 In Winter (1995), p. 164.
13 Otto Dix, cited in Cork (1994).
14 Cork (1994), pp. 305–06.
15 Some conscripts may have been motivated by patriotism, but they had no choice but to fight.
16 Ernest Hemingway, *The Short Stories of Ernest Hemingway*, 2nd edition (New York, 1925), p. 78-79
17 Song featured in the Dire Straits 1985 album with the same name, which became a huge success in UK and worldwide.
18 Hemingway (1925).
19 Samuel Hynes, *A War Imagined* (London, 1990).
20 Henry Reed, 'Lessons of the War', in Jon Stallworthy, ed., *Oxford Book of War Poetry* (Oxford, 1987)
21 From 1914 to 1918. Several of these are in A. J. P. Taylor's popular *The First World War: An Illustrated History* (London, 1963), 1st edition.
22 Pat Barker, *The Ghost Road* (New York, 1995), also *Regeneration* (New York, 1991) and the film *Regeneration*. It is also by implication depicted at the end of McGillie's film of Barker's story in *Regeneration*. In his PBS series on the war (Great War series, part 8), Jay Winter documented the scene that followed at Owen's home when news of his death arrived in Shrewsbury, Shropshire, England. The message arrived after the Armistice, as the church bells rang in celebration of the end of the fighting.
23 Hynes (1990).
24 Whether this was that true of all of Sassoon's war service or only these well-documented incidents he does not say.
25 Sassoon was never openly gay, but the homo-erotic aspect of his poetic genre discussed by Fussell in his chapter 'Soldier Boys' (*The Great War and Modern Memory* (Oxford, 1975)) may have caused further consternation and animus.
26 Adrian Gregory, *The Silence of Memory* (Oxford, 1994).
27 As critics of such events, and world advocates, such as Ted Harrison notes in his *Remembrance Today* (London, 2012).
28 The work of Thalia Campbell, the leading peace banner artist of the 1980s women's peace movement, was included also in the Imperial War Museum exhibition on peace protest.
29 For contemporary coverage, see *The Observer*, and *The Guardian* stories on Poppy displays (strong critique by Jonathan Jones; 28 and 31 October 2014, see also articles

by Mark Brown; 28 December 2014, and Rhiannon Lucy Cosslett; 9 November 2018).

30 The guaranteed wipe-out of MAD was lampooned in Kubrick's *Dr Strangelove* (1964).

31 The signs origins were never widely understood, nor their meaning once it had become associated with a counter-culture in the later 1960s. It later evolved during the Vietnam War years (1964–75), to be perceived as much as John and Yoko's enduring, if less specific, symbol both of 'hippiedom' and 'peace'. But its designer (1958), Gerald Holtom, in fact associated it with 'resistance'! A refusal to accept the nuclear arms race.

32 At that time, UK policy included 'first use' of atomic weapons in a military East/West conflict even against a conventional attack by the Soviet Union in Europe.

33 A sensitivity echoed in Susan Griffin's' work on US nuclear secrecy.

34 The ban was modified after 1966, so that the British Film Institute could distribute the film to private organizations that applied ('for educational purposes').

35 Barry Hines's prophetic *Threads*, like Watkins's films, involved local people as actors, some playing their actual roles officially assigned for them in 'civil defence' in an emergency nuclear scenario.

36 *The Hay Wain*, which had been painted over a century earlier, and near where the East Anglian movable missile and bombers were sited in England. Eventually shown in a retrospective 'Unofficial War Artist' exhibition at the Imperial War Museum. Peter Kennard, *Images for the End of a Century* (London, 1990).

37 Introduction by Jonathan Schell to Robert Del Tredici, *At Work in the Fields of the Bomb* (London, 1987). Del Tredici spent six years travelling, interviewing and taking pictures.

38 This style marked novels, especially science fiction, rock music, photography, cinema, posters and collage print. Not least an 'underground' press flourished, and peace-related music festivals from Glastonbury to Woodstock communicated to a new generation after 1968: Glastonbury (1972 onwards) was associated with, and raised funds for, both *Greenpeace* and the Nuclear Disarmament Campaign, though this linkage grew more tenuous.

39 In meetings in Oslo, where he had previously filmed *Edvard Munch*, and again during his own heroic global 'journey' in Sweden, Canada, Upstate New York near Hamilton and worldwide to recruit volunteers.

40 He eventually gained support from the National Film Board of Canada and CBS, to add to many in the growing peace movement groups of the early 1980s.

41 When it was completed with the help of both the NFBC Broadcasting Company in Quebec and many peace organizations, including the world's oldest peace group, Svenska Freds-och Skiljedomsföreningen – Swedish Peace and Arbitration Society (SPAS) in Sweden.

42 See Del Tredici's photo of Pantex plant (Image 7.7)

43 Del Tredici (1987). See his field notes, pp. 152–end. See photograph 60 of the 'White Train'.

44 Shoah historian Raol Hilberg focuses especially on the role of the train in the Holocaust.

45 *The Journey* script – especially the Hamburg interviews.

11

POSTNATIONAL MEMORY AND NATIONAL CONFLICT

Remembrance in a globalizing society

Cosmopolitan memory

In aspiring towards a more cosmopolitan memory, it is hard to escape the paradigmatic power of the nation state even after its sovereignty is dispersed, its territoriality become anachronistic, and its material relations largely transnational. Evolving a borderless, more universalizing memory that tries to avoid any 'nationalization' in representations of the past requires locating remembering in non-national sites and communities, in cross-frontier, transcultural networks and identities.[1] Reinforced by universalized mourning, cross-border events, acts of mutual recognition and shared grief, such ingredients of counter-cultural remembrance sustain critical narratives and de-territorialize past trauma, such as the Shoah. These in turn become global archetypes or cyphers of genocide remembered. By creating postnational rituals and symbols, art, music or non-linguistic imagery, transcends inherited framing. There is nothing necessarily shallow or ephemeral about such approaches to global mutuality and recognition. The idea that borders, boundaries and frontiers are essential to identity, as Antony Smith implies in his dismissal of global memory, is fraught with particularization of structural pasts. Such national and state versions are based on 'constructive forgetting', omitting all elements that contradict a unitary (e.g. ethnic or linguistic) narrating and concealing an inconvenient 'underside of history', slavery, forcible conscription, expropriation of land, patriarchal oppression and discrimination.[2]

Contested space: Beyond 'Good Friday'

Benedict Anderson's thesis of 'imagined community' proposes that any analysis of the construction of modern remembering is confronted by multiple, often severe, contests over symbols, icons, sites, monuments and martyrs, indeed 'histories: complex narratives of the collective past. An overwhelming number of these contestations have related to a 'national' cage or territorial frame of memory. As a boundedness constraining the historical or sociological imagination, such inventions do not necessarily represent a state memory, even a public majority memory. But they are almost inevitably linked to ethnicities, and to a territory (physical or cultural boundaries), or a common language, and are linked to these shared, even if only in imagined or invented, pasts. Territorial frames and myths of patriotic martyrs are a key part of such memories, as Anderson argues:

> The nation's biography snatches, against the going mortality rate, exemplary suicides, poignant martyrdoms, assassinations, executions, wars, and holocaust. But, to serve the narrative purpose, these violent deaths must be remembered/forgotten as 'our own'.[3]

Everyday uses of the terms 'nation' or 'nationalism' are almost always erroneous because they oversimplify. Nationalism is as complex and fraught with contradiction and ambiguity as memory itself. Ever changing, it is full of the internal tensions and ambivalences, of multiple and incompatible identities. When these emerge as representations in physical forms, contested spaces, these complexities and their layers of meaning become more obvious, and the boundaries more unclear.

Few places exhibit these iconic conflicts of historical memories and of violent deaths – national, communal, religious, ethnic, political and ideological – more clearly than the murals of the province of Ulster or the North of Ireland. 'Galleries' of street art, which I watched evolve over several decades, are painted mostly on the sides of homes and shops and peace walls. Whilst these existed earlier, they were created especially during the 'Troubles', after 1968 and the three decades that followed. This 'civic' art from divided cities (Derry/Londonderry, and Belfast especially) also represented three centuries of memory. From the iconized Battle of the Boyne (1680) to images of evictions and the Potato Famine, murals of 1916, both of the Easter Rising and the losses by both communities in the British Army who fought on the Somme in that year, are predominantly images of past conflict and military engagement: events commemorated from the seventeenth century up to Bloody Sunday and beyond. Each community also has its memorials to their 'side's' more recent martyrs – especially Bobby Sands and the hunger strikers at the Maze Prison (1981). In the Creggan estate and Bogside in Derry, along the Crumlin Road, Falls Road, in the Shankill in Belfast, in Andersonstown, or in the Ardoyne, which has its own special memorial to the Troubles – these are sites of commemoration. Almost mythical battlegrounds in a bitter civil war, each clash has its theatrical backdrop in this tribal yet layered wall art. But it is often interpreted in a purely binary way, yet some murals, especially since the Good Friday Agreement, are non-sectarian (Image 11.1).[4]

IMAGE 11.1 An atypically peaceful wall mural in Northern Ireland after Good Friday, commemorating those fallen in war – not only in Ireland but in places such as the Somme in 1916–18, in which Irish, north and south, suffered heavy casualties. This is memorialized in a number of murals. Photo by permission of Extramural Activity.

In one interpretation, the main frame of the images is a 'national' contest. But on inspection, the contests are plural and diffuse: Irish versus British, South versus North, Derry versus Londonderry, Republican/Nationalist against Unionist/Loyalist, and other post-colonial identities. But secular and sectarian sub-national and transnational narratives were overlain by other contests, especially the Catholic and Protestant religious divide. The 1916 secularist rising against British governance was not along religious lines – indeed many Catholics opposed it, while Republican Protestants joined, even led it. In the North, the historic conflict and subsequent Troubles *were*, at least in part, also about faith. The memories portrayed had continued from when the Presbyterian settlements began. But centuries of troubled relationships with England which intensified during the Great War, and the Irish civil war that followed, is symbolized by the Union Jack flag: 'British imperialism' confronts a mythically unified 'Republican' Tricolour, the green, the white, and the orange.[5]

Most of the invented nationalisms that face those who work on modern memory are similarly portrayed as binary constructs: other martyrs and heroes, mythologized and manufactured in contests that parallel those of Ireland. For example, the Serbian 'victim' myth of the battle of Kosovo would be muddied and confused, less stark, or one-sided, if the fact that Albanians fought fiercely on both sides at the 'Field of Blackbirds' (1389) had survived as part of the story. Equally the recurrent, deep divisions within Irish Republicanism since 1916 are not conveniently part of the 'memory' of the conflict, especially since the 1960s.

The simplistic bifurcation of 'identification memory' misses unifying and largely secular elements in an often-shared culture of mourning. In recent evolution, a Northern Ireland identity within Europe includes not only shared cultural experience, including two world wars, but also more specifically collective memory. Articulated during and after a terribly bloody and costly (as a ratio of population) civil war, this is exemplified in its remarkable and relatively bloodless symbolic competition of icons. This remarkable, and shared tradition of mural painting – like no other such image-contest that I am aware of – is one in which two blurred narratives, biased group memories and layered ambiguous traditions are established in paint.[6] But these collective memories exist juxtaposed in a shared space and, despite the occasional notable Gaelic phrase – in a common language. This is a shifting visual gallery of Ulster's rich communal identity, beyond British or Irish: it is itself, a unique site in a globalizing world. What is universal and human is common loss: it is this shared civilian memory that binds communities; not least for those volunteers, or conscripts, in 1916 on the Somme – or in the 1970s on the Falls Road or at Ballymurphy. Death was a leveller; shared loss can be part of a democratic process – not all funerals were military or political. The memory of civilians – in or out of uniform – locals as participants and victims, and of so many caught in the crossfire as collateral made that shared mourning possible. Ultimately the peace process was also a civic grassroots one.

The problem that this underlines is that a number of starkly dualistic frameworks for studying our contemporary memory exist. Most crucially these are universal versus particularistic, and international (or transnational) versus national, or ethnic. Of course both of these create simplified stereotypes: a 'peace' dimension lying with the former, stressing reconciliation and the suffering of war, while the latter tends to be implicitly more aggressive, chauvinistic, and militaristic – but also more territorial, stressing conventional frontiers and security. As I have shown, during the 1920s in the context of the rise of fascism, a binary version of divergent memory had been crystallized in the dichotomy between a 'pacifist' memory and 'militarist/nationalist' narratives (or myths) about the Great War.[7]

To re-state the paradox of modern memory, this is not – or not simply – a liberal/conservative divide. It is a recurring critical schism, in which two or more competing memory paradigms or 'myths' collide. Such frames of understanding give entirely different pictures of what has been – and is – occurring in political 'history', especially since 1914. It therefore impacts how we interpret and frame memory, and our pasts, both personal and public.

From a critical standpoint, history has been predominantly a tool of nation-states. Past historians suggested, even affirmed, that 'coherent' and legitimate' institutions through their historical foundation in the family, law, tradition, bound to locality or nation, are indispensable by giving firm frameworks for human action. With an emphasis on borders, history tended to reify given state entities as semi-permanent. These familiar manipulations of collective remembering, supported notions such as the mythical 'social oneness' of the nation, including racial purity or shared language. They were deployed both in representations constructing the 'national state' myth and in sustaining it.[8] Even in relation to nations, or as embodied in states, one can have no illusions about the negative impact of individual or collective 'blood revenge memory'. These are as often manipulated and sustained in chauvinistic nationalist narratives – from the fate of Armenia to the examples of Ireland, Bosnia and Palestine. Usually, even if in the background, or expressed with ambivalence, there exist alternatives to a 'national' memory.

Global Studies indicate how and where transnational experience and postnational sites of war and holocaust can generate such counter-memories. These allow for new discourse beyond the propaganda deployments of national or sectional tribalism, one which can confront ethnic hatreds. The militarization of struggle thrives on partisan memorializing of pasts and manipulation or repression of inconvenient facts. In the process, selectivity and denial in cultural diasporas play an increasing role, as do less partial transnational identifications. Regional and transboundary identities emerge and weaken or replace monolithic concepts of the 'national'. These frameworks are challenged not only in Europe by autonomous, local, transcultural and intermediary memories, but also even by multiple 'sub-nationalisms', such as the Kurdish, Palestinian, Quebecois, Catalan, Flemish, Breton, Welsh, Basque, or arguably Northern Irish identity.

At a supra-national level, European memorializing has evolved to challenge and demystify states, and help re-assess more local memory, especially given a century of shifting or dissolving boundaries. The impact of Ireland's membership in the European Community is a case of this new context, in which to be Irish is also to be European. By challenging the myth[9] of centralized unitary societies within 'natural' boundaries – or of homogenous communities locally – the increasing 'messiness' or imprecision of identified or inherited borders has given a plurality of opportunities, hopes and emancipatory possibilities that few scholars of memory acknowledge. Whilst Ireland, North and South, is a clear example of that postnational opening to peace, in another case, that of Macedonia, Serbia, Bosnia and Kosova, such an evolution is an unresolved process with inherent problems. In a global context such conflicts may never be resolved in terms of a narrowly traditional 'ethnic' concepts of nation; the role of subnational memories, or of memories based on other identifications, are potentially far more universalistic.

Decline of community based memory

Amongst sociologists of nationalism, A. D. Smith qualifies the notion of the 'modernity' of nations. The 'ethnic core' invoked by national identity is rarely modern and may accrue millennia of 'heritage' and symbols from which to derive its claimed past – these are partly communal ones. The decline of a community- or village-based memory, rapidly eclipsed by modernity, would seem to be a historical process outside the remit of a book on twentieth- and post-twentieth-century memory. Yet the puzzle of the relation between the concepts of national and postnational memory to each other and to 'the modern' has to be briefly contextualized. It can only be resolved by linking it to an analysis of the loss of traditional or 'folk' memory.

Infused with a sense of loss of this past, modern remembering was a reactive, but not in the main a reactionary response, to both the military and the civilian worlds, and not least to the impersonality of modern mass and mechanized war-making. If the collective form of memory in the sense used here is by its nature modern, it is because an alternative 'memory' existed in traditional societies, a pre-national shared memory that was essentially local, static or seasonally cyclical. Communal memory, largely, if not wholly, oral, was enclosed in agrarian life and its territorial boundaries. Religious calendars and myth, seasons, rituals and the cycles of birth, marriage, parenthood and death, as stressed by Halbwachs, rooted an unself-conscious 'group' memory in the locality, typically the village and the rural space. Modernity totally disrupted those patterns, territorially weakening the commemorative habits and frameworks of the community.

It is not too much to claim that globally, at the start of the twentieth century, most societies lacked any historical consciousness. Whilst elite memories or mnemonics co-existed with folk memory at the end of the nineteenth century, those people, largely 'without history', in truth also lacked a political or social memory in our sense. Whereas, however constructed, a civic memory or history is situated in a continuous sense of past, present and future. When we talk of folk or traditional memory, we describe the 'memory' of largely pre-literate communities, not states, but of collectivities, usually peasant societies, that lack such self-consciousness. We can talk of interpretation or stories of the past, rather than evidence.

Traditional remembering is not embedded either in a parish register or an ongoing historical process. It is of time 'immemorial': one marked by custom, ritual, myth; and ancestors and the constraints of seasons and life cycles. Religiosity and legend may need memorizing, as in oral traditions, but do not require remembering by each individual of their past experiences and relationships, or details of specific events. Modern memory, such as an acquired sense of temporality to which memory is related, is constructed, learnt; it is not innate.

However, as Nora comments, the France of village communities declined, especially as modern war took its toll; when peasant society was transformed a vacuum was created. Moreover with print and reading came various forms of public recollection and an idea of history, the memoir and the novel. Amongst elites, chronicles, written records, archives had evolved over centuries, but the new representations were of a different order and on a vaster scale. Shared public memory, beyond nostalgia and memoir, only emerged with new nationally framed societies, national history and the revolution in communications and mass literacy at the end of the nineteenth century. This memory only became possible because of new collective sensibilities. These changes overlap with the intellectual crisis and technological innovations of the late nineteenth and early twentieth century, including the mass circulation of newspapers. It was because of this conjunction that a more critical self-aware remembering became possible. This was typified in the work of the precursors of modern memory, discussed in Chapter 12.

Memory, in its modern meaning coincides with history as recorded witness, formal acknowledgement of past events and captured images such as photographs and testimony. As Walter Benjamin argues, these merged with mass production, representing past experience in the imagination, in literature, a memoir, a work of art.[10] Such representations of present and past in these shared and published images, whether literary or visual, become key for collective memory and changing consciousness. A state-framed memory is the dominant form disseminated, usually in the form of historical narrative, invoking the archive and presented as the 'nation's memory'. *Our Island Story* for Britain, for example, was the invention of a patriotic privileged elite; it was part of the myths of nation building.[11]

Such broad concepts as folk memory, national memory, and indeed a postnational or 'modern' memory, are all constructions – academic or cultural inventions.[12] Nevertheless they are more than mere scholarly categories since such constructions have their everyday representations, and real-life consequences. Yet equally, like all social frameworks, they are also ephemeral and imprecise. 'Folk memory' was to a large degree a retrospective category, invented after the fact, whereas 'national' – and a 'modern' – memory at least had a more dialectical relationship with actual events and experiences, evolving over time.[13]

Folk memory was nonetheless experienced and transmitted generationally. But as traditional societies are eroded by urbanism and industrialization, traditional forms of memory transmission, such as oral traditions, are reduced. They are largely replaced by public 'collected' memories, through modern mass society and media. Folk remnants co-exist in the present since collective memory is never monolithic,[14] but as a new critical form of remembering emerged in the early twentieth century, it challenged not only hegemonic national narratives or history, but also a mythologizing of the past. In some later cases it was consciously anti-hegemonic or made as counter-memory, as an alternative both to 'history' and to 'myth'. This was not necessarily postnational but an alternative narrative, and included at times, 'counter-hegemonic' or radical grassroots representations of the past. Generally these accounts arose initially as oppositional ones: often criticizing established positions with sceptical reactions to modern war and militarism, as well as preparations for war to come. Yet in a search for authentic memory, history was also involved in an invention of national tradition, however ersatz. The bond of the collective, and an idea of a national past, was promoted as current reality.

It is overly simplistic to suggest that the vacuum of folk memory was occupied by this invented nationalist 'memory' in a straightforward evolution. Many different forms of memory emerged to fill the spaces of modernity, but two main types need to be treated here. First, and historically prior to modern critical memory, the modern state's 'national' memory emerged as a territorial or linguistic one especially from 1870 to 1914. It was ideally embodied in an ethnically linked 'nation' to authenticate an 'imagined community'.[15] Such 'memory' was sustained through public ritual, referencing tradition.

If 'community memory' is defined as the only 'true' collective memory as Pierre Nora argues, it poses the paradox of a desperate modern search for a new memory in the absence of one. There would be no 'surfeit' of 'fake or inauthentic, proxy memory' if *national* history had been successful in entirely replacing folk memory; the need would have been met. But as Nora argues, it had not been adequately met – the memory boom of the late twentieth century was a search that created *lieux*, places and *objets* for finding lost memory, but it was not a genuine group-based collective memory itself. There is no concession by Nora that national memory had been in part an unsuccessful attempt to restore folk memory. New memory did not represent an attempt to reinvest in either national symbols or folk traditions of the 'patrie' with pilgrimages to sites of famous victories, or hagiographies of patriotic leaders such as Napoleon, Lincoln, De Gaulle or Churchill. Instead, a vacuum of memory and the inadequacy of national history favoured a more universalistic frame for remembering: it appeared an equally viable sensibility even if it stretched the concepts of group, community or collectivity far beyond Nora's idea of history or memory. Memory was in other words a threat to inherited frameworks. A postnational remembering was a threat even to 'modernity' itself, as Huyssen and other suggest.

National Memory: then and now

In any enquiry on new forms of remembering, problems arise in any use of the prefix 'modern' for 'memory'. The ambiguities of the notion of modernity are especially highlighted by the issue of nationalism. Whether we look for the origins of such sentiments in the 1590s, the 1780s – or later – the nation state and also its invention of the ideology of a 'bounded belongingness' remains essentially linked to the 'modern' – and indeed to the idea of 'modernity'. Convenient to an embattled Tudor monarchy, Shakespeare's history plays already revealed some modern orientations to 'national' identities; and especially his *Henry V* (1599) spoke to and for an imagined 'community' of England, an island nation, "set in a silver sea". This newly mythologized past was key to forming a state-based patriotism. This more popular version of public *memory* was gradually deployed as myth, history and tradition. Over more than three centuries, it helped legitimate a series of elite's ruling territorial and ethnic controls, or asserted an often-dubious linguistic identity and claims against others. In that sense, with for example the 'crusader flag', it presides over a militant English 'Nationalist' memory, not a British one. This 'patrie' was taken up by imperialist and populist movements of Right and Left.[16] Whilst today's patriots claim to be just as 'modern', to critics they appear, like the Balkan mythologies of the 1990s, to represent more plausibly a last gasp of dying identifications with a past, with the cross of St George, internal colonialism and memories of Empire. But nationalism re-invents itself, asserting claims over more contested symbols, and territorializing them. The 2014 Poppy display at the Tower of London, or films such as *Dunkirk* represent a part of a burgeoning English popular memory, exploiting a desire for social unity. In part, a reversion to the war heritage business, the display was a conservative project, promoted by patriotic media, and ultimately populist occasions.

Whilst modernizing state elites, their scribes, historians and activists created history and its legitimating myths, one must distinguish between this state-ordered 'national' memory and a more popular *nationalist* memory. The latter ideological memory is created for (and often by) the 'true believers', the grass-roots patriots, and often sustained by populist movements. National memory, equally constructed, evolves around each version. Both legitimizing modes are maintained by ritual and rhetoric; both are 'invented' and politically malleable, and yet 'social facts' in their consequences.

In opposition, different national and social myths of liberation competed in the formation (or dissolution) of unitary state identities. The rise and use of 'national memory', even if it was largely a nineteenth-century phenomenon, was, in Hobsbawm's phrase, an 'invention of tradition'. But in relative terms, it triumphed and so did the conceptualization of the 'nation state' as the natural frame of the polity. Such memory either replaced, or co-opted, much from traditional 'folk' memory. 'Folk' music fed into 'national music'.[17] Yet it was a predominantly state-centric process – from the top down, not from civil society, and it was a territorial one.

This book is based on the premise that modern memory represented a break with tradition in the twentieth century, but 'National Memory' was never 'modern' in that sense. Arguably, as Smith suggests, it is continuously 'modern' in that it simulated 'modernity' in each new re-invention of itself. Yet if it is essentially traditional – as he stresses – if nations are constantly renewed, even with new boundaries and ideology, they are forced to adapt old symbols, stories, traditions and myths and even re-enact inherited rituals; they are obliged to serve entirely new political and social circumstances. The artificiality of this process inevitably risks its own unmasking in a globalizing world.

As nations slowly lose their longer-term ethnic roots in processes such as inward and outward migration and globalization, they have to reconstruct or rediscover core values and memories and even the definition of the '*patrie*', the country itself.[18] It is this loss that Nora bewails: the loss of 'true' collective memory in the case of a 'nation' such as France, one based on a group culture and a core *ethnie*, and that is continuously 'French'. But such generational remembering and renewal is part of the national (state) institutions role in selling a 'unitary' past as a group's 'history'; and if it fails, popular movements will emerge to do so, with a growing angst that the core is being lost to migration, loss of sovereignty or 'alien' control.

At the end of the two world wars (1918, 1945) and of the Cold War (1989), there were felt to be renewed needs, not only by historians, to revisit memory and also to re-examine its links to nationality and nationhood: especially given the artificiality of post-colonial boundaries. The settlements of 1918–20, as in 1945–47, and in the early 1990s, involved reviving or preserving various 'national identities' which had been submerged or fragmented by war, population movement, migration, civil conflict and political re-alignments. But as these re-emerged they proved a source of friction. These were especially true of successive realignments in Europe, but also in post-colonial societies.[19] Other dimensions of reviving collective social memory tended to receive less attention. Like national ones, these were also linked to crises of identity and fostered agendas starting in the 1960s, around gender, and race, as well as 'sub-nationalisms'.

After 1989, a focus on national memory (as opposed to a nation's 'history') was often linked to 'identity'. Such an identity focus, partly reviving as a result of the emergence of further new nations also reflected *revived* nationalisms. Intellectual interest in them had been crystallized in Benedict Anderson's innovative mapping of the nation as an 'imagined community' (1983).[20] But more typical of an academic memory focus in the 1990s was Todorova's critical work on 'Balkan identity' and memory.[21] Whilst Anderson's examples related national identity to early nation-building, especially in Latin America, and Pierre Nora's writing focused on the evolution of the historical memory of one nation, French (national) and its collective memorizing and sites of memory;[22] in the 1990s the focus was on the crises of emergent identities, not least stateless ones.

Memory scholars of the 1990s have become less interested in war and Holocaust memory, and much more interested in linking the 'pseudo-community' of nationalism to 'identity' politics, drawing on the first narratives of a post-colonial 'memory'. Together with feminist analysis, such perspectives dominated the evolving field of memory studies for a decade. The Cold War and pre-Cold War experience and trauma studies still loomed in the background, but the new discourse rarely referred to these. Academic approaches in the last decades of the century, many oriented to post-modernist theorists, oriented to memory almost entirely in terms of identity conflicts.

Certainly this reflected a reality: – a revival of older ethnic identities re-ocurring from the 1970s and 1980s, started long before the dissolution of the Cold War blocs. But it was the post-1989 break-up of the Soviet Union and Yugoslavia and the creation of new states, not least the long festering survival of seven or eight identities in the multi-national Jugoslav civil wars of the 1990s, that was a key shaping context of 'nationalist identity' studies. Just as after 1945, new interest in such emerging identities typically reflected the impact of decolonization on cultural memory, now in particular new, sometimes pathological, forms of the *ethnie* became the locus of research. In many senses this tendency in the 1990s represents a paradox, given the postnational impact of renewed decolonization and the fragmentary effects of dismantling 'colonial' entities post-1989 – even in the former Soviet Union. From the multi-nationalist, multi-ethnic mosaic and cross-cultural identities in the post-Soviet break-up, and also in and after the Yugoslav civil wars, the creation of 'new' states, was also a decentralist and deconstructive process. But a civilian, *postnational*, perspective on memory would seem to have been an equally relevant, and indeed, an even more natural focus for postmodern critiques to adopt.

After the destructive and often futile proliferation of many such nationalisms, an intellectual lacuna in much of this obsession with identity was acknowledged. In later postnationalist discourse, Anderson's concept, whilst influential and timely, was also judged too restrictive and exclusionary: transnational change included many imagined or invented communities, other than nations – not least those of the refugee diasporas and of cultural cosmopolitanisms.[23] These were some of the key repositories of postnational memory. In Sturken's book *Tangled Memories* (1997), although the issues were still mainly framed within the national memory of the USA,[24] new collectivities of remembering are also looked at, such as the borderless community of memory formed around HIV/AIDS.[25]

Alongside new collectivities of mourning, studies showed how historic identities of memory, even industrial and working-class communities and movements, survive in the evolution of global society. The constructive project is not a uni-directional process, and it is one that helps articulate new needs. A focus on a *modern* and *transnational memory* can address such shared cultural needs, by disinterring and representing a more plural past. Inevitably these pasts include the 'national' fragments at all levels in a society, not only in relation to human identity, but also to the conceptual cages within which those migrant identities or transborder diasporas were sometimes trapped. To make the leap from describing predominantly 'national' orientations to memory, directly to those conceived of as constituting a universal or global memory, is of course a step too far. But equally to underestimate these multi-cultural, multi-ethnic dynamics is even more distortive.

Many anti-universalist scholars worked, uncritically at one point, on this type of national, and often chauvinist memory-making. By linking it to identity, they are dismissive of any reading that acknowledges the separate existence of a transnational 'counter myth'. This is a conceptual alternative subsequently emphasized by critics such as Andreas Huyssen as Barbara Misztal – theirs is an essentially anti-nationalist, cosmopolitan and demythologizing counter-memory,[26] which provides a postnationalist alternative. This parallels the much deeper appreciation of memory in the arts and historical writing of the second decade of the millennium. The popular emergence of cross-national genres including fusions in global music, in many societies worldwide, included in it crossovers between transcontinental cultural styles. It has also been echoed post-1945, politically, in numerous utopian schemes of global linkaging. One such was Gary Davis's 'World Passport' idea of the 1950s and 1960s, which sparked other campaigns for the institutionalization of dreams for an existence beyond frontiers. World Federalism, several UN agencies, Amnesty International, Greenpeace and Médecins Sans Frontières were typical of numerous non-governmental projects aspiring to give such postnational networks and practices substance, despite great power rivalries and conflicts.[27]

Postmodernism and memory

I have alluded to the seemingly perverse methodological nationalism of post-modernism in its initial focus on memory. This can be partly explained by its academic and disciplinary background: in social psychology, philosophy, textual analysis and linguistics. The contradiction in postmodernism's gravitation to a facile linkage of memory to 'identity' politics – first in the context of trans-national feminist radicalism, then post-colonialism – also extended the fetishization of a wide range of 'national' liberation struggles.[28] But there is a more deep-seated, conceptual source of the puzzle. Ideas of a postnational memory might imply for such critics a return to the universalistic narratives of the classic cosmopolitan approaches; these were part of a tradition most post-modernists rejected as an heir of the enlightenment. Since post-structuralist critiques treated nationalism, culturally, linguistically and psychologically, these perspectives as a consequence involved individualizing critiques of national identity. They were largely detached, either from any structural history and analysis of the state or from the sociology of collective memory.

For centuries public memories of war have been repeatedly turned to vengeful and chauvinist ends. As a result, departing from those seeing contemporary memory work as a more universal and empathetic project,[29] some theorists rejected that approach as unrealistic in the face of a reality of burgeoning conflicts and populist enthusiasms. A range of other perspectives on the role of national (ethnic) memory still divides those critics, some still stressing conflicting ethnicity or nationality as key to forming our cultural identities, and often this is linked to political, ideological agendas. As I have argued, latterly the work of Andreas Huyssen and others, and the growing critiques of Nora's work, began to challenge these positions, not least on how nationalism relates to modernity, identity and post-modernity. But only in the new millennium did this alternative approach become a significant focus of post-modern scholastic debates.[30]

Counter intuitively, in the wake of the Balkan civil wars, both postmodern and conservative critics ignored transnational perspectives. Notoriously, Kaplan (*Balkan Ghosts*)[31] and Isaacs (*Idols of the Tribe*)[32] provided popular and pessimistic views of conflicting identities. Later in the mood of a more liberal progressive 'Yugo Nostalgia' after the 1990s, it was possible to counter these texts that emphasized 'returns to tribal pasts'. An anthropology more representative and emblematic of the evolution of a 'modern' memory developed by the millennium with an emergent cultural Europeanism that countered, for example, Croatia's nationalism with its checker-board flag, that evoked memories of fascist symbolism.[33] Former Yugoslavia, initially an emergent 'new nation', was created as a multi-ethnic confederation with six republics and two autonomous provinces. This confederation was confronted by successive use of intense nationalist 'historical' and victim myths by its constituent 'nations', especially Serbs and Croats, but also others, even Bosnians, Macedonians and Albanians. Historically these tensions had fostered brutal episodes of inter-communal killing before, during and after World War Two. These conflicts eventually re-emerged as full scale civil war after 1992 until 1997 and erupting again in 1999. Undeniably, tapping into folk memory helped revive bloodletting in the Balkans. In Slovenia, Croatia, Bosnia, Serbia, Macedonia and eventually in Kosova, just as in many republics of the former Soviet Union, this nationalist revival had murderous consequences.

One of the more detached critical figures in analysing this process, Maria Todorova is rightly sceptical of how much of this genre is itself historical myth-making and part of the problem. In an analysis of the construction of collective identity, particularly in an age of electronic media, this raises the critical concept of 'post-memory'.[34] Post-memory implies a belated, retrospective, perhaps vicarious remembering by a second or third generation, some now living in diasporas. This raises the issue of what kind of moral purpose informs this re-remembering in an era of worldwide electronic communication. Is it a 'nation', a diasporic minority or elite that using social media can motivate post-memory; or is it something more independent, arising from the grassroots, or out of civil society?

Whilst clearly the 'invented Yugoslavia' was never effectively a 'nation', neither were the tribal sub-nations. Reactive throwbacks to a mystical past, some were violently, even cynically, to be re-imposed as mini-states by small political minorities or warlords. One of the popular and ongoing, if cheap, regional stereotypes about the societies of the Balkans is aptly caricatured by Todorova; as a culture, it is:

> [C]ursed with too much history per square mile, with an excess of historical memory and, as a result, with unmasterable ancient hatreds, and with a proliferation of intractable and incompatible ethnic and religious identities.[35]

What history lost was a major political project that was buried with the memory of Tito's reformist Yugoslavia. It had survived outside the Cold War blocs and played a global role in the non-aligned movement, staying positively neutralist in international affairs. It had identified itself with peacebuilding, non-alignment and decentralization, and even a certain political openness. Unlike the people of the Soviet bloc, or China or Albania for example, Yugoslavs were free to travel, and a measure of pluralism existed, despite censorship and repression of nationalism and the church – and a very limited free market.

Within such frameworks as 'nation' or 'state', collective memory is formed to some extent unconsciously or unintentionally, but not necessarily inertially. As these images and narratives of the Yugoslav/Balkan conflict reveal the remembered social past is malleable. Its very plasticity allows for creative selectivities. But intentionality in our construction of representations of the past is also part of the context in which a transformative counter-memory can coalesce. At issue here are the social or political ends to which a project of memory construction can be put or serve. As the conflicts in and after the Yugoslav disaster illustrate, memories and images are used to mobilize potentiality for purposes such as aggressive war, nationalist expansion, even to the point of fostering genocide. It is not only the memories of atrocity in Srebrenica or Knin that concern those who seek to counter or replace that process of manipulation of myth. Those who influence groups to collectively select certain things to remember and others to forget, have a narrative that rarely presents the story's larger frame. For those attempting to alleviate or reduce social violence and war, presenting a plural past, and a history beyond borders, opens up both a political choice of narratives and a potential for change.

Memories of liberation

Disillusion with the process of 'Liberation of Nations' by military means did not end with Beethoven's famous renunciation of support for Napoleon's emancipatory project for freeing European nations by war.[36] The study of post-colonial memory, or the memories of peasant wars in the aftermath of Empire, is often a story like Yugoslavia, Algeria or Ireland of a civil conflict in which previous state forces play a role, but where the cultural and ethnic diversity of society is used to politicize differences and create internecine slaughter. The tragedy of Algeria and Indochina (Vietnam) was not just that of its colonial legacies, and imperial interventions, but of imposed authoritarian solutions, local and regional that, as elsewhere in Africa and Asia, continuously and repeatedly disenfranchized and disempowered a majority of society.

Memories of the war, for example, narrated by people such as survivors, and veterans of the multiple armies involved in Vietnam – the tribal Montagnards, the ethnic Chinese, or the Khmer minorities, and of the Catholic community – and not least by voices from the overwhelming majority Buddhist community; it was never a 'national memory'. At times, the universalist Buddhists came close to cultural dominance, given their local rootedness: but they too were divided factionally. But equally divided after 1940 were the political (socialist/communist) Left, subsequently both between North and South and ideologically. A genuinely postnational memory ultimately derives from such stories of shared loss, and of a common, tragic, sense of divided humanity. The Indo-China war, or rather wars, like many conflicts represented so many sides, and so many conflicted and divided religious, political and ethnic loyalties, and not least, a social conflict of the towns against the villages and the countryside, as was revealed programmatically in Kampuchea. Such wars also draw in predatory and power-seeking elites who fly flags of convenience, rather than representing any 'nation'.[37]

A truth-seeking and truth-telling memory was most often heard from testimonies of the victims, refugees, emigres and deserters: the dispossessed, the defectors, and the betrayed. As a researcher on war resistance – partly through interpreters, I was able to record this voice. In the years 1965–75, I met a number of those witnesses, from the victims, the draftees and the Vietnamese peace movements, who were able to see beyond the perspectives of the big battalions, and who had often lost faith in state (or 'national') solutions. It was a very different narrative from those of the embedded journalists and even the bravest of war correspondents.

The personal narratives of returning GIs, former Vietnamese officers, émigré Buddhist monks and recent draftees were often shared memories, local stories, anecdotes: they were fragments of a complex tragedy that rather indicated the surrealism of a wilfully misrepresented conflict, and the distortions and denials on all sides.[38] "Who loses in Vietnam?" asked an anarchist placard in 1968 – "Always the people" was the answer; and in truth that conclusion was shared by millions in such conflicts not only in the two Vietnams, but also in Algeria, Kenya, Angola, Guatemala or Indonesia and dozens more. The lesson of Cuba's memory, on the other hand, was that the less protracted the war, the less the immediate suffering, and even the less draconic the 'emancipatory' regime, despite the hardships of blockade that followed.

After the 1975 ceasefire, the Indo-China war in particular stimulated a plethora of films purporting to narrate that shaping American 'memory' from the US (Hollywood) standpoint. Many, such as the fantasy *Apocalypse Now* (1979) or graphic *Full Metal Jacket* (1987), whilst mnemonic as events in themselves, captured the surrealism, but did not claim to be memories of a war – though the war journalist, (Michael Herr, *Dispatches*) helped write the scripts. Critics of *The Deer Hunter* suggested it propagandized and distorted the past. As a veteran, Oliver Stones's popular *Platoon* (1986) perhaps made a greater claim to approach veracity. Whether plausible representation or not, these were nevertheless solely 'prosthetics', in Landsberg's conceptual frame. She argues that film as an experienced event could be *real* and reinforce *screen memories* in both Freud's and Benjamin's (screening truths), and Sturken's sense. These are images which become invested by some actual and secondary witnesses with a 'truth'; and this acts as being a very 'actual', constituted, image of a 'real' past. Perhaps such reception of film memory represents it as a symbolic substitute for a reality that is yet too distant, too complex, muddled and ambiguous, to truly comprehend.

Previous examples of witness of the Shoah or Hiroshima suggest they may be too painful to reproduce in words or images (as Michael Herr implies in *Dispatches*). I have argued that *Schindler's List* is misleading in this way. Even if there were authentic description or photographs (of My Lai, for example) rediscovering that reality behind the screen metaphor, the memory itself will still very much depend on the standpoint of those witnesses who survive and feel free to talk about the particular atrocity.

From a postnational standpoint, in narratives of war, such as Vietnam, the memories we lack are those from 'the third way': the non-violent, non-aligned Buddhists. This was a perspective that was not part of the 'national' conceptual apparatus of Hanoi, Saigon or Washington – the White House, the Pentagon or other Western allies – and certainly not the southern National Liberation Front. Shamefully, this viewpoint was even largely ostracized in the Western peace movement. These unheard voices as always were those of the millions of victims caught in the middle: refugees fleeing war zones, or attempting another non-military or neutralist path – which included deserters and refusers.

Such trajectories in war replaced unitary or national narratives, not by a binary set of recollections, but by a plurality of stories, images, memories representing paradoxes, contradictions, ambivalences. Ken Burns's documentary on Vietnam moved us from one official (US) version, to two (US/North Vietnam) – apparently a step forward. But there were at least three, and it was the missing postnational and peaceful variant that left the vacuum unfilled.

In the absence of independent documentation of events, cinema of war can popularize it as accessible 'entertainment'. But can such prosthetic memory construction ever produce valid representations especially, given the dominance of commercial agendas in American TV and film? In contrast a European cinema of conflict is often more independent. The Polish trilogy, of its 'non-liberation' of the end of World War Two (Wajda's *A Generation*, *Kanal*, *Ashes and Diamonds*) more easily accepts complexity and ambiguity as memory construction, and confronts national contradictions in a more critical way. As invented memory, some powerful statements about the past emerged and forty years later, at the Gdansk shipyards, the narrative resumed, as did Wajda's filming of it.

Preserving an Algerian moment for a collective memory

One marker in memory cinema was an international film about a moment in the Algerian war of 1956–60. It is one of the most important exemplars available of a more nuanced, portrayal of war within one society. It does not claim to be more than a dramatized snapshot of a 'battle', not a war, and of a community, not of a nation. Neither fact nor fiction, it is an invocation of memory of a conflict; it is one that has a component of scrutiny beyond division. But it confronted French collective memory, and was shunned for six decades as a construct of an 'Algerian War', or civil war, that was widely denied.

It is significant that this contested reproduction of 'national liberation memory', so perceptively portrayed in Gillo Pontecorvo's *Battle of Algiers* (1966),[39] starts brutally but appropriately with a major theme of 1950s, yet not acknowledged or apologized for in France until 2018. The issues denied are the representations of French torture. The situation portrayed is in late 1956, the Algerian and Islamic revolution has burst out in the rural areas. In a peasant war, moving to the cities, as colonial society polarizes ten years after the massacres at Sétif (1945), the Front Liberation National (FLN) has decided on a desperate dual stratagem:[40] an armed urban coup in the old Muslim city of Algiers, and a general strike both in the Casbah and beyond. It aims to force attention from the UN, and support elsewhere, and a political resolution to the struggle. Ben Mehdi is the strategist behind this plan, and is later captured. Mostly non-actors, all the characters play real historical figures in the film, some even play themselves, such as Yacef Saddi. Ali La Pointe with an archetypical background (a biography very similar to that of Malcolm X's) is recruited in prison. The ex-pimp, pickpocket, dealer and thief has been converted into an Islamic revolutionary nationalist, helping to clean up the casbah in the cause of revolt. The three women, and the little boy, Youssef, are all historical figures. Others survived the 'battle', these four and La Pointe did not. 'Mathieu', the French paratroop general, a thinly disguised version of General Massu is played by the sole professional actor. The *Battle of Algiers* is not a re-enactment, but docu-drama: a historical memory of an innovative, if highly selective kind.

The film was banned in France in 1966 and not shown there until 1971; elsewhere in the West in the 1960s some radicals of the New Left in San Francisco cheered at the moment when the FLN's 'terror' bomb went off. Almost three decades later the Islamic Algerian fundamentalists took the movie as inspirational material in the 1990s for their opposition to the existing government: the movie was then banned by the Algerian authorities. In 2019, the film re-emerged yet again as a document of opposition, but this time as a politically secular one. Yet the narrative was not simply propaganda, documenting or endorsing either religious struggle or national liberation. The memorializing message of Pontecorvo is clearly cosmopolitan in its aspiration. In attaining independence, the 'national' revolution of 1960 'had devoured many of its own quarrelsome children'.[41] The potency of mass popular revolt of people power, both violent and unarmed non-violent, may be repressed, but it will only re-erupt again, often to be taken over by new oppressors. As a memory in 1956, the film points forward prophetically to a revival of such people power in the largely ill-fated Arab Spring fifty years later. The film, made with assistance of the then Algerian government, was at the time perhaps unique in incorporating individuals who survived the resistance and their recollections. A clue to the 'editorial' message is the use of the universal language of music that creates an aural symmetry between the bombs of the FLN and the bombings by the ultra-right French colonists ('Algerie Francaise') who themselves fought a covert, unofficial war against the rebels, also using bombs. Morricone's music condemns the bombs of both sides: the civilian deaths of either community are mourned, but blame is not shared equally.[42]

An unravelling of identities in conflict: a postnational memory project

Alternative frameworks for civil memory can and do arise out of conflict, as they did for example both in the Balkans and in Ireland after the 1990s. Such initiatives can even challenge the culture of militarism itself and the myths associated with the various ethnic, national or religious causes fought for. Potentially redemptive, more universalizing imageries recurrently emerge after such bloodletting simply because the contradictions of divided multi-layered identities are revealed. Public witness from below repairs a collective independent voice in a way in which it is rarely re-gained in formal commissions and inquiries.

More recent studies have confirmed this: even in former Yugoslavia in towns and villages post-war collective solidarities and expressions of grief and memorializing exist across ethnic divides. By renewing past accommodations and existing coexistence with neighbours, side by side with cross-frontier linkages, these continue as a basis for healing. Extraordinarily, despite the internecine savagery and xenophobia even in the war zones, positive counter-memories of a multinational past survived, and the international presence, however problematic its praxis was, overall, proved a factor in helping transcend division. The re-imagining of local culture started with the pre-war past: it occurred in a post-conflict society, which, whilst lacking legitimate borders, shared aspirations to 'integration' (European or 'Balkan', for example). In fact globally the proliferation of borderland conflicts and cross-boundary relationships have questioned not only the disputed frontiers of post-war arrangements, but also the very concept of borders themselves.

Of course, contradictory forms of social and cultural evolution may, as I argued previously, occur simultaneously in the same society. Politically divided, but not only binary, perceptions of the past defy an anachronistic myth of social unity: both denial and acknowledgement co-exist, each polarizing collective memory. Such perceptions grow and recede. Any simplifying of this contradiction enhances the apparent disappearance of 'doubt' – of the 'don't knows' – and a collapse of 'moderation'. Whilst often ambivalent about the costs of acknowledging the past, counter-memory-makers embark on a boundary-crossing process, not only in a physical, territorial sense, but also in a psychological and cultural one. To ask 'whose nation?' – to transcend a national framing of the past – each of the hypocrisies and double standards of 'state speak' which have tried to claim, revise or repossess a 'national' history'[43] need to be named and analysed, not least in the interests of pluralism.

But in making a postnational memory for a global society there is also a danger of an inversion of narratives. Undoubtedly memory is often linked to local identity formation. Through individual, autobiographical location and experience we may better establish who we are. But with collective memory, the link is more problematic, since different frames will give different identities power and meaning. As Theodor Adorno argued about authoritarian personalities, if that frame or memory is a nationalist, ethnic or chauvinistic one, it may reinforce a totalistic sense of collective identity. If, in this, personality lacks plural overlapping identifications, then individual self is subsumed or even reinvented in the rigid layers of collective identification.

This process too often occurs when hitherto mixed and coexistent communities become divided by conflict; group memories of a collective, but distinctive, past re-emerge or are revived. This can be well illustrated from the escalation of Balkan conflicts of the 1990s. A case in point is Tonë Bringa's exceptional anthropology of a mixed but divided Bosnian village near Sarajevo (in her book (1995) and her film *We Are All Neighbours*).[44] She documents how Catholic Croat and Bosniak Muslim neighbours and friends began to listen to traditional Bosnian music, or sing Croat nationalist songs as ethnic violence draws nearer. During the war and in a teaching course in an American University on the Balkans conflicts, the impact of this was brought home to me personally. The local Croats in the village's Catholic church are filmed by Bringa: they are singing the Croatian national anthem. At this point, an American student of Croatian origin, spontaneously stood up in class, hand clasped to breast and joined in with the filmed singing. It was a revelatory moment: the anecdote indicates how an armed escalation revives fierce emotions and ethno-nationalist allegiances and occurs not only at the site of the conflict, but also in key supportive diasporas, such as those in the USA.

Until recently there was scant acknowledgement of the manufactured artificiality of much of these 'national' historical pasts and the identities they sustain. The global internet progressively revealed, if not undermined, the local base of memory: yet the very process of economic globalization is linked to the adverse, a retreat into renewed populist *cul-de-sacs*, often involving protests of the marginalized and deprived. The disunited, plural yet overlapping communities of the British Isles, including the whole island of Ireland are a case in point. Powerful ethnically plural, regional (northern England), as well as Scottish, Irish, Ulster (Northern Ireland) and Welsh identifications co-existed,[45] but as each region became part of a European Union of 'nations', some of this historical artificiality was revealed, and tensions with metropoli increased.

At this point, de-synchronization can occur, invented 'national' memories can be variously mediated at differing levels at different times, and the pace of change can vary in intensity. That is clear in negotiating plural ethnic narratives in a post-imperial, post-colonial societies with imposed and artificial borders and post-colonial rivalries. Transitions to postnational memory create a context in which making or framing 'memory' is an active, challenging process wherever it occurs. But it is also ambivalent and conflicted and subject to facile co-optation. The global communicative setting, in which we remember our traumatic experiences, is changing ever more rapidly, yet our ability to abandon inherited cultural frames proceeds much more slowly. As a more critical approach aspires to influence the modern study of collective memory, it challenges and transcends these fixed national frameworks.

It is not only post-colonial, post-conflict societies which are reinventing a past beyond borders. Universally a different *modern* perception of the past, especially the immediate past, has emerged, or more specifically, it has been made. Beyond or despite actual and potential nationalist resurgences since the 1990s, such cultural evolution has continued simultaneously. One such linkage started with the twinning of bombed European cities; a process which began after World War Two, it helped promote postnational perceptions in Europe. In narrating the past of victims, the national is not the only focus of identity. A common sense of non-national civic history emerges, framing history or memory, even in in the midst of war. Even a community memory of loss is rarely 'set', but in a fluid and relative framework mixed with other collective loyalties and migrant experiences. Early in this book, I gave examples of Bradford as a community in 1914; now in the same city, ethnic neighbourhoods mark contemporary transnational identities with links to Wyke, along with Bradford Yorkshire, England, Britain, Europe, and often a previous home country, such as Poland or Bangladesh. These represent layers of a shared yet divided and plural belongingness. In such cities, this is not just the imagined, but also increasingly the 'real-life' experience. It is daily more multi-layered and multi-national in cities and societies worldwide. In post-conflict contexts solutions to practical peace concerns entail concrete proposals for conflict transformation and tension reduction. Those such as the Truth and Reconciliation Commissions were often linked to ongoing non-governmental peacekeeping efforts and peacebuilding, such as the 'Peace People' in Northern Ireland in the 1970s.

Politicized contests over war memories have also fastened on widely diverse objects and events; self-legitimating national narratives of war were countered by transcendence of inherited frames of understanding. Denying the legitimacy of military service, Roszika Schwimmer, a Hungarian pacifist and federalist, told the American Immigration Service, 'I have no country but the world'. Especially after World War Two, new proposals for World Federalism, international legal institutions, even world citizenship and courts, became widespread. The UN's new role focused on 'internationalist' interventions and peacekeeping. Whether or how such re-framing was represented culturally was particularly significant, and through the work of UNESCO, imaging and shaping a common humanity, or reconciliation projects transcending borders were stressed. Often criticized as utopian, popular remembrance of societies' loss was enduring and politically influential under occupation or colonial rule. Such memory is retained either largely unconsciously, or as uncomfortably juxtaposed to convenient state or elite justifications of past misrule. The radical alternative, re-conceptualization of past conflict often implies aspirations to explore other methods of change. Such political visions, frameworks and ideas were represented by the non-violent peace traditions of Gandhi, SNCC, King, Thich Nhat Hanh – the women's peace movement, and later, by the Greens. Their methodologies were embodied in the People's Power movements emerging globally since the 1980s.

By emphasizing such networks and affiliations, ones that transcend the conventions of national pride, patriotism and ethnic identity, alternative histories can emerge. Such was the episodic tradition of non-violent resistance in Central Europe as in 1953, 1956, 1968 and 1989 especially in Czechoslovakia. Non-violence, as Gene Sharpe's work illustrated, was used pragmatically in most cases, but also sometimes with a sense of national tradition.[46] But a transcendent idea of people power was the key to the transboundary popular revolts against Soviet rule, and were not predominantly chauvinist or militarist. They were internationalist and non-violent, whilst invoking 'national' solidarities (Czech/Slovak) and were represented in both the Prague Spring and the Velvet Revolution of 1989. Such complex loyalties became largely European ones, as these countries became accession states in the Union.

In another instance of postnational organizing, in 1955, in the Russell-Einstein Manifesto had, together with the Pugwash movement of 1957, articulated a post-atomic utopian vision of a more cosmopolitan empathy; it mobilized parts of the scientific community and was forged both by transnational connectedness and on urgent awareness of potential global self-harm. Conscious of the precedents of the Holocaust of the 1940s, a similar universalism prevailed in recording trauma and attempts to prevent further atrocity after 1945.

The promotion of postnational identities expressed in popular culture achieved innovations such as those in world music and dance (WOMAD). Like the recognition scene, these presented, a counter-articulated culture, celebrating a sense of common humanity, and both symbolically and practically transcending borders, not least through the non-verbal interaction of painting, sculpture, music and dance.

In the cultural aftermath of the 1960s, there was also a growing awareness of the selectivity of memorials. Aware that Washington's Vietnam wall is itself a comment on the dilemmas of national memorializing, the question was posed: 'Where are the Vietnamese, "the others", on the wall?' In Europe, the hundreds of thousands of Germans who died in the Great War were never effectively memorialized in Flanders, or the Somme. Or in Russia after 1940. Lacking were memorials to millions of women victims of violence in Korea, China, the Phillipines or 1945 Berlin. As noted earlier in this book, the memory of unacknowledged victims became a political issue in Spain, Russia, Turkey, Armenia, Indonesia, Chile, Argentina and Japan. Memorializing those victims remains a global challenge for memory work, beyond the previous constraints of templates.

Europe and twentieth-century memory

In that context of global forgetting after 1945, the search for a reconstituted civic memory was focused first and perhaps most intensively in Europe.[47] Europe's past of peace and war had radical political implications for the future, not only in rebuilding shattered social and economic relationships and actions, but also in re-casting its global role. The past of the continent as a community was nearing two millennia, but both denial *and* forgetting dominated its historical debates. A narrative about peace and security was dominated by 'coming to terms with' the implications of the incremental slaughter with wars which were, at their core, internecine, that is, European civil wars. But this evolution of sensibilities contained much longer trajectories and debates, beyond 1945 and before 1914.[48] The fragility of each post-imperial European peace, since 1815 was illustrated again in 1914, then after 1918 by the catastrophe of post-1936 Spain's continuing conflict to 1939. This insecurity was repeated in post-1945 colonial wars for Britain, for France in Algeria and Indo-China, for the Soviet Union in Hungary in 1956, and again across Eastern and Central Europe from 1960 to 1989. Finally the collapse of Yugoslavia during and after its civil war, accompanied by the fragmentation of the Soviet Union, which underlined conflicts along Russia's borders north to south. Each suggested that a pan-European peace order was still far from secure.

European societies are not simply 'nations', but constitute a cultural group with their unique character, and one aspect of transnational growth since 1994 has involved some reconstruction of, or reappraisal of, a common European memory. Europe, for all its histories of political turbulence and populist reaction, has a growing public acceptance of cultural affinity and a shift towards a new collective sense of confronting both an insecure present and an unsatisfactory past. Stirring an altered, but recognizably shared engagement in change, crises in Europe stimulated a more integrated polity, and eventually a European currency. This shift, despite populist reaction against it, reaches beyond 'high culture' to local community projects and organizational linkages. Europe's experiences of urban destruction are narratives it has shared worldwide. But change has been caused not just by bombs, but also by ruthless economic development beyond borders.

Rejection of purely nationalist perspectives and the loss of clear connections between a European past and a European future brings reorientations in writing both history and memory. This has become increasingly contextualized by corporate globalization. Reframing individual experience in shared and generational contexts is often mediated through popular TV and press journalism. Reconstructing collective culture through writing, filmmaking, theatre and music, such innovations have stirred an altered response to public events and rituals. These include new memorials and new museums. They become sites of contest over the implications of common remembering in a postnational world. To establish the European Community, Economic Zone and European Union, involving each of previously warring states was a watershed project. Potentially it was a marker in the construction of an enlarged zone of a more secure peace, a community of sharing.[49] But finding and articulating a common memory for that experience, one that can unify, on the basis of a shared loss has been difficult. In previous chapters, I discuss the internal centrality of co-operative memory work for countries such as Germany, Austria, Spain or France. This lay in the fact that it was also a struggle for civic dialogue and acknowledgement – against amnesia, denial and forgetting. The same contested discourse spread to former Yugoslavia and the rest of Eastern Europe in the 1990s.

Before 1914 a 'European cultural identity' was a social fact – at least for educated elites. But to recreate it, and the larger narrative of European societies risked ideological schisms. Confronting the past involved awakened memory: of atrocity, genocide and ethnic cleansing. Now as much part of collective experience as war, these required such templates as the Shoah and representing the atrocities of urbicide. As a result, European events of reconciliation were increasingly constructed and framed around shared remembering of these atrocities: a cross-border acknowledgement of traumatic loss and responsibility was marked by events such as Willie Brandt's apology for German actions, and request for forgiveness at the Warsaw Ghetto memorial. It has been seen as an authentic gesture to reconciliation as he knelt near the Umschlag Platz (the deportation site for Jews to the camps). Appearing to witnesses and media alike also to be spontaneous, rather than a staged occasion, it reinforced the centrality of German acknowledgement in Europe.

Europe has been profoundly re-configured in less than a century; the vast population relocations, the destruction of many major cities – which caused immense and continuing migration and re-settlement after 1940 – led to cultural transitions and transformed social life, with old frontiers dissolved. Regional environmental projects, for example, represent episodic transboundary co-operation beyond frontiers. They included utopian environmental schemes such as Gorbachev's proposed post-Cold War European Green Belt. Even the 'iron curtain's' remnants could be the basis for shared experiences from Finland to Black Sea. Moreover representations of refugees, and asylum seekers in the ongoing politics of 'national' polities in a postnational world could now be framed as bringing remembering pasts beyond borders back into the transnational political arena.

During the nuclear arms races of the 1960s, and once again in the 1980s, transborder autonomous social movements had evolved. Latterly they were within the parameters of the crucially important 'Helsinki process', and some were institutionalized. Helped initially by the OSCE, the escalating Cold War appeared to be finally transcended. INGOs and TRANGOs (international non-governmental and transnational organizations) were encouraged to play their own independent part. By linking peace concerns and human rights to détente, Helsinki empowered a recovery of memory for people in large areas of Europe after 1989.

In Czechoslovakia, the cultural movement of non-violent civilian resistance was part of a tradition in which the recapture of memory was linked to civic power. This was articulated by groups such as Charter 77, and Helsinki Watch, the Greens and many other groups, especially in Poland, East Germany and Hungary.[50] Acts of struggle, dissent and resistance were co-ordinated not only by dissident academics and a range of independent writers and critics alone, but also by autonomous social movement and local communities at the grassroots and in municipalities.

From 1979, the extensive *European Nuclear Disarmament* campaigns (END), self-consciously organized as a pan-European network ('Poland to Portugal' – or even further, 'the Atlantic to the Urals'). It was also a cross-frontier movement linking human rights (the Helsinki process) to plans for a nuclear-free Europe – including not only Eastern Europe, but also European Russia. It was an aspiration blocked by NATO, and on the takeover of the OSCE process, by the US State Department. Nevertheless END and the Helsinki groups effectively networked transnational NGOs, linking many independent peace movements with the dissident and autonomous groups in Prague, Berlin, Budapest and Warsaw.

For a decade before 1989, this movement was also far more locally based and spontaneous than has been recognized. Locally many smaller events occurred outside the large cities and connected, for example, with town-twinning visits and municipal nuclear free zones. These served to accelerate a boundary-defying commonality of purpose. For example the crescendo of linkages across the East/West divide were the 1989–90 iconic Berlin Wall celebrations, in December–January, which were as much a culmination of a European as pan-German process.

The impact of this event was symptomatic of activating common sensibilities at the grassroots. Across the Cold War division through memories of the post-1945 tragedies in Budapest, Warsaw and Berlin, as well as Prague, Bratislava and Gdansk, they were key parts the same active process of transformative remembering. The stories of post-1989 were as important generationally as those had been of post-1945. The political implications of reunification, and EU membership were real. But memories have proved fragile; the past slips from the holdings of the archive of memory, quickly, unless they are sustained culturally. Discourse about remembering the Cold War remains inchoate and ambivalent: widespread generational forgetting replaces that moment.

An incremental approach, using the past transformatively rather than for catharsis, implies a more redemptive and cosmopolitan identification. To some, a 'Little Europeanism' might appear as simply defensive protectionism. As contests over ritual transnational exercises in remembering expanded, were they to be multi-national or regional, or even claiming to be pan-continental events? For those wary of political unification, these debates were fraught with tensions over symbolic meanings. Famously these ambiguities attended the staged 'reconciliation' of Chancellor Kohl from Germany and President Mitterand from France at the symbolic memorial of Douaumont, Verdun, which remains an example of the dilemma of nationhood and memory, when ritualized (Image 11.2).

When the two met and embraced on the battlefield of Verdun, Kohl was standing at a 'national' site of memory; a place where France – to some extent – had, and still does, attempt to co-opt the memory of all the dead of Verdun. The mixed bones of the victors and the others, both in the graveyards and at

IMAGE 11.2 French president François Mitterrand and German chancellor Helmut Kohl at the Douaumont ossuary memorial event, near Verdun on 22 September 1984. Photo: Wolfgang Eilmes/DPA/PA Images.

Ossuary, remind visitors that the jumble of skulls are from a dozen nations. Yet all the remains of victims stored there, the spaces, and icons and voids, belong in a postnational memory. Indeed, Verdun had a history of centuries of German bishops and was a site in 1914–18 of an essentially European tragedy, but with American and African participants. The monuments remain symbolically French, except for American cemeteries nearby. But despite these, and other, not least, African casualties and of course, German, these cemeteries and monuments in the Argonne, are overwhelmingly linked to '*La Gloire*'.[51]

European leaders, Kohl and Mitterand, like Brandt in Warsaw, did at least attempt a symbolic crossing of boundaries. But most memorials and cemeteries have not yet achieved that postnational 'Europeanness' in their territories of mourning. The 'nationalized' ossuary at Douaumont (used in the 1930s remake of *J'Accuse*), not yet European but French, continues to be used as a 'patriotic' memorial. It was here that Abel Gance's apocalyptic army of the dead from the film *J'Accuse* (1919, 1938) depicted the ghosts rising against war. Should there ever be a third remake of the film, it might well include, as the dead armies arise, a mixture of uniforms; not only the distinctive uniform of *Horizon bleu* (blue-grey), but also this time of the whole spectrum of colours – grey, khaki and brown – to haunt the national politicians and protest the segregation of the wearers.

Indeed, a number of peace museums do confront this segregation by deconstructing and comparing national identities, symbolized by a range of military uniforms, as at the *Historial de la Grande Guerre* in Peronne (Somme). The effect of four national sets of these, with equipment laid out upon the floor with their packs and weapons, on the one hand serves to emphasize an order of institutional similarity of nations, yet also represents imposing a fleshless, inanimate, bureaucratic uniformity on the dead. Only the body and the face (both replaceable) are missing, and those can be perceived as interchangeable. It approximates a commonality in difference: the comparison is self-conscious, it not only gives equality,[52] but also indicates the very differences that themselves signify and reinforce conflict.

Towards transnational identity

Shared places of transnational pilgrimage which bring former adversaries together, even in largely constructed events, has become part of an acknowledged role for postnational memory. Nationalism, victimology and pathological mythmaking have been increasingly counterposed to a unifying or European narrative[53] in new centres and museums. To invoke further European memory, the desegregation of military cemeteries has been started, most notably in northern France at the '*Ring of Remembrance*', near Arras, at Notre Dame de Lorette. Unlike the Verdun Ossuaire, this is not a mystified jumbling of bones. It is one of the most important of recent postnational memory projects. Designed by Phillipe Prost in Paris, it was planned in 2011, and commissioned for the Nord-Pas de Calais Department in France. It was completed for 2014 and so far it names 600,000 dead from all combatant countries who died in the Artois region, in two huge steel crescents, forming a whole. The dead are listed alphabetically, regardless of rank, role or nationality: 294,000 from Britain and the Commonwealth, 110,000 from France (nearly 40,000 are buried there), 174,000 Germans buried in the area, as well as many thousands of Belgians, Portuguese, North Africans, and still many more to be added. This is a pilot project for a pan-European denationalization of memorial spaces.[54] Like Thiepval, its shape emphasizes spaces. Like the Vietnam Wall, it also emphasizes the individual names themselves. But unlike the Washington memorial, it includes both the so-called 'victors' and the other victims of the catastrophe.

In framing European memory-building as a critical process, one can trace its long gestation since 1918. With varied expression, wider than Europe, like the USA or Russia, its memory of war waxes and wanes. At times it is replaced or co-opted by other memories, as in the 1940s by Stalinism. Europe's colonial crimes, or those of the Jewish Holocaust, and those under Nazi occupation, were seen as less specifically European memories. Moreover equally global were the memories of decolonization. As noted earlier, memory of Europe's role in slavery was even more neglected. All these now compete for renewed priority and attention.

Moreover, after 1914, the way Europe's wars have been represented has altered. Over decades, reactions to patriotism were volatile, but in general memory began to lend less assurance of national rectitude to judging victor states. As times passed, the Great War tended to be remembered more and more in terms of mutual (especially European) loss rather than in terms of national justifications. This explains the essentially anti-militarist nature of much new memory construction in Europe and its increasingly transnational character.

An environment of postnational memory transforms pre-modern remembrance, offers contexts for ethnic reconciliation, and revives the theme of potential empathy or recognition developing between established or former enemies.[55] After World War Two, there were still political echoes of a pre-1914 internationalism, but they involved fewer utopian illusions about historical change. The spread of nuclear weapons across Europe was another factor that encouraged a more pragmatic political co-operation beyond borders, as the Helsinki process of the 1980s showed. Postnational trends – for example, city and town linkages – provided self-conscious spaces where civic memories, even if in tension, could be rehearsed, reflected on and shared. The obvious twinning of, for example, a bombed Coventry Cathedral with Dresden's Frauen Kirche, and indeed similar '*Mahnmals*' elsewhere, allowed very different stories to find a common space for rituals of mourning and reconciliation.

The European institutions of previously and recently warring states remains a most remarkable structural achievement of modern politics not least because states surrendered aspects of sovereignty for greater civic peace. A 'European Memory' beyond Cold War confrontation countered the sectional chauvinisms of national media and the ideologized productions of national pasts. Though, particularly in films relating to World War Two, narratives continue in purely nationalist frameworks,[56] the fact of the incremental growth of a European Community was not least forged because of both memories and fears of conflict. This peace principle was, and remains, missing from much day-to-day political debate. Preventing repetition of past traumas fostered a sense of shared experience for many of those who had suffered the 1939–45 war. The social democratic internationalism, renewed in Europe after 1945, was instrumental in consolidating group experiences, and the EC and the EU institutions represented in part a 'truth and reconciliation' project.

But there was also a demographic dimension: generational bonds that were constructed on the basis of mutual economic interest and the impact of the Marshall Plan, emerged naturally out of many post-conflict opportunities in the 1950s. These included travel and international education, with Erasmus and widespread 'study abroad' schemes. For a new context, a sense of the European culture, ruptured in 1914, slowly revived. For many, the events of 1989 and Schiller's 'Ode to Joy', sung at the Berlin Wall, and flying the new flag, symbolized an emerging multi-national, but not yet postnational, identity. But it was not without severe isolationist and nationalist challenges, not least in England.

This book has argued that the boundary defying character of nuclear weapons and their spread helped create a more universalist vision, so that orientation to such sites as Chernobyl, or even Nagasaki and Hiroshima, is an increasingly postnational one. Holocaust memory has also increasingly provided a global template for genocide and atrocity, and another shared framework for constructing a more cosmopolitan memory.[57] But this cypher was not alone sufficient to explain this change of consciousness.

Worldwide radioactivity resulting from atomic testing from 1946 onwards was a major source for a spread of environmental concern across borders and pre-dated ecological campaigns. Whilst the history of nuclear weapons has been critical in lessening territorial identification, multi-national corporate autonomy and so-called neo-liberalism beyond states' borders and from outside Europe has also decidedly weakened national sovereignty. Finally, so too have accelerating environmental threats to planetary existence, which make political frontiers a sobering anachronism in the face of climate change.

After World War Two and far beyond Europe, defensible territorial frontiers had, as George Kennan predicted in the 1940s, become in military terms archaic. The development of long-range missile technology made any atomic 'Maginot-line', an unproven, if not unfeasible alternative. Mutual oblivion, once war started, was the most plausible frame for collective fate and a shared narrative. However, the political contests for understanding this, responding to it and controlling such outcomes implied nothing about its success. This relied on a postnational vision, practical, institutional development and a postnational, less partial memory.

Notes

1 Thus Marita Sturken uses HIV/Aids as an example, a global memory community of victims; in contrast, I have referenced to localities of memory; a working-class community of loss including Bradford's 'Pals', or the North of Ireland.

2 A. D. Smith, *Ethnic Origins of Nations* (Oxford, 1986). A critique of this was published by Daniel Levy and Nathan Sznaider, *The Holocaust and Memory in the Global Age*, trans. Assenka Oksiloff (Philadelphia, 2006). See also Barrington Moore, *Social Origins of Dictatorship and Democracy* (Boston, 1966).

3 Marita Sturken, *Tangled Memories* (Berkeley, 1997); Benedict Anderson, *Imagined Communities: Reflections on the Origin and Spread of Nationalism* (New York and London, 1983), p. 206.

4 "Peace cannot be kept by force"; the image is in Belfast.

5 Yet orange is the colour that also represents the Protestant Unionist 'Ulstermen' and the orange order.

6 A brief discussion of the 'murals' and memory is in Graham Dawson, *Making Peace with the Past? Memory, Trauma and the Irish Troubles* (Manchester, 2007). See reference to the murals and to the Ardoyne memorial project on pp. 11–16.

7 As Adrian Gregory and others observe; Adrian Gregory, *The Silence of Memory* (Oxford, 1994).

8 Anderson (1983).

9 Andreas Huyssen, *Present Pasts: Urban Palimpsests and the Future of Memory* (Stanford, 2003), pp. 1–29; and his, *Twilight Memories in an Era of Amnesia* (New York and London, 1995)

10 Walter Benjamin, *Illuminations*, Introduction by Hannah Arendt (London, 1999).

11 *Our Empire Story* (London, nd) by Marshall, E. H. was the companion volume to E. H. Marshall's *Our Island Story* (London nd), and purveys similarly powerful popular myths.

12 Edward Shils, *Tradition* (London, 1979). One of the few conservative social theorists to approach memory (again in 1989), his sceptical voice nevertheless accepts the

social power of modern memory as few others do, and transcends structural functional systematization. See also E. Hobsbawm and T. Ranger, eds, *The Invention of Tradition* (Cambridge, 1983).

13 One example is the interaction of modern and national, with post-colonial memories as the globalization and end of empire impacted the structures of feeling in the West.

14 Nora, like Halbwachs, also describes an authentic group memory that was eclipsed by history. His detailed volumes on France awakened controversy, and broadened academic interest in the field. But his extensive focus on France and its mythology was criticized as 'nationalist'. However, it was plausibly argued that the analyses applied to any memory 'community'.

15 Anderson (1983).

16 It was revived in the movement of English opposition to membership in the European Union (2016), the so called "Brexit" campaign.

17 Such revivals, memories in song, occasionally deriving from the grassroots in popular music were not necessarily in opposition to each other until the new memorializing of the 1960s.

18 Austria: from empire to provincial mini-state, to Anschluss (and a leading role in the Third Reich) to occupation, partition – and eventual return to neutral provincialism.

19 Marked by 'new' 'nationhoods', emerging and submerged 'nations', especially in Central and Eastern Europe, Russia, Poland, Ukraine, the Balkans, the Baltic states, as well as in Asia, Africa and the Middle East, all sustained post-war crises. See also Peter Friztsche's review article, in 'The Case of Modern Memory', *The Journal of Modern History*, vol. 73, issue 1 (2001), 87–117.

20 Anderson (1983).

21 Maria Todorova, *Balkan Identities: Memory and History* (New York, 2004) and Fritzsche (2001).

22 In *Les Lieux de Memoire*. In the tradition of Maurice Halbwachs, Nora linked this to the issue of collective memory generally, to both 'high' and 'low' culture, but his approach has not been much applied outside France. Arguably this perspective, as in Samuel's work, and to some degree Sturken's, helped memory work to relate more to the detailed analysis of a nation's popular culture. See also Alison Landsberg, *Prosthetic Memory: The Transformation of American Remembrance in the Age of Mass Culture* (New York, 2004), who focuses on popular film in American remembrance, but fails to problematize Spielberg's construction of screen memory.

23 Huyssen, both in *Present Pasts* and also in *Twilight Memories*, see also p. l.

24 Landsberg (2004).

25 Sturken (1997).

26 Landsberg (2004).

27 Keith Lowe, *The Fear and the Freedom: How the Second World War Changed Us* (London, 2017), pp. 181–95.

28 This cult is one explanation of why the focus on 'national identity politics' predominated, but not why it became almost any obsession in the very different context of the 1990s post-Soviet and post-Yugoslav nationalist resurgences. See Nigel Young, 'On War, National Liberation and the State', *Christian Action* (London, 1971) for an earlier phase of this.

29 One may focus on this confluence of opinion as an 'aberration', yet it dominated much of the debate and literature on memory and identity. It was at the expense of more measured approaches to a wide range of other memories and longer-term trends emerging with globalization. See Fritzsche (2001).

30 Besides Huyssen, the work of Koselleck, Bauman and Habermas, referred to earlier, extended this debate from different perspectives. See especially Jurgen Habermas, *The Postnational Constellation*, rpt (Cambridge, 2007), ch. 4.

31 Robert D. Kaplan, *Balkan Ghosts: A Journey Through History* (New York, 1994).

32 H. Isaacs, *Idols of the Tribe* (Cambridge, MA, 1975)

33 Such comparisons include not only Balkan fascism, but also the use of the confederate flag in the South of the USA.
34 Maria Todorova, *Imagining the Balkans* (New York, 1997); see also Andreas Huyssen (2003); and 'Introduction' to *Twilight Memories* (1995). This work echoes some of Benjamin's and Sebald's perspectives.
35 Todorova (1997), and Huyssen (2003) 'Introduction', p. viii. On the FLN, see Eric Wolf, *Peasant Wars of the Twentieth Century* (Faber & Faber, 1973). See also Barrington Moore (1966).
36 When the composer deleted his *"Eroica"* Symphony dedication, to Bonaparte
37 For a short period in the Vietnam War, conflict was called the 'War of the Flags' since villages were forced to adopt surreptitiously more than one flag for self-protection.
38 Perhaps only cinema- as poetry could do that. Films such as *Apocalypse Now* and the second segment of *Full Metal Jacket* come closest to that unreal world.
39 *Battle of Algiers* (film) (dir. Gillo. Pontecorvo, 1966). The film shown again in Paris in April 2019 coincided with renewed popular pressure for change in Algeria.
40 On the FLN, see Wolf (1973).
41 The Kabyles, and the other ethnic rebels of the countryside and the mountains, amongst them. See Wolf (1973). As Saddi commented, the real problems start after the political independence.
42 The paradox is that fundamentalism as in Algiers also provides transnational identification, and with the large Algerian diaspora in France of four million, Arab and non-Arab, that memory survived, with contested narratives deeply embedded in French national consciousness: it is in that same sense both postnational and traditional.
43 My anecdote about the use of the 'Rest of the World' phrase illustrates the latent 'America-first' bias in the Academy
44 Tonë Bringa, *Being Muslim the Bosnian Way: Identity and Community in a Central Bosnian Village* (Princeton, 1995). The 1992 film *We Are All Neighbours* directed by Debbie Christie was also based on Bringa's work. See also Frische (2001).
45 Five nations are idiosyncratically permitted as the five separate soccer 'nations', but only four separate rugby 'national' teams; yet are not divided in the telephone directory.
46 Another example is the extraordinary decades of non-military civic resistance by Albanians in Kosovo before the paramilitary KLA emerged, or was created, to replace it. This replaced the memories of non-violence with the deeds of military heroes. See Howard Clark, *Civil Resistance in Kosovo* (London, 2000). It is too early to predict whether the balance will be redressed.
47 Even though most critical scholarly writing on it was in North America.
48 After 1648–1815 that continuity had been resumed. The legacies of the post-1945 settlements continued to dominate Europe from Germany eastwards into the next millennium.
49 Typical of the impetus to European cooperation was the founding of CERN in the early 1950s. A self-conscious project of a dozen European nations, it was located in Geneva partly because of that city's internationalist tradition; but straddling the borders of France and Switzerland its pure research function attracted involvement from over forty countries.
50 Recorded by Timothy Garton-Ash, *A History of the Present: Essays, Sketches and Despatches from Europe in the 1990s* (London, 2000).
51 Americans have separate patriotic cemeteries as at St Mihiel; German memory has failed to reclaim almost any space there, either symbolically or physically. So despite the reconciliation of the peace museums, as a site of postnational or memory of European loss, the lie is palpable. 'The Tricolor', even with the European flag, is no longer appropriate symbol for unknown thousands 'missing in action'. The European

memorial for the unknown dead mingled in the soil around them, and includes non-Europeans, is a project for future generations.

52 It is viewed in the third room at Peronne, after the savage trench sketches of the German dead, dying and half-living troglodytes: Dix's ragged, anonymous defiled creatures of the *Der Krieg* litographs.

53 Europe's problematic, which represents multiple narratives at one memorial site, is acute. Are postnational memories a fusion of national and other ones – or an invention juxtaposed or superimposed on national ones? See Jurgen Habermas *The Postnational Constellation* (Cambridge, 2007)

54 Paul Williams, *The Memorial Museums: The Global Rush to Commemorate Atrocities* (Oxford and New York, 2007); see also, Claudine Colin Communication, 'The International Memorial Notre-Dame-De-Lorette', (reprinted in Yearbook IFF- 2013) www.claudinecolin.com/en/1047-the-international-memorial-notre-dame-de-lorette (accessed: 11/03/2019).

55 Huyssen (2003).

56 Films about *Dunkirk* and *Churchill* were typical of this genre, sustaining the "England alone" myth.

57 Daniel Levy and Nathan Sznaider, 'Memory Unbound: The Holocaust and the Formation of Cosmopolitan Memory', *European Journal of Social Theory*, vol. 5 (2002), pp. 87–106.

PART 4

Towards a history of modern memory

12

TOWARDS A HISTORY OF MODERN MEMORY I

The work of the precursors

So much of modern memory springs from the images and absences of the Great War that it is easy to forget the setting; this included both the interest in memory that had developed before 1915 and the work of the key intellectual precursors. Yet theirs are notable and distinctive paths to memory work; and each have been equally associated with creating the context for the emergence of a cultural 'modernism'.

In 1900 the whole concept of the past, time, memory and the construction of history was at the heart of cultural and philosophical reflection. A discussion on remembrance and the nature of recalled experience was embedded in a context of both historical reappraisals - and a questioning of the future, and of our mythmaking about the past. These are all issues that preoccupied the forerunners of modern remembering. The process owes much to the inspirational work of these modern European memory-makers. I refer to just five here. Each influenced the emergence of an idea that there is a social or cultured memory, not necessarily a 'national' one. Even in the academy, these individuals did not collectively create a 'genre', as did later groups such as the 'Annales' group or the Frankfurt School. Nevertheless together their work acts as a clear reference point for the understanding of a crisis in personal remembering in an accelerating and often increasingly frenetic 'present', and – although less apparent at the time – an increasingly postnational world.

The problems of collective and individual consciousness

The best-known individual examples of this genre are Marcel Proust and his series of novels on *time past remembered* (or 'in search of lost time'), published over two decades; and, in parallel, Sigmund Freud's focus on 'forgotten pasts' buried in the individual subconscious. But the handful of figures most notably involved – a philosopher, a novelist, an expressionist painter, a psychoanalyst and a sociologist – despite their marked disagreements, collectively embodied a growing awareness of new dimensions of personal histories recovered. Quite independently, some American social psychologists were, in the same years, exploring similar questions of collective recall.[1]

Together these forerunners reveal the impact on society of the new approaches to individual memory, psychoanalysis and acknowledging the role of the subconscious on social sensibility. Most importantly, through Freud's analysis of the relationships between dream, trauma and memory, the role of past fantasies and nightmares, and their repression, are seen as crucial in untangling our past. Most of this work focuses on unconscious memory. In *fin de siècle* France, two precursors, the philosopher Henri Bergson (who explored our concept of time) and Proust (exploring individually *and* socially embedded memory, through a work of literature) clearly relate to Freud's work in Vienna. They analyse a past both recalled and suppressed yet still potentially represented and articulated – a latent memory revealed and acknowledged, triggered by reminders: mnemonics.

Such individual pursuits of memory should be seen in a wider cultural and intellectual context, and new breakthroughs in the arts. Even earlier than these publications are the dramatic visual perspectives of the Norwegian Edvard

IMAGE 12.1 Edvard Munch, *At the Deathbed*, 1895 One of numerous similar scenes from the 1890s by Munch, many focused on the death of his sister from tuberculosis. There are a dozen versions of it, as well as other scenes of childhood trauma and of deaths. Bergen Art Museum KODE, Rasmus Meyer's Collections. Photo © Munch Museum, Oslo.

Munch (Image 12.1). Painting his remembered dreams and nightmares, he asserted "I paint what I saw, not what I see".[2] Like Freud's patients, he confronts a recalled but otherwise suppressed deeply personal, disturbing past. They are examples of how the personal recall (so perceptively described in Proust's '*Petit Madeleine*' scenes) may become both public through art, and shared, even though in the case of Munch, and in many of Freud's patients, these were traumatic and previously repressed. A forerunner of similar facets in the later art of expressionism (Otto Dix), Munch's work of recollection such as his well known *Death in the Sick Room* (1893)[3] are typical examples.

The 'imperishability of recollection': Freud and Bergson

In his accounts of the talking cure, Freud's patient remembers an apparently insignificant yet suppressed and recalled moment or gesture. In his art, Munch remembers and paints an indistinct fleeting image – of shock and numbing pain from his trauma-ridden life, such as *Sick Child* (1885).[4] As Proust's character lifts a sweet cake to his mouth a whole chain of socially framed events and web of intricate relationships comes suddenly into focus, a whole 'time past remembered'.[5]

To focus on such memory moments by definition also represents a new focus on time – and concepts, as in Bergson – of the nature of temporality. This is the past of Munch's 'present experience' as he paints it,[6] recalling his remembered image of a dying sister. In Proust, the 'recovered past' is presented as a social image of relationships that link to the present and to potential futures. But what this outlook approached only tentatively was the *collective character* of that remembering – that even the personal sights, smells, tastes and touch images were *relational* images that they drew from *social* life.

It is a supreme irony, then, that in his analytical articulation of the collective nature of even individual remembering, the French sociologist of memory Maurice Halbwachs apparently repressed his own resentments and frustrations, and the shocking experience encountered when visiting the obscene physical horrors of the 'Battle' of the Marne in 1914.[7] That event which was partly revisited through Henri Barbusse's experience, and the novel *Le Feu*,[8] was to become a significant paradigm for collective memorizing. As an individual, Halbwachs could not acknowledge this memory as a model for his own work and in creating a theory for such collective remembering. It is likely this repression was, as was to be repeated on multiple occasions for others, because of the intensity of *personal* trauma in the witnessing of war. The role of such trauma in blocking both recall and personal testimony is widely observed. But that reality can distract us from the fact of an ongoing and essentially constructivist, cultural and creative process and in new forms of remembering, and representing, those events. Arguably this has transcendently human, ultimately universal implications, one that springs from shared templates of trauma. But still, even if it is unacknowledged, this memory has a subjective core, and as such individual pain is unavoidable. It is here that Freud's idea of 'Screen memories' which serve to screen out such painful individual recall, addresses such blocking processes.[9] Memory and forgetting are here linked, and they are implicitly social.

Without Freud's focus on such amnesia, and on remembering, a self-conscious, modern memory could not have emerged from the catastrophe of 1914–18 in the form that it did.[10]

Psychoanalysis coincided with a move beyond the literary 'memoire', and also beyond patriotic history. It points towards a postnationalist, yet self-critical narrative of humanity, against which the bloodletting of national wars clashed so brutally. The concern with dreams and nightmares, with the impact of trauma on the unconscious, pervades the writing of both Proust and Virginia Woolf. Later German expressionists such as Otto Dix followed Munch in drawing 'what they saw' to get 'rid of the demons'.[11]

Although Halbwachs's work on *group memory* was not published until the 1920s, he was already an established academic sociologist and statistician. He was the first major scholar to describe and deconstruct 'collective memories'. He has acquired the status of the first systematic modern memory worker – the first social scientist to examine the process by which groups or society (or societies) develop, sustain and transfer memory. Though surrounded by widespread public war memories that were too hard for him to personally process as examples of collective recollection, he argues that group life creates the context for individual memory. This social context of representation of memory determines who remembers – what, and when and why. An associate of Halbwachs, Walter Benjamin, writing in *Illuminations* on media and history, makes this nexus more explicit.[12] Halbwachs saw both physical space and relational spaces as settings for relatively stable relationships, even after the decline of traditional society and its supportive communities. Despite his focus on '*traditional*' groups, new forms of community could carry memory, including the issue of 'national' groupings.

Some indications of this connectedness between personal representations and civic public memory was also emerging in poetry; the opening of this book used Thomas's allusive 1915 poem *Adlestrop* as an example, in subsequent writing, of similarly mnemonic poetry.

Such precursors can also be viewed as expressing, and reacting to, a growing 'crisis of memory', emerging in the 1890s: one deepened by the Great War. The flourishing of the 'philosophy of history' debate, stimulated by Nietzsche, is symbolized by reference to the flight of Hegel's *Owl of Minerva.*[13] Reason is used as 'belated wisdom' to remind us of experience, through both hindsight and imagination – both reflecting on the past and questioning the future. Pointing forward to subsequent debates about grand narratives, all these became part of a new cultural consciousness, culminating in the birth of modernism, and eventually critical theory.

Freud, Bergson and Proust shared a fascination with the revelations of the individual unconsciousness; exemplified, mainly through the experiential present – time and memory. It was remembering brought into self-consciousness, but in tension with an urge to repress trauma. In this

Bergson acknowledged Proust as articulating the "flux of the inner life", the restoration of the past to the present – the recalled moment.

Many decades later, Peter Watkins the director of the biographical film *Edvard Munch* wrote of Munch's battles with this tortured experience "*he struggles to remember, he struggles to forget*", which is a contradiction reproduced consistently in memory-makers in every medium.[14] Bergson is obsessed with the concept of how the present includes the prolonging ('duration') of a moment in the past, in memory – how is this constructed? "The recollection of a single unique unrepeatable experience brings that past moment back and gives us '*identity*'". There are many examples in Proust's novels, which seem similar to Bergson's formulation (in *Matter and Memory*). Remembering becomes an 'activity', an operation, not the passive reproduction of memory 'responses': and this was what Proust repeatedly explored first in *Swanns Way* and then in other parts of 'Time-past'.[15] Proust's 'moment' was not so much a flashback as a holistic revelation of a buried past, not unlike Northrop Frye's formulation for a 'recognition scene' where our buried past is suddenly uncovered.[16] But for Proust's character, it is a personal context of memory, a milieu – not our human past as a whole – that reveals our 'humanness'. Such capturing, or recapturing, of a single moment in the past becomes part of the core of Benjamin's approach to the 'frozen' image. More recently the German theorist Andreas Huyssen continues this exploration in his aesthetic critique; he describes it as a *flash of recognition*, and how that, if represented, can become part of 'constructed' memory.[17]

Perhaps no subsequent medium of representation could reproduce such Proustian moments better than the emerging art of cinema and 'the flashback'. When many decades later Watkins edited his film *Munch* (1974),[18] he used the flashback to capture the artist's remembered traumas in an extraordinarily powerful use of photography: scenes are cut into episodes, sometimes quite randomly, some spurred by an event or a face. In a few frames, a glimpse of those, usually traumatic, scenes from past life – death, pain, sickness, bloodied images, insanity – are seconds that flashed past the conscious mind-reproduced trauma momentarily surfacing from the interior consciousness. After Proust and Bergson, and then in the coming decades, the flashback was introduced into cinema and was able to capture this Bergsonian interruption of consecutive time, image without temporality, perfectly.

It can be argued that the relation of Freud to Bergson and Proust is more by implication than evidence. What they shared was the search for '*Verstehen*' – critical understanding (which owed so much to Marx's early writings). But Bergson's *Matter and Memory* came extraordinarily close to Freud's analysis of dreams – written two years later. And it was Bergson who acknowledged Freud's breakthrough on unconscious memory as 'the total conservation of the past', and Proust who acknowledged the influence on him of Bergson's work on time and memory.[19]

Individual consciousness: collective remembering

That the uncovering of the individual 'unconscious' was a key part of the background to the creation of a 'modern memory' is hardly surprising. What is more surprising is the scattered, disconnected nature of its progenitors; for example, although Freud, Bergson and Proust were all contemporaries, Proust and Bergson were cousins and each aware of each other's work (although this is less clear in the case of Freud). Significant of memory work overall, Freud and Bergson were Jews, and Halbwachs converted to Judaism and died in a Nazi concentration camp.[20] For the philosopher, the novelist and the psycho-analyst, each worked in parallel yet on entirely separate paths, and each were more focused on individual experience and personally remembered experience than on a 'social memory', which was the basis of Halbwachs's critical breakthrough.

This establishes a pattern of disconnection exemplified in the subsequent history of memory work. Though memory for most precursors remains an individual activity, through the creative artistic transmissions of such experience, Munch's or Proust's for example, it can both reflect social context and potentially change it. It becomes, in other words, 'collective', in Halbwachs's definition through social relationships. Constructed memory became a conscious, active restoration of unique experience: traumatic in Freud's 'talking cure', less traumatic in Proust's novels, where the whole range of emotions are subjected to self-analysis. If it can be constructed, it can also become an alternative or counter-memory.

This, and Bergson's focus on the 'present-past' of each individual, may well be seen as the beginnings of all modern memory work. But on occasions, several of these forerunners (obviously Proust, but Bergson, and even Munch) betray a clear nostalgia for the lost, seductive 'past' of memory. Thus retrospection, which was to become such an important characteristic in much of the tradition examined in the century after 1914, always risked sentimentality, and that remained a pitfall for all memory workers ever since: the romantic attractions of the idealized 'before' (as in Siegfried Sassoon's or Vaughan Williams's pre-'Adlestrop' England) the bittersweet contradictions of resurrecting the past – sometimes best forgotten. The new task was to give purpose and meaning to that remembering; in other words, a human agenda for remembering, but only when it was necessary not to forget. It was left to Halbwachs to truly understand these broader collective implications for human consciousness: it was a divergent path from that of Benjamin or Adorno, or Karl Mannheim, yet these Frankfurt School theorists and critics represent the closest legatees of the precursors.

While postnational impulses were present before the August 1914 catastrophe began, it was the war that was the enabling occasion for this new prism of memory to become the means by which a modern nightmare would be seen, represented and perhaps understood. The post-1918 work of Freud and Proust also each reflect the deep impact of the war. Halbwachs was deeply affected by it: it was the collective trauma of the war's first months, especially on the Western Front, that Halbwachs, as I have noted, witnessed in person the fighting during the Battle of the Marne, but remarkably he did not record them, except in brief references in notes and letters. Though deeply affected by the war, he did not mention a social *memory* of it. The somewhat coded questions for Halbwachs were indeed postnational: they are about forcing "history and sociology to explore the hidden corners of frontiers and fronts".[21] As both a socialist and a social psychologist, he extended the methodological and conceptual issues of individual and group memory in detail to confront exactly these hidden corners he himself could not face, and perhaps to confront the covert nationalism of his mentor Emile Durkheim. Illustrated at the individual level not only by Proust in literature, in his *In Search of Lost Time*, but also in Bergson's philosophical concept of 'experienced time', recollection might be latent, but was 'imperishable' – it could be recovered.

A social concept of time had emerged which influenced Proust, and in turn must, it seems, have directly influenced Halbwachs's work. Ironically, despite his repression of experience, he describes how our pasts become part of the 'present', in consciousness, collectively as well as personally. In his theory, this is because of a complex cultural interchange that makes an individual experience 'universal', and thus communicates beyond an event, or a specific time period. His concept of social memory relates to everyday collective experience and also helps us understand collective amnesia.

Personal and collective memory: Halbwachs and group consciousness

As the key luminary of early memory studies, Halbwachs was a pupil of both the individualizing philosopher Bergson and the collectivizing sociologist Durkheim.[22] But in terms of the impact of this work on wider social analysis even in France, its publication was long delayed; indeed, when he died in a Nazi concentration camp (Buchenwald) in 1945, his work was not widely known and hardly translated. He wrote two major published works on memory in French, *The Social Aspects of Memory* (1925) and decades later his posthumous *Collective Memory* (1950).[23] His work on memory took over fifty years to be fully translated into English and decades to await a German translation; his reputation burgeoned with the memory studies of the 1980s. He was the first social analyst to emphasize memory as pre-eminently social: communitarian and cultural, rather than purely individual phenomenon. But he avoids the methodological tendency of Durkheim to anthropomorphize groups. In Halbwachs's work, groups do not remember *collectively* in any real sense: there is "collective mind", but shared and interactive memories. He thus avoids Durkheim corporatism ('group mind'), an idea so easily co-opted by nation states, even by Fascism.

Instead, Halbwachs argued that personal memories reflect group life and are located in experienced group events – and rituals – weddings, funerals, birthday celebrations, anniversaries. As in folk memory, the year provides markers – special days and festivals from winter to harvest and such fixtures as saints' days in the Christian calendar, or Bonfire Night in the English one. These are mnemonics that place individual remembering in the current of a group's life but are linked to time and place. Despite the rupture with traditional society, different groups or communities evolve a variety of structures for memory, some marked by the past. For example, the start of a traumatic war (1914) was for volunteer recruits in Britain, their families and neighbours to be remembered by many (not all) not as cataclysm but as an August 'bank holiday' event: a collective celebratory experience, sustained not by the state but by popular culture. It was due to be ended, it was popularly believed at the time, at the next large group celebration, 'When Christmas arrived'. That festival arrived with its own memorable narratives in France and Flanders, but as Philip Larkin put it, there would be "never such innocence again".[24]

The idea that remembering can be both individual and collective ('or cultural') raises both conceptual and methodical issues. Factors such as generational experiences and social class or demographic location are key determinants. But the idea of collective memory is not unproblematic. We risk giving concreteness (as Durkheim did) to something that is only 'socially' or culturally 'real'. It can be described, and has important effects on culture and human activity, but it is not itself material or measurable, but can have physical manifestations. The reality of collective memory is relational; it exists in the 'symbolic interaction' between people – individuals and groups – and in so far as it has explicit characteristics and narratives, they are 'made'; they are expressed in social action. But collective memory does not have clear boundaries, it is ever changing and is often intensely contradictory. The same imprecision is true of many of the major concepts in the social sciences, and it risks the error of a 'misplaced concreteness'.

Two issues arise in applying Halbwachs's concept of collective memory to the postnational 'modern' memory explored in this book. First, as a Durkheimian, Halbwachs's concept 'collectivity' is mainly, if not solely, the social group, which he has a tendency to reify, if not essentialize. This concept of the group can be privileged: not only at the expense of '*remembering individuals*', and the interactions between them, but also of postnational or non-territorial relationships; those transcend group identity or boundaries, and defy public loyalties. Sharing cosmopolitan or Universalist attitudes, includes remembering events of war or genocide. The second problem lies in the fact that, at times, his "group" model of memory is based on folk, communal or traditional forms of memory, which he himself sees as being replaced by history (state memory).

In other words, where his theory fits least problematically is with the rise of nationalist memory as a substitute group identity and overlaps with myths and 'history'. National memory has been relatively continuous, like traditional memory: yet nations especially 'nation states' in fact lack the rooted, enclosed character of the folk community and they are not *groups*. Nations may have shifting territorial borders; they are transient and not inclusive of all members. Since "invented communities", just as local or regional associations, may claim identity and continuity, they have to be 're-invented' constantly.

The problem with the 'collective' concept is that it could imply a unitary memory for a society or social group overtime. Yet for Halbwachs (who first used the term), and subsequently Pierre Nora, who is in many senses Halbwachs's successor, there are many group memories and they are complex and ever changing; many are shared memories but outside group life. Even postnationally a form of so-called collective memory may still remain an appropriate term, but my approach is as much about cultural, social or historical memory as a 'group' memory. The danger of the latter is that it can be confused with a corporate myths (such as that of the nation state), or as in Nora's case, is an implicitly 'national' memory.

Notes

1 These included Charles H. Cooley, who influenced the subsequent work of Herbert Blumer.
2 Edvard Munch, *Aphorisms on Art* (1886). Words said after the first exhibition of *The Sick Child* (quoted by A. S. Byatt, *The Guardian*, 29 June 2012).
3 Image 12.1, and in Peter Watkins's film *Edvard Munch* (1974), J. Gomez, ed., *Masters of Cinema* (London, 1974).
4 Munch (1886), and in Watkins, *Edvard Munch*.
5 Marcel Proust, 'Swanns Way', in *À la recherche du temps perdu* (*Remembrance of Things Past*), part 1 (London, 1951, first published edition in English). Virginia Woolf's writing, which appears at the same time as Proust's both in its interpretation of the flux of time, and mentioned phantoms, belongs in the same milieu, and is more directly related to the war.
6 Munch (1886), and in Watkins, *Edvard Munch*.
7 Annette Becker, *Maurice Halbwachs: Un Intellectuel en Guerres Mondiales 1914–15* (Noesis, 2003), Preface by Pierre Nora.
8 Henri Barbusse, *Le Feu* (*Under Fire*) (London, 1988).
9 Sigmund Freud, *The Interpretation of Dreams* (New York, 1965).
10 Given this anthropological framing of temporal events and practical sense of Freudian approaches, W.H.R. Rivers might be included as a precursor in his own right, as Winter argues in "Remembering War".
11 Otto Dix, *Demons*, quoted in Richard Cork, *A Bitter Truth: Avant Garde Art and the Great War* (New Haven, 1994), see pp. 302–07 and 251–52.
12 Walter Benjamin, 'The Work of Art in the Age of Mechanical Reproduction', in *Illuminations*, Introduction by Hannah Arendt (London, 1999), pp. 211–44, especially p. 229.
13 Proust (1951), on reference to Hegel see Herbert Marcuse, *Reason and Revolution* (London, 1965), Freud (1965), and Stuart H. Hughes, *Consciousness and Society* (New York, 1958).
14 Watkins, *Edvard Munch*.
15 The experiential characteristics of time are described in Hans Meyerhoff, *Time in Literature* (Berkeley, 1955) pp. 47–48, work on Bergson.
16 Northrup Frye, *Anatomy of Criticism* (Princeton, 1957).
17 Andreas Huyssen, *Present Pasts: Urban Palimpsests and the Future of Memory* (Stanford, 2003).
18 Watkins, *Edvard Munch*.
19 Henri Bergson, *Matter and Memory*, trans. Nancy Margaret Paul and W. Scott Palmer (New York [1910], 1968).
20 In this tradition Benjamin's critical work drew directly from theirs.

21 Becker (2003), p. 56.

22 Durkheim's collectivist sociology is an antithesis of Bergson's individualism. Halbwachs, and to some degree Freud, represent an interactionist view.

23 It is also wrong to argue as Sturken does to see Halbwachs as contradicting Freud's focus on individual memory: Freud too dealt with social forces – especially his 'civilization and its discontents' which deals with war (Sigmund Freud, *Civilizations and its Discontent* [New York, 1962]; Maurice Halbwachs, *On Collective Memory* (New York, 1980). Moreover Freud's concept of *screen memory* is essentially based on social interaction.

24 Philip Larkin, *MCMXIV,* poem 167, in Jon Stallworthy, ed., *Oxford Book of War Poetry* (Oxford, 1987).

13

TOWARDS A HISTORY OF MODERN MEMORY II

A memory–work timeline

Preamble

The purpose of this selective timeline, which includes many of the texts, memory works and workers covered in the book, is to give a sense of the chronology of memory-making, from the late nineteenth century through to the twenty-first century. It is based on dates cited in the text.

It provides the basis for my periodization of modern memory production about war and of the three memory booms I have focused on: 1928–36, 1955–68 and then the 1980s and early 1990s, as well as the generational implications of each.

It is predominantly of work in the USA, the rest of the English-speaking world and Western and Central Europe, possibly both a comment on the slow evolution of a postnationalist remembering elsewhere, and increasing recognition of the placement of blame.

It represents the episodic, diverse transnational and often disconnected tradition of memory work. This also gives some sense of a cumulative development. This could be misleading as it is not a single genre, but a heterogeneous, plural transnational output.

A selective chronology of modern memory as referenced in the book

1890 The Norwegian artist Edvard Munch starts to paint traumatic memories: *Aphorisms on Art* ('I paint not what I see, but what I saw').

1894 Munch paints *Ashes*, 1896 and other scenes of childhood loss. Henry Bergson publishes *Matter and Memory* (*Matière et Memoire*), English version 1908/1911, focused on the nature of 'time'.

1899 Sigmund Freud first publishes *Interpretation of Dreams* (*Die Traumdeutung*) (book) English version 1913; introduces in another psychological essay, the concept of 'screen memories' (blocking the past), (*Deckerinnerung*).

1902 Jan Bloch's International Museum of War and Peace opens in Lucerne/Luzern/Switzerland: 'the horror of new weapons will deter war'.

1904 The Stuttgart Resolution commits International socialism to prevent war.

1913 Marcel Proust publishes first volume of *In Search of Lost Times* (*À la Recherche du temps perdu*) 1913–27 (novel in seven volumes – last three posthumous; first translated into English with title *Remembrance of Things Past*), a panoramic view of social memory from the standpoint of the individual observer.

1914 The poet Edward Thomas's train, en route from Worcester, suddenly stops at an unanticipated station (June). H. G. Wells coins the phrase 'The War that will end War'. On 8 August, Walter Benjamin's friends in Berlin, Fritz Heinte and Carla Seligson, gas themselves as a protest against the announcement of war. Peter Kollwitz dies (October, Flanders). The sociologist Maurice Halbwachs observes the effects of modern war on the Marne, as does the writer Henri Barbusse (*Le Feu*). 'Bradford Pals' battalion was formed. The spontaneous Christmas Truce starts on 24–26 December in France and Belgium, and lasts longer in some sectors.

1915 Edward Thomas decides to join the war; he writes *Adlestrop* poem, (published 1917, the year he was killed); John McCrae poem *In Flanders Fields* written (killed 1917). On 24 April: Gallipoli landings, Turkey; Armenian genocide starts.

1916 Henri Barbusse's *Le Feu: Journal d'une escouade* account of the war published. On 1 July, Somme offensive begins; 'Bradford Pals' suffer catastrophic casualties. *Letters from Prison*, Rosa Luxemburg 1916–18 written in opposition to the war. The film *Battle of the Somme* causes shock when shown in Britain.

1917 Siegfried Sassoon renounces his military award; T. S. Eliot starts to write *The Waste Land* poem (1917–22); Sassoon publishes poem *Counter Attack* in volume of that name.

1918 Paul Nash paints *We Are Making A New World*, and reports on 'a bitter truth'. Gance works on filming *J'Accuse* near Verdun, France. In USA two women independently promote sale of poppies for war relief (Mona B. Michael, Anna Guérin). France Campaign to make a poppy symbol for the American Legion starts. November: the poet Wilfred Owen is killed: Armistice starts at 11am, on the eleventh of the eleventh. Event marked publicly in several countries and with silences in New Zealand. Carl Sandburg's poem *Grass* is published.

1919 Abel Gance *J'Accuse* film completed and shown; Peace Day London 19 July 19 – Construction of first, temporary, Whitehall Cenotaph; publication of *Michelin Guide to the Battlefields*; Siegfried Sassoon writes *Aftermath*; Liebknecht and Luxemburg murdered; 11 November first two minute silence in London. Käthe Kollwitz prints *Memorial Sheet for Karl Liebknecht* (*Gedenkblatt für Karl Liebknecht*) 1919–1920, woodcut.

1920 Lutyens's Cenotaph in London permanent structure (started 1919) unveiled; 11 November becomes permanent day of remembrance; opening of Imperial War Museum in London by King George V; Paul Klee painted *Angelus Novus* (owned by Walter Benjamin).

1921 11 November first UK Poppy Day; use of poppies on Remembrance Day. British composer Ralph Vaughan Williams *Pastoral Symphony*, with world war references (he had served as an ambulance driver).

1922 Proust finishes final volume of his *Recherche* and it is published; Eliot's *The Waste Land* completed.

1923 Hitler's *Mein Kampf* (*My Struggle*) written (publication starts 1925).

1924 Otto Dix, *Der Krieg* (*War*) cycle of fifty-one prints. Ernst Friedrich opens an anti-war museum in Berlin 1925; publishes *War against War* (mostly photographs of maimed, wounded and disfigured).

1925 Virginia Woolf writes *Mrs Dalloway*; Käthe Kollwitz starts *The Grieving Parents* memorial statues; Maurice Halbwach's *Les Cadres Sociaux de la Memoire* (*The Social Frameworks of Memory*) published in France; Ernest Hemingway *In Our Time* (short story collection including *Soldier's Home*).

1927 Vera Brittain completes autobiography, *Testament of Youth* (published 1933). Stanley Spencer starts painting Burghclere Sandham Memorial Chapel murals (completed 1929). Karl Mannheim's essay on 'political generations' published.

1928 *Journeys' End* (R. C. Sheriff's play), published 1929, at the Apollo theatre in London; such events signal the start of a 'War Memory' boom in publications and films across Europe and USA. Ernest Junger, *Storm of Steel* (novel). Kellogg-Briand Pact outlaws war.

1929 Ernst Junger, *Storm of Steel* (novel); Ernest Hemingway, *A Farewell to Arms* (novel); E. M. Remarque, *All Quiet on the Western Front* (novel); Robert Graves, *Goodbye to All That* (autobiography).

1930 Lewis Milestone's film, *All Quiet on the Western Front* banned in Germany; Siegfried Sassoon *Memoirs of an Infantry Officer* published.

1931 Film *Kameradschaft*, G. W. Pabst uses World War One flashbacks, with a transnational theme.

1932 *The Grieving Parents* memorial by Käthe Kollwitz installed in Flanders (Belgium); John Dos Passos, *1919* (novel). Completion of Lutyens's Thiepval memorial on the Somme.

1933 First use of white poppies (UK) Women's Cooperative Guild campaign, opposing militarization of Armistice Day. Nazis attack and destroy Ernst Friedrich's anti-war museum in Berlin. He is imprisoned.

1934 Nazi Party Congress Nuremburg, with Albert Speers *Theatre of Light* filmed.

1935 *The Triumph of the Will,* Leni Riefenstahl's film of 1934 Nuremberg congress.

1936 Otto Dix's *Flanders* 1917 (painting); Irwin Shaw, *Bury the Dead* (play), New York.

1937 Nazi *Degenerate Art* show (*Entartete Kunst*) includes works by Dix, Grosz, and Kollwitz; Pablo Picasso's *Guernica.* This painting protesting civilian bombing exhibited in the Paris World Exhibition along with Frans Masereel's *The Burial of War.*

1938 George Orwell, *Homage to Catalonia* (memoir of Spain); Ernest Hemingway *Old Man at the Bridge* (short story); Jean Renoir, *La Grande Illusion* (film).

1939 Halbwachs's final essay on memory published in French; 'Who, after all speaks today of the annihilation of the Armenians?' remark attributed to Hitler (possibly 1940).

1940 London Blitz. Virginia Woolfs last essay 'Thoughts on peace in an Air Raid' in *Death of a Moth.* Coventry Cathedral largely destroyed.

1942 Walt Disney makes film *Bambi* (not successful in USA and not distributed in Europe). USA joins war.

1943 Keith Douglas's *Vergissmeinnicht*, '*Forget me not*' (poem), Western desert. Allied bombs destroy Kaiser Wilhelm Gedächtniskirche church, Central Berlin (dedicated as memorial 1997). White Rose students executed, Munich University.

1944 Käthe Kollwitz 'Seed Corn Shall Not Be Sown' (anti-conscription poster), later used by anti-atom bomb campaign.

1945 Maurice Halbwachs dies in Buchenwald concentration camp (16 March). Yevgeny Khaldei photograph of Reichstag (May), Red Flag raising in Berlin. Belsen camp discovered and opened up. Newsreel of Bergen Belsen and other liberated camps (spring); first (Japanese) film footage of Hiroshima/Nagasaki bombs and aftermath (6 and 9 August) confiscated by US Authorities; limited reportage except for John Hersey's serialized account, *Hiroshima*

1946 First Bikini major Pacific atomic test 'Crossroads', images later used in Bruce Conner's 1976 film, *Crossroads.*

1947 Anne Frank's *The Diary of a Young Girl* (first published in Dutch as *Het Achterhuis*).

1950 Ira and Toshi Maruki begin work on the *Hiroshima Panels*, completed in 1982; M. Halbwachs', *La Memoire Collective* published in Paris, posthumously.

1952 Georges Franju's *Hotel des Invalides* (film); Anne Frank's *The Diary of a Young Girl* published in English.

1953 Israel's 'Law of Remembrance' establishes plan for Yad Vashem.

1955 Alain Resnais's film, *Nuit et Brouillard* (*Night and Fog*).

1958 Elie Wiesel's *La Nuit* (*Night*) in Yiddish first in 1956, published in France (first English publication, 1960 in USA).

1959 *Hiroshima Mon Amour* (directed by Alain Resnais, script by Marguerite Duras).

1960 *Neue Wache*, memorial dedicated to victims of war and Fascism (Berlin).

1961 Trial of Adolf Eichmann began in Jerusalem (Arendt records it in *Eichmann in Jerusalem*). Charles Chilton's *Oh! What a Lovely War* (radio version 1961 as *The Long, Long Trail*), Joan Littlewood (musical play, 1963) and Richard Attenborough (film, 1969) use same materials. First hydrogen bomb tested.

1962 Benjamin Britten's *War Requiem*, first performance, using Owen's poetry, at Coventry Cathedral; first 'Checkpoint Charlie' Museum, Berlin (moved in 1963).

1963 Peter Watkins's BBC film *The War Game* banned from TV.
A. J. P. Taylor's *First World War; An Illustrated History* published. Hannah Arendt's report on trial, *Eichmann in Jerusalem: A Report on the Banality of Evil* (book).

1966 Frances Yates's *Art of Memory* published. Gillo Pontecorvo *Battle of Algiers* (film) banned in France.

1967 Alexander and Marguerite Mitscherlich's *Die unfähigkeit zu trauern* (*The Inability to Mourn*) published in German.

1968 Robert J. Lifton's *Death in Life: Survivors of Hiroshima* (study of the Hibakusha).

1969 Kurt Vonnegut's novel *Slaughterhouse Five* (Vonnegut was in Dresden, 1945). Anselm Kiefer's controversial Hitler salute photos, *Occupations*.

1970 *Hiroshima Nagasaki, August 1945*: film footage released in 16 minute documentary.

1972 Jon Silkin's *Out of Battle* anthology and analysis of World War Two poetry published.

1973 Claude Lanzmann starts twelve years' work on his documentary *Shoah* (1985).

1975 Paul Fussell's *The Great War and Modern Memory* published. Alexander and Margarette/Mitscherlich's *An Inability to Mourn* published in English.

1976 Terrence des Pres's *The Survivor. An Anatomy of Life in the Death Camps* (analysis of Levi, Wiesel and others). Eric Bogle visits Great War battlefields, writes the song *No Man's Land*; Later to be known as *The Green Fields of France* (or *Willie MacBride*) performed by the Fureys and other Irish musicians. Bruce Conner's *Crossroads* film of 1946 A-bomb tests.

1981 1981–89 Anselm Kiefer's paints scenes based on holocaust memory: Shoah paintings (1983, 1989) several based on Paul Celan's poem 'Death Fugue', a tribute to Celan, and refers to Primo Levi. Yves Gibeau acquires the Presbytere at Roncy, his collecting continues on the Chemin des Dames until 1994. He is buried at Craonne's old cemetery in 1994.

1982 Vietnam Veterans Memorial Wall, Maya Ying Lin (Washington DC).

1984 Pierre Nora, *Les Lieux de memoires* (*Realms of Memory*) (1984–92) book (in four volumes).

1985 Ronald Reagan lays a wreath at Bitburg war cemetery, including SS memorial, with German chancellor Helmut Kohl. Claude Lanzmann's documentary *Shoah* (France); *Memories of the Camps* – USA documentary first scripted and edited in 1945, under direction of Alfred Hitchcock, later completed by PBS *Frontline* from fragments of Belsen material (segments shown in cinemas at the end of WWII in the UK).

1986 Spain's 'Pact of Forgetting' established. Japan's Yushukan (nationalist) shrine, and new revisionist Yushukan museum re-dedicated 1985–86 with executed war criminals rehabilitated. In Gemany 'historical re-appraisal' begins (1986–87). Jurgen Habermas and others.

1987 Peter Watkins's global peace film *The Journey* (14.5 hours) released. Robert Del Tredici's photographic book *At Work in the Fields of the Bomb* published.

1989 Bernard Tavernier, *La Vie et Rien d'Autre* (film); Modris Ekseins, *Rites of Spring: The Great War and the Birth of the Modern Age*; *War Requiem,* directed by Derek Jarman (silent film using Britten's music, Owen's poetry). Pierre Nora's *Between Memory and History* published.

1990 George L. Mosse, *Fallen Soldiers: Reshaping the Memory of the World Wars* (New York).

1991 Pat Barker's *Regeneration* (first in trilogy of memory novels: 1993, 1995), filmed in 1997.

1992 M. Halbwach's *On Collective Memory* published in English; Susan Griffin's *A Chorus of Stones*: *the Private Life of War* focused on American and European denial. Wannsee 1942 Conference House established as memorial and museum in Berlin.

1993 James Young's *The Texture of Memory*; Last volume of Pierre Nora's *Lieux de memoire* published; Neue Wache memorial re-dedicated in Berlin with new wording; Stephen Spielberg's film version of *The Schindler's Ark* story attracts large audiences (USA).

1994 Richard Cork's, *A Bitter Truth: Avant Garde Art and the Great War* (book and exhibition); Ralph Samuel's *Theatres of Memory;* Yves Gibeau dies, his Presbytere is recorded by Gerard Rondeau (until 2003–04). Douglas Haigh's name is removed from British Legion Poppy. Start of Smithsonian/ Hiroshima controversy *(Enola Gay)*, Washington DC 'Final Act' display.

1995 Pat Barker's *The Ghost Road*; Ian Buruma's *Wages of Guilt: Memories of War in Germany and Japan. Enola Gay* exhibit, Smithsonian, Washington, USA: fuselage remains, but exhibition cancelled, fifty years after the bombing. Curator Martin Harwittt resigns.

1996 TV series *The Great War and the Shaping of the 20th Century* (and book) by Blaine Baggett and Jay Winter (eight-part series airing on BBC in UK and PBS in USA). Visitors to Hiroshima museum reaches a million a year – atomic dome becomes World Heritage Site, Japan.

1997 Marita Sturken, *Tangled Memories: The Vietnam War, the AIDS Epidemic, and the Politics of Remembering.*

1998 In Flanders Fields Museum is established in the reconstructed medieval Cloth Hall, Ieper (Ypres), Belgium; Jay Winter's *Sites of Memory, Sites of Mourning: The Great War in European Cultural History* (book).

1999 W. G. Sebald's, Zurich lectures (1994) *Luft, Krieg Luftkrieg und Literatur,* (*On the Natural History of Destruction*) (book) published.

2001 W. G. Sebald's, *Austerlitz* published; Japan's PM Koizumi begins first of six annual visit to Yasukuni shrine.

2003 W. G. Sebald's *On the Natural History of Destruction*, Zurich lectures included (published in English). Visit to the Yasukuni Shrine by Japanese prime minister, also to the revisionist Yushukan museum which denies Japan's war guilt. Protests by China.

2004 Alison Landsberg introduces concept of 'prosthetic memory'.

2006 Spain's official 'Year of Historical Memory'.

2014 'Notre dame de Lorette', Arc of Remembrance, postnational memorial to the Great War dead (near Arras, Picardy, France) established. Mass poppy displays at the Tower of London and elsewhere, commemorating Commonwealth war dead, repeated in 2018.

2018 Decision in Spain to exhume Franco's body from the Valley of the Fallen mausoleum.

2019 French president acknowledges the use of torture and other crimes in Algeria, during and after the war (1950–60s).

Towards a modern history of memory: comment

This overview of 'memory works', based on materials cited throughout the book, helps give an impression of interrelated history across societies, especially in Europe and the English-speaking world. But except for Japan, the non-Western world is largely absent. It is a comment on how, for many reasons, much modern memory work itself has largely been produced in the West, and for Western audiences. Some dates selected are arbitrary, and even misleading in the sense that these are representative 'chosen' examples from a process – rather than a 'sequence' in a linked 'output' or a genre. Completion or publication of some works was long delayed (Halbwachs' for example). For others, on the contrary, completion long preceded their public impact; this was the case of much 1914–18 art and literature, especially poetry. Nevertheless, if it is treated as an impressionistic 'timeography', as a scatter of key examples, it well represents the episodic, idiosyncratic and often disconnected chain of representations in the evolution of 'modern memory' towards a more radically postnational narrative. I have only given limited references after 2000 when that narrative accelerated. This latter comment relates especially to my discussion in the concluding chapter, which follows, and relates to the context of new global media and electronic communication, in which selection becomes even more arbitrary and too influenced by the immediate pressures of an ever-changing historical 'present'.

14

THE PAST IN THE PRESENT – *METAMORPHOSEN*

Deconstructing the 'Angelus': clearing history's debris

In a philosophy of both memory and history, several later critics refer back extensively to a single beguiling, but ambiguous icon, the so-called *Angel of History* or *The 'Angelus Novus'*. It has been represented as symbolizing contradictory 'presents', concepts emerging from Walter Benjamin's essays in the 1940s.[1] The perverse, contested and eventually post-modernist image was supposedly derived from Paul Klee's playful puppet-like cartoon (1920). In this interpretation, the emergence of the modern, the rupture with the past symbolized by the 'Great War' is both backward looking and forward looking: the survival of traditional forms co-existing alongside the new; sometimes they are in tension, sometimes not. Benjamin refers to Klee's image in 1940 in a celebrated passage. He is perhaps linking it to 'memory', but clearly also referring to a friend's poem. Klee's trapped figure is seen to embody our frozen confidence in the present, as well as shaken faith in the future. It is stopped by Benjamin's 'post', or certainly non-Marxian, storm, "blowing out of paradise", which is 'sustained by an icy blast of pessimism'.[2]

Benjamin's original text seems to invite us to confront these contradictions. We too are caught in that continuous present; like the Angel, blown from paradise (Utopia): we are looking backwards at history, aghast; still driven 'back into the future' by the detritus of the past[3] – or is it rather back by a wind from the future? In any case, we are trapped by this historic debris, the mendacity of historical narrative, and its narrators. In either version the 'Angel' seems fated to be fixed, like us, in that contradiction, between a history (or barbarism) and a future blocked: fixated in a permanent present. We too are stuck, we can only stare at the destruction. Indeed, in Klee's painting the Angel gazes maniacally back at us. How apt a metaphor is this is for imagining the dilemmas facing postnational memory? It is true our contemporary existence rests upon the nature of those forces 'from the future', such as climate change, and how we confront them.

In fact the apocalyptic pessimist amongst us might see the wind blowing not back from 'paradise', or forward from 'history', but from Armageddon: a metaphor for aftershock driven by the blast from multiple thermonuclear explosions, and, to quote the Nobel Laureate, an irradiated cloud that is "blowing in the wind", or from tremors of impending environmental catastrophe. Few dare to re-interpret this contradictory and utterly ambiguous iconography as pessimism about our ability to transcend the past, or simply as an anguished, fatalistic response, more akin to Munchs' *Scream,* to our crises of historic existence (Image 14.1). Even as a metaphor for the sheer kaleidoscopic chaos of modern remembering it remains problematic.

IMAGE 14.1 Paul Klee, *Angelus Novus*, 1920. Puzzling, ambiguous cartoon-like figure probably lampooning Hitler, and quite unlike the Angel of History described by Walter Benjamin, who owned the sketch before T. W. Adorno. Later Gershom Scholem acquired the art work. Photo © Elie Posner/The Israel Museum, Jerusalem.

Perhaps the evolution of a postnational memory is to some extent trapped in that debris of history, between no future and dead pasts. Like the *Angelus*, we may be stranded and paralyzed, fixed in a moment of cultural 'memory'. Since 1914, 'Memory' has been fragmented in an ever-rushing overwhelming present. Potentially any effort at civilizing memory has to dwell amongst such obstacles and contradictions as nationalism. In that sense perhaps the concept can be still an appropriate myth. The 'debris' of national history, of 'barbaric' events, necessarily represents past horrors: the 'screened out' traumas; and denial.

There are immense, deeply ironic problems with all of this. First, neither of Benjamin's 'Angel of History' texts bear any resemblance to Klee's pictorial image. Benjamin writes of an image of an 'Angel of History', but without perhaps really looking back at the cartoon, or directly interpreting the intention of the original image of Klee's 'angel'. Klee's apocalyptic figure seems to be flattened against the glass wall of the present, with the continuum of future, possibly past, pressing chaotically behind, but there is no debris – the creature is staring at us, arms out stretched, a manic anti-prophet (anti-Fuhrer), quite at variance with Benjamin's heroic *Angel.*[4] Perhaps the separation was intentional?[5]

In this case, Benjamin's imaginative description seems to refer more to the words in his friend's verse. Adorno, complicates the story, and presents another, markedly different description of the Angel. These ambiguities and subsequent myth constructions only created a more complex and misleading set of misappropriations, as the narrative continued.[6]

Subsequently, relating to religion and psychoanalysis, Julia Kristeva and others picked up on what remained a fascinating literary trope, referred to by Jay Winter in his work on mourning. The icon transformed, symbolized a relation to trauma and truth.[7] Since 1940, the 'angel' has appeared in many guises:[8] in Anselm Kiefer's art and Carolyn Forché's narrative poetry of witness (*The Angel of History*[9]). For W. G. Sebald it carried connotations quite independent of Benjamin or Adorno, but closer to Klee's image, it was an impression of an ephemeral cinema of contemporary experience, stopped on its ever whirring reel: freeze-framed by mnemonic engagement, at a site of experience, or by a traumatic interruption – 'past and present' – flash back, and forward, behind Klee's paralysed figure.

Initially *Angelus Novus* (1920)[10] was, for two decades, virtually unknown. But it was in the anti-prophetic mood of the 1940s that Klee's ambiguous cartoon figure first gained notoriety. By the 1980s its intellectual status was even further enlarged. This sequence of events illustrates tensions between a postnational transformative vision of 'Modern Memory work' and the philosophical, post-Frankfurt and postmodernist's dismissal of it.[11]

I have elaborated on this story at length because it is more than merely a part of an intellectual 'coming to terms with the past' or Germany's own *Vergangenheitsbewaltigung*; rather, it illustrates a problematic and common issue in memory work of distortion, not only in the German post-history tradition of Benjamin, but also of Adorno and even W. G. Sebald (but not of Arendt). It is symptomatic of issues of an over-romanticized, even pretentious version of memory work generally – devising remembrance as dream-telling, wish fulfilment and as delusion. That is where Weber's sociology, Bloch's history, or that of the Annales, or Arendt's politically grounded writing are a salutary and necessary counterweight because they show how 'memory work' sits on the cusp or interstices of 'civilization' and 'barbarism', but it is not necessarily trapped. In that sense the concept, like the *Angelus*, can be only an appropriate metaphor for the flux of the moment: that a present is in the process of becoming past, yet may be frozen in memory, or alternatively, it can become a part of a creative archive for transformative politics.

An Exhibition in 2018 (Tate Britain in London) on the '*Aftermath*' art of post-war, included a far more appropriate and evocative memory 'angel'. It is a floating memorial figure: a bronze sculpture by Ernst Barlach; it was hung from the roof of Güstrow Cathedral in 1927.[12] It was taken down and destroyed by the Nazis in 1937. The Angels' face is that of Barlach's friend Käthe Kollwitz. Miraculously this angel was resurrected. Barlach had kept the cast hidden, and a new copy of the figure was created in Güstrow after 1945. Suspended in space, but not entirely without hope for the future, the "*Schwebende*" symbolizes a more optimistic flight.

Weber, Bloch and Hobsbawm

The innovations in human expression, especially in language, illustrating the thesis of a modern memory, respond to a dramatically changing world; one which contained what the political sociologist Max Weber called 'a loss of magic', in a bureaucratic and technological universe.[13] This cultural 'disenchantment' was expressed in often darkly pessimistic writing and painting in the *fin de siècle* of the 1890s, and the immediate pre-war period. It was filled with apocalyptic prophecy, reacting to the evolution of modernity and rationalization. From the 1890s to the 1930s such apocalyptic preoccupations accompany not only a recurrent scepticism about progress in the West, but also the role and character of 'history' itself. As Bloch explained in his classic account of the culture of the Middle Ages, *Feudal Society*;[14] social existence could become dominated by such an apocalyptic consciousness. Reinforced by myth, epic and legend, a pervasive 'folk memory' had focused imagination on the past. There was no point in looking forward to Armageddon; the Day of Judgment blocked off any future beyond. The now, the present, had little relevance without referring back to these myths and 'histories'.

After 1945 such obsessive pre-occupations accompanied the aftermath of the Manhattan project, and nuclear testing. Creators and critics repeatedly react to comparable problems. In the 1940s Adorno, Arendt, Benjamin – even Camus – comment on a collective amnesia induced by the traumas of 1945; not only the destruction in the camps, but also of whole cities. Later Klee's or Benjamin's 'Angel' appears as the same lodestar as referenced by Sebald or in Anselm Kiefer's paintings. Both the future, shaken by war and genocide, and the past, except in invoking 'tradition' – no longer had discernible pattern or meaning – other than that which we imposed on it. Life's sequence was broken; we were, like Kurt Vonnegut's post-war Billy Pilgrim, lost in the flashbacks of time:

> Billy Pilgrim has come unstuck in time.
>
> Billy has gone to sleep a senile widower and awakened on his wedding day. He has walked through a door in 1955 and came out another one in 1941. He has gone back through that door to find himself in 1963. He has seen his birth and death many times, he says, and pays random visits to all the events in between.[15]

In representing memory, cinema is the ideal medium for the use of 'flashback' images of the past re-represented. Novels also successfully use the device – Vonnegut in *Slaughterhouse 5*, through Billy Pilgrim, returns to his own wartime traumas. Lost in time, memory is fragmented and distorted: flashing forward and flashing back. But the cinematic image provides the most powerful memorable uses: setting up a dialogue between past and present – and even – prophetically, future. Subsequently echoed in millennial dystopias, or a post-nuclear scenarios in film, these images were symptomatic of continuing and terminally numbed moods of despair, and potentially soothed only by doses of forgetting. Suspended between 'history' and oblivion, the very act of remembering both paralyses action and represses imagination; it challenges memory itself. As Vonnegut remarks in *Slaughterhouse 5*:

> I think of how useless the Dresden part of my memory has been …
>
> People aren't supposed to look back. I'm certainly not going to do it anymore.
>
> I've finished my war book now.[16]

This perplexing set of paradoxes is summarized in the term 'modern memory'. Peter Fritsche speaks of our being 'stranded in the present', by a nostalgia for the past. But after 1945 perhaps 'trapped' in the present by an unmoveable past might be more apt. Yet if memory and memory workers are stuck at the crossroads of past and future, then for collective memory to have any chance of empowering the anti-forgetter, it has to seek and find empathic understanding.

Powerful as it was, Max Weber did not assume that this process of 'rationalization' was an irreversible one.[17] Indeed, traditionalism and the vast power of radical revivalist Islam has long been confronting US exceptionalism, which has its own modes of anti-rational fundamentalism. Such revivals of the past may also question Chinese, Russian and other 'national' hegemonies. These suggest that any assumption of 'directionality' in analysing memory's past and future evolution would be foolhardy. In a postnational world, the present nation state 'system', itself a problematic and artificial arrangement, may be in many or most respects, obsolescent, but it has continuing political effects and for the time being, these continue, and are powerful enough to pre-empt alternatives.

Such current crises of global culture coincide with the arrival of worldwide electronic communicators intruding our individual lives. Hobsbawm the critical historian fears even the loss of a historical past trampled in an ever rushing 'now'. By implication he fears that it also signifies the loss of prospects of a more enlightened future. A new 'historyless' generation has, like Vonnegut's metaphorical Pilgrim, 'lost its way in time': it has lost history, or at least stands at the interstices of memory and history, experience and life, without clear direction. For historians such compression of time was an uncrossed border: as Andreas Huyssen argues, these changes – living in and for the moment – began to demote or threaten everything but the latest experience, fad or novelty – whatever could be purveyed.

For Hobsbawm, as Marxian, by 1992 this implied that even a 'historical imagination' (or even memory) was 'dead'. The decline of historical continuity, or the sense of it, that he bemoans, not only undermines traditional remembering and achieves a loss of 'history', but also leaves as its legacy a truncated experience for people growing up in the new millennium.[18]

> The destruction of the past, or rather the social mechanisms that link one's contemporary experience to that of earlier generations, is one of the most characteristic and eerie phenomena of the late twentieth century. Most young men and women at the century's end grow up in a sort of permanent present lacking any organic relation to the public past of the times they live in.[19]

In the preface to his survey of 1914–89 (the 'short twentieth century'), he gives examples of the historical referents that were important in his own left-wing life and travels; he points out for example in Paris, how memorable these markers, such as significant street names or metro stations were.[20] Notably, however, many reference national battles, treaties or events. But crucially, such signs have now 'lost all relevance' in a generation fixed on the ever-rushing overwhelming present. These repress memory and, in Huyssen's words, leave experience "tumbling rapidly into an irreversible past".[21] For many, in what seems to have been a historical period of public memorizing of national events, that past is in danger of being irretrievably lost. For others, the memorializing process continues at the same time, but in new forms.[22]

Hobsbawm, writing in 1992, observed a specific decline in the 'archival' community. But was he correct in asserting that the 'historical imagination was therefore dead'? Much has undermined traditional remembrance and history, and leaves an altered experience of the past, but he misses the degree to which *memory* now occupies the void – attaching itself particularly to new generations, as a replacement. Denying the 'telos' that history still represented to Adorno in 1953, the process threatened a crisis not only for Marxism, but also for liberalism and social reform: memory work is dramatically questions any evolutionary present. Grossly intensified by the excess of 1914–45, this critical reaction and the juxtaposing of memory and prophecy, which had started fifty years earlier in *fin de siècle* Europe, was now a conversation about social death.

The discourse about 'progress' in history, grand narratives of social evolution, had been challenged long before. In the Europe of the 1890s, especially among the key precursors of a modern memory, little connection was made between history and the future. The questions raised in the crisis of memory in the 1940s, included not only Theodor Adorno's questioning 'of a future for poetry', but also whether, after Auschwitz, one kind of history might now be dead or dying. What Hobsbawm is bewailing is the loss of that one kind of historical memory: it is a nineteenth-century public, essentially nationalist, or militarist, memory. He does not acknowledge the invention of new, less historically specific versions; expressed not in street or metro names, recalling national triumphs, but of sites of mourning, in counter-monuments, texts and images: markers of an alternative remembering, created to oppose the hegemony of inherited narratives.

In other words, paradoxically a new age of radical remembering co-exists with an age of radical forgetting, and a conscious erasure of forms of the past – to allow re-framing the present. This form of collective memory, endorsing counter-values, uses a borderless 'past in the present' to shape a postnational future. In so far as memory becomes part of the global 'now' in its representation, its role is in creating imaginable, more cosmopolitan alternatives. Modern memory work, the formal task of re-presenting those pasts in daily life, also enables a recognition of even proxy or prosthetic remembering as a *present* experience.

However selective, unreliable, and manipulated – selectively amnesiac – our constructions of the past are, they provide a basis for envisioning futures – however uncertain. They are part of what Hobsbawm himself had called an 'invention of tradition', a tradition of *remembering*. This provides an alternative continuity to that presented by 'history': a counter-memory of unfulfilled projects or utopias, including postnational ones.

At the end of the twentieth century, the task of modern memory became in part, to re-discover its roots in the creative work of an earlier period. Whether or not it represents an evolution, a 'history of memory' is possible. But, unlike history, 'modern memory' represents a process of ever changing, critical cultural construction and reconstruction. From 'truth-telling' linked to critical reactions to the phenomenon of mass industrialized killing, it stretches out to include our dreams of events unfulfilled in the present, and to uncertain visions of the future.

As I have argued, twentieth-century war – its art and its literature, the European Holocaust, and the Atomic Age after 1945 – dominated this memory. Its evolution in modern Japan and North America represented an important counterweight to a purely European memory. This reaction resonated in the 1950s and

1960s in many other modern industrial societies, but especially amongst victims; those groups which had suffered the impact of war and colonial rule, and in which the fear of a war using nuclear weapons now spread worldwide. These renewals and innovations in memory were echoed in post-colonial or post-imperial remembering.[23] Such changes reflect some of the same forces that brought modern memory into being after 1918: an era of renewed crisis, not only in the European Community of nations, with the resurgence of populist nationalism since 1989, even in the USA, but also the renewed threat of a global conflict involving new now nuclear armed states in Asia and the Middle East.

Joe's war: the demography of the memory boom

Those societies initially revealing most interest in social memory, and active in memory creation, have been those such as Britain, France, Germany, the Netherlands, Belgium and Japan, with predominantly ageing populations, and marked by recent histories of intense conflict and violence. The transformation of collective memory not only reflects that demographic and generational social change, but also the cultural shifts which accompanied them: it reveals postnational orientations in youth culture, as globalization influences so much in popular music, electronic discourse, and social media.

Whilst such demographic factors after the 'baby boom' have to be seen as a major contribution to this broadening of public interest in historical memory, there is also a multi-cultural fusion of genres – or 'cross over' between various kinds of cultural memory construction. These were quite dissimilar from, and in tension with previous production of 'public history'. Much of it adopted a more detached critical stance to inherited frameworks both of understanding the world and, the ways we structure our feelings about the past. By the 1990s, memory activity, as I have described it – visits to sites and memorials and anniversary events, new kinds of museumalization – increasingly became part of the global 'curriculum' and impacted on a third, even fourth, generation of modern memory beyond 1914.

Contemporary public life responds increasingly to a cultural imperative, a need to recapture lost pasts. Global memory travel proliferates, whether real or virtual, to sites of mourning and trauma: to new museums or new sites of resistance. Generations of students and young people, helped by online searches, began pursuing such 'memory' projects as family trees: connecting with such related pasts to enhance personal 'memory' and revisiting a once experienced event involved increasing numbers of those (especially grandparents) whose reflections on horror at such sites are an anchor for their own experience, in a series of bewildering yet ultimately linked episodes of total violence.

To re-instate Hiroshima, or Nagasaki, in the mind or consciousness, for example, or lesser known special places of visitation such as Langemark, the Chemin des Dames, Plötzensee, or Brzinka, is to make them territories in our imagination. We, together with witnesses to the events, fulfil a 'prosthetic' need to return there. These attract generations of veterans and survivors, not least from diasporas, especially in the Western world, but also from Japan, Russia and even China. They live longer, and can respond to the opportunity to visit memory sites. Though no less controversial, memorials have become better presented and preserved, and new ones are constantly created. For over sixty years of such change, memory 'traditions' have been transformed or re-invented. They reflect an older generation constituting itself as a more self-conscious cohort; encouraging others to remember, write, speak and 'bear witness'. Such are the groups that often return or are 'returned' (taken by family) to the sites, with a revised memory of the camps and the killing fields; and 'new' facts recalled.

One individual tale of recall of such transgenerational memories from the 1940s was only finally re-told in 2005. These were a long delayed Polish father's accounts of a journey from 1939 to 1940. In them he tells his daughter of his terrifying escape across a divided, occupied, terrorized Europe East to West. It took more than a decade to record the journey, which was reproduced as a vivid biography/ autobiography, *Joe's War.* Joe's journeys are retraced by his daughter, the author, Annette Kobak, across the reconfigured terrain of Central and Eastern Europe.

This story, a model of its kind, illustrates how an itinerant transborder memory can be retraced – not as memory tourism or indulging in the memory industry, but as biography and autobiography – linking past to present,[24] generation to generation, time to place – a process replicated in so much of modern memory work. Frequently survivors, victims of trauma, veterans who visit sites personally or with relatives, or are invited as witnesses – or finally rehearse oral testimony in media; however varyingly accurate that recall proves, do so as anti-deniers, as family mourners or commemorators, and many have postponed breaking their silence for decades. [25]

Such stories, and wisdoms transmitted to these next generations are an essential alternative to the cyberspace. They encourage a third, or even fourth (the great-grandchildren) generation to visit, across almost a century of experience.[26] As Marc Bloch emphasized, multiplication of grandparents was a very traditional, inter-generational, source of such memory-bearing; and oral 'traditions' are not entirely dead. Whilst memories of the Great War remained recurrently 'generational', in the 1930s, 1940s, 1950s and 1960s, and even beyond the death of the last veteran, they also became cultural facts, 'a past in the present'. As the last survivors from 1918 died, and those from 1945 grew fewer, the continuation of contemporary memory work owed much to a corpus of 'memory' passed on by individuals helped by an increasing, collective, human longevity. Pilgrimages to sites of evil provide cross-border opportunities for cathartic and redemptive understanding; for mutual survivors themselves; and empathy for those in ongoing crises – as in the terrible aftermath of war in Korea – still seriously neglected, because of six decades of division and repression.

Critical journalism as memory work: historicizing the moment

This book has tried to correct the unacknowledged relevance in much writing on the role of journalism to *memory work.* This lack of acknowledgement extends even to journalists themselves. But the exceptions, the self-conscious journalistic memory-makers and memory preservers, their reporting and analysis are key to postnational memory.

International journalists and photographers have long played this active, creative role: moments captured when Martha Gellhorn wrote about her experience in Spain, or much later, when Timothy Garton-Ash described his participatory witnessing in Central/Eastern Europe, and Misha Glenny wrote his own 'Histories of the Present', in former Yugoslavia.

The critical role of the journalist – historian as global witness is ever more important, and is in the tradition of Hemingway and Orwell. Supported by photojournalists such as Khaldei or Del Tredici, eye-witness writing in war captures this new perception of a compressed time, crucial to re-memorizing history as a *present* and remembering it as an act of witness. A recorded moment moulded by place, by observation, conversation, and presence: it states 'I was there', in ways other history can rarely do. In the staccato descriptions of Joan Didion's *Salvador,* or Michael Herr's *Dispatches* (from Vietnam), it is the anecdote, the demythologizing of a story or of an event, or a photojournalist's iconic picture, which enshrines a historically critical moment in memory. Whilst historians have always selected facts to construct history, these culture makers also select perceptions, re-presentations, images, perceived facts and representations by witnesses to help construct or reconstruct public and private narratives, such as the stories of refugees and returnees from conflicts. But the dilemmas and limitations of such external investigative journalists, writers and historians are clear: the dangers of war reporting are well known – there are threats far more serious than censorship. Nevertheless, these front-line memory workers are better seekers and guardians of concealed truths and awkward facts than many historians.

So many inconvenient and unreported memories have been secured, not by historians; but survivors and victims. Sometimes archival records can be resurrected, and forgotten events remembered; but what we often rely on, is the testimony of an individual alone. In representing truth in modern remembering, Orwell argued that newspapers had little to do with recalling real events. His remarks on 'Newspeak' and the rewriting of history, in *1984* and in essays, were drawn directly from his experiences in the Spanish Civil War. Against this, it has been claimed that the "The newsroom provides the missing link between the future and representation of the past". In Todd Gitlin's phrase from 1968, "The whole world is watching": memory of an event becomes linked to manipulation of images: memory is staged for access, at primetime TV viewing. 'Mass media' is often seen as key to the larger problem of an indiscriminate surfeit of proxy experience, and often is. As Ash comments, loss of memory flattens journalism – it strips away 'identity'.

Such journalists, who endeavour to reveal the significance of a remembered present, provide an antidote to the fears of Hobsbawm and alleviate the sense that an overwhelming constant 'present' is erasing both memory and history. Orwell, Hemingway, Gellhorn, Ash, and others in that tradition were present to confront the distortions of the myth-makers, with which of course we collaborate.[27] The corpus extends and expands the work of journalists in conflict – reporting globally both of war and of social change; Gandhi's non-violent campaigns would have been far less influential in the West without the correspondents who accompanied him.

In the last decades of the twentieth century and during the end of the Cold War, using witness stories and oral testimony, the fusion of such memory work and 'histories of the present' became clear. It was illustrated during 1990s Yugoslav conflict, and the 'Velvet Revolution' of 1989; it made memory work more accessible globally.[28] This represents the ways in which an increasingly critical transnational journalism can provide the bridge between 'memory' and 'history'.

A sense of the growing importance of movements beyond borders marks Garton-Ash's work on 1989, and shows an ability to cover an experienced memory of historical cross-frontier transitions. This postnational approach is notably transparent in his personal reports of the 'Magic Lantern', the theatre in Prague where independents both debated and then planned and acted change. This site and other sites in Central Eastern Europe during the autumn of 1989 were critical to our understanding of what was happening in Warsaw, Berlin, Budapest and later Bosnia; and then later Garton-Ash's signal role in uncovering of the record of the Stasi, in East Germany.[29] Each reported episode brought a wider political and human engagement in the dramatic changes in civil society. Whilst hope for powerful truth-telling, narratives of people power revolutions and of the Yugoslav wars were short lived, the memory of 1989 was preserved. More recently, the Arab Spring and events that followed in Middle East and North Africa brought new challenges to journalism beyond frontiers, where the courage, tenacity and death of reporters has become part of the story of memory itself.

Martha Gellhorn argued in her critique of war in 1988 that "Memory and imagination, not nuclear weapons are the great deterrent".[30] It is a rare 'war' correspondent who is so fundamentally opposed to war – the very institution that they report on, live off, but aspire to understand – that they radically reject it. It reminds us of the creative potential role of anti-militarist journalism, despite its imbrication into the structures of power. This tradition of memory – recording can in part be seen as deriving from the terse immediacy of the language that marked some of the 1914–18 poets and writers discussed earlier in this book. Such journalism can also be defined in terms of a new media voice after the 1960s, one which involves defying both commercial pressures and academic carping. Gelhorn understood that 'memory' and 'imagination' constituted a coherent cultural presence with a global impact. Like Hemingway, and Orwell and more recent practitioners, she sought an ethical, compassionate and political way of truth-telling about war, and preserving it through writing.

Postnational memory draws on the pared-down prose about war produced by writers who were also journalists, using ironic pieces, writing on the borders of reportage and creative writing. Theirs is the work of writers consciously contributing to civic memory, about war and social struggle for change. When Orwell writes about Spanish comrades in his essays, poems, or the book *Homage to Catalonia*, he, like Hemingway, has his own place in the demythologizing of war, the deconstruction of the warrior and the demilitarizing of our imagination.

Vignette:

Yevgeny Khaldei – the malleability of memory and the Reichstag photo, 1945

Some of the most memorable photographs of symbolic moments, such as the iconic flag raising after the battle for Iwo Jima (1945) were re-staged for national public relations; earlier (authentic) flag raising photos in combat were either censored or suppressed. In this notable case, Yevgeny Khaldei's reconstituted and demythologized photograph of Berlin and the 'Flag over the Reichstag' (May 1945) is a much more complex story. Unlike the Iwo Jima photos, the original picture was taken under fire, not later. Stalin's extraordinary, key front-line photographer Khaldei shot the first few pictures in a severe combat situation. However, the full and ironic story of its 'doctoring' confirms the ambiguity of what makes such 'mnemonic images' even more memorable.

At the end of World War Two in Europe, during the Fall of Berlin (1945), there were several photographs by different photographers of the Soviet *Red flag* being raised over the roof of the German Reichstag. But Khaldei's was the first taken, and it revealed (before *Tass* censored it) that Soviet looting was occurring right at the time of a great patriotic moment. The first photographs documented, and thereby seem to confirm, another truer memory through the negative and the photo; it was a photojournalist's story,[31] but a dangerously problematic one. To potentially confuse matters, several other, much poorer photos by other cameramen were staged – but later – and promoted after the fighting subsided. Superficially, they look fairly similar to Khaldei's original, except for the normal traffic in the streets, no smoke from explosions, no tanks left in the photographs.

Khaldei had clambered up the crumbling and slippery blood-soaked steps of the shattered parliament building, to the roof, during the battle whilst fire fights continued below. It is true that he had with him in Berlin a pre-prepared red flag with hammer and sickle sewn on – made from a red table cloth, specifically for the occasion. This, after all, was Stalin's big moment! The moment that symbolized victory in the Great Patriotic War; they had won the race to Berlin, but at a vast cost in Russian lives.

Once in position, an officer assisted a soldier to hoist the flag up for Khaldei's photo (Image 14.2). The story circulated at the time that when the negatives were printed, a string of looted watches on the officer's wrist and arm were in the foreground. But which arm and wrist? Later Khaldei was ordered to 'airbrush' out the offending watches and the image was sent out to the world. But word got out.

IMAGE 14.2 Yevgeny Khaldei, Raising a flag over the Reichstag in Berlin, May 1945. Courtesy Picker Art Gallery, Colgate University. ©Getty Images, Photo: Richard Walker.

In his book, *The Wages of Guilt*, Ian Buruma, the Dutch historian, recounts hearing the very same story in the 1980s about this. By then, Khaldei's had become the most famous image of the flag being displayed on the roof of the devastated Parliament Building. In an interview with an anonymous East German, who had been in conquered Berlin, whom he does not identify, he heard:

> [T]hat one of the soldiers in the photograph was wearing looted watches on his arm like a stack of bracelets ... I looked at the picture again and could not see any watches. Forty years of Soviet rule must have played tricks with his memory.[32]

Ten years after Buruma's book was published, in 1995, I met the amazing veteran. Khaldei as a twenty-nine-year-old Jewish Russian had travelled with the Red Army in combat: from Moscow to Murmansk, to the Crimea and the advance into Germany. He also documented Jewish liberation in Budapest and the occupation of Vienna. I heard first hand his dramatic account of his involvement in events around the Reichstag. When I heard that story told personally, it was vividly relayed by Khaldei, through his personal interpreter. Heavy fighting was still underway when they reached the area between the

Soviet troops and tanks, and the remnants of the German defence guarding Hitler's bunker and key strong points near the Brandenburg Gate.

He confirmed that he had retained a copy of an original print of the notorious picture and several negatives in his personal archive. He told us that the story of the multiple watches was absolutely true. Watches were indeed on the arm or arms of the officer, the figure who is supporting the soldier putting up the heavy flag on a crumbling pedestal. The officer is looking away (Khaldei smiled). The ascent had been treacherous, the staircase shattered and the banner awkward. The position was still precarious. Fighting continued in the building, they were the first Soviet soldiers there. But he captured the genuine moment. The photographer signed a copy of the photograph for me which I still have, and is reproduced here.

Later, meeting the photographer, I began studying the several widely published versions of the Khaldei Photo. Like Ian Buruma, I could not see multiple watches anywhere. There were (as Buruma said) either none, or in one case only one. That one was all clearly still visible (but on the wrong wrist!). Khaldei said he had scratched them all out with a pin on orders from TASS, Stalin's news agency. Yet despite this detail, I could still clearly remember seeing an image of the right arm with multiple watches. Were there other versions that he retained from his negatives, before retouching? I began to doubt the story myself, and even Khaldei's exact telling of it – though official censorship of the picture was extremely plausible even for purely patriotic reasons – 'good Soviet soldiers'[33] would never loot. There were also good reasons for Khaldei to self-censor, before, and subsequently. The more watches on either arm the more de-mythologizing both of the Fall of Berlin and the 'Great Patriotic War'. Even after Stalin's death, that was still a very sensitive topic.

Given the record of widespread looting elsewhere, it is likely that extensive individual looting did take place in Berlin. To cover that up in the heat of battle would then be very conscious self-censorship. Probably, for that anonymous officer, it was not a priority. A year after my meeting with Khaldei, the modified versions of the photo and the story re-appeared in two places. One was both in the photo book of Khaldei's work, *Witness to History*,[34] and the other a TV documentary featuring a new interview with the photographer, entitled *Yevgeny Khaldei: A Photographer under Stalin*, 1997. It was on the officer's left wrist that there was (only) one watch.[35] No string of watches appeared on the right wrist which was the image Khaldei claims he deleted (with a pin) for the official version, to avoid speculation of looting. Several published versions are murky on both arms and wrists: there is residual indistinctness on the left arm validating my clearly remembered imaged that was of the bracelet of watches on the left wrist and arm. The single watch on the right in one 'official' photo remains. So do the details of

Khaldei's original verbal account and the story, which also chimes with Buruma's original heard story.

It appears now the multiple watch story is at least three-quarters truth. but I do wonder if the original picture or negative still exists somewhere – to prove a point. What a memory researcher's dream it would be to find it!

As my discussion of Sebald's use of images also suggests, the photograph was never a reliable source for constituted memory. Sebald emphasizes the ambiguity and ephemeral character of the photograph in memory. The malleability of Khaldei's famous photo reinforces its historicality, but with several mnemonic twists. The photo, which seemed to contradictorily both support selective amnesia, conspiracy theory, and official 'nationalist' manipulation, captures the contradictions. Yet it also indicates witness and truth-telling. At least Khaldei *was* there: in Berlin at the symbolic moment; and in combat – admittedly with a prepared, if home-made, flag. But despite other Soviet re-staged versions, this was not a staged re-run of the event after the fighting had stopped: it was his original authentic photographs (in several versions). That became, and has remained, the historical image: the iconic, if slightly doctored one.

When we talk of photo myths, we can compare the Reichstag story with the controversial re-staging of the picture of the flag at Iwo Jima. This, a cynical official re-enactment of the real moment, which the original photographer photographed in combat, but with a smaller flag, having arrested the ever rushing pressure of events, he and the original soldiers who captured the hill were all passed over, even humiliated, and their authentic memory was ignored. Such is the state arrangement of national constituted memory, the original image rearranged with a larger flag, and despite protests, Rosenthal, who photographed the fake version, was awarded the Pulitzer Prize. In the same sense, photographers and photojournalists such as Khaldei were typical witnesses to the same authentic 'memorable truth'. Ironically their stories show both how truth even in photographs can be the first casualty of war and how memory through ethical journalism can re-adjust faked evidence to reconstruct a repressed truth.

Shooting the instant present: memory, conflict, and the past as image

In the context of postnational representation, such wordless images have a special power. The potency of depicting the past without any spoken or written language is that it gives us, if not universality, at least immediate global accessibility. Heterogeneous examples exist – such as Paul Nash's pictorial art; film stills, archive photographs, hand-drawn sketches – and now immediate electronic relay of worldwide happenings, events and places. All constitute new 'sites of memory'. Like music, they universalize but need not homogenize. However, the electronic media problem is also that of overload: a plethora of imagery converges without selectivity, criteria, explanation or historical context. The benign and pathological potentialities of this are obvious.

In an age of 'viral images' and electronic social media, the film-still, cartoon, or the photograph can still interact with a multitude of new online witnesses. Visual images entering in our social engagement and transmissions as online news inevitably become an active ingredient in our memory-making. Often these visual representations relate to places and events. Used in this book are such memorable images: Khaldei's historic photograph of that Berlin moment, Watkins and Del Tredici's more expansive images of a global atomic landscape, and Gerard Rondeau's intimate photographs of the otherwise lost local memory work of Yves Gibeau. In understanding modern memory, these become part of a global archive of the past in the present. In conceptualizing a changing time–space relationship, image-making is a central ongoing process of construction transcending linguistic divisions. A plethora of mnemonic images can be broadcast extra-territorially or in cyberspace as an aide memoire, or as documentation, as national propaganda or anti-militarist testament.[36]

The postnational 'archive' comprises worldwide sources, photographs from dozens of war actions and atrocities, and also peacemaking projets: focusing on moments in time in one hundred years of conflicts. We can compare the temporal spatial dimensions of them, some reframed in this book. For example, Japanese photographers would revisit Hiroshima shortly after Pikadon – days, months, years and then decades after the event, to represent the site – and often produce books of images, as the place transformed. Similarly visceral images of war, oppression and genocide and their aftermath, the ruins, the skeletons, are presented to us in random historical order of the events themselves. But they are timed from the instant after a violent event, through a century of 'distance'. Ordered by length of lapsed time from the event, one is a second after the shock of an explosion in Afghanistan – and another taken at a site near Ypres, ninety-nine years after an event, the executions of supposed "deserters".

I have described in previous chapters, the memory work of photographers visiting sites of mourning and trauma to uncover meaning – hidden truths. In Flanders, for example, French, British and Belgian soldiers who were accused of cowardice, desertion or disobedience were *Shot at Dawn* (the title of the work). In 1914 in one small area alone, there were thirty British executions (there were hundreds elsewhere). The first victim was Private Highgate, a seventeen-year-old British soldier. Chloe Dewe Matthews returned to the same site of executions, at more or less the exact time of day. She then fired the 'shots' securing that revisited moment (November 2013).

Memory installations that involve the passage of time and the reciprocities of sites of memory point towards creative usage of sounds and images together. Railways, as I have stressed, are apt symbols of the twentieth century, and in 'Distant Trains' by Bill Fontana they appear in a 1984 art installation in a then still ruined Anhalter Bahnof: a railway station that had sat at the hub of Berlin city life before the 1940s bombing. A 'past in the present' was linked to another site by an installation and the sounds of today's Cologne railway station (rebuilt since 1945) was relayed across the eerie empty space between what was East and West Berlin. Broadcast are noises of a peopled present with trains, communicated to a de-populated past in a present; in a silent space without people, trains or activity.[37]

There is both continuity and discontinuity between such urban wastelands of 1940–45 and the sites both of the genocides and of the Great War. The full extent of similar urbicides in Tokyo, Hamburg, Frankfurt and Warsaw could not be grasped without photograph or film shot at the time; imagining the landscapes of mass bombing, otherwise without visual records of the remnants, the charred waste, the 'deadman's dump', the piles of shoes, the charnel houses, is impossible. Paintings such as Nash and Dix of Flanders, supplement our visual testimony after 1914–18, but the recorded visual image becomes an indispensable prop to imagination; these reside as a permanent part of modern collective memory, because mere visitation of most contemporary sites is either inadequate, or often impossible.

However, a postnational memory reconstruction of a past without frontiers contains a major contradiction. Such construction 'beyond borders' is created, and still largely framed in 'national' media spaces, and within language boundaries. Imagining a future beyond the nation state requires a reconceptualizing of the time and space in which the historical process occurs. This transition too needs representation.

'Border crossing' discourses about memory require active demobilizing of those histories that are essentially mythical constructions for chauvinist purposes. Therefore gender, as a postnational category, is crucial, as are other affinities that are borderless; cultural identity links that are not summarized by 'nation' are essential as enabling such sensibilities, and de-territorialising them.

History or memory? What to remember, what to forget

The problem of social memory in the modern world is not the fact that we have a surfeit of memory, nor of forgetting, amnesia and denial. We resort to memory not least because of the inadequacies and limitations of history as a method of dealing with the recent past. Yet the problem with both history and memory lies in the process of selection. The framing and controlling of the past has limited our ability to learn about social evolution. It is not that history repeats itself, or that we fail to learn from it, but that a lack of the sociological imagination prevents critical cultural remembering. If we do not have too much memory, nor forget too much, the selection process itself becomes the issue and that addresses the development of political and cultural structures.

Wiping the slate clean, creating an intentional amnesia about twentieth-century war and atrocity would not solve the problem. Because of the inadequacies of a manipulated remembering culture or co-optation of our rituals of commemoration by the state, reframing memory represents the alternative. As Vonnegut pleads: "People shouldn't have to look back". A modern memory offers some paths to re-possessing shared memory outside traditional or national frames. Like history, much twentieth-century memory was controlled by purely national narratives and served the needs of states in an interstate system. But personal stories, community narratives and cross-border recollections afford a stark alternative, and an alternative outlook notably sustained by the creative arts since 1915.

Increasingly reflexive and self-conscious, making an interdependent and alternative public memory is a creature of later modernity, but the sense that to some degree memory is replacing history, far from reinforces Fukuyama's thesis of an 'end of history'. The project of actively constructing counter-memory is a dynamic, engaged and critical process. It reshapes lives and cultural settings, despite the contested voices, despite a welter of words and images spread by the modern technologies of global communication. Memory work still relies on human selection: the key anniversary, poem, painting, photograph, classic film, novel, not least the authentic memoir.

History's claims were always inflated and partial – memory's claim beyond caveats, and qualifications, was too often limited to an alternative framing of social feeling. Social or cultural memory is by definition collective. Insofar as it deals with experience of public events and their commemoration it is also 'historical'. But specific to it is the siting and timing of personal memories in civic frameworks, events or representations.

History prevailed over 'memory' in the later nineteenth century, and then especially in the scientistic atmosphere of the early twentieth century. Like some other social 'sciences', history was seen as authoritative. In contrast, memory was deemed to be about privately experienced events, and individual perspectives (and opinions): unauthorized memories were narrated based on indistinct recollections and unreliable witnesses, whereas history was public, civic, legitimated, evidential and, not least, part of an authenticated national narrative. Even when dissected, it too was found to be secondary, inauthentic and strongly influenced by its patronage, its funding and its framed sources – it was the predominantly accepted version of the past. Any power of social memory was counter-hegemonic – and in that sense subversive: 'history may state that', but 'I was there and I saw this'. Radical counter-remembering after 1914 was the incipient force that broke the unchallenged dominance of any official history (and official silences) forever. That was the first great achievement of modern memory and owes much to individual reactive genius. A breakthrough for popular truth-*seeking*, it created a non-bounded space for global truth-speaking, not only about war and atrocity, but also about postnational potentials and a species fellowship, a recognition across boundaries.

Notes

1 This reference appeared in 'Theses on the Philosophy of History' in the collection *Illuminations,* with an Introduction by Hannah Arendt (London, 1999), p. 245.

2 Benjamin (1999).

3 Benjamin (1999); see also Martin Jay, 'Against Consolational: Walter Benjamin and the Refusal to Mourn', in Jay Winter, and Emmanuel Sivan, *War and Remembrance in the Twentieth Century* (Cambridge, UK and New York, 2000), pp. 221–39.

4 The Angel's relationship with the past, if any, is unclear, and Klee's technical innovative skill and modernist playfulness adds to the puzzle. There is no 'debris' depicted in the sketch. That was Benjamin's impression of Klee's experimental graphics, and his ignorance of Klee's techniques was perhaps the cause of his misinterpretation of a remembered image. If the debris is derived from Klee's technical experiments in art, then the whole process provides a telling comment on the memories: 'the Angel' was a purely fictional creation.

5 T. W. Adorno, quote on Angelus (Hitler), see notes 1 and 2, p. 271 in Jay Winter, *Sites of Memory, Sites of Mourning* (Cambridge, 1995). The cartoon which Adorno links somewhat uncritically to a cartoon of Bismarck is ambiguous and it seems intended to be sardonic: Klee's hints that his new *Angelus* was in fact intended to be a manic depiction of Adolf Hitler as the new saviour.

6 After Benjamin's (who had acquired it in 1921) suicide in 1940, Klee's picture passed on to Adorno (in 1945). Through Adorno, *Angelus* transferred in 1969 to a previous art collector (an earlier colleague and friend of Benjamin, Gershom Scholem). It was eventually (1982) given to the Israel Museum in Jerusalem.

7 Benjamin's text was cited in the 1980s, see Julia Kristeva, *Black Sun. Depression and Melancholia* (orig. pub. 1986), trans. L. S. Roudiez (New York, 1989) on the post-Holocaust crisis.

8 For example, cited by Winter in describing the role of memory in modernist culture, on Kristeva (1995), pp. 225–27.

9 Carolyn Forché, ed., *Against Forgetting: Twentieth-Century Poetry of Witness* (New York, 1993); and *The Angel of History* (New York, 1994).

10 Paul Klee (Image 14.1) discussed in Winter (1995), pp. 223–56; cited by Kristeva (1995). The perverse mythology of Klee's 'Angel' is an interesting, even entertaining image and Benjamin's literary version is extraordinarily powerful – but perhaps that needs its own, more ambitious, painting than Klee's. The mix helped to create, in the end, its own mythology and memory: a metaphysical mishmash of Hegelian dialectics, Jewish mysticism, and then misappropriations from a critical theory to a post-structuralist metaphor. It is a detour that, rather than further memory work, weakens, or mystifies it. Hopefully the '*Angel*' will be given an appropriately counter-monumental final burial.

11 Even if only metaphorically the story illustrates the deep tensions within critical theory from Adorno to Kristeva and beyond – and the tendencies within this tradition to create confusion within the memory project quite independent of metaphors of the Angel. See comments in Andreas Huyssen, *Twilight Memories in an Era of Amnesia* (New York and London, 1995). Adorno's 'possession' of the artwork itself and elision of the Angel picture, both image and the attribution of the idea to Klee's enigmatic cartoon, is distorting.

12 For an image of the war memorial (entitled *Der Schwebende* (The Hovering)), see Cork (1994), p. 293, Plate 391.

13 Max Weber in H. Gerth and C. W. Mills, *From Max Weber* (New York, 1946) – disenchantment and loss of magic is discussed in Edward Shils, *Tradition* (London, 1979). A very useful political summary of Weber's rationalization thesis, Shils raises many ideas about the future present, the present past that are taken up by theorists twenty years later (see Chapter 15).

14 Marc Bloch, *Feudal Societies* (1961), ch. 6, vol.1. Bloch was a key member of the Annales School, which not only paralleled the Frankfurt critics but also had links to Halbwachs.
15 Kurt Vonnegut, *Slaughterhouse Five* (London, 1970).
16 Vonnegut (1970), pp. 2 and 19. It had taken twenty-four years from Vonnegut's Dresden experience, and he vowed not to write about war anymore.
17 Max Weber in Shils (1979).
18 See also Shils (1979), pp. 314–41.
19 Eric Hobsbawm, 'The Century: A Bird's Eye View', in *Age of Extremes* (New York, 1998), pp. 3 and 15.
20 Introduction to Hobsbawm (1995).
21 Introduction to Huyssen (1995). Nora makes similar points in his later articles.
22 In the north of England new airports are named after *John Lennon* or *Robin Hood*, a Beatle and a bandit, both in their way 'primitive rebels'.
23 Of course 'modern memory work', as traced in this book, continues to evolve since 1989, but often in more contentious, contradictory and critical ways. Post-Cold War, various nationalist resurgences threatened again as in the 1930s to subvert the memory project.
24 Annette Kobak, *Joe's War* (London, 2005).
25 As a good example of this genre of a family biography focused on wartime experiences, see H. Miller "Harry and Norah Miller" (self-published, Blurb books, Nottingham, 2018). It is based mainly on letters (1940-1946)
26 In an earlier chapter I used the example in Kobak (2005). Based on these memories, Kobak retraces her father's dangerous untold journey across Europe at the outbreak of World War Two.
27 Also of course, Garton-Ash, Chris Hedges and the less celebrated (outside Eastern Europe) hero of 'objectivity', BBC reporter Misha Glenny (World Service).
28 Todd Gitlin, *The Whole World is Watching* (New York, 1980). Without first-hand accounts, we select – or have selected for us – what to remember, and what to forget. Yet journalism also poses the questions of who does the selecting? Can we as civil society usefully have greater possession of this process? Probably only through direct experience.
29 Misha Glenny's reports during the collapse of Yugoslavia. Misha Glenny, *The Fall of Yugoslavia* (London, 1992) continued previous work in the Balkans.
30 Martha Gelhorn, 'The Face of War', in *Atlantic Monthly* (New York, 1986), p. 6.
31 Buruma had come to doubt the story *because* of the retouched photograph; Ian Buruma, *Wages of Guilt* (New York, 1994), p. 48.
32 Buruma (1994), p. 48.
33 Various accounts of the fall of Berlin confirm the widespread looting and other worse crimes.
34 Yevgeny Khaldei, *Witness to History: The Photographs of Yevgeny Khaldei* (New York, 1995).
35 See Image 14.2 and caption.
36 As a way of representing this genre, *Conflict. Time. Photography* was an exposition of work on visceral time–space comparisons (Tate Modern in London, November, 2014).
37 Bill Fontana, 'Distant Trains' (1984), discussed in Joan Gibbons, *Contemporary Art and Memory: Images of Recollection and Remembrance* (London, 2007).

ACKNOWLEDGEMENTS

This project has been helped by so many: scores of people, in dozens of countries over the several decades that the ideas for this book gestated; of the fifty or so names listed, many deserve lengthy individual acknowledgements and specifics. Instead I have simply listed them in alphabetical order, with immense gratitude.

Joyce Apsel, Peter Balakian, Doug Becker, Melissa Bruemmer, Fred Busch, Piet Chielens, Tom Cloutman, Laurie Cohen, Richard Cork, Terrence des Pres, Martha Dietz, Tracy Downs, Arthur Eyffinger Don Ferencz, Elmer T. Frasch, Martin Gilbert, John Gittings, Welling Hall, Ben Hayes, Jeff Henderson, Curtis Hinsley, Herb Hirsch, Anna Hodgkin/Davin, Dirk Hoffmann, Justin Hoover, Martyn Housden, George Hudson, Richard Johnson, Isobel Johnstone, David Joy Angela Kendall, Yevgeny Khaldei, John Knecht, Annette Kobak, Jan Krebs, Robert Jay Lifton, Mervyn Love, Robin Luckham, Jeff Makala, Scott MacDonald, Iri Maruki, Toshi Maruki, James S. C. Pappas, Wendy Price, Faith Rees-Evans, Lucy Rees-Evans, Nancy Ries, Paul Rogers, Melanie Rohse, Gerard Rondeau, Tim Ryback, Alice Salt, Douglas Schulz, Julie Shouldice, Susanna Siddiqui, Donavon Slaven, Ken Smith, Cheyenne Stewart, Philip Stirups, Alan Taylor, Marek Thee, Terra Tolley, Sanna Tukiainen, Larenda Twigg, Peter van den Dungen, Martin Van Harten, Chloë Vereker, Sebastian Vereker, Zelie Vereker, Alison Walling, Alan Williams, Peter Watkins, Tom Wengraf, Lucy Whetton, Antonia Young, Ursula Young.

My thanks to Earlham College for inviting me to teach a seminar (2015) on themes covered in this book and to the students who took part. The list contains several of my helpers linked to the Peace Studies Department at Bradford University, England and also colleagues and students at Colgate University, New York – whose imaginative Study Abroad tours and Visiting Lecture Series were an important part of enabling my memory work to proceed. These both stimulated and delayed this book!

Groups and individuals who gave free permissions for reproducing images and text include:

The Picker Art Gallery, Colgate University, Yevgeny Khaldei: Reichstag, 1945, Jane Ewart and the Gavin Ewart Estate for the poem 'Imperial War Museum', Paul Williamson for his father H. S. Williamson's 'German Attack on a wet morning 1918' (painting in IWM), the late Gerard Rondeau and Madame Rondeau, for the marvellous photo of Yves Gibeau at Roncy. Liz Gauffberg (Estate of Terrence des Pres) for his 'Landscape, Self, Grid' (excerpt), Alison Culllingford on behalf of the University of Bradford Archive/Library: 'Reconciliation' statue (photograph); the Commonweal Collection Bradford and Ellie Clement; the Bradford Peace Museum and Carol Rank for 'Remembrance' peace banner (Thalia Campbell); In Flanders Fields Museum in Ypres/Ieper and Piet Chielens; for their ideas, five images (listed) - and permissions and other generous support for the project; I am deeply grateful to all the above.

Invaluable financial support came from the Samuel Rubin Foundation, the Planethood Fund, the Biosophical Foundation, the Peace Education Fund and the Guerand Hermes Peace Foundation, as well as Christian CND. This help is gratefully acknowledged.

IMAGE CREDITS

Paul Williamson: 10.5
Maruki Gallery for *The Hiroshima Panels*: cover art, 7.1, 10.4
The Peace Museum Bradford: 10.7
Judy Dean (2016), Flickr: 0.1
Imperial War Museum: 0.2, 2.6, 2.8, 5.5, 9.3
Michelin Travel Partner UK Ltd: 1.1
bpk – Bildagentur für Kunst, Kultur und Geschichte/DACS: 1.2, 2.4, 2.11, 3.2
Martin Siepmann/Nordpool: 9.6
In Flanders Fields Museum (IFF): 1.3, 2.7, 4.1, 9.5
Australian War Memorial/Brendan en Bourgogne, Travel et travail WordPress (in Wikimedia Commons): 2.3
PA Images: 2.5, 6.5, 11.2
Gerard Rondeau: 9.2
Estate of Georg Grosz, Princeton, NJ/DACS: 3.1
Bridgeman Images: 9.1
Robert Del Tredici: 4.3, 7.7
Nigel Young: 5.2, 8.1, 9.7
National Army Museum: 5.3
Canadian War Museum: 5.4
US Library of Congress: 6.1
Archival Collection of the State Museum Auschwitz-Birkenau: 6.4
Anselm Kiefer/The Doris and Donald Fisher Collection, San Francisco Museum of Modern Art: 7.5
US Air Force: 7.8
Johann H. Addicks (JHA) in Wikimedia Commons: 9.4
Richard Walker/Picker Art Gallery, Colgate University/Getty Images: 14.2

J. B. Priestley Library, University of Bradford: 10.2
Käthe Kollwitz Museum Berlin/Studio Bartsch Berlin: 10.3
Extramural Activity: 11.1
Bergen Art Museum KODE, Rasmus Meyer's Collections/Munch Museum, Oslo: 12.1
The Israel Museum, Jerusalem: 14.1

ABBREVIATIONS

BBC	British Broadcasting Corporation
CND	Campaign for Nuclear Disarmament
EC	European Community
END	European Nuclear Disarmament campaign
EU	European Union
FLN	Front de Libération Nationale – National Liberation Front (Algeria)
IFF	In Flanders Fields (Museum)
INGO	International non-governmental organization
INPM	International Network of Peace Museums
IWM	Imperial War Museum
NATO	North Atlantic Treaty Organization
ND	Nuclear Disarmament
NGO	Non-governmental organization
OIEP	Oxford International Encyclopedia of Peace
OSCE	Organisation for Security and Cooperation in Europe
TRANGO	Transnational (non-)governmental organization
TRC	Truth and Reconciliation Commission
UN	United Nations
WRI	War Resisters International

BIBLIOGRAPHY

Adorno, T. W., *Prisms* (Cambridge, MA, 1981).

Adorno, T. W., E. Frankel-Brunswick, David Levinson and R. Sanford, eds, *The Authoritarian Personality* (New York, 1950).

Agilar, Paloma, 'Agents of Memory: Spanish Civil War Veterans and Disabled Soldiers', in Jay Winter and Emmanuel Sivan, eds, *War and Remembrance in the Twentieth Century* (Cambridge, UK and New York, 2000).

Alleg, Henri, *La Question* (London, 1958).

Anderson, Benedict, *Imagined Communities: Reflections on the Origin and Spread of Nationalism* (New York and London, 1983).

Apsel, Joyce, *Introducing Peace Museums* (London, 2015).

Apsel, Joyce and Amy Sodaro, *Museums and Sites of Persuasion: Politics, Memory and Human Rights* (Abingdon, UK, 2019).

Arendt, Hannah, *Origins of Totalitarianism* (New York, 1951).

Arendt, Hannah, ed., *Illuminations: Walter Benjamin* (London, 1999).

Arendt, Hannah, *Eichmann in Jerusalem: A Report on the Banality of Evil*, Introduction by Amos Elon (London, 2006).

Ashplant, Timothy G. et al, *The Politics of Memory: Commemorating War* (New Brunswick and London, 2009).

Ashworth, T., *Trench Warfare 1914–18: The Live and Let Live System* (New York, 1980).

Balakian, Peter, *Black Dog of Fate* (New York, 1997).

Baker, Simon and Mavlian Shoair, eds, *Conflict. Time. Photography* (London, 2015).

Barbusse, Henri, *Le Feu* (*Under Fire*) (London, 1988).

Barker, Pat, *Regeneration* (New York, 1991).

Barker, Pat, *The Ghost Road* (New York, 1995).

Barker, Rachel, *Conscience, Government and War: Conscientious Objection in Great Britain, 1939–45* (Abingdon, 1982).

Becker, Annette, *La Guerre et la Foi: de la Mort á la Memoire*, Preface by Pierre Nora (Paris, 1994).

Becker, Annette, *Maurice Halbwachs: Un Intellectuel en Guerres Mondiales 1914–15*, Preface by Pierre Nora (Noesis, 2003).

Benjamin, Walter, *Illuminations*, Introduction by Hannah Arendt (New York, 1968).
Benjamin, Walter, *Illuminations*, Introduction by Hannah Arendt (London, 1999).
Berger, Peter, *Pyramids of Sacrifice: Political Ethics and Social Change* (London, 1976).
Berger, Peter and Thomas Luckmann, *The Social Construction of Reality* (New York, 1967).
Bergson, Henri, *Matter and Memory*, trans. Nancy Margaret Paul and W. Scott Palmer (New York [1910], 1968).
Bloch, Marc, *Feudal Societies Volume l* (Chicago, 1961).
Blunden, Edmund, *Undertones of War* (London, 1928).
Booth, Alyson, *Postcards from the Trenches* (Oxford, 1996).
Boulding, Elise, *Cultures of Peace: The Hidden Side of History* (Syracuse, 2000).
Broyles, William, *Brothers in Arms: A Journey from War into Peace* (New York, 1986).
Bringa, Tonë, *Being Muslim the Bosnian Way: Identity and Community in a Central Bosnian Village* (Princeton, 1995).
Brittain, Vera, *Testament of Youth* (London, 1933).
Brock, Peter and Nigel Young, *Pacifism in the Twentieth Century* (Syracuse, 1999).
Brown, Malcolm and Shirley Seaton, *Christmas Truce: The Western Front December 1914* (London, 1984).
Buruma, Ian, *Wages of Guilt* (New York, 1994).
Campbell, Joseph, *The Power of Myth* (New York, 1988).
Ceadel, Martin, *Pacifism in Britain, 1914–45: The Defining of Faith* (Oxford, 1980).
Clark, Howard, *Civil Resistance in Kosovo* (London, 2000).
Cobb, Humphrey, *Paths of Glory* (London, 1935).
Cole, Tim, *Selling the Holocaust* (New York and London, 2000).
Connerton, Paul, *How Societies Remember* (Cambridge, 1989).
Connerton, Paul, 'Seven Types of Forgetting', *Memory Studies*, vol. 1, issue 1 (2008), pp. 59–71.
Cork, Richard, *A Bitter Truth: Avant Garde Art and the Great War* (New Haven, 1994).
Coser, Lewis A., ed., *Maurice Halbwachs on Collective Memory* (Chicago and London, 1992).
Crownshaw, Richard, Jane Kilby and Antony Rowland, eds, *The Future of Memory* (Oxford and New York, 2010).
Cubitt, Geoffrey, *History and Memory* (Manchester, 2007).
Curle, Adam, *Mystics and Militants: Awareness, Ideals and Social Action* (London, 1972).
Dawson, Graham, *Making Peace with the Past? Memory, Trauma and the Irish Troubles* (Manchester, 2007).
Del Tredici, Robert, *At Work in the Fields of the Bomb* (London, 1987).
Des Pres, Terrence, *The Survivor: An Anatomy of Life in the Death Camps* (New York, 1976).
Des Pres, Terrence, 'Landscape/Self/Grid', in *Writing into the World* (New York, 1991), p. 175.
Didion, Joan, *Salvador* (New York, 1982).
Douglas, Keith 'Vergissmeinicht', in Jon Stallworthy, ed., *Oxford Book of War Poetry* (Oxford, 1987).
Dyer, Gwynne, *War* (London, 1985).
Eksteins, Modris, *Rites of Spring: The Great War and the Birth of the Modern Age* (Boston, 1989).
Eksteins, Modris, 'Memory and the Great War', in H. Strachan, ed., *Oxford History of the Great War* (Oxford and New York, 1998).
Eliot, T. S., *The Wasteland and Other Poems* (London, 1922).
Erll, Astrid, *Memory in Culture*, (Basingstoke, UK, 2011).
Fanon, Frantz, *The Wretched of the Earth* (New York, 1963).

Faulks, Sebastian, *Birdsong* (New York, 1993).
Feller, Gordon, Sherle R. Schwenninger and Diane Singerman, eds, *Peace and World Order Studies: A Curriculum Guide*, 3rd edition (New York, 1981).
Felman, Shoshana, *Judicial Unconcious* (Cambridge, MA, 2002).
Felman, Shoshana and Dori Laub, *Testimony: Crisis of Witnessing in Literature, Psychoanalysis and History* (New York, 1992).
Forché, Carolyn, ed., *Against Forgetting: Twentieth-Century Poetry of Witness* (New York, 1993).
Forché, Carolyn, *The Angel of History* (New York, 1994).
Foucault, Michel, *Discipline and Punish: The Birth of the Prison* (London, 1977), English version.
Frank, Anne, *Diary*, 1st edition, English translation (New York, 1952).
Freedland, Jonathan, 'Finkelstein: The Row Rumbles on', *The Guardian* (19 July, 2000).
Friedrich, Ernst, *War Against War* (Seattle, 1987).
Fritsche, Peter, 'The Case of Modern Memory', *The Journal of Modern History*, vol. 73, (March, 2001), pp. 87–117.
Fritsche, Peter, *Stranded in the Present* (Harvard, 2004).
Freud, Sigmund, *Civilizations and its Discontent* (New York, 1962).
Freud, Sigmund, *The Interpretation of Dreams* (New York, 1965).
Friztsche, Peter, 'The Case of Modern Memory', *The Journal of Modern History*, vol. 73, issue 1 (2001), 87–117.
Frye, Northrop, *Anatomy of Criticism* (Princeton, 1957).
Fukuyama, Francis, *End of History* (New York, 1992).
Fussell, Paul, *The Great War and Modern Memory* (Oxford, 1975).
Fussell, Paul, *Wartime: Understanding and Behaviour in the Second World War* (New York, 1989).
Garton Ash, Timothy, *The Magic Lantern* (New York, 1990).
Garton Ash, Timothy, *We the People: The Revolution of '89 Witnessed in Warsaw, Budapest, Berlin and Prague* (London, 1990).
Garton-Ash, Timothy, *The File: A Personal History* (London, 1998).
Garton-Ash, Timothy, *A History of the Present: Essays, Sketches and Despatches from Europe in the 1990s* (London, 2000).
Gellhorn, Martha, *The Face of War* (New York, 1986).
Gerth, Hans and C. Wright Mills, eds. and trans., *From Max Weber* (New York, 1946).
Gibbons, Joan, *Contemporary Art and Memory: Images of Recollection and Remembrance* (London, 2007).
Gilbert, Martin, *The Holocaust: The Jewish Tragedy* (New York, 1986).
Gilbert, Martin, *The Holocaust: A History of the Jews of Europe during the Second World War* (New York, 1986).
Gilbert, Martin, *Holocaust Journey* (New York, 1997).
Ginsberg, Alan, *Howl and other Poems* (New York, 1956).
Gitlin, Todd, *The Whole World is Watching: Mass Media in the Making and Unmaking of the New Left* (New York, 1980).
Glenny, Misha, *The Fall of Yugoslavia* (London, 1992).
Glover, Jonathan and Jon Silkin, *First World War Prose* (London 1989)
Gomez, J., ed., *Masters of Cinema* (London, 1974).
Graham, Helen, *The Spanish Civil War: A Very Short Introduction* (New York, 2005).
Graves, Robert, *Goodbye to All That* (London, 1929).
Gregory, Adrian, *The Silence of Memory: Armistice Day, 1919–1946* (Oxford, 1994).

Griffin, Susan, *Chorus of Stones* (New York, 1992).
Habermas, Jurgen, *The Postnational Constellation*, rpt (Cambridge, 2007).
Halbwachs, Maurice, *On Collective Memory* (New York, 1980).
Halbwachs, Maurice, *The Collective Memory* (Chicago, 1992).
Harrison, Ted, *Remembrance Today* (London, 2012).
Haug, Frigga, 'Australian Feminist Studies', *Memory Work*, vol. 23 (2002), pp. 537–541.
Haug, Frigga, et al., *Female Sexualisation: A Collective Work of Memory*, trans. Carter (London, 1999).
Hedges, Chris, *War Is a Force That Gives Us Meaning* (New York, 2002).
Hein, Laura and Mark Selden, eds, *Censoring History: Citizenship and Memory in Japan, Germany and the United States* (New York, 2000).
Heller, Joseph, *Catch 22* (London, 1962).
Hemingway, Ernest, *In Our Time* (New York, 1970).
Hemingway, Ernest, *The Short Stories of Ernest Hemingway*, 2nd edition (New York, 1953).
Hemingway, Ernest, *A Farewell to Arms* (New York, 1957).
Hersey, John, *Hiroshima* (New York, 1946).
Hilberg, Raul, *Destruction of European Jews* (New York, 1985).
Hirsch, Herbert, *Genocide and the Politics of Memory: Studying Death to Preserve Life: Why Genocide Occurs and a Vison of How It Can Be Prevented* (Chapel Hill and London, 1995).
Hitler, Adolf, *Mein Kampf* (Berlin, 1925).
Hobsbawm, Eric, *On History* (London, 1997).
Hobsbawm, Eric, *Age of Extremes* (New York, 1998).
Hobsbawm, Eric and T. Ranger, eds, *The Invention of Tradition* (Cambridge, 1983).
Hochschild, Adam, *King Leopold's Ghost* (Boston and New York, 1999).
Hodgkin, Katharine and Susannah Radstone, *The Politics of Memory* (London and New York, 2003).
Hudson, Ralph. N., *The Bradford Pals* (Bradford Libraries, 2000).
Hughes, Stuart H., *Consciousness and Society* (New York, 1958).
Huyssen, Andreas, *Twilight Memories in an Era of Amnesia* (New York and London, 1995).
Huyssen, Andreas, *Present Pasts: Urban Palimpsests and the Future of Memory* (Stanford, 2003).
Hynes, Samuel, *A War Imagined* (London, 1990).
In Flanders Fields, Handbook, IFF Museum (Ieper, 2013)
Isaacs, H., *Idols of the Tribe* (Cambridge, MA, 1975).
James, Wilmot and Linda van de Vijver, eds, *After the TRC: Reflections on Truth and Reconciliation in South Africa* (Athens and Ohio, 2000).
Jay, Martin, 'Against Consolation: Walter Benjamin and the Refusal to Mourn', in Jay Winter and Emmanuel Sivan, eds, *War and Remembrance in the Twentieth Century* (Cambridge and New York, 2000).
Joll, James, *The Second International* 1889–1914 (London, 1974).
Junger, Ernst, *The Storm of Steel* (London, 1929).
Kaplan, Robert D., *Balkan Ghosts: A Journey Through History* (New York, 1994).
Keen, Sam, *Faces of the Enemy* (New York, 1988).
Kennard, Peter, *Images for the End of a Century* (London, 1990).
Khaldei, Yevgeny, *Witness to History: The Photographs of Yevgeny Khaldei* (New York, 1995).
Kiefer, Anselm, *L'Exposition* (Paris, 2015).
Kipling, Rudyard, *Barrack Room Ballads and Other Verses* (London, 1892).
Knightley, Philip, *The First Casualty* (New York and London, 1975).
Kobak, Annette, *Joe's War: My Father Decoded* (London, 2005).

Koselleck, Reinhard, *Futures Past: On the Semantics of Historical Time*, trans. Keith Tribe (New York, 2004).
Kramer, Jane, *The Politics of Memory* (New York, 1996).
Kramer, Jane, *The Politics of Memory: Looking for German in the New Germany* (New York, 1998).
Kristeva, Julia, *Black Sun. Depression and Melancholia* (1986) trans. L. S. Roudiez (New York, 1989).
Kundera, Milan, *The Book of Laughter and Forgetting* (Middlesex, 1981).
LaCapra, Dominick, *Representing the Holocaust: History, Theory, Trauma* (New York, 1996).
LaCapra, Dominick, *History and Memory after Auschwitz* (New York and London, 1998).
Landsberg, Alison, *Prosthetic Memory: The Transformation of American Remembrance in the Age of Mass Culture* (New York, 2004).
Langenbacher, Eric and Yossi Shain, eds, *Power and the Past: Collective Memory and International Relations* (Washington DC, 2010).
Langenbacher, Eric, et al., eds, *Dynamics of Memory and Identity in Contemporary Europe* (New York and Oxford, 2012).
Lanzmann, Claude, *Shoah* (New York, 1985), English edition.
Laslett, Peter, *The World We Have Lost* (Oxford, 1983).
Leed, E. J., *No Man's Land* (Cambridge, 1979).
Levy, Daniel and Nathan Sznaider, 'Memory Unbound: The Holocaust and the Formation of Cosmopolitan Memory', *European Journal of Social Theory*, vol. 5 (2002), pp. 87–106.
Levy, Daniel and Nathan Sznaider, 'The Institutionalization of Cosmopolitan Morality: The Holocaust and Human Rights', *Journal of Human Rights*, vol. 3, issue 2 (2004), pp. 143–157.
Levy, Daniel and Nathan Sznaider, *The Holocaust and Memory in the Global Age*, trans. Assenka Oksiloff (Philadelphia, 2006).
Lewis, C. Day, *The Collected Poems of Wilfred Owen* (London, 1963).
Lifton, Robert, *Death in Life: Survivors of Hiroshima* (New York, 1968).
Lindquist, Sven, *History of Aerial Bombing* (London, 2002).
Linenthal, Edward, *Preserving Memory: The Struggle to Create America's Holocaust Museum* (New York, 1997).
Lowe, Keith, *The Fear and the Freedom: How the Second World War Changed Us* (London, 2017).
Luci, Nita and Linda Gusla, 'Our Men Will Not Have Amnesia', in S. Ramet, ed., *Civic and Uncivic Values in Kosovo* (Budapest and New York, 2015).
Lyotard, Jean-François, 'Re-Writing Modernity', *SubStance*, vol. 16, issue 3 (1987), pp. 3–9.
MacLeod, Kirsty, *The Last Summer* (London, 1983).
MacNamara, Robert, *The Fog of War* (Lanham, MD, 2005).
Mannheim, Karl, 'The Sociological Problem of Generations' (1928), partially excerpted in Olick et al., eds, *Collective Memory Reader* (Oxford, 2011).
Marcuse, Herbert, *Reason and Revolution: Hegel and the Rise of Social Theory* (London, 1965).
Marshall, E. H., *Our Empire Story* (London, nd).
Marshall, E. H., *Our Island Story* (London, nd).
Maruki, I. and T. Maruki, *Hiroshima Panels: The Joint Works of Iri Maruki and Toshi Maruki*, 2nd edition (Saitama, Japan, 1991).
Meyerhoff, Hans, *Time in Literature* (Berkeley, 1955).
Mills, C.Wright, *The Sociological Imagination* (Oxford, 1959).
Misztal, Barbara A., *Theories of Social Remembering* (Maidenhead and Philadelphia, 2003).

Mitscherlich, Alexander and Margarethe Mitscherlich, *The Inability to Mourn* (New York, 1975).

Moore, Barrington, *Social Origins of Dictatorship and Democracy* (Boston, 1966).

Morpurgo, Michael, *War Horse* (London, 2007).

Morton, H. V., *In Search of England* (London, 1927).

Mosse, George, *Fallen Soldiers: Reshaping the Memory of the Great War* (Oxford, 1990).

Munch, E., *Aphorisms on Art* (1886).

Nettl, J. P., *Rosa Luxemburg* (Oxford, 1966).

Nora, Pierre, *Realms of Memory: The Construction of the French Past* (New York, 1996).

Nora, Pierre, 'The Reasons for the Current Upsurge in Memory', *Transit-Virtuelles Forum*, 22 (2002).

Olick, Jeffrey K., V. Vinitzky-Seroussi and D. Levy, eds, *Collective Memory Reader* (Oxford, 2011).

Orwell, George, *Homage to Catalonia* (London, 1962).

Orwell, George, *Politics of English Language* 1984, in *Collected Essays, Journalism and Essays and Letters of George Orwell*, Sonia Orwell and Ian Angoa, eds, vol. 4 (New York, 1968), pp. 127–140.

Owen, Wilfred, 'Strange Meeting', in C. Day Lewis, ed., *The Collected Poems of Wilfred Owen* (London, 1963).

Proust, Marcel, 'Swanns Way', in *À la recherche du temps perdu* (*Remembrance of Things Past)*, part 1 (London, 1951).

Radstone, Susannah, ed., *Memory and Methodology* (Oxford and New York, 2000).

Radstone, Susannah, 'Memory Studies: For and Against', *Memory Studies*, vol. 1 (2008), pp. 31–39.

Radstone, Susannah, 'What Place is This? Transcultural Memory and the Locations of Memory Studies', *Parallax*, vol. 17, issue 4 (2011), pp. 109–123.

Radstone, Susannah and Katherine Hodgkin, eds, *Regimes of Memory* (New York and London, 2003).

Raw, David, *Bradford Pals: A Comprehensive History of the 16th, 18th and 20th (Service) Battalions of the Prince of Wales' Own West Yorkshire Regiment 1914–1918* (Barnsley, 2005).

Remarque, Eric. M., *All Quiet on the Western Front* (New York, 1958).

Ricoeur, Paul, *Memory, History, Forgetting*, trans. Blamey Kathleen and David Pellauer (Chicago and London, 2004)

Rigby, Andrew, *Justice and Reconciliation: After the Violence* (London, 2001).

Rondeau, Gèrard, *Les Fantômes du Chemin des Dames, Le Presbytère d'Yves Gibeau* (Paris, 2003).

Rosenbaum, Alan S., ed., *Is the Holocaust Unique? Perspectives on Comparative Genocide* (Oxford, 1996).

Rousso, Henry, *The Vichy Syndrome: History and Memory in France since 1944*, trans. A. Goldhammer (Cambridge and London, 1991).

Rűrup, Reinhard, ed., *Topography of Terror: Gestapo, SS and Reichssicherheitshauptamt on the 'Prinz-Albrecht-Terrain' A Documentation* (Berlin, 1987).

Ryback, Tim, 'Report from Dachau', *New Yorker* (3 August 1992).

Samuel, Raphael, *Theatres of Memory* (New York, 1994).

Sassoon, Siegfried, *Memoirs of an Infantry Officer* (New York, 1930).

Sassoon, Siegfried, *Collected Poems* (New York, 1949).

Sartre, J., *Réflexions sur la Question Juive* (trans. as *Anti-Semite and Jew*) (New York, 1946).

Scannel, Vernon, 'The Great War' (1962) in Jon Stallworthy, ed., *Oxford Book of War Poetry* (Oxford, 1987).

Scarry, Elaine, *The Body in Pain* (New York, 1985).
Schley, Jim, ed., *Writing in a Nuclear Age* (Hannover and New England, 1984).
Schwartz, Lynne, ed., *The Emergence of Memory, Conversations with W. G. Sebald* (New York, 2007).
Scott, Peter Dale, *Coming to Jakarta: A Poem about Terror* (New York, 1988).
Scott, Peter Dale, *Poetry and Terror: Politics and Poetics in Coming to Jakarta* (Lanham, MD, 2018).
Scott, P. D., *The Sleep of Reason: Denial, Memory Work, and the Reconstruction of Social Order. In Literary Responses to Mass Violence*. Report of the symposium held at Brandeis University (Waltham, MA, September 2003).
Sebald, W. G., *Austerlitz* (London, 2002).
Sebald, W. G., *On the Natural History of Destruction* (German edn 1999; New York, 2003).
Sheriff, R. C., *Journey's End* (London, 1929).
Shils, Edward, *Tradition* (London, 1979).
Silkin, Jon, *Out of Battle* (London, 1972).
Silkin, Jon, ed., *Book of First World War Poetry* (London, 1979).
Smith, A. D., *Ethnic Origins of Nations* (Oxford, 1986).
Sorel, Georges, *Reflections on Violence* (Glencoe, 1950).
Stallworthy, Jon, ed., *Oxford Book of War Poetry* (Oxford, 1987).
Strachan, Hew, ed., *World War I: A History* (Oxford and New York, 1998).
Sturken, Marita, *Tangled Memories* (Berkeley, 1997).
Swiebocka, Teresa, Jonathan Webber and Connie Wilsack, eds, *Auschwitz: A History in Photographs* (Oswięcim, Bloomington, Indianapolis and Warsaw, 1995).
Taylor, A. J. P., *The First World War: An Illustrated History*, 1st edition (London, 1963).
Thompson, E. P., *The Making of the English Working Class* (New York, 1966).
Thomas, Edward, *Poems of Edward Thomas* (Oxford, 1978).
Todorova, Maria, *Imagining the Balkans* (New York, 1997).
Todorova, Maria, *Balkan Identities: Memory and History* (New York, 2004).
Touraine, Alain, *Critique of Modernity* (Oxford and Cambridge, MA, 1995).
Tremlett, Giles, *Ghosts of Spain* (New York, 2006).
Vandenbroucke, R., 'The Hiroshima Panels', in Nigel Young, ed., *Oxford International Encyclopedia of Peace* (Oxford and New York, 2010).
Van den Dungen, Peter, 'Peace Museums', in Linus Pauling, Ervin Laszlo and Jong Yoo, eds, *The World Encyclopaedia of Peace* (Pergamon, 1986).
Vonnegut, Kurt, *Slaughterhouse Five* (London, 1970).
Walzer, Michael, *Just and Unjust Wars* (New York, 1977).
Watkins, Peter, 'Edvard Munch', in J. Gomez, ed., *Masters of Cinema* (London, 1974).
Watkins, Peter, *Film Guide to 'The Journey'* (Auckland, New Zealand, 1990).
Weber, Max, in H. Gerth and C. W. Mills, eds and trans., *From Max Weber* (New York, 1946).
Wells, H. G., *The War that Will End War* (New York, 1914).
Williams, P., *Memorial Museums: The Global Rush to Commemorate Atrocities* (Oxford and New York, 2007).
Williams, R., *Culture and Society* (London, 1958).
Willsher, Kim, 'French Town Tries to Save First World War Soldier's Room', *The Guardian*, December 2014.
Winter, Jay, *Sites of Memory, Sites of Mourning* (Cambridge, 1995).
Winter, Jay, *Remembering War: The Great War between Memory and History in the Twentieth Century* (New Haven, 2006).
Winter, Jay, *War Beyond Words: Languages of Remembrance from the Great War to the Present* (New Haven, CT, 2017).

Winter, Jay and Blaine Baggett, *The Great War and the Shaping of the 20th Century* (New York, 1996).
Winter, Jay and Emmanuel Sivan, eds, *War and Remembrance in the Twentieth Century* (Cambridge and New York, 2000).
Wittner, Lawrence, *The Struggle against the Bomb. Volume 1, One World or None: A History of the World Nuclear Disarmament Movement through 1953* (Stanford, 1993).
Wittner, Lawrence, *The Struggle against the Bomb. Vol. 2: Resisting the Bomb: A History of the World Nuclear Disarmament Movement, 1954–1970* (Stanford 1997).
Wolf, Eric, *Peasant Wars of the Twentieth Century* (Faber & Faber, 1973).
Woolf, Virginia, *Mrs Dalloway* (London, 1925).
Woolf, Virginia, *The Death of a Moth and Other Essays* (London, 1970).
Yates, Frances, *Art of Memory* (Oxford, 1984).
Young, Geoffrey Winthrop, *The Grace of Forgetting* (London, 1953).
Young, James E., 'Memory and the Monument after 9/11', in R. Crownshaw, Jane Kilby and Antony Rowland, eds, *The Future of Memory* (New York and Oxford, 2010).
Young, James E., *Texture of Memory* (New Haven, 1994).
Young, Nigel, 'On War, National Liberation and the State', in *Christian Action* (London, 1971).
Young, Nigel, *An Infantile Disorder: The Crisis and Decline of the New Left* (London, 1976; 2nd edition, 2018).
Young, Nigel, ed., *Oxford International Encyclopedia of Peace* (Oxford and New York, 2010).
Zigrosser, Carl, ed., *Prints and Drawings of Käthe Kollwitz* (New York, 1969).
Zinn, Howard, *Peoples' History of the United States* (New York, 1980).

Other key sources and background works

Eksteins, Modris, the Cultural Impact of the Great War, in *Film and the First World War*, eds. Karel Dibbets and Bert Hagenkamps, (Amsterdam, 1995) (pp. 201–212)
Hirsch, Herbert, *Genocide and the Politics of Memory* (Chapel Hill and London, 1995).
Hobsbawm, Eric, *Interesting Times* (London, 2002)
Hughes, H.Stuart, *Consciousness and Society* (New York, 1968).
Hynes, Samuel, *The Soldier's Tale* (New York, 1997).
Kammen, Michael, *Mystic Chords of Memory: The Transformation of Tradition in American Culture* (New York, 1991).
Mannheim, Karl, *Ideology and Utopia* (New York, 1952)
Lowenthal, David, *The Past is a Foreign Country* (Cambridge, 1985).
Steiner, George, 'A Season in Hell', in *Bluebeard's Castle* (London, 1971), pp. 29–48.
Touraine, Alain, *Critique of Modernity* (Oxford and Cambridge, MA, 1995).
Virilio, Paul, *War in Cinema* (London, 1991)

FILMOGRAPHY

A Generation [Polish: *Pokolenie*], dir. Andrzej Wajda. Zespól Filmowy 'Kadr', 1955.

All Quiet on the Western Front, dir. Lewis Milestone. Universal Pictures, 1930.

Apocalypse Now, dir. Francis Ford Coppola. United Artists, 1979.

Ashes and Diamonds [Polish: *Popiól i diament*], dir. Andrzej Wajda. Zespól Filmowy 'Kadr', 1958.

Bambi, dir. James Algar et al. Walt Disney Productions, 1942.

Battle of the Somme, dir. Geoffrey H. Malins. British Topical Committee for War Films, 1916.

Behind the Lines [original title: *Regeneration*], dir. Gillies MacKinnon. BBC Films, 1997.

Born on the Fourth of July, dir. Oliver Stone. Ixtlan – Universal Pictures et al., 1987.

Comradeship [German: *Kameradschaft*], dir. Georg W. Pabst. Nero-Film AG – Gaumont-Franco Film-Aubert, 1931.

Crossroads, dir. Bruce Conner. Canyon Cinema, 1976.

Disappearing World War: We Are All Neighbours, dir. Debbie Christie. ITV, 1993.

Dr. Strangelove or: How I Learned to Stop Worrying and Love the Bomb, dir. Stanley Kubrick. Columbia Pictures – Hawk Films, 1964.

Edvard Munch, dir. Peter Watkins. Norsk Film et al., 1974.

Frontline: Memory of the Camps, dir. Alfred Hitchcock and Sidney Bernstein. PBS – US Office of War Information, 1985.

Full Metal Jacket, dir. Stanley Kubrick. Natant – Staley Kubrick Productions – Warner Bros, 1987.

Gandhi, dir. Richard Attenborough. Columbia Pictures et al., 1982.

Hiroshima Mon Amour, dir. Alain Resnais, written by Marguerite Duras. Argos Films et al., 1959.

Hiroshima Nagasaki August 1945, Dir. Erik Barnouw, Japan Film Co.\Columbia University, 1970.

Hope and Glory, dir. John Boorman. Columbia Pictures et al., 1987.

Hotel des Invalides, dir. Georges Franju. Forces et voix de la France, 1952.

Hotel Terminus, dir. Marcel Ophuls. The Memory Picture Company – The Samuel Goldwyn Company, 1988.

In Country, dir. Norman Jewison. Warner Bros, 1989.
J'accuse!, dir. Abel Gance. Pathe Freres, 1919.
J'accuse!, dir. Abel Gance. Forrester-Parant Productions, 1938.
Kanal, dir. Andrzej Wajda. Zespól Filmowy 'Kadr', 1956.
King & Country, dir. Joseph Losey. BHE Productions, 1964.
King of Hearts [French: *Le Roi de Coeur*], dir. Philippe De Broca. United Artists et al., 1966.
La Grande Illusion, dir. Jean Renoir. RAC, 1937.
Life and Nothing But [French: *La Vie et Rien d'Autre*], dir. Bernard Tavernier. Hachette Premiere et al., 1989.
March to Aldermaston, dir. Lindsay Anderson and Karel Reisz. Film and TV Committee for Nuclear Disarmament, 1959.
Memories of the Camps, dir. Alfred Hitchcock and Sidney Bernstein. Ministry of Information, 2014.
Memorial Day, dir. Samuel Fischer. Perspective Films, 2012.
Night and Fog [French: *Nuit et Brouillard*], dir. Alain Resnais. Argos Films, 1955.
Oh! What a Lovely War, dir. Richard Attenborough. Accord Productions – Paramount Pictures, 1969.
Paths of Glory, dir. Stanley Kubrick. Bryna Productions – United Artists, 1957.
Platoon, dir. Oliver Stone. Hemdale – Cinema 86, 1986.
Rosa Luxemburg, dir. Margarethe von Trotta. Bioskop Film et al., 1986.
Schindler's List, dir. Steven Spielberg. Universal Pictures – Amblin Entertainment, 1993.
Shoah, dir. Claude Lanzmann. BBC et al., 1985.
Sophie's Choice, dir. Alan J. Pakula. IFC Entertainment – Keith Barish Productions, 1982.
Star Wars: Episode V – The Empire Strikes Back, dir. Irvin Kreshner. Lucasfilm, 1980.
Testament, dir. Lynne Littman. Paramount Pictures et al., 1983.
The Atomic Cafe, dir. Jayne Loader, Kevin and Pierce Rafferty. The Archives Project, 1982.
The Battle of Algiers [Italian: *La battaglia di Algeri*], dir. Gillo Pontecorvo. Casbah Film – Igor Film, 1966.
The Day After, dir. Nicholas Meyer. ABC Circle Films, 1983.
The Deer Hunter, dir. Michael Cimino. EMI Films – Universal Pictures, 1978.
The Fog of War: Eleven Lessons from the Life of Robert S. McNamara, dir. Errol Morris. Sony Pictures Classics et al., 2003.
The Great War and the Shaping of the 20th Century, dir. Carl Byker et al., written by Blaine Baggett and Jay Winter. BBC, 1996 (UK), PBS, 1997 (USA).
The Journey (original title: *Resan*), dir. Peter Watkins, Canyon Cinema – Folkets Bio et al., 1987.
The Sorrow and the Pity [French: *Le Chagrin et la Pitie*], dir. Marcel Ophuli. NDR – TSS – Television Rencontre, 1969.
The Triumph of the Will [German: *Triumph des Willens*], dir. Leni Riefenstahl. Riefenstahl-Produktion, 1935.
The War Game, dir. Peter Watkins. BBC, 1965.
Threads, dir. Barry Hines. BBC et al., 1984.
War Requiem, dir. Derek Jarman. BBC et al., 1989.

INDEX